E BANK

LLARS. *on demand*

Lecompton K.T. Nov. 1st 1856

w York.

3

3

Pres.t

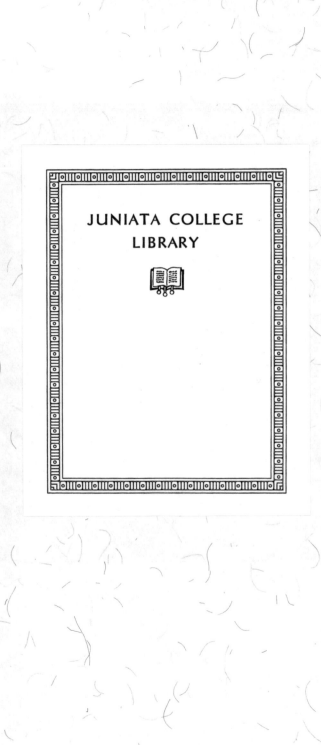

A FINANCIAL HISTORY
OF THE
UNITED STATES

FIVE SHILLINGS.

To Counterfeit is Death.
Printed by JAMES ADAMS, 1776.

A FINANCIAL HISTORY OF THE UNITED STATES

by MARGARET G. MYERS

COLUMBIA UNIVERSITY PRESS, 1970

New York & London

MARGARET G. MYERS IS EMERITUS PROFESSOR
OF ECONOMICS AT VASSAR COLLEGE

COPYRIGHT © 1970 COLUMBIA UNIVERSITY PRESS
LIBRARY OF CONGRESS CATALOG CARD NUMBER: 70-104900
ISBN: 0-231-02442-8
PRINTED IN THE UNITED STATES OF AMERICA

PREFACE

THIS book departs from the narrow definition of financial history which limits the field to public finance. This is not to deny that the state, in a modern industrial society, is the most important financial unit—the largest income receiver, the largest borrower, and the largest spender. But its activities bind it closely to the institutions of the money market, and it can never operate as a separate entity, however much it might like to do so.

Nor can the financial community be independent of the government. Although the United States is very self-conscious about its role as exponent of the free enterprise system, the amount of governmnt regulation in many areas of the economy is greater than in nations which give less lip service to *laissez-faire* principles. In earlier years there was very little government control, and the unhappy results in the fields of banking, stock trading, and corporate organization inevitably led to one legal restriction after another, backed up by court interpretations and enforcement procedures.

Federal finance has increased in importance as the result of the increasing size and population of the country. State and local units are unable to cope with such large-scale interstate problems as highways, health, welfare, and education. Even the most ardent advocates of states' rights have been obliged to turn to the central government for assistance in solving these problems.

Public and private finance affect each other so intimately that financial history must include the history of the principal financial institutions— their origin, their development, and perhaps their decline. Some of them arose by specialization in one activity of an existing institution, others out of a need to fill a gap or to provide a more efficient mechanism. Changes in technology and in forms of business organization have affected the kinds of credit needed for production.

An important factor in the development of financial techniques and institutions has been social change in attitudes toward debt. A mortgage on the family home was once regarded as either a tragedy or a disgrace. Now families go into debt not only for a home, but for a car, a pool, a television set, travel, even for clothing. An American without debt is sometimes suspected of having such low credit rating that no one will trust him. Consumer and mortgage credit increased rapidly after the second world war, bringing changes in commercial banking and in many financial intermediaries. The shift in the labor force had much to do with the changed feeling about debt. There was a steady decline in the proportion and even in the number of workers in agriculture, where income is subject to erratic fluctuations of weather and crops. The corresponding increase in workers in the service sector (the proportion in industry was almost unchanged) made debt less dangerous because income was more stable.

Easy access to credit is frequently justified as an incentive to growth. Certainly, inadequate provision for credit, or the lack of any, may impede the free flow of goods and services through the economy and have a negative effect on growth. The positive relationship between financial institutions and growth is more difficult to evaluate, in part because the concept of growth itself is difficult to define. If growth means better nourishment, housing, and education for a population which is not straining at its resources, it should and can be aided by sound credit, wise taxation, stable prices. If growth has for one of its chief results an increase in the area of solid cement where there were formerly forests, fields, and homes; if growth destroys irreplaceable natural beauty in order to save a few pennies on consumer electric bills, or add a few pennies to corporate profits, it had better not be aided by financial devices.

The measurement of growth became a matter of almost hysterical concern in the United States in the 1950s when it was reported that the rate of growth of the Soviet Union was greater than that of the United States; if this continued, it would be only a few years before the Soviet Union was ahead. The assumption of a straight-line trend for the growth of either country was quite unjustified, and a comparison of growth rates for two such different countries had even less justification. Even for one series in one country it is difficult to obtain a precise measure of change. Such a complicated figure as that for Gross National Product is made up of many series subject to statistical error, and it cannot be assumed that they have all canceled each other out. It is an extremely useful figure, but it must be used with full awareness of its limitations.

Discussion of the influence of financial factors on growth has taken many forms over the years, and the vocabulary has changed with the times. Paper money controversies of the colonial period gave way to those on bullion versus paper, silver versus gold, sound money versus cheap money, fiscal policy versus monetary policy. During the latter half of the nineteenth century the apparently unavoidable alternations of prosperity and depression were studied in terms of "crises," and in the first half of the twentieth century in terms of the "business cycle."

The painful instability of the economy was blamed by some writers on the instability of iron production, or crop production, or some other factor. Often it was ascribed to the price level or the quantity of money. During the 1920s Professor Irving Fisher popularized the idea that the business cycle was basically a "Dance of the Dollar" and that it could be eliminated by stabilizing prices through the mechanism of a currency based on varying amounts of commodities. During the deep depression of the 1930s John Maynard Keynes, in "The General Theory of Employment, Interest and Money," emphasized the importance of investment, by the government if necessary, in order to maintain business activity and prevent unemployment. This was a fiscal policy for depression.

A few years after the war, with the depression far behind, the danger became inflation. Monetary controls again came into use, sometimes in conjunction with fiscal devices, in an effort to maintain stable prices without increasing unemployment. A new variant of the quantity theory of money was proposed by the Chicago school, which would maintain stability in the economy by increasing monetary circulation at a constant rate. There was some disagreement as to the definition of money; all agreed that it should include currency and demand deposits, but time deposits, savings bank deposits, and funds of other intermediaries were not so clearly money. There was also disagreement as to the rate of increase which should be selected. How the velocity of circulation was to be kept constant, and how the quality of credit was to be maintained, were questions left without satisfactory answers. There seemed little hope that the problem of economic instability had received a permanent solution.

Any attempt to trace within the limits of one volume the financial history of the United States, with its rapid increase in size and wealth over three centuries, involves difficult choices of method and treatment. A strictly chronological presentation has some advantages, but loses the thread of development for any one institution, while a study of one institution after another makes it difficult to see interrelationships. On another level, evaluation presents problems if not dangers, yet complete objectivity—if there is such a thing—is lifeless and even cowardly. I have tried to steer a middle course among these dangers.

MARGARET G. MYERS

Poughkeepsie, New York
February 3, 1970

ACKNOWLEDGMENTS

I SHOULD like to express my appreciation and gratitude to my husband, Benjamin Haggott Beckhart, for his help, to my publishers for their patience, to the staff of the Vassar College Library for their skillful assistance, and to Hugh G. Dobbins for his design of my book.

The illustrations of coins, currency, and checks were supplied through the generosity of the Chase Manhattan Bank Money Museum and its director, Helen V. Foote.

M. G. M.

CONTENTS

Pine tree shilling, 1652

CHAPTER 1

THE COLONIAL PERIOD

THE hundred and fifty years before the Declaration of Independence saw the early development of most of the factors which have given this country its distinctive character. In the realm of finance as in the realm of politics, the history of these formative years is essential to an understanding of later events. The financial squabbles often led to political violence; the famous Boston Tea Party was only one act in the long drama of conflict between sovereigns and proprietors in the mother country and colonists in the new country. The shortage of capital and the even more obvious shortage of currency, resulting from the constantly unfavorable balance of payments, all made the colonists resentful of taxes and duties and pushed them into a series of financial expedients which were often inimical to the interests of the English and sometimes hurtful to the long-run welfare of the colonists themselves. But they also provided a fund of experience which was extremely valuable when the time came to draw up a permanent constitution for the union.

Early Payments: Barter and Wampum

The first colonists brought with them to North America a meager supply of tools, supplies, and seeds, but little actual currency. They soon began to send back to England a few local products to repay the loans which had helped to outfit the voyages and to pay for essential imports.

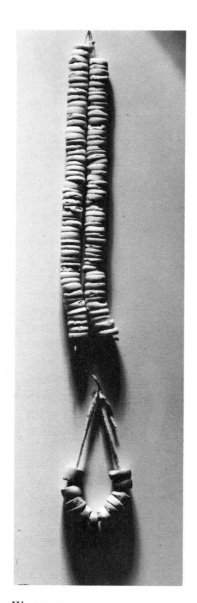

Wampum

In this earliest period the trade was two-way; only later did the triangular trade involving the West Indies become the typical pattern.

Domestic trade was carried on by barter, and by the use of the shell bead currency of the Indians. According to the account of Governor Bradford of Plymouth colony, the Dutch settlers were the first to adopt this wampum or "Wampampeake" money. The black beads were made of the inside shell of clams or mussels and were rarer and therefore more valuable than the white beads from conch shells. The beads were strung on leather thongs and were sometimes worked into belts to be exchanged as tokens of friendship when treaties were signed. Both Indians and Europeans accused each other of dyeing the white wampum to make it pass for the more valuable black. The ratio of black to white shell was usually two to one, but it varied considerably, as did the prices quoted in wampum. New Netherland merchants complained to the "High and Mighty Lords States General of the United Netherlands" in 1649 that "Wampum, which is the currency here, has never been placed on a sure footing."[1] By 1664 wampum had depreciated by about one-fourth in relation to the Dutch guilder but was still used for many transactions. Peter Stuyvesant, the Director-General of New Netherland, in that year asked Van Renselaer, a merchant in Albany, to raise a loan of five or six thousand guilders in wampum and send it to him in New York to pay the laborers on the fort; he promised to repay the loan either in slaves or other goods. Nine years later the Dutch proposed an excise tax payable in beavers or wampum, and the forced loan of 1674 was made payable in "merchantable Beaver or Wheat, at Wampum price."[2]

The use of wampum seems to have spread to the neighboring colonies early. Connecticut in 1645 set the value of white wampum at six to the penny, and of the black at three to the penny. In 1648 Massachusetts required that it must be "strunge sutably" in parcels worth one, three, or twelve pennies.[3] Pennsylvania complained in 1672 that New York ports were collecting import duties of "four guilders in Wampum, upon each Anker of strong rum."[4] Gradually wampum was replaced by coin and paper money. The Reverend Andrew Burnaby reports that he saw it being made by Indians on Staten Island as late as 1760, but it was seldom mentioned after that date.

Along with the wampum, many staple commodities were used as means of payment, although most of them were too perishable to serve as a unit of account or a store of values. Corn was in such demand as currency in Massachusetts in 1633 that feeding it to swine was prohibited. New England merchants also found it necessary to receive payment in bullets, peas, flax, wool, codfish, beef, and pork. Tax collectors in spite of their protests sometimes had to accept bulky products and even live animals.* Beaver skins were a currency as well as a principal export from New York and neighboring areas.

The colonies in which tobacco could be grown early adopted it as an official medium of exchange. Its relatively high value in small bulk, and the fact that it could be dried and stored with small danger of spoilage, made it far superior to grain, meat, or animals as a currency. Virginia collected taxes and imposed fines in terms of tobacco. After 1632, official warehouses were established, receipts were given to individuals who brought their tobacco to the warehouse for safe-keeping, and these receipts began to circulate from hand to hand in the settlement of accounts between individuals as well as in the payment of taxes. The receipts became in effect a paper money based on tobacco; they became a legal tender after 1730 and fluctuated in value with the price of tobacco. Maryland was another colony which relied on tobacco for settling domestic accounts.[5]

Whether payment was actually made in wampum, in commodities, or in specie, prices were by 1700 normally quoted in the English units of pounds, shillings and pence. Efforts were made to maintain a legal ratio of wampum and commodities to the standard unit, but they were seldom successful for long. One way of evading the law was simply to adjust the price according to the payment offered. Madame Knight, in a lively account of her uncomfortable journey from Boston to New York in 1704, reported that merchants along the way raised their prices if they were offered anything but specie. To the unlucky buyer who had no coin, the six-penny knife cost twelve pence in "country pay" of commodities.

Currency Confusion

The variety of coins in circulation and the worn condition of many of them resulted in enormous confusion. In addition to the common English and Spanish money, Portuguese and Dutch coins were also in cir-

---

* See p. 21.

culation. Spanish dollars were often broken into quarters or even eighths, so that "two bits" were equivalent to a quarter of a dollar. The eight-real piece of Portugal was almost identical in weight and fineness with the Spanish dollar, and also resembled the taler which had been minted by the successive Counts of Schlick of Joachimsthal from the fourteenth century on. All these pieces contained about 17.5 pennyweight of silver, the equivalent of 4s. 6d. of English money, according to the official report of Isaac Newton in 1717. The rix-dollar, originally coined at Augsburg, was similar, as was also the Mexican pillar dollar stamped with the Pillars of Hercules and the boastful motto "Plus Ultra." There were also lion or dog dollars from the Netherlands. Merchants had to weigh these clipped and sweated coins every time they were received or paid out.

In an effort to provide more good coin, Massachusetts in 1652 had established its own mint under the supervision of John Hull. He purchased silver in the form of bullion or plate and made it into pieces of three and six pennies and shillings stamped with the famous pine tree. The fineness of the silver was the same as that of the English shilling, but only three-fourths as much was used in each coin. For a generation these pieces circulated throughout the colonies, until in 1684 the charter of Massachusetts was revoked by the King, and the mint had to be closed. A few of the coins remained in circulation down to the Revolution.

No other coins were actually minted in America in the colonial period. The charter of Virginia gave it the privilege, but it was not used. Maryland was authorized by a law of 1661 to establish a mint, but never did so. Lord Baltimore had a few small coins, with his portrait on one side and the family arms on the other, minted in England for the use of the colony, but they were inadequate for its needs, and the New England shilling and, later, tobacco were made legal tender.[6] The Rosa Americana, a copper penny issued by George I, was in spite of its name coined in Ireland, not in America.

Since most of the colonies had not been granted the right to mint their own coins, some of them attempted to attract the existing coins by a more generous rate of exchange. This led to competitive devaluation and a situation (described by the harassed merchants of New York in a Memorial to the British Board of Trade in 1700) resulting in "a piece of eight in the Bahamy Islands being about five shillings the same in

Carolina, in Maryland and Virginia four shillings and sixpence, in Penn-silvania Seven shillings, in New York and New England six shillings and sixpence."

Their proposed solution was to recoin all the foreign pieces into English coin, but the petition to do so was not granted. Instead a Royal Proclamation, followed by the Act of 1708, set a maximum rate for the Spanish dollar at six shillings, with smaller pieces to be valued pro-portionately. Neither Proclamation nor Act was effective, and the mer-chants continued to complain even more bitterly than before.[7]

Equally ineffective was the attempt made by some colonies to main-tain a legal ratio between gold and silver. Gold coins came into the country in large amounts after the opening of the Brazilian mines about 1700. The market value of the two metals varied frequently during the eighteenth century, and colonies which had made both a legal tender, found it almost impossible to keep the legal ratio in line with the market ratio. Pennsylvania changed the ratio seven times during the first half of the century. Massachusetts after several changes settled on 15.38 to 1 in 1732. Silver was rising in value in Europe, and tended to be drained away from the colonies, in spite of laws and regulations. The confusion of the currency continued throughout the colonial period and into the years of revolution.[8]

Colonial Paper Money

The serious inadequacy of the circulating media stimulated a variety of experiments to alleviate the shortages, with varying results. The American colonies have the dubious distinction of being the first gov-ernments of modern times—the Chinese are supposed to have been the first of all time—to print and issue paper money. The idea probably came from the London goldsmiths who had been giving receipts for gold and silver deposited with them; these receipts often passed from hand to hand like coin. Pamphlets by various English authors suggested that this device might be extended. William Potter, for example, in 1650 published in London a rather repetitious little pamphlet of 84 pages en-titled "The Key of Wealth, or, a new Way for Improving of Trade: Lawfull, Easie, Safe and Effectuall, shewing how a few Tradesmen agreeing together may both double their Stocks and the increase thereof.

. . ." His plan was really a proposal for mutual guarantee of bills of credit to be issued by a group of tradesmen "of known and sufficient credit" who "bind themselves jointly to make good the same. . . ." The bills would be loaned out only against good security, thus avoiding depreciation, and the result would be that "the dore (or rather a wide gate) is opened unto the storehouse of riches."

A similar plan was proposed for Massachusetts a few years later by the Rev. John Woodbridge of Newbury, a friend of Potter. In his pamphlet, "Severals relating to the Fund," he recommends "erecting a Fund of Land, by Authority, or private Persons, in the nature of a Money-Bank; or Merchandise Lumber,* to pass Credit upon, by Book-Entries; or Bill of Exchange, for Great Payments: and Change-bills for running Cash."[9]

During the last third of the seventeenth century several attempts were made by Boston merchants, and at least one by Philadelphians, to put such a plan into operation. The chief obstacle was to find enough eminent and wealthy persons to provide the cash, land, or commodities necessary to get started. In 1733 a group of Boston merchants was finally successful. They issued their own notes for £110,000, to be redeemable in 10 years in silver at the rate of 19 shillings to the ounce. When silver rose in price to 27 shillings per ounce, the notes went to a premium and were hoarded, so that they disappeared from circulation.

In 1741, after a great deal of public controversy over the relative merits of private and governmental issues, a private land bank was established in Boston in spite of the opposition of the Governor of the colony. Each of the subscribers, among whom was Samuel Adams, put in £2 of actual currency, and paid for the rest of the £1000 share in hemp, flax, cordage, iron, or certain other commodities; or they borrowed the rest in notes of the Bank itself on mortgages for 20 years at 3 percent. The Bank issued £150,000 of notes but, when the Bubble Act† was made to apply to New England as well as to England, the Bank was forced to wind up its affairs.

In the meantime the Massachusetts colonial government had stepped into the breach and begun to issue its own paper money. The expenses

---

* That is, a Lombard loan, secured by merchandise.
† See p. 11.

of the colony had been heavily increased by the unsuccessful military expedition into Canada at the outset of King William's War in 1689, and the expected spoils of war had not materialized. Borrowing was impossible, and heavier taxation almost equally impossible, so in 1690 the historic decision was made to print £7000 of certificates of indebtedness with which to meet the colony's obligations. These notes were receivable for taxes and were to be destroyed within the year as taxes were paid. Another £33,000 were issued in the following year; of them, £10,000 were actually burned as they were turned in for taxes. No new notes were issued during the following decade, although a few were reissued instead of being destroyed. Because the total was a modest amount, the growing business of the colony was able to absorb them, and these Old Charter or Colony notes suffered little depreciation.

The next series of issues was less successful. Massachusetts was given a new charter as a Province, not a Colony, under William and Mary. The Province Bills, issued after 1702, were to be redeemed from the proceeds of a special tax levy, but the redemption dates were frequently postponed, new issues were made, and by 1714 when the total had reached £194,000, the discount on the notes was 30 percent.

In order to provide the needed currency for circulation, a new device, the public land bank, was tried; it was organized under public rather than private auspices. The provincial government issued notes to the counties, and later also to the towns, to be loaned by them to individuals against good real estate security, in amounts of £50 to £500, for 5 years at 4 percent. Even these precautions did not prevent overissue and depreciation, and in 1730 a Royal Instruction set a limit on the annual issue at £30,000, to be used only for current provincial expenses; previous issues were ordered to be withdrawn on schedule, and the mortgages canceled. Moreover the Provincial Assembly was no longer to be permitted to issue paper money by mere "resolves" of its own; thenceforth it had to pass a formal Act which required the approval of Governor and Council before it could be put into effect.

The Province Bills nevertheless continued to depreciate and by 1740 had lost one-third of their value. They began to be referred to as Old Tenor bills when a new series of New Tenor bills was issued in 1742. As the value of the paper deteriorated, judges were admonished to take account of the rate of depreciation in cases involving financial settlements; the price of silver and the rate of exchange on London were to be used as measures. Finally in 1749 the British Parliament granted the province a sum to reimburse its military expenses. With this help all its outstanding paper was redeemed at the rate of 7.5 to 1, and after 1750 all debts and contracts were paid in silver coin. From that time until the Revolution, Massachusetts currency enjoyed relative stability.

Other New England colonies followed the example of Massachusetts in currency as in most other matters. Connecticut, Rhode Island, and New Hampshire used various types of credit bills after 1709–10, and all deteriorated severely, since they were issued in "immoderate quantities." Those of Rhode Island were described by Reverend Burnaby in 1760 as being "as bad as it is possible to be"; they were outlawed, not very successfully, by Massachusetts and Connecticut.[10]

Legislative decrees and legal penalties had little effect in maintaining a sound currency unless they were reinforced by the imposition of taxes or other measures to provide funds for redemption of the notes. This was demonstrated by the record of the middle colonies, where the paper money of the early colonial period was very much better than that of New England. New York began to issue bills of credit during Queen Anne's War in 1709, when a tax levy on the counties was unsuccessful in raising funds. The colony therefore issued £13,000 to be legal tender for all payments and to be redeemed with interest. Another £11,000 was issued 2 years later. These first notes were paid off promptly and did not depreciate.

No new issues were made between 1724 and 1734, although a few of the worn bills were reissued. In 1734 the need to defend New York harbor was the occasion for another issue of £12,000. After 1737 the colony adopted the public land bank system of issuing notes against mortgages. Funds were allocated to the counties, which appointed commissioners to make individual loans of £25 to £100 for 12 years at 5 percent against mortgage security. In spite of the security behind them these notes did not avoid depreciation since the mortgages securing them could not be readily sold. They were bitterly denounced by Governor Clinton in 1747, when he could not even ascertain the amount still outstanding. More notes were issued as military expenses increased, and only about half of the £800,000 total had been canceled by 1771; the rest continued to circulate until the Revolution at varying discounts.

New Jersey followed a pattern similar to that of New York but on a more limited scale. As a result of her moderation her notes were at a 12.5 percent premium over New York's in 1741.[11]

In Pennsylvania no paper money was issued until 1723 when there was a severe depression in America associated with the collapse of the South Sea Bubble in England and the reduced demand for American goods. The Governor of this colony was sympathetic, and encouraged the Assembly to enact legislation providing for three series of land-bank notes of £45,000, £30,000 and £30,000 by 1729. They were loaned for 8 years at 5 percent, in amounts ranging from £12 to £100, against mortgages for not more than one-third the value of the land. The system was so carefully administered and the issues so promptly redeemed as the loans were repaid that the notes depreciated very little and were reported to have had "a prodigious good Effect" on business activity.[12] Moreover the interest earned by the colony on these loans was sufficient, with a small excise tax on liquor, to pay all the expenses of the government in some years, according to the Governor's Report to the British Board of Trade in 1731. Later issues were equally well managed; although the total eventually reached £950,000, more than half of them had been redeemed by 1774. During the fifty years preceding the Revolution, Pennsylvania enjoyed prices as stable as in any half-century afterwards.

The moderation shown by Pennsylvania in its issues of paper money was due in part to the influence of the pacifist Quakers, who refused until 1746 to meet military expenses by this device. It stemmed also from the good advice of men like Benjamin Franklin. In 1729, when he was only twenty-three years old, he had written a "Modest Inquiry into the Nature and Necessity of a Paper Currency"[13] in which he defended "prudent issues" but pointed out that large additions to the circulation merely depreciated the currency and inflated prices. His good sense so impressed the legislators that they gave him the contract for printing the paper money.

In the south, the Carolinas began to use paper money at about the same time as Connecticut and Rhode Island, with the same result of extreme depreciation resulting from overissue and failure to carry out the redemption provisions of the laws. In Maryland, early issues of the 1730s were backed by a tax on tobacco, but the fluctuating price of that commodity made depreciation inevitable. The issues after 1750, however, made mostly in the form of loans, were secured by a reserve of Bank of England and other British stocks and were maintained at par down to the Revolution. The notes were issued as one, two, four, six, or eight dollars, making Maryland the first to circulate a currency in dollars.

Virginia was in a more favorable situation than most of the other colonies, with her valuable crop of tobacco which served not only as a means of exchange at home but also as payment for her imports from abroad. She was therefore under less pressure to meet governmental expenses with paper money and did not do so until 1755. She was able to redeem the issues promptly from the proceeds of special land and poll taxes and, after 1761, from regular taxes. Although there were some of the usual complaints about the scarcity of currency in Virginia, her money was on the whole better managed and less depreciated than most.[14]

One reason for the colonies' currency problems was that the mother country was able to give them only intermittent attention and guidance. England was having recurrent monetary troubles of her own during this period, and they were made worse by frequent wars. Colonial governors were often sent out with instructions to stop further issues of paper money, but most of them had no effective powers with which to enforce such an order. Indeed many of the most bitter conflicts between colonies and their royal governors centered around the paper money question. The Governor of South Carolina was deposed in 1719 as the result of such a quarrel; when South Carolina became a royal colony the quarrel was continued, and the legislature adjourned for three years without making any provision for paying the expenses of the government. Much the same thing happened in New Hampshire when for the five years 1731–36 the representatives refused to vote supplies because the governor would not approve an issue of notes. There was a similar controversy in New Jersey. The governors were usually forced to submit, or at least to compromise, since their own salaries were involved.

The Bubble Act of 1719, which forbade further issues of bills of credit in England, did not apply to the colonies until 1751, and even then it was made enforceable only in New England. The anger aroused in New England by this prohibition was not greatly alleviated when in

1764 all the colonies were brought under the ban. Parliament tried to temper the blow by reimbursing the colonies in specie for the military expenses they had incurred, thus removing the reason for many of the issues. Although the specie was used in some of the colonies to redeem their outstanding notes, the payment did not soften the hearts of the colonists.

No longer able to issue legal tender paper money, some of the colonies used their own treasury bills as a partial substitute. Massachusetts paid its creditors in promissory notes bearing interest, redeemable in silver after 2 or 3 years. These notes did not depreciate and were much sought after as an investment; they were redeemed from the proceeds of taxes. Most other colonies issued similar notes and, by the outbreak of the Revolution, Pelatiah Webster estimated that 50 to 60 percent of the country's circulating medium of 12,000,000 dollars consisted of this type of paper.

There is no doubt that the paper money which was handled in such a manner as to avoid depreciation was of great service to the American colonies during the difficult years of their early growth. Whether the heavily depreciated issues had a net effect which was good or bad has been a subject for warm debate.[15]

Account Keeping and Credit

The day-to-day embarrassments which arose from the lack of a uniform, stable, and adequate currency were reflected in the books kept by the merchants of the period. For example, Thomas Hancock, uncle of John, was a Boston merchant during the first half of the eighteenth century. He kept his accounts in "Old Tenor" until about 1750, then shifted to "Lawful Money" which remained relatively stable at the rate of 133 to 100 sterling, down to the Revolution. But the fact that the accounts were kept in pounds, shillings, and pence did not mean that currency was actually exchanged. His wholesale purchases and retail sales were sometimes carried on by barter, as when a carpenter was paid for repair work with books, cider, beef, molasses, candles, and a gun; sometimes by a triangular exchange of goods; at still other times with bills of exchange which were payable in commodities as well as in currency.

Book credit by one merchant to another played an important role in the trade of the colonies, not only because of the scarcity of currency but also because of the lack of adequate working capital. A man who wished to set himself up in business had to rely on his own savings and perhaps on those of relatives and friends. He therefore depended on his suppliers to grant him credit, usually by means of book entries without even such visible evidence of debt as a note. Prompt payment of accounts seems to have been the exception rather than the rule. Even the post offices granted credit in those days. Benjamin Franklin, as postmaster at Philadelphia from 1739 to 1753, had great trouble in collecting sums due for postage. At the end of his term of office there were 700 accounts still outstanding, with a total of over £800 in arrears; one of the principal recalcitrants expressed great resentment when his mailing privilege was withdrawn.

Since there were no commercial banks in the colonies before the Revolution, many of the better-known merchants carried on what were essentially banking operations in making loans and in handling payments. In 1775 Nathaniel Littleton Savage, a Virginia businessman of wide commercial interests, had outstanding loans to 100 individuals, usually on the security of notes or bonds. In Philadelphia the merchants who frequented the London Coffee House often made loans to each other as well as to the public.

Many of these merchants also carried on what amounted to a foreign banking business. John Hull, who had made a fortune by minting the pine-tree shilling, settled one of his own accounts by shipping over a mixed bag of silver and gold coins; not long after, he issued a letter of credit for £300 to two Americans traveling to London. Thomas Hancock often sold bills of exchange to travelers bound for England or to merchants with accounts to settle there. His funds abroad were replenished when his associate in the West Indies drew sight drafts on Hope and Company of Amsterdam, sent them to London, and had them credited to Hancock's account.[16]

Business Organization

The organization of business enterprise in the colonies was as informal as that of credit. Of true business corporations before the Revolution there seem to have been only six. *The New York Company for Settleing a Fishery in These Parts* was chartered in 1675 by the Governor and Council of York, acting for the Duke of York; its shares were sold at £10 each. In 1682 the governor of Pennsylvania chartered *The Free Society of Traders* with a capital stock of £5400; only shareholders who resided or owned land in Pennsylvania were permitted to vote, and then only on a sliding scale which gave no stockholder more than three votes regardless of the number of shares he owned. The company did well for a few years as operator of a tannery, a gristmill, a sawmill, and a glass factory, in addition to its business of importing goods from England, but it was unable to handle such a variety of activities and failed in 1722. Another Pennsylvania company was the first American insurance corporation, *The Philadelphia Contributionship for the insuring of Houses from Loss by Fire.* Benjamin Franklin headed the list of subscribers to its stock and it continued to be active down to the twentieth century.

In New England the *New London Society United for Trade and Commerce* was chartered in Connecticut in 1732. The *Union Wharf Company* of New Haven, chartered in 1760, built and operated a long wharf for the convenience of shippers. Another wharf company, *The Proprietors of Boston Pier,* was equally successful under its charter of 1772.

Several other corporations were established during the colonial period for purposes other than business. One of them, chartered in 1759, had the impressive title of *Corporation for the Relief of Poor and Distressed Presbyterian Ministers and of the Poor and Distressed Widows and Orphans of Presbyterian Ministers.* By surviving into the twentieth century it became the oldest life insurance company in continued existence in the world. Another nonprofit corporation was the *New York Chamber of Commerce* which received its patent from the Crown in 1770 and thus became the second oldest Chamber of Commerce in the world.

The large joint-stock companies originally chartered by the British government for the settlement of the colonies were corporations. The *Hudson's Bay Company,* chartered by Charles II in 1690 for seven years, the *Massachusetts Bay Company,* which later became the colony of Massachusetts, and the *Ohio Company* of 1749, were examples of the type of organization which created in the American mind the impression that corporation and monopoly were inextricably linked. The dramatic failure of the South Sea and Mississippi companies about 1720, and the

Bubble Act which was inspired by the failures, also contributed to the public suspicion of corporations.[17]

Government Revenues

Many of the bitter controversies over paper money, land banks, and taxes arose not only from the scarcity of currency but also from the heavy expenses of establishing new governments. Courts had to be set up with judges and clerks, roads had to be made, forts had to be constructed and equipped, prisons had to be built and staffed. Some of the expensive services of modern governments such as education and water supply were seldom demanded in the colonial period, but it was necessary for public officials to raise sums which were large in relation to the income, and especially large in relation to the cash income, of a community so predominantly agricultural.

The property tax was the main support of the government in all the New England colonies. In Massachusetts the earliest taxes were levied by the general court of the colony on the towns in rough proportion to their population and trade; the town selectmen then made the assessments on the estates of the individual freemen, that is, of adult male white church members. The tax itself was set in terms of "rates." One rate was one penny to the pound of assessed valuation, or the equivalent of 4⅙ mills per dollar. During the late seventeenth century the tax varied from half a rate in 1670 to sixteen rates in 1676 at the time of King Philip's War. By 1750, when Douglass was writing his *Summary,* the method of assessment had been somewhat systematized; the estate was considered to consist of real and personal property. Houses and lands were valued at six times their annual income, and personal property in the form of slaves and cattle was valued at standard figures. This type of tax bore most heavily on the farmers whose houses, barns, and cattle could be easily seen and counted.

A poll tax was also levied in terms of rates. A person was valued at £20, so that a rate of a penny per pound amounted to a poll tax of 20 d. per person. When the rate on property was changed, the poll tax was usually changed also. Some persons were exempted from both taxes—usually the governor and lieutenant of the colony, the president, fellows and students of Harvard College, and ministers, school teachers, and invalids.

From 1646 on, there was also a tax on "faculty," or ability to earn. This was a kind of primitive income tax. Anyone earning over 18 d. per day was required to pay an annual tax of 3s. 4d. in addition to the poll tax. The basis for assessment and the rate of tax were frequently changed, and eventually the faculty tax became a tax on wages and profits. In some form it was used in seven of the thirteen colonies.

Excise taxes were used in some of the New England colonies for control rather than for revenue. Wines and spirits were usually taxed, but not beer or hard cider. Imported luxuries like citrus fruits were also subject to a tax paid by the vendor. Excise taxes, like the others, were supposed to be paid in gold and silver coin, but even as late as 1750 the tax collectors of New England were obliged to accept payment in iron, ironware, cloth, whalebone, cordage, beeswax, bayberry wax, wool, tallow, leather, peas, corn, grain, pork, and beef, all at values not to exceed half of their market price.[18]

New York, because of its Dutch background, had a somewhat different tax system in the early years. The Dutch West India Company was so eager to obtain immigrants that it promised them a ten-year exemption from all taxes. The system of quitrents for land was, however, roughly equivalent to a tax on land. In addition, export duties were collected on beaver skins and tobacco, and some import and transit duties were levied. Excise taxes had to be paid on beer and wine.

When the colony came under British control in 1664, a system of property taxes was developed similar in many respects to that of Massachusetts. The high Sheriff of the county was to instruct the Constables to require the Overseers of every town to draw up a list of assessed values in which males over sixteen were to be rated at £18, cows over four years old at £4, sheep over one year at 6s. 8d., and so forth. Two years later, in 1666, another law required that "the publique Rates shall henceforth be payable att one Certayne tyme of the yeare. . . . That the payment of the Rate for publique Charges shall be made in Corne beefe or porke, att the price herein mentioned (that is to say) wheate not exceeding 5s. the bushell Rye and pease 4s: Indian Corne 3s. and oates 2s. 6d. beef att 3s. and porke att 4d. per pound and no other payment shall bee allowed of."

A graduated poll tax was levied in 1702 in order to fortify the Narrows, the approach to New York harbor; it was heaviest on lawyers, well-to-do bachelors, and wearers of wigs. In 1709 a tax was laid on chimneys or hearths and on slaves; it was in this period that the first paper money was issued. The governors of New York had the same difficulty as the others in meeting expenses, especially when military costs mounted. New Jersey used much the same combination of revenue-raising devices as New York.[19]

Pennsylvania resorted to the property tax early in its history. Assessors were elected in each county to evaluate the property, real and personal, and rates were determined by the ratio of assessed valuation to estimated expenses. A poll tax was also collected in most counties. The first provincial tax was levied in 1693 on real and personal property; exempted were the proprietors, and persons who had "a great charge of children, and become indigent in the world." This tax was not collected every year. A great conflict arose over the exemption of the estates of the Penn heirs who were the proprietors, but they were eventually forced to submit to the property tax like all other property owners of the colony.[20]

In the southern colonies the large landowners were opposed to the property tax; hence the poll tax was often the first to be levied. In Virginia, for example, the expenses of the Assembly in 1623 were met by a tax of ten pounds of tobacco per male head. Four years later any man who did not help to build the fort was required to contribute five pounds of tobacco toward its cost; one pound of tobacco also had to be paid for every absence from church. Not until 1645 were property taxes levied in Virginia. At that time every landowner was taxed four pounds of tobacco for each hundred acres of land, and three pounds for each breeding sheep or cow. But Virginia never relied on property taxes as did New England. The export tax on tobacco not only provided ample revenue for the government right down to the Revolution, but also saved the colony from the excesses of paper money which plagued so many of the colonies. Tobacco was grown in some other colonies, but it was particularly suitable to the soil and climate of Virginia. Maryland grew some tobacco, but relied almost entirely on the poll tax during the colonial period.[21]

A revenue device which was popular early in all the colonies was the lottery. The English Act of 1709 which forbade private lotteries did not apply in the colonies unless the colonial legislature had passed a similar law. However, Cotton Mather and most of the Quakers were opposed to lotteries, either private or public, and gradually restrictions were imposed. Massachusetts and New York in 1719 and 1721, respectively, forbade lotteries unless they were specifically authorized by the government; between 1727 and 1732 Connecticut, Rhode Island, and Pennsylvania forbade them altogether but were not able to enforce the prohibition.

In 1744 Massachusetts used the first of the government lotteries to raise money for King George's War; New York was unsuccessful when it tried the same device two years later. Many official lotteries were devoted to the financing of education. King's College in New York (later Columbia University), Yale in New Haven, Harvard in Boston, the College, Academy and Charitable School of Philadelphia (later the University of Pennsylvania), Princeton in New Jersey, and Dartmouth in New Hampshire, all benefited from the funds raised with the approval of the colonial legislatures through lotteries.[22]

Import Duties

All the colonies added to their revenues at one time or another during the colonial period by levying import duties. Most of the colonial charters specifically granted this power, and it was used not only in the case of goods imported by sea, but often in the case of goods brought by land from "foreign" territory, that is, from another colony, unless reciprocal exemptions had been given. From the point of view of the government, import duties had a number of advantages over internal revenues. They were more apt to be paid in specie, and any source of specie was welcome in a community where there was a shortage of hard currency. Moreover the import duty was a relatively constant source of revenue, in spite of the European attempts at military and naval blockades, and the depredations of pirates who infested the seas. And, finally, the import duty made possible some control over the type and amount of goods purchased by the colonists.

Massachusetts, New York, and South Carolina were the colonies which relied most heavily on duties. Massachusetts used them early in her history as a means of controlling what were regarded as "the immoderate expense of provisions brought from beyond the seas."[23] Any person who imported fruit, sugar, wine, strong water, or tobacco had to pay a duty of one-sixth of the price, and if the goods were destined for resale, one-third of the price. This duty was repealed in 1638, but high duties continued to be levied on wines and liquors. Retaliatory rates were enacted against goods from Connecticut and Plymouth in 1649 and were not removed until the offending duties on Massachusetts goods had been repealed by those areas. Double rates were charged on all goods imported by "foreigners" from Rhode Island, New Hampshire, and Connecticut from 1715 to 1774. And, like New York and Pennsylvania, Massachusetts set high duties on the importation of slaves in order to discourage the traffic.

In New York the system of import duties began with the Dutch West India Company, which set specific rates on imports of codfish and furs. There was little change when the British took over the colony, but the administration was improved. All imported goods had to go through a weigh-house, and each shipmaster was required to file a sworn statement of dutiable goods on board.

Other northern colonies relied less on import duties. New Hampshire adopted a policy of free trade after 1722. Rhode Island had duties only on ship tonnage and on slaves. New Jersey put duties on rum and on slaves, more for control than for revenue. Pennsylvania had duties on ship tonnage and on sugar, spirits, and slaves; in 1718 it also imposed a 10 percent duty on imports from New York and Maryland, which had put a similar tax on Pennsylvania products.

Among the southern colonies, South Carolina was most dependent on import duties. Unlike the northern colonies, the duty on slaves was set at the high figure of £50 per slave, not for control but for revenue; by 1731 two-thirds of the government income came from this source.

When import duties were levied on goods from other colonies, the rate was usually lower than on goods from beyond the seas. Goods from other British territories were not always given a lower rate, although tariff legislation affecting British goods had to be approved by the Crown. Many colonies granted lower rates on goods of whatever origin, if they were brought in by their own citizens or in ships owned by their own citizens. In any case, drawbacks or refunding of duties on goods which were reexported was a common practice.

It is of course impossible to determine how effectively the customs regulations were enforced, and how much they were evaded by smuggling. A tax like that of £50 per slave in South Carolina must have offered a strong incentive to illegal entry. Even in New York where the rates were moderate, it has been estimated that total imports in the period just before the Revolution amounted to about £500,000 annually, on which duties of about £25,000 should have been levied. Actually only £5000 were collected. Molasses and sugar were undoubtedly smuggled into New England in large quantities to provide material for the rum industry.

Many colonies used taxes on exports as well as on imports. Six colonies laid export duties on lumber in order to conserve the trees for their own shipyards, but after 1750 New England colonies abandoned all export duties. In 1714 New Jersey put an export tax on wheat in order to encourage milling at home, and in 1725 on wooden staves to encourage the manufacture of casks. Virginia relied heavily on export duties, not only on tobacco, but also on iron and on wool, in order to encourage home manufacture.[24]

Foreign Trade

The first exports from Massachusetts were the plant products used as drugs–ginseng, sassafras, sumac, and sarsaparilla; beaver and otter furs; clapboards; and dried fish. By the middle of the eighteenth century, iron and naval stores had been added to the list, and the building of ships for export had become one of the important occupations in several of the New England colonies. And of course, rum. As the disapproving Dr. Douglass summed it up in 1749:

Rum is a considerable article in our manufactures. It is distilled from molasses imported from the West-Indies islands; it has killed more Indians than the wars and their sicknesses; it does not spare white people, especially when made into flip, which is rum mixed with a foul small beer, and the coarsest of Muscovado sugars; it is vended to all our continent colonies to great advantage.[25]

The middle colonies, with neither rum nor tobacco, had to develop a variety of products and manufactures to sell abroad. Furs were an important export to England and Europe in the earliest years, as they were to China after the Revolution. New York developed the manufacture of cloth, hats, shoes, and glass, but lagged behind Pennsylvania with its bar and pig iron manufactures. Maryland and Virginia also produced iron articles, some of which they exported. The southern colonies and especially the Carolinas with their virgin pine forests became the great source for the pitch and tar which were essential to the sailing ships of the period.

Much of the foreign trade of the colonies was conducted in a roundabout fashion, some of it triangular, some of it in still more complicated patterns. Macpherson in his *Annals* for 1764 describes the situation as it existed at that time:

The old northern colonies in America, it is well known, have very few articles fit for the British market; and yet they every year took off large quantities of merchandize from Great Britain, for which they made payments with tolerable regularity. Though they could not, like the Spanish colonists, dig the money out of their own soil, they found means to make a great part of their remittances in gold and silver dug out of the Spanish mines. This they effected by being general carriers, and by a circuitous commerce, carried on in small vessels, chiefly with the foreign West-India settlements, to which they carried lumber of all sorts, fish of an inferior quality, beef, pork, butter, horses, poultry and other live stock, an inferior kind of tobacco, corn, flour, bread, cyder, and even apples, cabbages, onions, &. and also vessels built at a small expense, the materials being almost all within themselves; but the greatest part was remitted home to Britain, and, together with bills of exchange generally remitted to London for the proceeds of their best fish, sold in the Roman-catholic countries of Europe, served to pay for the goods they received from the mother country.

He adds that New England, New York and Pennsylvania usually had to pay more than they received from England, while Maryland, Virginia, the Carolinas, and in later years Georgia, usually received a balance from England.[26]

It was not only the limitations of resources and capital with which the American colonies had to cope; it was also the mercantilist policy of the mother country. Every colonial power in this period considered it a right, if not a positive duty, to build up its own power by using its colonies to that end. One of the policies of England was therefore to discourage in the colonies any manufacturing which would compete with her own products, especially in the vital field of wool, yarn, and cloth. An Act of the Virginia legislature in 1684, for example, which would have encouraged the manufacture of textiles, was annulled by the British Parliament; at the same session, Parliament forbade the exportation of wool from one colony to another.

The control of shipping was even more important to English policy. The Ordinance of 1651 and the Navigation Laws of 1660 were designed to thwart the Dutch, their chief competitors; they limited the carrying of goods between the mother country and the American colonies to British ships or ships of British colonies. This encouraged shipbuilding in New England, and by 1720 Massachusetts was launching 150 ships per year. British shipbuilders complained in vain against this competition from the colonies.

Other legislation was aimed at the control of specific commodities. The various Enumeration Acts listed the articles which had to be sent directly to England, not to other countries. The principal exports of New England—fish, rum, timber, and ships—were not among the enumerated articles, but the Carolinas lost their Portuguese market when rice was enumerated in 1706. Although tobacco was on the list, the damage done to American producers was offset at least in part by the prohibition of tobacco growing in England after 1660, and the tripling of tariff duties on imports of Spanish tobacco into England. Tobacco, like the other enumerated articles, could be sent on to other markets after it had been delivered to England, but the southern colonists believed that their profit was less than it would have been without the restriction. This may not have been the case, for in 1776 Adam Smith criticized the legislation on the opposite grounds, that the price of tobacco would have been lower, not higher, had there been no restriction.

During the seventeenth century the colonists were so dependent on England that they expressed little resentment against policies which were taken for granted among colonial powers. But, as the colonists became economically stronger, they became increasingly restive. The passage of the Molasses Act in 1733, which put a duty on rum, sugar, and molasses from non-British sources, aroused such opposition that no attempt was made to enforce it for several decades. When finally put into operation, it caused serious damage to the economic interest of New England by increasing the cost and reducing the profit in the manufacture of rum.

The prohibition in 1750 of the manufacture of iron products was aimed at the middle and southern colonies. They were beginning to take pride in their ability to make their own nails and utensils, and saw no reason why they should be obliged to purchase all their manufactured iron from the mother country.

During the third quarter of the eighteenth century the economic restrictions on the colonies were more onerous and more strictly enforced than previously. Moreover the mother country expected the colonies to pay the costs of the British army in America since it was ostensibly there to protect them from French and Indians. On the other hand, the rapid growth of the colonies was making them more than ever dependent on England for capital and for credit. English investment in ships, in land companies, and in manufacturing in America was heavy, and Adam Smith believed that it was actually inimical to English progress. Even more essential to the colonists was the financing of trade by British merchants, who often waited as long as two years for their payment from the Americans. At the outbreak of the Revolution the amount owed to British creditors was estimated at 28,000,000 dollars, an amount nearly equal to the value of two years' imports. Many British officials believed that such economic and financial dependence would make it impossible for the colonies to break away from the mother country,[27] but they were soon proved to be mistaken.

CHAPTER 2

"Piece of eight," 18th century

REVOLUTION AND CONFEDERATION

Continental Currency

T HE FINANCIAL situation of the country at the outset of the Revolution was not a favorable augury for the success of an extended war. When the delegates met early in 1775 to demand from Great Britain redress of their grievances, one of their first actions was to appoint a financial committee to cope with the increasingly urgent matters of expense and revenue. Since Congress had no power to levy taxes, and since it also had no power to borrow even if there had been anyone willing to lend, within four days the committee brought in a report recommending an issue of bills of credit to the value of two million Spanish milled dollars. The only real debate was over method; every state might issue for itself a sum apportioned by Congress, or Congress might issue the whole sum and apportion to each state the amount which it was obligated to redeem, or all of the states might be jointly obligated to redeem all the notes. The last plan was the one adopted as most likely to make the paper acceptable to the public, and to provide a further bond of union among the states. Benjamin Franklin's effort to make the notes bear interest was unsuccessful. By the end of 1775, 6 million dollars had been issued, to be redeemed between 1779 and 1786. As they were paid to the Treasury, they were to have a hole punched in them, then be burned in Philadelphia. Expenses continued to mount faster than revenues and, during 1776, another 19 million of bills was issued on four different dates. At first the bills were numbered by hand, and signed by two members of the Congress at 1.33 dollars per thousand signatures. As the volume of issues increased, only one signature was required, but even so the labor of signing the bills was tremendous and often delayed their circulation.

In the meantime, Congress had begun to discuss the financial sections of the Articles of Confederation. Article XI (printed in the *Journal of the Continental Congress* for July 12, 1776) proposed that "All charges of War and all other Expences . . . shall be defrayed out of a common Treasury, which shall be supplied by the several Colonies in Proportion to the Number of Inhabitants of every Age, Sex and Quality except Indians not paying Taxes . . . The Taxes for paying that Proportion shall be laid and levied by the Authority and Direction of the Legislatures of the several Colonies." In the draft of this Article as it was revised on August 20, the word State was substituted for Colony.

The proposal to levy taxes in proportion to population was recognized as inequitable but was designed to expedite the process of assessment, since the population of each state could be more quickly and correctly estimated than its taxable wealth. The objections to this proposal were so strong that it had to be dropped, and for it was substituted "the value of all land within each State . . . as such land and the buildings and improvements thereon shall be estimated according to such mode as the United States, in Congress assembled, shall, from time to time, direct and appoint."

Unfortunately, whatever the mode of assessment, no revenue could be expected from the states for some time. Not only would the process of levying and collecting taxes within the states be a slow one, but many of the states, now free of British control, had reverted to the issue of paper money because they had so little hope of meeting their own needs by taxation. Indeed some of the new states were asking and receiving loans from Congress until they could collect their tax levies.

The only financial powers granted to the central government were those included in Article XIV: "The United States Assembled shall have the sole and exclusive right and power of . . . coining money and regulating the value thereof, . . ." and the right "to agree upon and fix the necessary sums and expences . . ." and "to borrow Money or emit

Continental currency, Philadelphia, 1778

bills on the credit of the United States . . ." provided that at least nine states assented.

The administration of the finances was equally inadequate; it was reorganized during the early months of 1776 and put under a standing committee of five, later of ten, members of Congress, usually referred to as the Board of Treasury. Their work became more important and more onerous after independence was declared, when it became clear that a long and expensive war was in prospect. The unwillingness of Congress to place any effective power in the hands of one man made it difficult for the Board to function efficiently. Members had to audit all accounts and make provision for their payment, as well as to estimate future expenses. Many of the fundamental problems regarding the division of responsibility between legislative and executive branches were faced in this committee. Some of them were resolved when it was replaced in 1781 by a single Superintendent of Finance, Robert Morris, who was able to bring a certain amount of order into the chaotic finances.*

Late in 1776 Congress tried also to raise money by a lottery, a device which had frequently been used in the colonies to support schools and

---

* See p. 33.

churches. It was hoped that 1.5 million dollars might be raised through the sale of 100,000 tickets selling at 10, 20, 30, or 40 dollars each in "ready money." Prizes were to be paid in Continental bills or in treasury certificates bearing interest at 4 percent for 5 years. Unfortunately, the Continental bills had already begun to depreciate, and very few persons were willing to risk their ready money for a chance to win a prize of doubtful value. Tickets continued to be offered through 1781, but the revenue obtained in this way was insignificant.

Congress never gave up its attempts to collect from the states at least part of the funds needed for financing the war, but their contributions came in so slowly that there seemed no alternative except further issues of paper. During 1777 these amounted to 13 million dollars; although the issues were made cautiously, a million or two at a time, by the end of the year the notes had fallen to one-third of their face value. In 1778 the rate of issue was increased, and fourteen separate lots amounting to 63 million were put into circulation. During this year the government met its expenses almost entirely with paper money, and by the end of the year the value of the bills was down to one-fifth. It was becoming clear that the Continental bills were reaching the end of their usefulness. Redemptions of the early issues had not been made on schedule. The attempt made by Congress at the end of 1778 to take out of circulation two issues of more than 41 million, made in 1777 and 1778, on the excuse that they had been frequently counterfeited, had little effect except still further to weaken public confidence in the bills.

Finally in September 1779 Congress decided to place a ceiling of 200 million dollars on the total circulation. The amount outstanding at this time was already 160 million, and by the end of the year the limit had been reached; of total issues of 241 million, 200 were still outstanding. In March of the next year Congress resolved that it would redeem all bills of credit at one-fortieth of their face value. This was open repudiation, made more reprehensible by the fact that Congress had been declaring with vehemence almost up to that moment that it would never repudiate its obligations. Funds for the exchange of the bills into a new issue were to be obtained by a monthly levy on the states of 15 million of the old bills during the next thirteen months. As old bills came in, new ones were issued, but to only one-twentieth of the face value of the old. Within a year, the old bills had practically disappeared from circulation. George Washington, who had begun to keep the accounts of the army in Continental dollars in 1777, made the last entry in paper currency in his current account record in May 1781. After that date, specie was again in circulation, thanks in large part to the specie sent from France.[1]

State Issues of Paper Money

The depreciation of the Continental paper was aggravated by the fact that most of the states also issued inconvertible paper money during the Revolution. When the colonial governments were superseded by special revolutionary assemblies, they found themselves without the usual sources of income, but faced with the necessity of raising militia, obtaining supplies, and paying officials. The restraints of royal governors and British laws were no longer operative. The battle of Lexington was hardly over when the Connecticut Assembly met and voted, among other items, an issue of £50,000 in bills of credit redeemable in two years. During the summer it issued another £100,000 to be redeemed by a special tax levy within 5 years. Massachusetts, which had been on practically a specie basis for a quarter of a century, issued £26,000 of paper early in 1775 in order to make advance payments to newly recruited soldiers. Rhode Island followed suit, but made the new issues bear interest at 2.5 percent for 5 years; later issues bore no interest. By the close of 1775 every one of the colonies from New Hampshire to Georgia had issued some paper money. The total for the Revolutionary period was estimated at more than 200 million dollars, not far below the total for the Continental bills of the Confederation.

Congress grew concerned about the state issues when they became an important factor in the inflation which was occurring. In 1777, therefore, Congress requested the states to discontinue their issues and to make the Continental bills a full legal tender. Gradually the states acceded to this request and either stopped their issues altogether or substituted for them treasury notes bearing interest. The notes already outstanding were not redeemed according to schedule, but remained in circulation until worn out or paid for taxes. By mid-1780 most of them had fallen to less than 2 percent of their face value.

Inflation and Price Controls

The rising prices which accompanied the increase in paper money brought about efforts to regulate them by law. New England, accustomed to legal control over many aspects of life, called one of the first price conventions in Providence in December 1776 when the increase in prices was still moderate. It recommended more taxation, and restriction of paper money, and formulated a set of prices for farm labor, wheat, corn, rum, and wool; "all other necessary articles" were "to be in reasonable accustomed proportion to the above." These recommendations were enacted into law by the New England states and were recommended by Congress to states in other areas as well. For its own part, Congress invited the states to pass even more severe laws to regulate retail trade, and to confiscate hoarded goods in order to control the profiteers who were using every means of "oppressing, sharping and extortion." Several other states followed the example of New England and passed laws of varying degrees of severity.

In addition to these legislative efforts to punish the merchants who hoarded goods or refused to sell at legal prices and the speculators who took advantage of scarcities, many communities resorted to direct action. Mass meetings were held in some towns, merchants were threatened or haled into court, irate women raided shops in which goods were said to be hoarded, and the specie dollar was hanged in effigy in Philadelphia to protest the refusal of dealers to accept paper money.

The general ineffectiveness of all these measures may be judged by the fact that a second price convention was held in Connecticut in January 1778 which drew up another long list of approved prices. Congress itself authorized the calling of a price convention in Philadelphia in 1780 and urged the states to set guide lines for prices of domestic produce and wages of farm labor at twenty times the rates which had prevailed in 1774. In the same year, however, Congress also advised the states to repeal their legal tender laws, since the notes to which they referred were being withdrawn from circulation. After that date the attempt to legislate prices was generally abandoned.[2]

The inflation was disastrous for those living on fixed incomes—widows, retired persons, creditors of any sort. For farmers, laborers, and others living on current earnings there was little difference, and for debtors there was an actual advantage since they could pay off their debts with a fraction of the real value which they had borrowed. The general confusion and dishonesty engendered by the situation was of course a disadvantage to the whole community.

State Support of the Confederation

The Continental Congress had been given no power to levy any kind of tax or to collect any kind of revenue. Yet it was expected to carry on the war, to send commissioners abroad, and to handle a considerable volume of domestic business as well. It had therefore to rely on the contributions of the states, and it was often reduced to the humiliation of begging them to fulfill their obligations. The quotas for each state were set by Congress but, in the absence of any precise measure of either population or wealth, the resulting figures often represented a hope for an amount to be forthcoming, rather than an equitable distribution of the tax burden.

Early in January 1777 Congress recommended to the state legislatures that in order to provide the funds for redeeming their shares of notes already in circulation, they should

raise by taxation, in the course of the current year, and remit to the treasury, such sums of money as they shall think will be most proper in the present situation of the inhabitants; which sums shall be carried to their credit, and accounted for in the settlement of their proportion of the public expenses and debts, for which the united [sic] States are jointly bound: . . . .[3]

The November exhortation of Congress to the states was somewhat more specific; the states were requested to raise by taxation a total of 5 million dollars, allocated roughly by estimated population. This and similar subsequent appeals brought only a small amount to the national treasury, and it was therefore followed in 1779 by more formal requisitions of 15 million in January, 45 million in May, and 30 million in October. In response to these ever more insistent requests, about 3 million was actually paid in paper money, and another 10 million in supplies. By this time the depreciation was so far advanced that the specie value of the supplies was probably less than 1 million.

Further requisitions from the states during 1780 were made in the form of supplies of beef, pork, rum, flour, and tobacco. This method of provisioning the troops seemed to Congress to have the double advantage of shifting to the states the problem of collecting the supplies and of relieving the quartermaster of the administration of the funds. The waste and incompetence in this department had been subjects of constant complaint. But the new system did little to improve the financial situation. On April 24, 1780, Congress again appealed to the states in a letter reported in the *Secret Journal* but not released for publication:

It is unnecessary to mention our embarrassments. They are known to you. . . . To the means of relieving them we wish your attention. The whole of the moneys due on the quotas of taxes to the first of March last, are become of immediate and indispensable necessity. Numerous debts have accumulated on the publick departments, and justice requires they should be forthwith discharged. Large sums are also requisite for the purposes of transportation, and to continue the purchases of supplies for the army until the states are prepared to furnish them.

A month later a resolution of Congress called on the states "to collect and pay into the continental treasury immediately, if possible, and at all events within thirty days of this time, ten millions of dollars for . . . bringing the army into the field, and forwarding their supplies."[4]

If the situation was desperate for the federal government, it was not easier for the individual states. Several of them were occupied by British troops at various times and were therefore unable to contribute to the general expense even if they had wished to do so. The states which were not occupied also found it difficult to raise enough by taxes to pay their own and the federal expenses. Since one of the prime reasons for the revolt of the colonies from British rule had been objection to taxation, the state assemblies often had trouble in explaining to the citizenry why, after the Revolution had taken place, taxes were higher than before. There was a great deal of muttering and complaint, as well as outright resistance.

There was undoubtedly reason for complaint. The methods of collecting taxes in this period were extremely varied, and they were often inequitable by any standard. The Marquis de Chastellux who visited the country in 1781 was quite shocked at the high rates and the careless methods of assessment. In Boston, he reported:

Twelve assessors have full powers to tax the people according to their ability; they estimate on view, the business transacted by each merchant, and his probable profits. Mr. Brick for example being agent for the French navy, and interested besides in several branches of commerce, amongst them that of insurance, they calculate how much business he may be supposed to do, of which they judge by the bills of exchange he endorses, and by the policies he underwrites, and according to their valuation, in which neither losses nor expences are reckoned, they suppose him to gain so much a day and he is consequently subjected to a pro-portionable daily tax. During the year 1781 he paid *three guineas and a half per day.*[5]

Some individuals in all states had suffered heavily from occupation by enemy troops, or from the requisition of supplies by their own armies, and were unable to meet tax assessments. When Benjamin Franklin wrote to the French monarch asking for a loan, he declared that it would be impossible for the new government to finance the war for independence through taxation alone.

There were of course some citizens like John and Abigail Adams who saw clearly that inflation did more harm than taxation. John Adams wrote to his wife in August 1777, "Taxation as deep as possible is the only radical cure. I hope you will pay every tax that is brought to you, if you sell my books or clothes or oxen, or your cows, to pay it." And Abigail, on June 8, 1779, wrote to her husband in Paris of the high rates she was paying, "That, I suppose, you will rejoice at; so would I, did it remedy the evil" [of inflation].[6]

Loan Certificates

The inability of Congress to obtain from the states the funds needed for the war, and the rapid depreciation of the Continental currency, caused Congress as early as October 1776 to attempt the sale of loan certificates, or short-term Treasury obligations. The first offer, in units of 200 dollars and up, had little success because the rate of interest was only 4 percent. When on the advice of John Adams the next issue bore 6 percent, most of the 15 million was sold through loan offices set up in each of the states. The rate was really better than 6 percent because from September 1777 to March 1778 the interest was payable in specie, obtained by bills of exchange drawn on the American commissioners in Paris who had finally succeeded in negotiating a secret loan from France.

Although the offer of interest in specie was withdrawn after the first six months, 67 million of the certificates were sold; their value in specie amounted to about 11 million dollars. A large part of the total came not from cash sales, but from the issue of loan certificates to pay for requisitions of supplies and even for wages. They were paid out to state governments and to individual merchants and contractors by army quartermasters, commissaries, and other officers. Congress also used loan certificates to cover some of its own expenses during the difficult winter of 1780–1781. There was very little control over the goods received or the services rendered, either as to quality or to quantity, and waste and inefficiency, if not downright corruption, increased under the system. It was impossible to determine the total amount of certificates issued, or how many had been returned in payment for taxes. Their effect on the economy was the same as if paper money had been added to the circulation. After the war, the certificates still outstanding were merged into the body of the federal debt according to a table of depreciation showing the value of paper money at the time each certificate had been issued.[7]

Robert Morris

Little improvement in federal finance was made until Robert Morris became Superintendent of Finance in 1781. He was already a leading figure among Philadelphia merchants. He had come to America with his father when he was only thirteen years old, and had been apprenticed to the firm of Charles Willing. Ten years later he became a partner, an unusual achievement for a young man of twenty-three. Willing and Morris dealt in a wide range of commodities, on their own account or as correspondents, with operations in the West Indies, Spain, and Portugal as well as Great Britain. They also handled marine insurance and bills of exchange, combining commerce and finance as was customary among merchants of the period. Both Willing and Morris had been active in opposition to the British colonial policy, and were among the earliest signers of the Non-Importation Resolutions. Morris became a member of the Pennsylvania delegation to the Continental Congress, and one of the signers of the Declaration of Independence.

He was therefore familiar with the problems of federal finance when he became Superintendent of Finance. As a responsible executive, he was able to introduce much needed improvements in the government accounts and in the methods of raising and handling funds. He even initiated a budget system, so that each department was obliged to estimate its expenditures, and the whole was presented for the approval of Congress before any funds could be paid out. He risked his personal fortune by underwriting government obligations which could not have been sold without his guarantee. There were some transactions in which it was difficult to distinguish his personal and his public interests, for he did not abandon his own business when he took over the public office. Although some of his activities could certainly be criticized by modern standards, they seem to have been kept well within the limits of the business ethics of their day. He gave up his position in 1784 in order to rebuild his own fortune, but several of his ventures were unsuccessful and he died a bankrupt.[8]

Foreign Loans

Even before the Declaration of Independence was signed, Congress had sent a Committee of Secret Correspondence to France to obtain sympathy and, if possible, more tangible aid. Congress certainly did not expect the French king to feel any kindness toward revolutions, but there was reason to hope that France would be glad to assist in embarrassing and weakening its hereditary enemy, England. This hope was justified, and early in 1776 the French representative Beaumarchais arranged for the secret shipment of 1 million livres* worth of supplies and munitions from the royal arsenals, to be repaid in shipments of produce from America. About the same time, and for similar reasons, Spain gave 1 million livres to the French secretary of state to be used to assist America. Such secrecy surrounded these transactions that no adequate accounts were kept, the public and private transactions became hopelessly intermingled, and it was not until 1831 that Congress finally settled with the heirs of

---

* A livre was worth one-fifth of a Spanish milled dollar in September 1777.

Beaumarchais by paying part of their claims. It should be noted that these loans involved only commodities on both sides and were never included in the total of foreign loans negotiated by Congress.

The good relations between France and the United States were further strengthened by the treaty drafted in September 1776 and signed on May 4, 1778, which gave to France reciprocal rights to commerce and shipping. This was also kept secret, as were further loans of 2 million livres and supplies worth nearly 5 million livres.

By this time the principal European powers were preparing for their own wars. Not only were they unable to lend more to America, but also they were attempting to borrow in the European money markets and offering to pay higher interest than the Americans. It was therefore not until 1781 that more help could be obtained from France. In that year the King made a loan of 4 million livres and an outright gift of 6 million livres, part of it to be used for the purchase of supplies in France, and part to be sent in cash to the United States for the use of the army. Since the King had observed the confusion and inefficiency in the handling of American finances on both sides of the ocean, he stipulated that only George Washington himself, the commander-in-chief, should be permitted to draw on the fund. Benjamin Franklin, then a commissioner in Paris, protested indignantly against such an unusual arrangement, but in vain. Another loan of 6 million livres in 1782 and a final loan of 6 million livres in 1783 brought the total French loans to 18 million livres, the equivalent at that time of about 3.3 million dollars.

In addition, the French monarch agreed to serve as security for a Dutch loan of 10 million livres, to be floated in Amsterdam. The American commissioners had been trying for several years to raise money there, the financial capital of Europe. The Dutch regency, however, refused to help the American cause, and Dutch bankers, closely allied with British financial interests, were not willing to handle an American loan. The credit of the United States was not high, and on a strictly business basis hardly merited consideration. Nor was it improved by the fact that several individual states, as John Adams indignantly reported, had sent emissaries "running all over Europe, asking to borrow money" which gave the impression that distress and poverty prevailed throughout the country.

The difficulties and discouragements of the American commissions in

Europe caused John Adams to write home at one point, "I can represent my situation in this affair of a loan, by no other figure than that of a man in the midst of the ocean negotiating for his life among a school of sharks." Nevertheless in July 1782 he was able to report to Congress that he had arranged for a loan of 5 million guilders, approximately 2 million dollars, at 5 percent, to be put on the market in sections. If the first section went well, the second would be offered. In spite of Adams' pessimism the loan was a success and the proceeds became available just in time to pay the interest on the loan made earlier by France, and to pay the drafts which had been drawn against the American commissioners in Europe, to meet bills payable in America. The letters of the commissioners to each other and to Congress in this period suggest that the situation of Adams, and others, was not so much that of a man among sharks as of a man on a tightrope. Bills of exchange were drawn in America by supply and treasury officials and sent to Europe to pay for purchases and to pay the interest on certificates and bonds held by foreigners. The commissioners often had no ready cash with which to meet these bills and had to borrow the funds after the bills were drawn; their own salaries and expenses had also to be met by such borrowing. Foreign lenders had ample reason for hesitating to invest their funds in America. France, Holland, and Spain, the only countries which gave any aid or made any loans to the United States in this early period, would hardly have done so on purely economic grounds; fortunately, their political interests were involved and so help was forthcoming.[9]

Business Conditions during the Revolution

Although both state and federal governments had such difficulty in meeting their regular and military expenses, the revolutionary years were far from being a period of deep depression over the whole country. Indeed they were marked, in some areas at some times, by many symptoms of boom. The occupying British forces in Boston, Providence, and New York spent large amounts when they were provisioning their troops in those cities. French troops who came to aid the American army also spent liberally. Even the American army, although it had little to spend but paper money and loan certificates, created a flurry of business activity around its various headquarters.

When military operations interfered with ordinary business in the seacoast town, merchants moved inland. The Marquis de Chastellux reported that the interior roads and inns of the northern states had been greatly improved as a result of this shift. He found also that a great deal of manufacturing was starting up as a result of the curtailment of imports. In Connecticut "some common cloths and other woollen stuffs are fabricated here, but of a good wear, and sufficient to clothe the people who live in the country, or in any other town than Boston, New York and Philadelphia. I went into a house where they were preparing and dying the cloth. This cloth is made by the people of the country, and is then sent to these little manufactories, where they are dressed, pressed and dyed." He concluded, "On the whole it is difficult to conceive the state of increase and the prosperity of this country, after so long and calamitous a war."[10]

The prosperity was not confined to domestic business. Foreign, and especially English, goods were still in great demand, and the ports that escaped British occupation became centers for privateering as well as for legal shipping. The business of marine insurance developed rapidly in connection with the legal voyages. Privateering voyages, although they could not be covered by insurance because of the high risks they ran, were extremely profitable if they were successful, and a number of New England fortunes were based on this activity. The development of shipping was furthered by the abolition of customhouse monopolies at such ports as Annapolis and Newport, and by the opening of all the ports to the ships of all friendly nations. This action, a natural revulsion against the hated mercantilist policies of England, had been one of the first steps taken by the new Congress in April 1776.

The end of hostilities in 1783 marked the end of the heavy military expenditures, and released from the army many soldiers, causing a readjustment of economic life. In some sections of the country there was a surge of building of houses and taverns and roads. There was also a pent-up demand for imported goods. But the erstwhile colonies soon began to feel the effect of their exclusion from British markets, and the newly gained right to trade directly with European countries did not at first make up the difference. Prices of American exports such as wheat began to fall in 1785. Bankruptcies of small merchants increased notably in 1784 and 1785. Bitter complaints were sent to Congress, but with its limited powers it was helpless to take any effective action.

Coinage

During the Revolution as before, there was a shortage of coin. What was left in circulation consisted of worn or clipped coins from all corners of the world, especially England, Spain, and Portugal. The moidores and and six-and-thirties had holes punched in them, while others were actually cut into halves, quarters, and even eighths. Congress itself ordered that coins destined to be paid out by the quartermaster be clipped down to the "standard weight." When Mr. Timothy Pickering asked for punch and anvil with which to perform this operation, he was informed that it could be done very easily with shears. It was no wonder that many traders still used tobacco as the basis for their pricing.[11]

The colonial paper which was still in circulation only added to the confusion. Lieutenant Thomas Anburey from Burgoyne's army, who as prisoner of war was marched from Massachusetts to Virginia in 1778, wrote:

We have been greatly perplexed in our march through the various provinces by the dollars being of such various value; in some it is only six shillings, in others seven, seven and sixpence, and eight shillings. The provinces entertain little opinion as to the value of their neighbor's money, as it will not pass in the next province; the New-York money will not pass in the Jerseys, nor that of the Jerseys in Pennsylvania, and so on.[12]

It was not until 1782 that Congress took up the matter of coinage. It called on Robert Morris for a statement of the values of all the coins then in circulation, with recommendations for a national currency. He proposed as the unit a silver dollar of 373 grains of fine silver, with smaller coins of copper. Congress approved his request for the establishment of a Mint, but made no decision regarding the coins to be minted. Thomas Jefferson earned the eternal gratitude of his countrymen by amending Morris' plan to make the small coins decimal fractions of the dollar, with the half-cent the lowest in value. The actual value of the dollar as established by Congress in 1786 was 375.64 grains of fine silver, to be minted with one-eleventh part alloy, into dollars, half-dollars, double-dimes, and dimes. Five- and ten-dollar gold pieces were also to be minted, with 24.6268 grains of pure gold to the dollar. This made the ratio of gold to silver 15.253 to 1.

The only coins actually minted under this legislation of the Confederation were a few tons of copper cents and half-cents. Foreign copper coins were no longer to be current after September 1787, and any copper coins struck by the states were to pass by weight. The shortage of these small coins was a great hardship.[13]

New Issues of State Paper Money

Although the signing of the peace treaty in September 1783 greatly reduced the current expenses of the central government, it did not put an end to the financial problems. Nearly 1 million dollars of debts from 1783 were still unpaid in 1784, in addition to the 3 million dollars of overdue interest on debts contracted during the war. The total expenses for 1784 were expected therefore to be about 5.5 million. With no certain income in view, Congress had no recourse except to call again on the states, and they were as unable or unwilling to meet their quotas as they had been during the war.

The states had financial difficulties of their own. Many of them had large unpaid war debts, and in many of them the taxes were heavy and uncertain. A renewed demand therefore arose for issues of paper money, and paper money parties gained control of a number of state legislatures. Pennsylvania was the first to yield to this demand; in spite of the strong opposition of Pelatiah Webster and other urban representatives, the rural spokesmen from the western part of the state combined with the enemies of the banking interests to approve an issue of £150,000 of bills of credit in May 1785. One-third of the amount was to be loaned on mortgage security, and two-thirds to be used to pay interest on the outstanding debt. The bills were not made legal tender, and a sinking fund was established for their redemption. Nevertheless they depreciated by 12 percent by the end of 1786, and by 1789 had practically disappeared from circulation.

New York also used paper money to meet its expenses in this period. After much public discussion, in which Thomas Paine led the opposition, sterling bills for £200,000 were issued in 1786, to be redeemed at 8 shillings to the dollar; three-fourths of the amount was to be loaned on real estate security. About the same time, New Jersey issued a modest amount of £100,000 which depreciated so little that some of it remained in circulation down to 1800. North Carolina and Georgia used paper issues to pay their returning soldiers, and in both states the notes depreciated rapidly. The issues of South Carolina were better managed than those of her neighbors; they were circulating at a premium by 1789, and the interest paid on the loans which secured the notes brought the state a revenue of 300,000 dollars by 1808, when some were still outstanding.

In Rhode Island the controversy over paper money was heated and violent. The paper money party won the election of April 1786 and at once issued a "paper bank" of £100,000, to be loaned against mortgages of twice the value, for 14 years at 4 percent. Most of the loans went to the farmers, who had been the strongest advocates of the issue. Merchants in the towns refused to accept the paper, although it was declared to be legal tender. The embattled merchants still refused it; some of them closed their shops; creditors hid from debtors who were trying to repay loans in the rapidly depreciating paper; even the farmers refused to bring their produce to market. In a celebrated case, brought against a butcher who refused to take the money at par, in September 1786 the court refused to uphold the legal tender clause. The Assembly threatened to impeach the judge, but finally capitulated and repealed the law in 1789.

Not all the states succumbed to the pressure for paper money. Massachusetts, Connecticut, and New Hampshire in New England, Virginia and Maryland in the south, were able to avoid it.[14] The new constitution settled the question by reserving to the federal government the right "To coin Money, regulate the Value thereof, and of foreign Coin" and by expressly forbidding the states to "coin Money; emit Bills of Credit; make any Thing but gold and silver Coin a Tender in Payment of Debts."*

---

* Notes issued by state-chartered banks were not prohibited by this clause, according to the court decision in Briscoe v. Bank of Maryland in 1837.

Early Banking

Down to the Revolution the word "bank" in the colonies had usually signified a mere batch of paper money, and the appropriate phrase was "to issue a bank." Abroad, however, there were several banks in the modern sense of the word; the Bank of England had been established in 1694, Sweden and France had public banks, and the functioning of the Bank of Amsterdam had been described by Adam Smith in his *Wealth of Nations*, which was widely read in America after its publication in 1776. Well-educated Americans were therefore quite familiar with the services which could be performed by a commercial bank.

Alexander Hamilton, Gouverneur Morris, and Robert Livingston were among the Congressional leaders who advocated the establishment of a bank as of possible assistance in the difficult task of financing the war. A despairing letter from General Washington brought the problem sharply to the attention of Congress, and persuaded it to establish the Bank of Pennsylvania in June 1780. This Bank was far from being a modern commercial bank, however; it was more like a subscription list to a loan fund for the army with the repayment guaranteed by Congress. It had no charter, and the subscribers merely received bonds to the amount of their subscription. Robert Morris himself subscribed £10,000, and the total amounted to £300,000. Congress directed the Board of Treasury to put up as security £150,000 of bills of exchange drawn on the United States ministers in Europe—which of course depended on their ability to borrow the money there. The Bank nevertheless was of great assistance. Thomas Paine reported that "By means of this bank the army was supplied throughout the campaign, and being at the same time recruited, was enabled to maintain its ground." Most observers agreed with Thomas Paine that the Bank of Pennsylvania, in spite of the rather primitive form which was so disappointing to Alexander Hamilton, had been of inestimable service to the revolutionary cause at a moment of crisis.

Many would also have added that one of its chief services had been that of preparing the way for the establishment of a true commercial bank, the Bank of North America. That charter was granted by a narrow majority of Congress in May 1781 with very little debate. Many of the subscribers to the Bank of Pennsylvania merely exchanged their shares for those of the new bank; others paid for them with government loan certificates. In order to complete its capital of 400,000 dollars, Morris subscribed 254,000 on behalf of the government, and the Bank was thus enabled to begin operations in January 1782. Each 400-dollar share was entitled to one vote in electing the twelve Directors. Two of them were chosen each quarter to "inspect and control" the business, this involved reporting to the Superintendent of Finance at the close of every business day the state of the cash account and the notes issued and received. No limit was set on the note issue, and there was no requirement as to reserves; the notes were made receivable for all taxes and debts due the United States.

Since there was some question about the power of the Continental Congress to charter such an institution, the Bank obtained charters or recognition of its national charter from many of the states; some of them granted it also a monopoly of banking within the state. Its business increased rapidly and in its second year it paid a dividend of 14 percent. This attracted more private investors who bought out the government shares. In 1784 the capital was increased by 1000 new shares which sold at 500 dollars, a premium of 20 percent above par.

Robert Morris as Superintendent of Finance found the Bank enormously useful to him in the handling of government finances. One of his business partners, Thomas Willing, was its president. The Bank loaned the government money to tide it over temporary deficits, discounted its bills, and helped to bring order into the collection and expenditures of the federal treasury. It handled funds of state and municipal agencies as well, and its commercial business was large. Pelatiah Webster, the Philadelphia merchant, wrote of it in his *Political Essays* in 1791:

So great was its success, and so amazing were its affects, that it appears by the bank-books, that its cash-account in one year, viz. from Jan. 1, 1784 to Jan. 1, 1785 (the third year of its operation) amounted to the almost incredible sum of 59 570 000 Mexican dollars; and its transactions from Jan. 1, 1785 to Jan. 1, 1786 amounted to about 37 000 000 dollars.[15]

It remained in operation until it was absorbed by the First Pennsylvania Banking and Trust Company (established in 1812) in 1929.

The success of this bank, and the need of more banking service for the expanding commerce of the country, soon brought about the chartering of two similar institutions. In New York, Alexander Hamilton had long been interested in establishing a commercial bank. Chancellor Livingston and his friend tried to set up a bank based on mortgage security, like some of the land banks of the colonial period, but Hamilton was able to get this proposal defeated by the legislature. In its stead he drafted a charter for a "money" bank based on specie subscribed for its stock. Because his political opponents were able to prevent the bank from obtaining a legislative charter, it began as a private company, but one which nevertheless succeeded in obtaining its 500,000 dollar capital from more than 200 subscribers within a few weeks. Each stockholder was entitled to seven votes for the first ten shares, and one extra vote for each five additional shares. The discount rate was set at 6 percent, a thirty-day limit was set on loans, and no renewals were to be permitted. The cashier was sent to Philadelphia to learn the details of operation from the Bank of North America, and the Bank of New York opened for business at Franklin Square on June 9, 1784. It finally obtained a charter from the state of New York in 1791.*

The third bank established during the Confederation period was the Bank of Massachusetts in Boston. It was chartered by the state legislature in February 1784 with a capital of £500,000, but its accounts were kept in Mexican dollars. Discounting rules were similar to those of the New York bank, and some of its customers complained that the bank subtracted the interest at the time of the loan—a practice which became universal in the United States. The Bank of Massachusetts merged with the First National Bank of Boston in 1903.[16]

Business Organization

There were few corporations other than banks in the years of the Confederation. The urgent need to improve transportation led to several attempts to raise funds for the purpose by private subscription, without formal incorporation. General Washington, as early as 1772, had been instrumental in obtaining from the Virginia House of Burgesses permission to collect money and open a navigable way in the Potomac river as

---

* See p. 69.

far as Fort Cumberland. Technical problems, as well as the jealousy of Maryand, were responsible for so long a delay that the war intervened and the project had to be abandoned.

As soon as the war was over, this and similar plans were revived, and by 1790 six charters had been granted by legislatures of five southern states for corporations to improve inland navigation. Other states soon joined in the drive for internal improvements, and a number of companies secured charters. There was little difficulty in securing subscriptions to the stock of these corporations, but actual payment for the shares came in very slowly. Few of the projects were ever completed, and many of them were not even started. Not until the state and local governments undertook the building of roads and canals in a later period were they successfully carried through.*

The corporations chartered for the construction of toll bridges—three before 1790, and 73 by the end of the century—were somewhat more successful. Building a toll bridge was less expensive and less difficult than constructing a road or a canal, and offered the investor a much quicker return on his capital. The first toll bridge was constructed across the Charles River to connect Boston and Charlestown. It was opened in 1786, on the anniversary of Bunker Hill, with a parade, music, and a banquet for eight hundred. The celebration was quite justified; annual profits were reported as more than 10 percent for many years.

The corporate form of organization was seldom used for manufacturing enterprises in this period. Many of them started as household activities; spinning, weaving, knitting, and shoemaking carried on by a family developed into the manufacture of larger amounts for a cash income. The putting-out system was also common in this period; such articles as nails made from rod iron, and wool cards and cotton cards (so important before the invention of the cotton gin), could be made at home from materials supplied by an employer. Even the heavier activities like those of gristmills, sawmills, paper mills, and glassworks were customarily begun as family enterprises or as partnerships using local capital. Almy and Brown of Providence which in 1789 began to manufacture corduroys and other heavy fabrics, the Aera and Aetna Iron Works of North Carolina, the hat factory of Burr and Company in Danbury, Connecticut,

---

* See p. 109 ff.

were all unincorporated. In some cases the enterprise was run as an unincorporated joint-stock company. Three corporations which formed exceptions to the general rule were a cotton manufacturer chartered by Massachusetts, and in Connecticut, one chartered for the manufacture of silk and another for mining iron ore.[17]

Public Lands

One source of revenue which had been heavily counted on by the Continental Congress was the sale of public lands, those vast and largely uncharted areas of the West. Even in the preliminary draft of the Articles of Confederation prepared by Benjamin Franklin in 1776, there had been a hint that the lands of the colonies "which by Charter or Proclamation, or under any Pretence, are said to extend to the South Sea" should be under the jurisdiction of Congress. However, when the vote on the question was taken on October 15, 1777, the states denied to Congress the power to fix their boundaries. The same question was raised again in the finance report of September 19, 1778—the same report in which it was proposed to "cry down" the currency emissions of the states and to levy a percent tax on imports. The report called on the "several States having large uncultivated Territory, beyond what is in their Power to govern . . . to cede the same to the United States." This recommendation, like most of the others in the report, went unheeded. The question became more urgent when in 1780 and 1781 Maryland was hesitating to ratify and thus complete the Confederation. Maryland had feared the size and power of the larger states like Connecticut, New York, and Virginia and was persuaded to join the Confederation only after they ceded their western lands to the United States.

The lands thus acquired by the federal government created many problems, political as well as financial. No part of them could be sold until plans were made for organizing and governing them. An elaborate scheme for the eventual formation of ten new states, complete with classical names suggested by Jefferson, with slavery forever excluded, was modified in debate until it became little more than provision for temporary government of any territory which had a population of 20,000 or more free inhabitants. In this form it was passed on April 23, 1784. Washington made a trip into the West during the latter part of that year and was concerned about the speed with which speculators and squatters were taking up the land. There was also danger of renewed Indian wars if just dealing with the tribes was not enforced. Congress finally stopped its wrangling and passed the Land Ordinance of 1787 which made pre-survey unnecessary and thus made possible large grants. Among the provisions of the Ordinance which became the land policy of the United States was one which required one section of every township to be reserved for the maintenance of public schools. A similar proposal for the support of religion was rejected.

As a result of this legislation it became possible to open the area to the public. There was great potential demand for the land, and several companies were organized almost as soon as the war was over to buy large tracts and sell them in subdivisions. The Ohio Company offered to buy 1 million dollars worth of land in 1787, to be paid for in paper, with an allowance of one-third for bad lands and incidental expenses; the actual cost to the company amounted to 8 or 9 cents per acre. The Scioto Company was another which was early on the scene with a purchase of 5 million acres. Just how much revenue was obtained altogether from this source in this early period is not easy to determine. Jefferson in 1787 declared that 5 million acres had been sold in private sale for a dollar an acre, but in certificates not in specie. Hamilton in his *Report on Public Credit* of 1790, estimated 960,000 dollars as the amount received from the sale of land and other properties. Gallatin gave the receipts from sales of public lands up to 1790 as 1,100,000. Whatever the total, these sales did not bring in enough actual cash to meet the pressing financial needs of the Confederation government.[18]

Import Duties

Since the hard-pressed Continental Congress had exhausted the possibilities of paper money issues, and public land sales had proved disappointing, the most promising source of income in the immediate postwar period seemed to be a resort to import duties. Congress had shifted its position on this question several times. Most of the early Revolutionary leaders, with the possible exception of Alexander Hamilton, were free traders in principle. They welcomed the release from Britain's trade restrictions, and hoped that free trade might be established in the United States, even if during the war it was necessary to stop imports from Britain. One of the first actions of Congress when it assembled in Philadelphia in September 1774 had been the passage of a nonimportation resolution against all goods from Great Britain and Ireland. In October this became a nonconsumption and nonexportation resolution as well. Merchandise from other countries, however, was to be freely admitted, and

any goods, wares and merchandise, except such as are of the growth, production, or manufacture of, or brought from any country under the dominion of the King of Great Britain, and except India Tea, may be imported from any other part of the world to the thirteen United Colonies, by the inhabitants thereof, and by the people of all such countries as are not subject to the said King; liable however to all such duties and imposition as now are, or may hereafter be laid by any of the said colonies.

Slaves were specifically excluded.

Unfortunately, this recognition by Congress of the right of the states to put a levy on imports encouraged many of them to reinstate the duties which, in the first flush of their independence from England, they, like the Congress, had abolished. Virginia had been an exception; even during the war she had continued to tax most imports except salt, iron, and firearms, as well as the exports of tobacco which had long been her chief source of revenue. Other states now joined Virginia in exacting import duties, not only to raise the needed revenue but also, after the first few years of reviving trade, to protect the infant industries which had sprung up during the war. The Pennsylvania Act of 1785 was designed "to encourage and protect the manufactures of this state." Massachusetts in the same year set a duty of 25 percent *ad valorem* on many manufactured articles, and high specific rates on others. By 1788, nine of the thirteen states, including all in New England and the middle area, had passed one or more tariff laws.

By this time, even such earlier advocates of free trade as Franklin, Madison, Jefferson, and John Adams had become convinced that at least temporary protection was needed from the flood of imports if American manufacturing was to survive. They would not admit that Lord Sheffield was correct, in his *Observations on the Commerce of the American States* of 1783, when he wrote rather smugly that Americans could not get along without imports of manufactured goods, and that only the

British could provide the credit which Americans needed in order to pay for them; the British therefore had little to fear from French or Dutch competition, and there was no reason for them to make any concessions to Americans in order to keep their trade. The Americans were determined to prove Lord Sheffield wrong and, like Pitt, foresaw the day when they would be able to supply their own woolens, cottons, shoes, hats, stockings, buttons, jewelry, books, porcelain, glass, cutlery, iron and steel, cordage, and wine.

Congress did not therefore disapprove the import duties of the states; rather it coveted the power to raise revenue for itself by the same method. Even during the war, in exhorting the states to meet their quotas of military expenses, Congress had suggested that the levy on the states would be less onerous if the central government could collect import duties. Gouverneur Morris as early as September 1778 proposed that, along with the usual devices of foreign loans, loan certificates, state quotas, and a federal poll tax, Congress be empowered to levy a 2 percent import duty. Little attention was paid to any part of this report except that which dealt with the Continental currency. A similar recommendation was made in March 1780, and this time it was discussed at intervals for nearly a year. In February 1781 the states were requested to "vest a power in Congress to levy" an import duty of 5 percent *ad valorem* to be used for the payment of the public debt. Such a duty at this time would have produced only 600,000 to 700,000 dollars annually, and the interest on the public debt already amounted to about 2 million annually, but Congress hoped that, as foreign trade increased, more adequate revenue would be provided. However, the measure never went into effect because it was never able to obtain the consent of all the states.

In April 1783 Congress made another attempt to obtain the requisite authorization from the states. Debts were mounting, the army was threatening mutiny if it was not paid, and the possibility of further foreign loans seemed remote. The new version of the tariff proposed specific duties on each of the seven principal kinds of imports—liquor, sugar, tea, coffee, cocoa, molasses, and pepper—and a 5 percent *ad valorem* duty on less important kinds. The act was to run for only twenty-five years, and the collectors at the ports were to be named by the states in order to alleviate the fear of a strong central government which was voiced by many members of Congress. In spite of these provisions it was over two years before twelve of the states had given their approval. New York was the recalcitrant; she finally gave her consent in May 1785 but hedged it about with severe restrictions. Then it took Congress nearly a year to name a committee to draft the law. By this time the whole financial situation had changed so much for the worse that a far more effective remedy was required than a tariff, and the first steps were being taken toward a complete rewriting of the Articles of Confederation.[19]

Assumption of State Debts

Although the war had been won, revenues were still inadequate, but they were not the only financial problem of the Congress. Accounts still had to be settled among the states for the expenses incurred during the war. The Articles of Confederation had provided only that the total cost of the war was to be allocated among the states in proportion to the value of their land. States which had already contributed more than their allocation were to receive the difference from states which had not yet paid their quota.

This principle left the way open for much dissension. Some of the expenses had not been authorized by Congress, as, for example the expedition of George Rogers Clark sent by Virginia to the northwest. Some expenses had not been properly recorded, or essential records had been destroyed by enemy occupation, especially in the south. There were many perplexing problems relating to the accountability of the commissary officers: the relative rates of depreciation of the funds allotted to them for supplies; the reliability of the records, if indeed there were any records at all, of the amounts and kinds of goods purchased; and the credits to be assigned to the states for the goods and services which they had provided. Superintendent Morris knew that the states were anxious to be credited with all the supplies they had furnished, and that no state was willing to contribute more than its share. He submitted a report to Congress as early as November 1781 in which he emphasized the necessity of settling these problems so that the public credit could be restored. Congress followed his advice and in the Act of February 27, 1782, provided for a commission to examine all the accounts and determine the balances due to or from individuals and states. Its work was difficult and time-consuming. The Ordinance of 1786 made the task somewhat easier by relaxing some of the rules regarding proof of expenditure; no longer did the states have to present vouchers for each outlay. A year later the rules were still further eased, leaving the Commissioners with authority to follow "principles of general equity." One of the results was to make possible a host of individual claims which had not been made earlier for lack of documentary proof. It is worthy of note that, once the amounts of the claims had been settled by the Commissioners, they cannily destroyed the papers on which their decisions had been based.[20]

It was found that seven of the states had made contributions in cash or in kind which exceeded their share of the expenses. These seven— New Hampshire, Massachusetts, Rhode Island, Connecticut, New Jersey, South Carolina, and Georgia—accepted public securities in the amount of their respective balances. The six debtor states were expected to reimburse the federal government for the amount of their debit balance, but only New York ever did so; eventually all of them were released from the obligation. The settlement of these state and individual accounts was an important step in putting the finances on a sound basis. Although it did not provide the funds with which the claims could be met, it made possible the final settlement by Alexander Hamilton when the new Constitution gave the federal government an adequate revenue and a reorganized Treasury.*

The Cost of the Revolution

The total cost of the war was difficult to compute precisely because it depended on the rate at which the depreciated currency was valued in each period. In a Report made to the House of Representatives in 1790 the whole expense of the war to the United States was stated as 135 million dollars, made up of 5 million of expenditures abroad, 21 million expended by the states, 17 million of supplies paid for by certificates, and 92 million of wages and supplies paid for in cash, that is, in specie or in paper money at its specie value. This estimate was based on the official table of valuation of the paper currency, which was generally considered to have been overgenerous. Gallatin, who made a study of the same subject in his *Sketch of the Finances of the United*

* See p. 54.

States in 1796, accused Hamilton of "wasting" 11 million by overpaying the states without checking more carefully the amounts they had actually spent. Modern estimates have tended to put the total at a higher rather than a lower figure, since expenditures abroad may have amounted to 10 rather than to 5 million, and state expenditures should have included many items which were never entered in the official accounts.

These figures do not include the cost of the aid given by France in the form of army and navy reinforcements. The French Comptroller of the Treasury said that it cost his country 60 million livres annually to maintain its army in America. Over five years, this would have amounted to about 60 million dollars. Vergennes is reported to have told Lafayette in November 1782 that France had expended 250 million livres, or about 50 million dollars, in the course of the war. The peace treaty of 1783 made formal recognition of gifts and loans of about 6 million dollars, to be repaid with interest by 1798.

On their side, the British, in addition to the expenses met from current income, saw their national debt increase by 115 million pounds, the equivalent of almost 500 million dollars.[21]

Whatever the total, it appears that a large share of the real cost of the Revolution was borne by the luckless holders of the Continental and state paper money which depreciated so rapidly. Benjamin Franklin saw this clearly at the time, but could devise no alternative since Congress had no effective taxing power. In a letter to his friend Thomas Ruston, written on October 9, 1780, he took an optimistic view:

Congress . . . is, as you suppose, not well skilled in finance. But their deficiency in knowledge has been amply supplied by good luck. They issued an immense quantity of paper bills to pay, clothe, arm, and feed their troops, and fit out ships; and with this paper, without taxes for the first three years, they fought and buffeted one of the most powerful nations of Europe. They hoped, notwithstanding its quantity, to have kept up the value of their paper. In this they were mistaken. It depreciated gradually. But this depreciation, though in some circumstances inconvenient, has had the general good and great effect of operating as a tax, and perhaps the most equal of all taxes, since it depreciated in the hands of the holders of money, and thereby taxed them in proportion to the sums they held and the time they held it, which generally is in proportion to men's wealth.

Breck, who wrote a history of the Continental currency in 1843, took an even more cheerful view. He estimated the Continental issues at 200 million, and the state issues at 100 million, which is almost certainly too low. This total of 300 million he valued at 15 million specie, assuming an average value of 20 to 1. Since the issues covered a period of six years, and the population averaged about 3 million at that time, the actual burden according to his calculation was about 1 dollar per capita per year. This, he admits, is "a severe tax; yet, when examined with care, it will be found less heavy than it seems at first sight." He does not, like Franklin, attempt to argue away the inequality of the actual burden, which was far heavier on the lower-income groups than on the wealthy who could protect themselves from the inflation by investment in land or goods.[22]

The End of the Confederation

Alexander Hamilton, like many others, had become convinced of the need for a revision of the Articles of Confederation as a result of his experience with war finance problems. As early as 1783 he drafted a summary of the defects of the Articles, insofar as they related to financial needs, as follows:

Fourthly: In vesting the United States in Congress assembled with the *power of general taxation* . . . and yet rendering that power, so essential to the existence of the Union, nugatory, by withholding from them all control over either the imposition or the collection of the taxes for raising the sums required: whence it happens that the inclinations, not the abilities, of the respective States are, in fact, the criterion of their contribution to the common expense; and the public burthen has fallen, and will continue to fall, with very unequal weight.

Fifthly: In fixing a rule for determining the proportion of each State towards the common expense, which, if practicable at all, must, in the execution, be attended with great expense, inequality, uncertainty, and difficulty.

Sixthly: In authorizing Congress "to borrow money, or emit bills on the credit of the United States" without the power of establishing funds to secure the repayment of the money borrowed, or the redemption of the bills emitted. . . . Indeed, in authorizing Congress at all to emit an *unfunded* paper as the sign of value, a resource which though useful in the infancy of this country, and indispensable in the commencement of the revolution, ought not to continue a formal part of the Constitution, nor ever, hereafter, to be employed, being, in its nature, pregnant with abuses, and liable to be made the engine of imposition and fraud, holding out temptations equally pernicious to the integrity of government and to the morals of the people.

. . . .

Eighthly: In not vesting in the United States, a general superintendence of trade, equally necessary in the view of revenue and regulation. . . .[23]

No action resulted from these resolutions in the Congress, and Hamilton took up the subject again in a speech before the New York Legislature in 1787. He declared that in the previous five years the states of North Carolina and Georgia had paid nothing into the federal treasury; South Carolina, only a few supplies; and New Hampshire, 7000 dollars. Connecticut and Delaware had paid about one-third of their requisitions; Massachusetts, Rhode Island, and Maryland, about one-half; Pennsylvania, nearly all; and New York, more than her quota. Total payments into the treasury, according to this report, had declined steadily in each of the five years. For the preceding three years, only 1,400,000 dollars had been paid in specie (New York again contributing more than her share). Connecticut and New Jersey had declined to pay at all because they disapproved of the system. He ended the report by recommending again that import duties be levied by Congress. This should provide a revenue of about 1 million annually, which would be of material help in meeting the annual payments of $1,600,000 for principal and interest of the foreign debt.

It was not until September 1786 that a meeting actually assembled to consider "the trade and commerce of the United States" and "how far an uniform system in their commercial intercourse and regulations, might be necessary to their common interest." Commissioners from New York, New Jersey, Pennsylvania, Delaware, and Virginia met in Annapolis, a location carefully selected to be neutral, far removed from the party factions of New York and Philadelphia. Indeed it was so far removed that the Commissioners from three New England states and North Carolina never got there. The others drew up the resolutions for a full convention to meet in Philadelphia the following spring, and thus the new Constitution was made possible.[24]

CHAPTER 3

Liberty penny, 1806

A NEW CONSTITUTION AND A NEW ERA IN FINANCE, 1789-1811

The Treasury Department

AFTER more than a decade of experience with the weak Confederation, the need for a government which would have more power and more revenue had become evident even to those who feared it. The new Constitution gave Congress the specific powers, among others,

To lay and collect taxes, duties, imposts, and excises, to pay the debts and provide for the common defense and general welfare of the United States; but all duties, imposts, and excises shall be uniform throughout the United States;

To borrow money on the credit of the United States.

To coin money, regulate the value thereof, and of foreign coin, and fix the standard of weights and measures.

The power of Congress to tax was limited by the provision that "No capitation or other direct tax shall be laid unless in proportion to the census or enumeration hereinbefore directed to be taken."

The states were expressly forbidden to coin money, emit bills of credit, or make anything but gold and silver coin a tender in payment of debts.

The case for the new constitution was brilliantly argued in the *Federalist Papers* by James Madison, John Jay, and Alexander Hamilton, who stressed the advantages of the proposed changes both for public

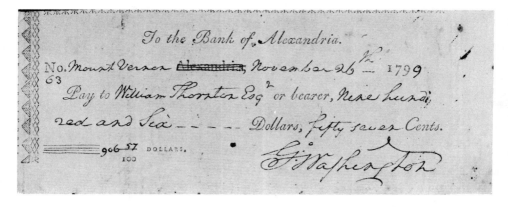

Check signed G. Washington, 1799

credit and for private enterprise. Ratification was secured in one state after another, and in April 1789 Washington was installed as President and delivered his inaugural address in Federal Hall at the corner of Wall and Broad Streets in New York City. The Department of State under Thomas Jefferson, and the War Department with Henry Knox as Secretary, were the first to be set up.

It was not until September 2 of that year that the Treasury Department was established. The enabling Act provided that it should be headed by a Secretary whose duty it should be:

to digest and prepare plans for the improvement and management of the revenue, and for the support of public credit; to prepare and submit report estimates of the public revenue, and the public expenditures; to superintend the collection of the revenue; to decide on the forms of keeping and stating accounts and making returns; . . . to make report, and give information to either branch of the legislature, in person or in writing (as he may be required), respecting all matters referred to him by the Senate or House of Representatives, or which shall pertain to his office; and generally to perform all such services relative to the finances, as he shall be directed to perform.

The same law provided for a Comptroller, an Auditor, a Treasurer, and a Register; required the Secretary to post a bond of 150,000 dollars and to make reports to each session of Congress.

Alexander Hamilton took over management of the Treasury when he was still in his early thirties, but he had had many years of experience in government and finance. In 1772 at the age of fifteen he had come from the West Indies to attend King's College in New York, bringing letters of introduction to the leaders of politics as well as of society. He was not yet through college when his first political pamphlet appeared anonymously, defending the Congressional boycott of British goods with many of the same arguments which were later developed in his *Report on Manufactures*. During the Revolution he was a Lieutenant-Colonel in command of New York regiments, an aide to General Washington, and a member of the Continental Congress. In 1782 Robert Morris appointed him a Receiver of Continental taxes for New York, for which he was to receive one-fourth of 1 percent of the state's quota of 373,598 dollars. This experience with the practical difficulties of obtaining revenue for the central government convinced him of the need to strengthen the Articles of Confederation, and he was one of the leaders in the convention which drafted the new Constitution.

When the new Constitution was adopted, Hamilton's training and background made him the obvious choice for Secretary of the Treasury. He found the Treasury entirely without funds to meet current expenses, and was obliged to arrange temporary loans from the Bank of New York and the Bank of North America with which to pay the first instalments of salary to the President and the members of Congress which was meeting in New York.[1]

The First Tariff

The new Congress spent only a few weeks on the details of its organization before turning to the problem of revenue. The imposition of import duties and excise taxes was generally accepted as inevitable, but there was great difference of opinion as to which commodities should be taxed, and how heavily, in order to "secure the object of revenue" without being "oppressive to the constituents," as Madison phrased it. The tariff debate began even before the bill was introduced into the House in April 1789, and quickly developed the sectional strains which became typical in American politics. The manufacturers of the northern and eastern states wanted protection from the manufactured imports which competed with their own products—Massachusetts on nails, Maryland on glass, Pennsylvania on steel—but they did not want to pay higher prices on imported raw materials like molasses. The southern planters wanted low prices for the manufactured articles which they had to import, since they produced few of their own.

The Act which was approved on July 4 was a compromise measure. Duties up to 15 percent were required on a few manufactured articles. A moderate duty of 5 percent was to be levied on all imported goods except a few raw materials such as saltpeter, lead, tin, brass, copper, wool, dyes, furs, and raw hides, which were on the free list. Specific duties were levied on thirty-two commodities considered luxuries—liquor, coffee, sugar, cheese, candles, soap, footwear, cordage, thread, gold and silver lace, buttons, paper playing cards, carriages, and the like; a duty of 2.5 cents per gallon had to be paid on molasses, and up to 45 cents per pound on tea, depending on quality. All duties were to be decreased by one-tenth if the dutiable commodity arrived in an American-owned vessel. Vessels built and owned by Americans paid a duty of only 6 cents per ton, as against 50 cents per ton for foreign-owned vessels. After some Congressional hesitation, the actual collection of the duties was entrusted to federal officers in order to ensure uniform methods of valuation.

A year later some of the specific duties were increased, but the basic 5 percent *ad valorem* was retained until March 1799 when the whole tariff schedule was revised slightly upward. The objective was still revenue rather than protection, although Hamilton, in his *Report on Manufactures* in 1792, had made a closely reasoned argument for protection of infant American industries. Even Jefferson, in spite of his free-trade principles, had begun to advocate higher duties on goods from any nation which "imposes high duties on our productions, or prohibits them altogether."[2] Nevertheless protectionist sentiment did not become dominant until the Embargo and the War of 1812 changed the pattern of trade and created a new group of manufacturers who were not yet able to compete with imported products.

Foreign Trade

In the years before 1812 the relatively mild import duties did not dampen the growth of foreign trade. Merchants were still the leading men of affairs, and the term business was practically synonymous with foreign commerce. The wars among the powers of Europe in the 1790s threw into the hands of the Americans a large share of the trade of the world. In some of these years the reexport of foreign products, mostly West Indian, was greater in value than the export of American products.

The American products themselves were variously received in the countries of Europe. Jefferson, the Secretary of State, summarized the restrictions against them in his *Report* of 1793. Great Britain, the most important trading partner, had no duties on the tar and pitch needed by her ships, but levied heavy duties on tobacco, rice, bacon, whale oil, grain, and bread. Salted fish and meat imports were prohibited altogether, and American-built ships were not permitted to enter her ports. France had low rates on bread, rice, wood, and ashes but high duties on whale oil, indigo, salt fish, and tobacco. Spain and Portugal had light duties on most American products, but prohibited imports of American tobacco. Holland had high duties on many commodities and forbade the importation of pickled beef and pork, meal, and bread.

The statistics of American foreign trade are very unsatisfactory for this early period. Only the total customs duties collected at each port were available, and these not until 1791. Imports subject to *ad valorem* duties were reported at their value, and those subject to specific duties were reported by quantity. No reports were made for imports not subject to duty. The value of exports was reported for each article. After 1821 the statistics were more carefully collected, and more details were given.

In spite of the unsatisfactory nature of the early figures, it is clear that tobacco had lost its leading position among American exports and had been replaced by wheat and flour. Cotton exports were still far behind and would remain so until the cotton gin was perfected. Britain continued to be the best customer, taking one-fourth of all the exports from the United States. British official figures show that American exports to Britain and its dominions rose from the £750,000 of 1784 to £1,200,000 by 1790, and to a peak of nearly £5,000,000 in 1807. (The British pound of this period was worth 4.44 dollars. France was the next best customer, in some years taking almost as much as Britain from the United States. The grand total of American exports had reached at least 20 million dollars by 1796, in Gallatin's estimation; on a per capita basis this was slightly above that of the British, and triple that of the French, exports. In 1807, the peak year for this period, total exports amounted to 108 million; it was not until 1835 that the total was again so high.

Although exports and the earnings of the carrying trade were increasing, the balance of trade was consistently against the United States because of its heavy imports of raw materials and manufactured goods. Britain continued to be the chief supplier, as Lord Sheffield had predicted.* The customary channels of trade had been less disturbed by the Revolution than might have been expected, and the long credits which British merchants were willing and able to give to American customers confirmed their habit of buying from Great Britain, until the Napoleonic wars and the Embargo interfered with shipping.

Imports from other countries were, however, increasing rapidly. Tea was being brought directly from China in American vessels by such firms as N. L. and G. Griswold and Archibald Gracie, and no longer had to go through British ports. European countries sent their goods to the United States whenever they were not too occupied with wars. The total of imports rose almost steadily, carrying customs receipts from 3.4 million dollars in 1792 to 16.4 million in the peak year, 1808. The grand total of customs duties for the years through 1815 was 223 million, and all other federal revenues amounted to only 24 million. By this time New York was the leading port, and the collections at her customs house were by 1797 greater than those of either Boston or Philadelphia.

Excise Taxes

In order to increase its revenue and provide for the repayment of the debts it had assumed, Congress turned to internal excise taxes as well as to duties on imports. In 1791 a tax of 25 cents per gallon was levied on whiskey if it was made from foreign materials, 18 cents if made from domestic supplies. The tax on distilled spirits aroused a fury of resentment in many groups, but especially among the farmers of western Pennsylvania. They found it almost impossible to get their heavier products— grain, lumber, and meat—across the mountains to a market, whereas whiskey represented a relatively high value in much less bulk and was an important source of cash income. Its manufacture was carried on by

* See p. 47.

the most respectable elements of the community, it was used in barter dealings, and even ministers' salaries were sometimes paid in it. The genuine economic burden of the whiskey tax was seized on as an occasion for political opposition to "Mr. Hamilton's excise." Popular opinion was aroused to violence against the hapless collectors of the tax; rioters were jailed. It was not until the army was sent in to the Monongahela area beyond the Allegheny Mountains that the "Whiskey Rebellion" was quelled in the winter of 1794–95. The tax was not repealed until 1802, but the opposition to it gradually became less vociferous. Other products of the western counties were becoming more important, and possibly the whiskey distillers were becoming less visible.

In 1798 a tax on houses was introduced at the suggestion of Gallatin, who was then in the House from Pennsylvania. It was one of the first progressive taxes, and it rose from two-tenths of 1 percent annually for houses valued at 100 to 500 dollars up to 1 percent on houses valued at 30,000 dollars or more. By 1813 the range of excise taxes covered snuff, sugar, carriages, and proceeds of auction sales, as well as a stamp tax on legal documents.[3]

The Funding of the Debt

With an adequate revenue assured to the central government for the first time, the new Congress turned its attention to the next task and instructed Hamilton to study the problem of refunding and repaying the debt. In his *Report on the Public Credit* of January 1790 he faced squarely the many difficult aspects of the question which had been a source of embarrassment over many years.

The least controversial part of the debt was that owed to foreign governments; every one agreed that it had to be paid as soon as possible. By this time the outstanding loans had increased to more than 10 million dollars, with accrued interest of 1.6 million. About two-thirds of it was due to France, and one-third to Holland, and a negligible 174,000 dollars due to Spain. Interest payments on the debt to France had been suspended in 1785, and installments of the principal had not been paid after 1787. Both principal and interest were payable in foreign currencies. Hamilton proposed that for fifteen years the President be authorized to borrow enough to repay the principal of the loans, and that the interest be paid out of any current income over the 600,000 dollars annually needed for expenses at home. There was little opposition to this plan, and it was carried out much as Hamilton had advised.

The more controversial part of the debt was the domestic one involving the amounts owing to individuals and states as established by the Commissioners under the Confederation.* The new Constitution provided that debts contracted under the Confederation should be valid under the new regime. The total owed to individuals amounted to more than 40 million dollars, of which about one-third was accrued interest. Many of the certificates had originally been issued to pay soldiers and officers of the army; others had been given to farmers and merchants by commissary officers. Many of the bonds had been purchased by patriotic investors who had later been obliged to sell them at a loss; some of the securities, like some of the certificates and warrants, had changed hands several times. There were charges that speculators in the northeastern states had bought up much of the debt from the more guileless and needy investors of the south and were urging refunding in order to obtain a huge unearned profit. It was well known that foreigners had purchased many of the certificates, and that active trading in them was being carried on in New York for foreign as well as for American accounts.

To Hamilton it seemed impossible to search back through the history of each bond and certificate to find the original holder, and even had this been possible it would have been unfair to the intermediate holders. He proposed therefore that new securities be issued, to be exchanged for outstanding obligations at their specie value at the rate of 100 to 1. Two-thirds of the new loan would bear 6 percent interest from the starting date of January 1, 1791; one-third would bear interest only after 1800. The arrears of interest would be paid in securities bearing only 3 percent.

The third and most difficult question with respect to the debt was whether the federal government should assume the state debts still outstanding. Massachusetts and South Carolina had large unpaid obligations on the war account; North Carolina, Virginia, Maryland, and Georgia had paid off most of their war debts; the other states had less at stake. An acrimonious debate went on in Congress for six months, with Madison, much to Hamilton's dismay, joining Jefferson in opposition to

---

* See p. 49.

assumption. A compromise was finally reached in behind-the-scenes negotiations which gained the support of the Virginians by giving them the national capital at a site on the banks of the Potomac, after a ten-year interlude in Philadelphia. On that basis it became possible to win the assent of Congress to the assumption of state debts estimated at 21.5 million dollars. The amount actually assumed was slightly less; it amounted to 18.2 million by 1793. The obligations of the states were turned in for a new federal issue; on four-ninths of the principal and accrued interest the holders were to receive 6 percent; on two-ninths, the same rate, but deferred; and on the remaining one-third, 3 percent. Congress expected that most of the principal could be repaid from sales of public lands.

Throughout this period the prices of government securities fluctuated widely in the limited market of the day under the influence of every rumor and every resolution of the Congress, which was meeting in New York. As the prospect of funding became more certain, the prices rose until they stood at a premium of 20 percent for the 6 percent securities. Many individuals abroad as well as at home benefited substantially from the refunding. Some of the relatives and business associates of Hamilton were among them, but he himself was not, and when he left the Treasury he declared that he was poorer than when he had entered.

The total of the federal government debt after assumption, with accrued interest, was about 75 million dollars. Since the population at the first census of 1790 was nearly 4 million, the debt amounted to less than 20 dollars per capita. Formidable as the total seemed to the struggling young republic, it was relatively less than that of England or France. On a per capita basis the debt of Great Britain was six times as large, and that of France was two and one-half times as large. Fortunately the income of the federal government was adequate; four-fifths of all federal revenue could be devoted to debt service in the decade 1790–1800. The burden of the debt was considerably offset by the refunding which settled many troublesome questions for the Treasury. Hamilton had advocated it as part of his plan to attach the "monied interest" to the new government and thus strengthen it, and this he undoubtedly accomplished. The success of his operation gave an impetus to the securities market and to the ownership of securities, and probably increased the importance of that form of wealth and of its owners, in comparison with the landed interests represented by Jefferson and the gentlemen farmers of Virginia. It is doubtful, however, that the direction of development of the expanding economy was changed; industry was already growing rapidly and the process of industrialization could not be stopped.[4]

The Management of the Debt

Hamilton had obtained the authorization he needed from Congress for the refunding and repayment of the debt. A large part of his work as Secretary of the Treasury was the carrying out of this task. In order to have funds always available for payment of principal and interest, a Sinking Fund was established, an idea borrowed from the British, based on the miracle of compound interest by which a relatively small sum would grow rapidly into a much larger one.*

Hamilton's Sinking Fund was to receive surplus revenues from import and tonnage duties, interest saved on government securities which were redeemed, and proceeds from the sale of public lands. In 1795 it was authorized to receive also the dividends on government-owned shares of the Bank of the United States, and excise taxes on liquor distilled in the country. Although enthusiasm for the blessings of the Sinking Fund were not shared by all of Hamilton's contemporaries, especially those of the opposite political party, the Commissioners were able to use the funds thus accumulated to meet most of the due dates of the various debts. The small Spanish debt was completely liquidated within a few years. The French debt maturing in 1791 was converted into a dollar debt at a longer maturity and a higher rate of interest. It was not possible to convert the Dutch debt due in 1795 from florins to dollars, so Wolcott, who had succeeded Hamilton at the Treasury, bought government bonds from the Bank of the United States; they were sent to Amsterdam and sold there in order to pay the debt.

The chief critic of Hamilton's debt management was Albert Gallatin,

---

* Benjamin Franklin was another enthusiast for this idea, and on his death in 1790 left £1000, or 4440 dollars, to the city of Philadelphia, and the same to Boston, out of which loans were to be made to "married artificers" in order to encourage them to go into business. By 1960 his legacy amounted to nearly a third of a million dollars and was a source of embarrassment to the city fathers who found few applicants for such loans.

who later became Secretary of the Treasury under Jefferson. A native of Switzerland, Gallatin had come to the United States in 1780 and, after some years of work in New England, had settled in Pennsylvania and become a member of its Assembly in 1791. There he sponsored legislation for the funding of the state debts and the redemption of the outstanding paper money of the state. When he went to the House of Representatives he played a similar role of financial leadership. Under his guidance the House Committee of Ways and Means became an important factor in determining national fiscal policy. In 1796 he wrote a *Sketch of the Finances of the United States* in which he demonstrated that, if the accrued interest was correctly calculated, the total debt instead of declining had actually been increasing. He recommended that the debt be repaid as rapidly as possible by cutting expenses, especially those of the army and the navy; that the Treasury be required also to make regular detailed reports in clearer form than those of Hamilton.

As Secretary of the Treasury after 1800, Gallatin had the support of President Jefferson in working for economy and debt repayment. He estimated that the national debt, which in 1801 stood at about 83 million dollars, could be reduced by 38 million in eight years and be almost completely paid off by 1817, if annual appropriations of 7.2 million could be devoted to the payment of principal and interest. During the first half-dozen years of his incumbency he was able to carry out this program. He was also able to reduce internal taxes in 1802, including the unpopular excise taxes on whiskey and salt; the difference was more than made up by an increase of 2½ percent on imported goods subject to *ad valorem* duties. This extra tax was called the Mediterranean Fund, to imply that it was a mere temporary levy for the expenses of the war against the pirates in Tripoli. The Louisiana Purchase of 1803 was made with 2 million in cash and the proceeds of 13 million 6 percent bonds. In spite of this, the total of the debt was down to 57 million by the end of Jefferson's second administration. By 1812, when financing of the war interfered with further debt retirement, all the bonds payable in foreign currencies had been redeemed. Only 45 million of dollar bonds were still outstanding; this was called the domestic debt, although a large part of it was held by foreigners, particularly Dutch and British investors. Gallatin had carried out his plans, aided by unusual returns from customs duties during a period of flourishing trade.[5]

State and Local Finance

State treasuries had been relieved of much of their burden by the federal government's assumption of their war debts. When Secretary of the Treasury Wolcott made a survey of state finances in 1796 he estimated that the annual expenses of the states were about 1 million dollars, without including the capital expenditures on schools and jails. State income was more than adequate in most cases.

The sources of revenue varied, as they had always done, from one section of the country to another, and continued to follow the patterns set up in colonial times. In New England the chief reliance was on the property tax. Assessments were made annually in Vermont, every five years in New Hampshire, at least every ten years in Massachusetts. Some of the states set a fixed value on certain kinds of property such as land; others left it to the judgment and discretion of the assessors, who were elected. Vermont set the assessed value of a "poll" at £6 for males between ages 16 and 60 but exempted from the poll tax all ministers, teachers, students, and the sick. Massachusetts specifically exempted Harvard property and personnel. Most New England states continued to include in the property assessment some form of income or profit or faculty tax. When the list of assessed valuations had been drawn up, and taxpayers had had an opportunity to protest, the amount needed by the state was divided by the total assessed valuation to obtain the rate for that year. The actual collection was usually left to local authorities, who used the same list as the basis for their own assessments.

The middle states tended to rely less on the property tax and more upon license and other fees. New York had sufficient income from public lands and investments to cover its annual expenses of 75,000 dollars, and to make grants to hospitals, schools, and universities of an equal amount, between 1788 and 1796. New York never used the poll tax. New Jersey had no poll tax, but levied a tax on single men, slaves and shopkeepers, as well as on such property as land, horses, cattle, and mills. When Pennsylvania found taxation necessary, it levied a tax of 10 to 30 shillings on free men, and included slaves and indentured servants in the property which was taxed; it also levied a tax on "profits of offices and posts" which resembled an income tax; however, it specifically exempted ministers, teachers, mechanics, and manufacturers. Delaware levied a tax on estimated annual income, as well as on real and personal property.

Southern states relied less heavily on the property tax. Maryland had a system of license fees for lawyers and tavern keepers in addition to a modest tax on real and personal property, and fees for certain activities. North Carolina and Georgia had a poll tax on both white and Negro males, and specific taxes on land, houses, merchandise, and cattle; Georgia also collected a duty of 10 dollars on each slave imported. South Carolina taxed land and buildings, and used the same rate for taxes on faculties and professions, which were assessed according to estimated income; slaves were taxed as a form of property.

In all the states the method of assessment was crude and variable, and the subject of constant complaint from the taxpayers. While population was small, the locally elected assessors were well known and there was little danger of fraud. Difficulties increased as cities grew and citizens demanded increasing services from their state and local governments.[6]

The Bank of the United States

An integral part of Hamilton's plan for the organization of finances under the new Constitution was the establishment of a large bank chartered by the national government, drawn on the model of the Bank of England which had been established in 1694. Hamilton saw that the Treasury would need to look to such an institution for short-term loans and for bills of exchange with which to make payments on that part of the debt which was held abroad. In December 1790, therefore, he presented to Congress his *Report on a National Bank* in which he made a strong case for the usefulness of "public" (i.e., incorporated) banks. They increased the "circulating capital" of a country, and facilitated payments for business and government. They did not, he declared, increase usury or prevent other kinds of lending, or encourage overtrading. Indeed the list of charges against which he defended banks throws much light on the financial problems of the period, many of which arose from the lack of capital rather than from the activities of the few banks then in existence.

He turned then to the reasons for establishing a national bank. He firmly believed that Congress had the right to issue such a charter. He rejected the idea of using the Bank of North America for special services to the Treasury, because by this time it was operating under a Pennsylvania charter instead of under the charter originally granted by the Continental Congress. He pointed to the examples of several European banks which had been successful and particularly recommended the Bank of England as a model because its notes were redeemable in specie, and were limited by the provision that its total debt must not exceed its capital.

Hamilton's own party, the Federalists, who believed that a strong central government was essential, supported him in his effort to obtain the charter for the bank from Congress; they interpreted the Constitution broadly and considered that the power "to coin money, regulate the value thereof and of foreign coin" implied the right of Congress to do anything necessary to implement that power. Opposed to a national bank were the strict constructionists like Jefferson and Madison who would reserve to the states every power not explicitly granted to the central government.

Hamilton won the charter by a vote of 2 to 1 in the House, and received a majority in the Senate where at that time the votes were not recorded. After some hesitation, President Washington rejected the opinions of the Attorney-General and of Secretary of State Jefferson that the Act was unconstitutional, and signed the bill incorporating the Bank on February 25, 1791. Its capital was set at 10 million dollars, of which one-fifth was to be subscribed by the government, paid for in its own obligations. Twenty-five directors were to be elected by the stockholders but, as in many corporations of the period, voting rights did not increase in proportion to the number of shares owned, and no one had more than thirty votes. Nonresident shareholders might not vote at all.

The charter contained few restrictions on the operations of the Bank, nor did it specifically define the "business of banking." However, it was forbidden to trade in anything except bills of exchange, gold or silver bullion, or goods pledged for loans and not redeemed. Interest was limited to 6 percent. Even more important was that the Bank was forbidden to purchase the public debt, or to lend to the United States or to any state more than 100,000 dollars unless specifically authorized to do so by Congress; this would save the Bank from ever becoming a mere engine of inflation for the Treasury. The total debt of the Bank was not to exceed the sum of the capital and the "moneys then actually deposited in the bank for safe keeping." There was no requirement for specie redemption of its notes, or for a specie reserve against deposits.

When books were opened for subscription to the stock of the Bank in July 1791, such was the demand that the whole four-fifths of the public capital was oversubscribed within an hour. Among the subscribers were the state of New York, the Bank of Massachusetts, Harvard College, thirty members of Congress, merchants, and professional men. They had to pay one-fourth in specie; the rest might be in government obligations. Eventually much of the stock was held by foreign investors. The head office was opened in Philadelphia, then the capital of the United States. The President of the Bank, Thomas Willing (who had been president of the Bank of North America) and eight other directors were from Pennsylvania, seven were from New York, and four from Massachusetts. Branches were opened one after the other in the principal cities, the eighth and last in New Orleans in 1805. Hamilton had opposed the establishment of branches of the Bank, but his influence was unavailing against the strong demand from the growing cities, many of which had no other banking facilities.

The establishment of the Bank of the United States in Philadelphia and of its branches in New York, Boston, and Baltimore caused deep concern among the four banks which up to that time had been holding Treasury deposits and conducting foreign exchange operations for the government—the Bank of North America, the Bank of New York, the Bank of Massachusetts, and the Bank of Maryland, which had opened in 1791. When the Bank of New York expressed its fear of losing Treasury deposits, Hamilton wrote a reassuring letter to its officers: "Ultimately it will be incumbent upon me to place the public funds in the keeping of the Branch; but it may be depended upon that I shall precipitate nothing, but shall so conduct the transfer as not to embarrass or distress your institution." The Treasury deposits were accordingly allowed to run down gradually as the Treasury drew checks on its account, and most of the new deposits were made in the New York branch of the Bank of the United States after it opened in April 1792. The same policy was followed at the branches in Baltimore, Boston, and Providence, as well as at the head office in Philadelphia. By 1804 nine-tenths of the Treasury deposits were in the Bank or its branches. However, in special cases, deposits were made in state banks to help them over a temporary shortage of specie. For example, in August 1792 the Collector of Customs was instructed to make his deposits in the Bank of New York for a time, instead of in the branch of the Bank of the United States. Commercial banks were also given some of the foreign exchange business of the Treasury. Even Jefferson, when he became President, advocated a "judicious distribution" of favors among the state banks in order to bind them to his administration. Although most of its transactions consisted of commercial loans for the financing of domestic and foreign trade, the Bank had many attributes of what nowadays would be considered a central bank.[7]

The establishment of the Bank of the United States did not prevent or even discourage the formation of other commercial banks. The success of the four existing banks, which had been evidenced by their dividends of 9 and 10 percent in some years, inevitably attracted capital into this field. Not only were investors anxious to have new banks established, but also businessmen were eager to have more banking services. New charters in this period had to be granted individually by the state legislatures, and obtaining a charter from an unfriendly legislature was sometimes difficult if not impossible. In several cases a bank started business without a charter at all, as the Bank of New York had done in 1784.*

New banks increased rapidly in number; by 1794 there were 18 banks; by 1800 when Jefferson took office, there were 29 banks in 24 cities. By 1804 it was estimated that there were 45 banks, and by 1811 there were 90 throughout the country.† Since most of the bank charters contained few restrictions on loans, or any requirement for reserves except

---

* See p. 43.

† Since there were few official bank reports in this period, the exact number is hard to determine. In the *Journal of Economic History*, XXV 3, September 1965, J. Van Fenstermaker gives figures which are slightly different from those of Gallatin. He ascribes the disparity to the probable inclusion of nonincorporated banks, of which about 64 are known to have operated in part or all of the period before 1830, most of them in Ohio, Virginia, and Pennsylvania.

the usual obligation of redeeming notes in specie on demand, the standard of banking operations was not high. Banks made most of their loans in the form of notes rather than deposits, and their notes made up a large part of the circulating medium, even for small transactions. Not until 1813 did the law of New York forbid the issue of notes of less than one dollar in value. There were many complaints about the "bank rags" which passed for money at various rates of discount. Many banks issued far more than they could hope to redeem, some of them postdated so that there was not even a promise to redeem them until the more or less distant future.

The quality of the bank notes in circulation would have been even lower without the influence of the Bank of the United States. Its sysmatic presentation of their notes for redemption made it a kind of regulator of their issues, a circumstance which was not always appreciated by the country banks. The larger banks in the big cities were accustomed to meeting daily demands for specie, and were for the most part glad to have the country banks under control. In spite of the competition which its sheer size offered ,them, the large banks recognized the aid which they had received from the Bank, and the services it performed in steadying the money market and making remittances to all parts of the country.

These large banks were therefore among the supporters of the renewal of the Bank's charter when it came before Congress in 1811. Those sympathetic to the Bank included many Jeffersonians like Madison and Gallatin who had formerly opposed the Bank but now recognized its value. Gallatin would even have increased its capital from 10 to 30 million dollars. Mathew Carey and Condy Raguet, prominent publishers and writers in Philadelphia, also supported the cause of the Bank.

The opponents of the Bank were equally diverse in their interests, and far more vocal. Among them was John Jacob Astor of New York who had had a personal feud with the New York branch, Jacob Barker, a New York speculator, and Henry Clay of Kentucky, leader of the opposition to the Bank in the Senate.

In both Houses of Congress the issue most often raised in the debate over the recharter was that of constitutionality. The foreign ownership of much of its stock was also considered a glaring fault in spite of the fact that nonresident owners might not vote for directors. Serious economic questions were glossed over in the discussion. When the vote was finally taken in the House, recharter lost by only one vote. In the Senate, several weeks later, the vote was a tie and was decided in the negative by Vice President George Clinton of New York who had never forgiven Gallatin and Madison for opposing his nomination for the Presidency. In 1811, therefore, just when the services of the Bank were most needed as the country faced the prospect of war, the Treasury was obliged to find new depositary banks for its funds, and to send abroad the 7 million dollars owed to the foreign stockholders, unless they chose (as many of them fortunately did) to reinvest in other American securities or real estate. And this was at a time when, it was estimated, there was no more than 10 million dollars in specie in the whole country.

The Bank asked for two years of grace in which to liquidate its affairs, but this was refused. The branches were sold to new banks set up in their communities. Stephen Girard, who owned 400,000 dollars of the Bank's stock, took over the staff as well as the building of the head office in Philadelphia. By 1815 all the stockholders had been repaid in full for their capital, although the final liquidation was not completed until 1852.[8]

Coinage

The unsatisfactory state of the bank note circulation was made worse with the ending of the control formerly exercised over state bank issues by the Bank of the United States. Moreover the coins in circulation were inadequate in amount and varied in quality. The state of the currency had been of concern to Hamilton from the start, and in 1791 his report proposing that a Mint be established was accepted by Congress. He followed Jefferson in recommending a bimetallic standard, but thought the ratio should be 15 to 1, as closer to the market ratio, which was then 14.88 to 1.

The shortage of pennies caused particular hardship. Most of those which had been privately minted before 1789 in various parts of New England, New Jersey, and Pennsylvania had disappeared from circulation by 1790, leaving such a gap that the Common Council in New York City issued paper tickets for 1, 2, and 3 pennies. When the United States Mint was established, therefore, its first task was to coin pennies.* Gold and silver coins began to be minted in 1794, but not in sufficient amounts to fill all the needs for currency. Although the law had provided that, three years after United States coins had gone into circulation, no foreign coins should be legal tender, the Presidential Proclamation of July 22, 1797, was much more limited in its prohibition; it withdrew the legal tender quality from foreign silver coins but excepted the "Spanish milled dollar and parts thereof," thus leaving the most common foreign coin as it had been. Foreign gold coins were not mentioned in the Proclamation, and they continued to circulate as full legal tender until 1857. The presently customary sign for the United States dollar ($) was not even in common use before 1811.

The shortage of coin was particularly troublesome in the southern and western states where there were few banks to fill the gap with their note issues. There were frequent complaints that their specie was drained off by the northern and eastern areas from which they had to purchase manufactured goods. State governments as well as merchants found themselves handicapped by the shortage of circulating media, both in collecting their revenues and in paying their accounts. In Ohio, for example, an Act of 1809 authorized the State Auditor to issue warrants for 5, 10, and 20 dollars with which to pay individuals; they were designed to circulate as currency and to be receivable for taxes. The warrants were used during several periods, and the Act was not finally repealed until 1831.[9]

Foreign Payments and Foreign Exchange

One of the reasons for the continuing shortage of coin was the necessity of sending large amounts of specie abroad to meet the unfavorable balance of trade. Part of the deficit was offset by foreign investment in the United States and by commercial credit extended by foreign bankers and merchants to American importers, but in these early years there was usually a net export of specie as well.

England continued to be the principal trading partner of the United States, and sterling exchange was the principal medium for the financing of foreign trade in the American market, whether with England or with

---

* A few pennies and half-pennies had been coined under the Confederation. See p. 39.

other countries. The currency legislation of July 31, 1789, had defined
the dollar in such a way that the mint par between the dollar and the
pound was 4.44 dollars. This figure continued to be used as the basis
for exchange rates in spite of the several changes in the ratio of silver
in the two currencies. From 1792 until 1830 the true mint par was
4.57 dollars or 2.73 percent above the nominal par, but the published
rates continued to be given as a premium or discount on 4.44 dollars.
(The situation was even worse after 1834, when the mint par became
4.8665 dollars or 9.46 percent above the nominal par which nevertheless
remained the basis for quotations of exchange until 1874.) The unfavorable balance of payments in the American trade with Britain gave rise
to a genuine premium on sterling exchange much of the time, but it was
far less than the nominal premium of the published rates.

The long and hazardous voyage from the United States to Europe
made the shipment of specie very expensive. The cost was estimated at
5 percent in 1811; this meant that gold exports would not normally take
place until the price of sterling bills had risen by that much over the
true par, nor would gold be imported until the price of sterling bills had
fallen proportionately. There was also a seasonal variation in the rates
of exchange; the price of sterling bills was higher in the autumn when
American merchants were stocking their shelves with British goods, and
it was lower in the spring when shipments of cotton were being made
to Europe.

Much of the exchange business in this early part of the century was
carried on by merchants with international connections. Alexander Brown
and Sons started out as linen merchants with offices in Great Britain and
in the United States, and gradually shifted from merchandising to finance.
Prime, Ward and King were originally merchants but, like the Browns,
became bankers with offices on both sides of the Atlantic. Baring Brothers
in London, connected by marriage with the banking Binghams of Philadelphia, were correspondents of the Bank of the United States. Some of
the big commercial banks in the port cities also handled foreign exchange
bills and acted as correspondents for banks in the inland cities. Treasury
transactions involving foreign exchange were usually carried on through
the Bank of the United States, but occasionally through commercial
banks.[10]

The first two decades under the Constitution were years of exuberant economic growth, to which the solution of the pressing financial problems made a substantial contribution. The energies of the increasing population might have been turned to exploiting the rich natural resources of the continent which was gradually being made accessible, had not the War of 1812 intervened. A new period of financial difficulty then began.

Silver three-cent piece

CHAPTER 4

THE WAR OF 1812
AND THE SECOND BANK
OF THE UNITED STATES

Financing the War of 1812

THE NEW international dispute in which the United States now became involved not only increased its expenses but also sharply decreased its revenues. There had been great demand for American exports during the Napoleonic wars in Europe. It had made Americans prosperous—indeed, had produced its first half-dozen millionaires—and had enabled them to increase their imports so that government receipts from customs duties rose sharply. Suddenly the situation changed. In a desperate effort to stop British and French interference with American ships and sailors on the high seas, short of declaring war on either one or both, President Jefferson proclaimed an embargo on most foreign trade. The exports of 1808 were only one-fifth as large as those of 1807, and imports were cut in half. Imports recovered slightly during the next few years but fell again until in 1814 they were down to one-tenth of the 1807 peak.* Customs duties fell proportionately and reached a low point of 6 million dollars in 1814.

---

* See p. 104.

Although Gallatin, as Secretary of the Treasury since 1801, had followed with Jefferson's approval a policy of debt repayment and economy especially directed toward army and navy expenditures, he saw that war with England was imminent. He was willing to borrow to cover the increase in defense costs, but his Swiss conservatism made him unwilling to borrow for current expenses. To cover the loss of revenue from customs duties, he urged Congress to restore some of the internal taxes which had been abolished in 1802. Congress, with little realization of what a war would cost, paid no heed to the Secretary; he was obliged to borrow in order to meet ordinary expenditures in 1809. It was not until war was actually declared in June 1812 that Congress raised tariff rates, but by that time there were so few imports that the gesture was futile, and further borrowing became necessary.

It was a poor time to borrow. The credit of the Treasury was at the lowest point since the Revolution. Much of the country was opposed to the war; New England was particularly bitter about the Embargo and the Non-importation Acts, which had destroyed her commerce. New York, Philadelphia, and Baltimore were almost equally stricken. In March 1812 Congress authorized a war loan of 11 million dollars in 6 percent bonds to mature in 12 years, with a down payment of only one-eighth. In spite of the effort to make the purchase of the bonds easy and attractive, they were not at once taken. The New York *Evening Post* of April 28 advised: "Let those who are for war subscribe—let those who dread it, avoid doing so, as they value all they hold dear." Four days later it reported with sour satisfaction, "Yesterday (excepting the subscription of the Manhattan Bank, which is probably a loan by the left hand to the right) the subscription did not amount to $100,000; to-day some French gentlemen have added, say, $40,000 more and there we stick." However, within two weeks banks had taken over 4 million and individuals nearly 2 million, which Gallatin considered an amount "as great as might have been expected within so short a period."

A new 16 million dollar loan authorized in February 1813 was equally unattractive to investors and was placed only after David Parish and Stephen Girard in Philadelphia, and John Jacob Astor in New York, had arranged to take more than half. A second loan of 7.5 million dollars at 6 percent could be sold only at a discount of nearly 12 percent. Of the total borrowing of 61 million authorized by Congress through 1814, only 45 million were sold, and a large part of that only at a heavy discount. Another 32 million (9 million of it at 7 percent) was authorized in 1815, bringing the nominal debt to a peak of 132 million by the end of that year.[1]

Treasury Notes of 1812

The difficulty of raising money from the sale of long-term bonds caused the government to try the expedient of short-term Treasury notes. These seemed to offer a solution to several problems. They had the advantage that many members of Congress would approve them as a method of increasing the circulating medium. They would also relieve the Treasury of the embarrassment caused by its ill-advised agreement to reimburse subscribers to earlier bond issues if later issues were sold at a heavier discount; since bonds were selling only at progressively increasing discounts, this would have amounted to a heavy drain on any new funds obtained through bond sales.

The Act of June 30, 1812, which authorized the first issue of 5 million of Treasury notes, provided that they be redeemable within 1 year, and that notes of 20 dollars or more should bear interest of 5.4 percent. They were legal tender for all government dues. Another 5 million were issued in 1813, 18 million in 1814, and 8 million in 1815. In spite of these relatively modest amounts, the notes depreciated and did not long remain in circulation. Most of them were used for payment of taxes, or for subscriptions to the 7 percent bonds. In 1816 the Treasury itself reissued some that had been received for taxes—a "breach of public faith . . . the payment of the public creditors yesterday in treasury notes instead of current money," according to the *Evening Post* of April 3, 1816. Fortunately, by the end of 1817 only 2 percent of the total issue was still outstanding.

The resort to fiat money in the form of irredeemable Treasury notes might have been avoided had Congress been able to levy direct taxes on individuals.* Since it did not have this power under the Constitution,

---

* An income tax was levied during the Civil War under the guise of an indirect tax. The income tax of 1894 was ruled unconstitutional by the Supreme Court. A constitutional amendment was required to make an income tax possible. See Chapters 7 and 10.

Congress could assess the states only on the basis of their population, leaving it to them to decide how the burden should be shared among their citizens. A direct tax of 3 million dollars was levied on the states for the year 1814 and twice that amount for the following year. They were given the option of collecting it themselves, or of having it collected by federal officers; in spite of the implied threat of federal action, the direct tax produced less than expected.

Internal excise taxes were also increased, especially on manufactured articles which had long been protected by the tariff. Sugar refined within the country was to pay 4 cents a pound; distillers and merchants of liquor and wine were required to buy licenses; taxes were laid on bank notes, bonds, and bills of exchange, and even the unpopular salt tax was increased. But only gradually and reluctantly were these charges imposed, after the Treasury had been reduced to a situation described in November 1814 by Mr. Hanson, Federalist member of Congress from Maryland:

So completely empty was the Treasury and destitute of credit that funds could not be obtained to defray the current ordinary expenses of the different Departments . . . the Department of State was so bare of money as to be unable to pay even its stationery bill . . . the Treasury was obliged to borrow pitiful sums, which it would disgrace a merchant in tolerable credit to ask for. . . . The Paymaster was unable to meet demands for paltry amounts—not even for $30. . . . In short it was difficult to conceive a situation more critical and perilous than that of the government at this moment, without money, without credit, and destitute of the means of defending the country.

It was only the willingness of the Secretary of State, James Monroe, to pledge his personal fortune as security that enabled General Jackson to obtain funds for moving his troops to New Orleans, where he fought the important land battle of the war.[2]

The Banking Situation

A large part of the financial difficulties of the Treasury and of the country during these years must be ascribed to the banking situation after the demise of the Bank of the United States. Although many of the foreign stockholders of the Bank did not demand the return of their funds, some specie had to be sent abroad at this inopportune moment. A more serious misfortune for the Treasury was the loss of the expe-

State bank notes, 1839

rienced and expert services of the Bank in handling its funds, and the necessity of using state banks as depositaries. Most important of all, the absence of the restraining influence of the Bank encouraged a rapid increase in the number of small state banks.

The number of banks in 1811 had been estimated at 90. By 1816 they had increased to 250. In New York alone, 6 banks were chartered in 1811 and 4 in 1812. One of the latter was the Bank of America, which offered 4 shares of its stock in return for 1 share in the Bank of the United States. Governor Tompkins, convinced that the only result of this increase in banks could be inflation, prorogued the New York legislature in an effort to prevent the issue of any more bank charters.

Since the purpose for which banks had been incorporated was to earn interest on loans which were largely extended in the form of notes, the volume in circulation inevitably increased during the next five years; from an estimated 28 million in 1811 it rose to 68 million in 1816. Many of the notes were of small denomination, less likely to be presented for redemption; some of them were postdated so that they could not be presented for redemption until a future date. Few of the bank charters contained any requirement that the issuing bank redeem its notes on demand, or that a specie reserve be maintained in order to ensure redemption. Some of the charters required that part of the initial capital be paid in specie, but this was often evaded. Massachusetts had led the way in 1809 by setting a tax on circulation of 2 percent per month for a bank which could not redeem its notes on demand, but not until 1816 did New York, which liked to consider itself financially more sophisticated than its neighbors, include in bank charters a provision that the charter would be forfeited if notes were not redeemed on demand.

Even more difficult to control than the note issues of incorporated banks were the notes of unincorporated companies—not only banks but canal companies, academies, railroads, and even blacksmiths. A note was evidence of debt, and going into debt was a common-law right which it was hard to stop by legal enactment, although Virginia in 1785, Massachusetts in 1799, and New York in 1804 had made efforts to do so. Eventually the privilege of note issue was restricted in most states to corporations specifically authorized for the purpose, that is, banks, and the matter ceased to be a problem. However, it continued to exist in a few states for several decades after this period.

By the year 1814 the banking situation of the country had so deteriorated that Thomas Jefferson wrote to his old friend John Adams:

I have ever been the enemy of banks; not of those discounting for cash; but of those foisting their own paper into circulation, and thus banishing our cash. My zeal against those institutions was so warm and open at the establishment of the bank of the U. S. that I was derided as a Maniac by the tribe of bank-mongers, who were seeking to filch from the public their swindling and barren gains. But the errors of that day cannot be recalled. The evils they have engendered are now upon us, and the question is, how are we to get out of them? Shall we build an altar to the old paper money of the revolution, which ruined individuals but saved the republic, and burn on that all the bank charters present and future, and their notes with them? For these are to ruin both republic and individuals. This cannot be done. The Mania is too strong. It has siesed by it's delusions and corruptions all the members of our governments, general, special and individual. Our circulating paper of the last year was estimated at 200. millions of dollars. The new banks now petitioned for, to the several legislatures, are for about 60. millions additional capital, and of course 180. millions of additional circulation, nearly doubling that of the last year; and raising the whole mass to near 400. millions, or 40. for 1. of the wholesome amount of circulation for a population of 8. millions circumstanced as we are: and you remember how rapidly our money went down after our 40. for 1. establishment in the revolution. I doubt if the present trash can hold as long. I think the 380. millions must blow all up in the course of the present year. . . . Should not prudent men, who possess stock in any monied institution, either draw and hoard the cash, now while they can, or exchange it for canal stock, or such other as being bottomed on immoveable property, will remain unhurt by the crush? . . . You might as well, with the sailors, whistle to the wind, as suggest precautions against having too much money. We must scud then before the gale, and try to hold fast, ourselves, by some plank of the wreck. God send us all a safe delivrance. . . .[3]

Jefferson's prediction of a breakdown in the banking system was soon fulfilled. The British attack on Washington in August 1814 caused the suspension of banks in that city and in Baltimore. Banks in Philadelphia soon followed, and then those of New York. Only in New England were the banks able to maintain specie convertibility. Gallatin, who had resigned from the Treasury in 1813, thoroughly disheartened by his lack of Congressional support, was probably correct in believing that if the Bank of the United States had still been in existence, the suspension might have been avoided.

The treaty of peace was signed six months after the suspension, so that federal expenses were reduced and income gradually increased. However, the difficulties of the new Secretary of the Treasury, A. J. Dallas, were not yet over. He was obliged to use many banks as depositaries and to carry with them special accounts for each type of paper: for local bank paper if it was still at par, for notes of other banks, for Treasury notes bearing interest, and for small non-interest-bearing Treasury notes. Since he was prohibited by statute from accepting depreciated bank notes, he was frequently unable to withdraw his deposits. The banks were in no hurry to resume specie payments, and there was no way by which the national government could put pressure on them if they were unable or unwilling to do so. Many state legislatures authorized the issue of small bills for change, since small coins had practically disappeared from circulation.[4]

Second Bank of the United States

Under these circumstances, even the former opponents of a national bank began to change their attitude. Several proposals for a new Bank of the United States had been offered to Congress in the years after 1811 but none had been able to gain its support. Now a group of financiers took the lead, including John Jacob Astor in New York and Stephen Girard and David Parish of Philadelphia, all of whom had been enemies of the first Bank. They had subscribed heavily to Treasury obligations in order to finance the war and were now quite reasonably concerned about maintaining the quality of their investments. Jacob Barker of New York, Henry Clay of Kentucky, and John C. Calhoun of South Carolina also changed their position and joined Secretary Dallas as supporters of a new national bank.

When the charter for the Bank came to a vote in the House on March 14, 1816, it was the party in power which supported it and the opposition party which voted against it. This was like the division on the charter of the first Bank, except that now it was the Jeffersonian Republicans who were in office and the Federalists who were the opposition. The majority of the members of Congress from the south and the west approved the Bank, and from the north, with its large commercial banks, opposed it, Mr. Webster leading the opposition. It is worthy of note that the debates in Congress gave little attention to the question of constitutionality; even President Madison admitted that time and judicial decisions had resolved this particular difference.

The Second Bank was similar in many respects to the first. It was granted a twenty-year charter, and was subject to inspection by the Treasury. Of its larger capital, 35 million dollars instead of 10, one-fifth was to be subscribed by the government and five of the twenty-five directors appointed by it. Par value of the shares was set at 100 instead of 400 dollars in order to encourage wider ownership; to prevent control by a few wealthy stockholders, no person was to have more than 30 votes, and foreign stockholders were not permitted to vote at all. Books for subscription to the stock were opened in twenty cities in July 1816. Every state was represented among the 31,000 persons who put down their names. Individual subscribers had to pay one-fourth in specie, the remainder in specie or in government securities.

The charter of the Second Bank of the United States would never have gained the necessary votes in Congress if the state banks had not received assurance that no sudden resumption of specie payments would be forced on them. The Second Bank was as gentle with the state banks at the beginning of its operations as its predecessor had been. The head office of the Bank was opened in Philadelphia in January 1817, but it was not until February that representatives of the state banks met in Philadelphia and agreed on a date for resumption. The Treasury promised that public balances would be withdrawn gradually from the state bank depositaries, and that the Bank would come to the aid of any state bank which found itself in difficulties. The Bank sent an agent to London to sell some of its stock; he brought back more than 7 million dollars in specie to aid in specie resumption.

Banks in the northeastern part of the country resumed in the latter part of February as they had agreed to do, but many banks in the south and west continued in such poor condition that they could not resume, and many of them failed. There was strong popular resentment in some states at the losses caused by the depreciated or worthless bank paper. As a result, the new constitutions of Indiana and Illinois, in 1816 and 1818, prohibited the establishment of privately owned banks, whether incorporated or not. Both states then organized state banks; this first Bank of Indiana failed after a few years, and that of Illinois never opened.

Check signed by Andrew Jackson, 1831

Alabama, Mississippi, and Georgia also started banks in which the state owned part of the capital, but they had small success. Missouri established a Loan Office in 1821, against the opposition of Senator Thomas Hart Benton, but it was declared unconstitutional within the year. Michigan Territory issued its own scrip. Much of the antibank sentiment on which Andrew Jackson was able to capitalize can be ascribed to the corruption and confusion of the banking situation during this period.[5]

History of the Second Bank of the United States

The Second Bank got off to a poor start. A majority of the public directors were elected by a clique that was committed to putting into the presidency Captain William Jones, a Philadelphia merchant who had been Secretary of the Treasury briefly after Gallatin, and who had recently gone through bankruptcy. Girard, who had purchased 3 million of the stock and was one of the five government directors, promised to use his influence to replace the majority of directors with "the most prudent, independent and well qualified gentlemen" but was unsuccessful, and refused to serve another term.[6]

By that time eighteen branches of the Bank had been established, one in each of the principal commercial cities; after 1825 seven more were opened. The central office at Philadelphia could exercise very little restraint over the operations of its branches in this period, even had it wished to do so. Both President Jones and James McCulloch, cashier of the Baltimore office, had been critical of the "timid and faltering course" of the first Bank in making loans, and were "not at all disposed to take the late Bank of the United States as an exemplar in practice."[7] They were therefore quite prepared to encourage with generous loans the business expansion which followed the resumption of specie payments and the increase in foreign and domestic trading after the war.

By 1818 the Bank was in a very weak position, with demand liabilities of more than 22 million dollars, and specie of only 2.4 million; indeed, it was on the point of stopping payment. A Committee of the House of Representatives appointed to investigate the Bank found that it had loaned very little on discounts of good business paper, but had preferred to loan against notes with stock collateral. The discounting of notes of stockholders, to enable them to evade the requirement of specie down payments for their stock, was especially censured, as well it might have been. Stockholders had even received dividends on their stock before it was paid for. State banks were found to have no grounds for their complaint of oppression by the Bank; if anything, the Bank had shown excessive forbearance in paying out the notes of state banks instead of sending them home for redemption, and this had contributed to the over-extension of the circulation of some western banks.

The Baltimore branch had been most seriously at fault, not only in its choice of paper for discount but also in its loans to officers who were speculating in Bank stock. James W. McCulloch, the cashier, was forced to resign; by the time the affair was settled his activities had cost the Bank 1.5 million dollars. Jones resigned as president of the Bank, and Langdon Cheves succeeded him. He had been Chairman of the House Committee of Ways and Means during the war.

Before McCulloch resigned, his name as representative of the Baltimore branch had become attached to a controversy which produced one of the great legal decisions of American history. The state of Maryland had imposed an annual tax of 15,000 dollars on any bank operating without a Maryland charter. The Bank of the United States refused to pay the tax, and took its case to the state court, where it lost. It then appealed to the Supreme Court of the United States. Chief Justice Marshall, after selling the seventeen shares of Bank stock that he had held, presided at the trial which involved some of the best lawyers of the day—Daniel Webster, who had by this time become a supporter of the

Bank, William Pinkney and William Wirt for the Bank; Luther Martin, Attorney General of Maryland, for the state. Martin had been one of the opponents of the Constitution a generation earlier, and much of the argument was similar to the controversy of that period. The Supreme Court brought in a unanimous decision in favor of the Bank, on the grounds that the power to tax was the power to destroy and that no state might destroy a creature of the federal government. *McCulloch* vs. *Maryland* set a precedent that still affects many aspects of American life.[8]

With this question settled at the very beginning of his term of office, Cheves was able to concentrate on the administrative problems he had inherited. He made drastic cuts in salaries and expenses, collected outstanding loans and was cautious in making new ones, and succeeded in getting new officers and directors appointed who would support his policy. "The Bank was saved and the people were ruined" was the way William Gouge (a rabid anti-Bank man) described it a few years later, blaming the Bank for the depression which followed closely on the change of administration.[9]

The Bank had certainly contributed to the expansion which preceded the depression, but it alone was not responsible for the collapse of the postwar boom. The pent-up demand for foreign goods on the American side, and the eagerness of British manufacturers to dispose of their stocks, had enormously increased imports into the United States, most of them on credit. Such a situation could not last indefinitely in any case, and the boom was soon succeeded by forced sales, bankruptcies, and general distress. The extent of the crisis may be judged by the decrease of the volume of bank notes outstanding (and there was little other currency) from about 68 million in 1816 to about 45 million by the end of 1819.

Condy Raguet,* Chairman of a Pennsylvania Senate Committee appointed to study the causes of the distress, put the blame not on the Bank, but on the banks, in his report of January 29, 1820.

That cause is to be found chiefly in the abuses of the Banking System, which abuses consist first, in the excessive number of Banks, and second in their universal bad administration. For the first of these abuses, the people have to reproach themselves, for having urged the legislature to

---

* See p. 70.

depart from that truly republican doctrine which influenced the delibera-
tions of our early assemblies, and which taught that the incorporation
of the moneyed interest, already sufficiently powerful of itself, was but
the creation of an odious aristocracy, hostile to the spirit of free government and subversive of the rights and liberties of the people. The second
abuse, the mismanagement of the Banks, is to be ascribed to a general
ignorance of the true theory of money and Banking, and to the avarice
of speculators.[10]

Cheves gradually restored the financial soundness of the Bank, and
when Nicholas Biddle succeeded him as president in 1823 it was in good
condition. The next seven years were the great days of the Bank. Biddle
had been one of the government directors of the Bank as well as a stockholder, and he had assisted the Congressional committee which investigated it in 1818. He was not only a banker; he was also a widely educated
man of the world, with an excellent position in that Philadelphia society
which regarded itself as the most select and sophisticated in the United
States. But he was not at all a practical politician. A greater contrast to
Andrew Jackson could hardly have been found, and it was small wonder
that they came into conflict.

During these first seven years, half of his whole term of office, Biddle
conducted the Bank with a strong sense of its special responsibilities and
privileges, and in many ways made it something like a modern central
bank. Since the great Bank of England itself had not yet come to recognize its unique position in the money market, the achievement of Biddle
was all the more remarkable. The term "banque centrale" was even used
to describe the Bank in 1834 by Michel Chevalier, the French traveler,
in his *Lettres sur l'Amérique du Nord*.[11]

Biddle himself was quite explicit that "beyond a certain limit the convenience of the customers of the Bank, however desirable it may be to
promote it, is only a secondary consideration" and that the general public
interest came first. When money was tight, the Bank limited its discounts
and let the public revenue accumulate in its coffers so that it could certainly meet all demands for redemption of its notes. Only the head office,
and not the branches, was permitted to sell specie, in order to centralize
the nation's specie reserves. In the autumn of 1825, the Bank was called
on to repay 7 million dollars of the public debt—the largest single

payment it had ever had to handle. When refunding rather than repayment of the debt was the policy of the Treasury, this too was entrusted to the Bank.[12] Biddle's aim was always to "pay off a considerable amount for the Government without diminishing the facilities which it is accustomed to give to the community." In addition to managing the public debt, the Bank performed many routine services for the Treasury. It transferred without charge funds from New York, where customs collections were heaviest, to other parts of the country, where payments were to be made. The handling of government pensions alone required a staff of forty employees.

Biddle felt special responsibility for the effect of movements of foreign exchange on the money market. When imports increased, and the rate on sterling bills rose to the gold export point, the Bank took steps to control "as far as possible the exchanges so as not to let them long remain beyond the rates which induce large shipments of coin and where a reduction of issues must take place to render it as gradual as possible and not greater than the occasions may require: these are among the functions and benefits of the Bank. They have been often employed with signal benefit."

A practice strongly encouraged by Biddle was the use of the acceptance in domestic as well as in foreign trade. This was common among European banks but had never been popular in the United States, where the promissory note was the customary credit instrument. It was a promise to pay a given sum, at a specified time and place, and was a recognition of a debt arising out of a transaction between two indiviluals, or between an individual and a bank. The promissory note was often unsecured, or secured by a mortgage or a chattel lien; "going on a friend's note" as coendorser was a risky way to show friendship. The acceptance, on the other hand, was a draft or order to pay, and had to be "accepted," or signed across its face, by the person or bank on whom it was drawn, or by an agent of the drawee in the place where the bill was drawn. It could then be discounted at a bank. This kind of "bill of exchange" was very useful in making payments between individuals and firms which were unknown to each other and separated by long distances.

With its network of branches over the country, the Bank was well equipped to handle acceptances, and the increase of cotton exports from southern cities provided a stimulus. Biddle thus explained how the process worked, before a Congressional committee in 1832:

The crop in Tennessee is purchased by merchants who ship it to New Orleans, giving their bills founded on it to the branch at Nashville, which furnishes them with [bank] notes. These notes are in time brought to New York for purchasing supplies for Tennessee. They are paid in New York, and the Nashville bank becomes the debtor of the branch at New York. The Nashville branch repays them by drafts given to the branch at New York on the branch at New Orleans, where its bills have been sent, and the branch in New York brings home the amount by selling its drafts on the branch at New Orleans; or the New Orleans branch remits. Such an operation so far from "disturbing the regular course of trade," is its best auxiliary.[13]

The volume of acceptances handled by the Bank quadrupled in amount between 1823 and 1830, and doubled again by 1833. After the demise of the Bank and the closing of its branches, the trade acceptance fell into relative disuse and the promissory note again became the chief form of domestic business paper in the United States.* J. S. Gibbons, in his treatise on *The Banks of New York,* declared that "Commerce, in its broadest sense, is carried on by promissory notes. The multiplication of this form of credit is beyond all control." And the *Bankers' Magazine* in 1860 confirmed this: "In the United States the promissory note has become the favorite negotiable paper, and in transactions for the purchase and sale of merchandise these instruments are the common and usual forms of settlement of accounts."

Charter Renewal Fight

In spite of its accomplishments in many fields, the Bank had a number of enemies. Some were state banks which resented the fact that the Bank, through its branches, made a practice of sending their notes home for redemption once a week. The well-managed banks were glad to have their competitors kept in order by this device. There were enough of the others, however, to cause Gallatin, writing in 1831, to refute the "general complaints on the part of many of the State banks" and to

---

* See p. 119.

declare that he had never known of a solvent bank to be injured by this policy of the Bank of the United States but that it had "effectually checked excessive issues." Gallatin at this time was president of the National Bank of New York (which in spite of its name had a state charter).

Some other banks in New York City opposed the Bank because its head office was in Philadelphia. New York, the largest city in the country since 1810, had with the start of its regular packet sailings to Europe and the south by 1820, and the opening of the Erie Canal route to the west in 1825, taken the leadership in domestic and foreign trade from Philadelphia. Most of the import duties, the principal source of federal revenue, were collected at the port of New York and deposited in the New York branch of the Bank, thus increasing the funds under the control of the parent bank in Philadelphia.[14] Nicholas Biddle believed that the charter fight was a contest between Wall Street and Chestnut Street rather than, as the Jacksonians implied, a contest between the humble agrarians and the moneyed aristocracy.

The most powerful opposition to the Bank was political, as became evident when President Jackson sent his first Message to Congress in 1829. Although he gave due credit to the Bank for the "judicious arrangements of the officers" in aiding the Treasury to pay off the last of the public debt, he raised again the question of its constitutionality, doubted its expediency, and added "it must be admitted by all, that it has failed in the great end of establishing a uniform and sound currency"—this in a period when the currency was better than it had ever been, or was to be during the next generation. Jackson himself knew little of banks, and he confessed to Biddle on one occasion that he had been suspicious of banks ever since he had read about the South Sea Bubble.

His own party included a few like "Old Bullion" Benton, the doughty Senator from Missouri, who honestly disapproved of all paper money and the banks which issued it. There were others who had no doubts about the constitutionality of a federal bank, but wanted one under their own control; they petitioned Congress for a charter even before the Bank charter expired. The closest advisors to the President were men who saw a contest over the Bank's recharter as an opportunity to gain a political victory over their Federalist enemies. Among them was Martin Van Buren, once a personal friend of Biddle, who had already tangled with the Federalist banks of New York when as governor he pushed through the legislature the Safety Fund System.* He resigned to be Secretary of State under Jackson, later became Vice-President and then President, and helped to establish the Independent Treasury.[15]

Biddle and his advisors were understandably disturbed by the attacks on the Bank and by other indications of hostility which began to appear in administration newspapers. They decided not to wait until 1836 when the charter would expire, but to apply for a renewal well in advance of that date. Daniel Webster and Henry Clay helped to prepare the petition for recharter which was presented to Congress in January 1832. The lengthy debate over the petition resulted only in a resolution to investigate the Bank, and in March a Congressional committee was appointed. After a month of hearings in Philadelphia and Washington, the majority of the seven-member committee brought in a report which damned the Bank as it had been appointed to do, although two of the majority members later disavowed the charges of corruption made in the report. The minority of three members, however, defended the Bank, and John Quincy Adams, one of the three, filed in addition a supplement to the minority report because he was so indignant at the treatment of Mr. Biddle during the hearings. Hezekiah Niles, although a staunch Democrat and "no partizans of the bank" commented in his weekly *Register* of May 12, 1832, ". . . we regard this 'report' as the strangest mixture of *water-gruel and vinegar*, the most awkward and clumsy and exaggerated *ex parte* production that we ever read." The report is of importance in financial history because it laid the basis not only for the destruction of the Bank but also for a series of governmental actions which within a decade completely changed the relations of the government to the money market.[16]

In spite of the adverse report of the Congressional committee and the campaign of abuse in certain newspapers, the bill for the recharter of the Bank passed in the House by a vote of 167 to 85, and in the Senate by 28 to 20. A week later on July 10, just as Congress was about to adjourn, Jackson sent a long veto message. He gave as one of his reasons his doubt about the constitutionality, but stressed the association of the

---

* The Safety Fund System required banks to contribute annually to a fund for protection of bank creditors, and to submit to inspection. The large city banks objected that this was unfair to them.

Bank with the "monied oligarchy" and with foreigners. One-fourth of the stock was owned by foreigners, it is true, but they had no voting rights, a point which the President did not mention. It was impossible to rally a two-thirds vote in the Senate to override the veto, and so the charter was lost. In the Presidential election of that autumn, Jackson easily defeated Henry Clay, the friend of the Bank.

In one sense the "Bank war" has never been ended. Historians have continued to analyze the personalities of Biddle and Jackson and their supporters, the merits of Bank policies, and the blame for the troubles which followed its demise. New material keeps turning up to throw new light on one aspect of the case or another. Few events in the financial history of the United States have been discussed at such length with such passion.

Removal of Treasury Deposits from the Bank

Jackson entered on his second term of office in March 1833. His dislike of the Bank had been increased by the political campaign with its violent diatribes and invectives on both sides. There was uneasiness in the financial community as it became clear that the President was planning further attacks on the Bank. The uneasiness was proved to be quite justified when in September (during a recess of Congress) the Washington *Globe* carried an official announcement that government deposits were no longer to be placed in the Bank and its branches, but in state banks as depositaries. Congress was not officially informed of this action until it convened again in December.

Some of the seasoned bankers in Jackson's own party, like Gallatin in New York, were not at all enthusiastic about the prospect of handling funds for the Treasury. However, they were persuaded by Amos Kendall, a subordinate officer in the Treasury but a confidante of the President, that it would be to their advantage to do so. The Secretary of the Treasury, Louis McLane, and his successor, William J. Duane, were as reluctant as the bankers to embark on this scheme. Duane was forced out of office and replaced by the former Attorney General, Roger B. Taney, who was willing to cooperate. He was rewarded later by an appointment to the Supreme Court.

The Bank had been assured that the funds then on deposit would not be immediately withdrawn. However, Secretary Taney entrusted to five of the new state depositaries drafts on the Bank of the United States for 3,200,000 dollars to be used in case there was retaliatory action by the Bank. The Union Bank of Maryland, headed by Taney's friend, Thomas Ellicott, was in serious difficulties because of Ellicott's speculations. It violated Taney's instructions and presented two of its drafts at once. Biddle had not been told how many such drafts were outstanding, as he customarily had been by previous Secretaries. The Bank was therefore reluctantly constrained to reduce its loans more rapidly than it had planned to do.[17]

This reduction occurred before the depositary banks were in a position to expand, and the result was a short financial crisis which was especially severe in the importing cities. The tariff of 1833 had made customs duties payable at the moment of importation, rather than, as before, after the goods were sold. New York merchants who sent a delegation to Washington to appeal for relief were told by Jackson that the fault lay entirely with the Bank and that nothing would induce him to restore the government deposits to it.

Eventually the depositary banks were able to increase their loans on the basis of funds deposited by the Treasury. After October 1, 1833, all new deposits were made in seven state banks, one each in Philadelphia and Baltimore, two in Boston, and three in New York; six of them were closely associated with Jackson's advisors and were popularly referred to as the "pet banks." The depositary banks expanded, as they had been admonished to do by Secretary Taney. At the three pet banks in New York City, loans and discounts rose from 8.2 million dollars on October 1, 1833, to more than 12 million six months later, and the expansion continued until it was stopped by the crash of 1837.

By June 1836 thirty-three banks were being used as depositaries. The new Secretary of the Treasury, Levi Woodbury, urged them to build up their specie reserve and to curtail their issue of small notes, but had no way of enforcing his request unless he withdrew the deposits altogether. Both the President and the Secretary professed to be delighted with the manner in which the banks were handling Treasury funds and making transfers from one part of the country to another. Not until the following year did the Secretary admit publicly that the new system was unsatisfactory. In his Report for 1837 he said:

The operations of the deposite act . . . will probably prove very deficient. In some other respects they have, by first requiring to be speedily collected and subdivided among more numerous banks from ten to fifteen millions of dollars, and then compelling, within the short period of nine months from the 1st of January last, another collection and transfer of nearly forty millions more, and much of it from merchants, and to places not situated in the usual channels of trade or of large fiscal operations, unquestionably aggravated many of the distresses which had their principal origin in other causes. Those operations necessarily aided to produce the derangement that occurred in the domestic exchanges, and imposed a task upon the banks unprecedented for its amount and difficulty.

The Secretary put the chief blame on Congress which had required, in the Act of June 23, 1836, that no bank receive deposits to more than three-fourths of its capital. This limited his discretion so that the transfers of funds could not be made in ways best adapted to meet the needs of the financial community.

The Bank of the United States, after the veto of its charter renewal and especially after the removal of the Treasury deposits, could take little responsibility for the money market and made little effort to control the note issue of the state banks. Their number had more than doubled, and their note issue had nearly tripled, between 1830 and 1837.

The boom in business which accompanied the increase in banks and bank note circulation carried the price of cotton from 9 to 18 cents per pound.* Exports rose in value from 72 to 124 million dollars between 1830 and 1836, and imports increased even more rapidly from 63 to 177 million. Banks could not meet all the demands for credit, even with the funds which Treasury deposits made available to them. The Bank of the United States came under renewed criticism because it too was not expanding its loans, although it had provided 2 million to save the New York insurance companies after the great fire of December 1835.[18]

The Distribution of the Surplus

The second important financial measure of the Jackson regime was the distribution of the surplus which had accumulated in the Treasury. Jackson had advocated this as early as his first Message in 1829. By

---

* See p. 118.

the middle of his second administration the surplus was still larger. The national debt had been paid off; sales of public lands were increasing; and the high tariff of 1828, even after some reduction by the Compromise Act of 1833, was bringing in far larger revenues than were needed for current expenses. Both parties were concerned about the size of the surplus, the Jacksonians because they were opposed to federal expenditures for internal improvements, and the opposition because they feared the power which the surplus gave to the party in office.

It was also becoming difficult to find banks in which to deposit the growing funds of the Treasury, since many of them could not meet qualifications as to capital. Both parties in Congress, therefore, in spite of the opposition of the Secretary of the Treasury, agreed on the plan which had originally been proposed by Jackson but which he now opposed—the distribution among the states of the surplus revenues of the federal government. To meet the objections of the President, it was called a loan; any sum in the Treasury, above a balance of 5 million dollars, was to be distributed to the states in four quarterly installments, in proportion to the number of their representatives in Congress.

When the law was passed in June 1836, the surplus was about 50 million dollars. By the time the distribution began in January 1837, the depression had reduced it to 37 million. The first installment of 9 million was paid on schedule, and the depositary banks in New York, from which most of the money was drawn, met the Treasury draft without difficulty. During March the Mechanics Bank protested that it had been paying out large sums on government account and would find it hard to make the second quarterly payment of the surplus. The Secretary politely regretted the plight of the bank, but said he was helpless, as the bank still held a government deposit which he was obliged to draw out under the law. All the banks met the April draft in spite of their protests.

A few weeks later the New York banks were complaining again that the heavy withdrawals of Treasury funds, one-fourth of them in specie, had forced a reduction in their loans of nearly 5 million dollars and was producing extremely tight money in the city. Their specie reserve had fallen so low that they would be unable to meet the Treasury draft for the third quarter. In fact, they suspended specie payments completely on May 10, 1837, and their action was soon followed by banks in some other parts of the country. The Treasury managed to make the third quarter payment in July by using funds in banks outside New York. When the fourth installment was to be paid in October, the Treasury had on deposit in the fifteen northern states only 3 million, and was obligated to pay out to those states a total of 6.5 million. The depositary banks in the eleven southern and western states held 9 million of Treasury deposits, but only 3 million were required to be paid out to those states. Since the Treasury could not accept the notes of suspended banks, it was impossible for it to transfer the needed 3.5 million from the south and west to the north. After lengthy and acrimonious debate, Congress finally, on October 2, postponed the fourth installment until January 1839. When that date arrived, there was no longer any surplus in the Treasury. The depression of 1837 had cut the revenues of the government far below its expenditures, and the fourth installment was never paid.

Although the sums distributed to the states were technically loans, most of the states treated them as gifts and made no effort to repay them. Some states used the money for railroads and other internal improvements; a number invested in bank or railroad stock and used the interest in support of public schools. Louisiana and Maryland used part of the money to pay off the state debt. Maine, Massachusetts, New Jersey, and Ohio divided the money among the counties, which used it for the most part for schools. Vermont and Rhode Island divided the money among their towns. The judgment of contemporary observers was almost unanimous that in the majority of cases the distribution of the surplus had encouraged waste and extravagance.[19]

The Specie Circular

The third financial measure of Jackson's administration followed shortly after the distribution of the surplus. It was the Specie Circular, which was issued as an executive order forbidding any government officer to accept "for land sold, any draft, certificate, or other evidence of money or deposit . . . unless signed by the Treasurer of the United States." Congress had no opportunity to discuss this order until after it had been issued; it then passed a bill which partially repealed the order, but Jackson delayed signing until Congress had gone home, so the Circular remained in operation.

There had long been difficulty in collecting sums due the Treasury for public lands. Of the 48 million dollars owed to the government for the 20 million acres sold between 1796 and 1820, only 28 million dollars had been actually paid. After 1820 the government refused to sell on the installment plan and insisted that purchasers pay cash, which consisted usually of notes of state banks. With sales of public lands increasing very rapidly during his administration, a fact to which he had earlier pointed with pride as evidence of "real abundance of capital and ease in the money market," Jackson became concerned about the quality of the bank paper being paid to the Treasury. His first step in September 1835 had been to forbid the acceptance of bank notes of denominations below 5 dollars. This accomplished very little in improving the quality of the circulation; less than a year later, on July 11, 1836, he issued the Specie Circular.

The result of the ban on bank paper for land payments was to reverse the normal flow of funds within the country. Few purchasers of land would take the risk of carrying specie west in their saddle bags. The banks of the west therefore had to pay out specie in large amounts, in return for notes of eastern banks brought by the purchasers. The specie was then paid to the Treasury representatives who locked up most of it, since the law limited the amount which could be deposited in any bank. The only way to get the coin back into normal circulation was for the Treasury to pay it out to government employees or suppliers, but there were few of these in the west. It became increasingly difficult for the western banks to maintain their supply of specie.

Another factor aggravated the currency situation just at this time. The Act of 1834 had raised the ratio of gold to silver, tending to drive out the silver coin which was now worth more abroad than at home.* Since there had never been enough gold coin in the country to meet the need (foreign gold coins were still in common use), the new law made it even more difficult than before for the banks to maintain reserves of specie with which to redeem their notes. The Treasury felt no responsibility for this situation. It had moved rapidly toward a policy of refusing aid to all banks, even the pet banks. Indeed, the Act of June 23, 1836, expressly forbade transfers of Treasury funds "for the purpose of accom-

---

* See Chapter 6.

modating the banks to which the transfer may be made, or to sustain their credit, or for any other purpose whatever, except it be to facilitate the public disbursements." The Treasury insisted on receiving specie for itself, but how the banks and the citizens were to obtain the specie was no longer of any concern to it.[20] Sales of public lands immediately fell off sharply and never again reached the 1836 peak of 25 million dollars.

The Crisis of 1837

In March 1836 the national charter of the Bank expired and it began to operate as the United States Bank of Pennsylvania under a charter from Pennsylvania. During the next few months Biddle attempted to prepare the Bank for the difficulties he foresaw resulting from the Specie Circular and the Distribution of the Surplus. He was unable to prevent the suspension of specie payments in May of 1837 by the New York banks, and was obliged to follow their example although his own bank was sound. It was not until a year later, after the Specie Circular had been repealed by Congress, that resumption was possible, with the aid of 1 million pounds sterling in gold imported by Prime, Ward and King on the guarantee of Barings.

During these months Biddle had been making a valiant effort to support the price of cotton, on which both the United States and England depended. The cotton was sold at a handsome profit and the Bank seemed to be in excellent shape. Biddle, after more than twenty years at the helm, seized the opportunity to resign and retire.

The depression was far from over, however. Banks in the west were hard-pressed to meet their obligations and, when the price of cotton again declined, banks and merchants in the south were in difficulty. The Bank of England was refusing credit on American imports. The banks of New York, determined to avoid another suspension, curtailed their loans, but banks in Philadelphia, including the United States Bank, were forced to announce another suspension in October 1839. With Biddle gone, the Bank was soon in serious trouble, and it went down in bankruptcy in 1841. Banks and business all over the country were in difficulties and no help could be expected from the central government. The states, heavily in debt, were powerless.

The difficulties of carrying on business activities during this period are epitomized in a letter written in December 1838 by James W. King of Clinton, Michigan, to the New York firm of Phelps Dodge from which he had purchased 500 dollars worth of tin:

Your letter came to hand Requesting an answer Respecting your Clame In Regard to it I ecknolage you had ought to had your pay Long time ago - But oing to the wild Cat Curincy and some of the Chartered Banks it Bin impossible to do eny thing with money wee Sold our goods to Smith & Landon They wur to pay the Demand on account of they Being ingaged in the Wild Cat Banks they had to Leave the country. I had to take the goods to secure myself & Sold them out on a Credit in preference to take the kind of money that was in Curculation - untill some two months pas I have stopd the lending Business and am making my Colections this winter if you want it before I Can Colect it I will Sattisfy the Demand By good notes against good farmers & Back them myself if it wood make them enny Better - or if you will Be patient Little Longer I will Pay you as soon as I Can Colect it money is scarce hear Mr. Shelly has not paid me for the *tin* I hold his note now - But that is nothing to do with you & If you must forbar with me a Little Longer and it Shall Come together with the inress.[21]

This depression was one of the worst in the history of the country. It was described years later by Hugh McCulloch, who had been head of the second Bank of Indiana at the time, in these words:

The depression which prevailed from 1837 to 1843 cannot be understood by any who did not witness it. It was widespread and all-pervading. It affected all classes, but the greatest sufferers, next to the day laborers, were the farmers. Everything which the farmer had to sell had to be disposed of in barter or for currency at ruinous prices. I witnessed in 1841 a sale to a hotel-keeper in Indianapolis of oats at six cents a bushel, chickens at half a dollar a dozen, and eggs at 3 c a dozen. Other farm products were proportionately low; two c and ½ a pound net for fat cattle and hogs was the ruling price at Cincinnati. . . . Day laborers were the greatest sufferers, for wages declined more than the prices of the articles which they needed for their own support and the support of their families. Many were out of employment.[22]

The United States was to undergo other depressions, but few were so long or so severe. The combination of heavy borrowing from England on long-term by American states and corporations, with heavy imports of goods on short-term credit, created a top-heavy structure of debt which collapsed when it could no longer be supported by British banks. The complete lack of understanding of money market functions on the part of the United States government, and the absence of any centralized monetary control, prolonged the recovery period.

APPENDIX

Federal Debt

The program of debt repayment so carefully designed by Gallatin was seriously interrupted by the embargo and the war. The total had been reduced to 57 million dollars at the beginning of Madison's administra-

TABLE 1. TOTAL OF PUBLIC DEBT AT CLOSE OF EACH ADMIN-ISTRATION FROM 1793 TO 1841 (*in millions of dollars*)

As of Jan. 1	Public Debt at Close of each Administration	Total Revenues of 4-Year Period		
		Customs Receipts	Public Lands	Total
1793	80.4	7.8	—	18.9
1797	82.1	21.2	.004	33.9
1801	83.0	30.3	.096	42.0
1805	82.3	44.8	1.0	50.8
1809	57.0	59.8	2.4	62.6
1813	56.0	38.2	2.9	57.0
1817	123.5	62.8	5.0	183.2
1821	90.0	75.7	9.5	100.9
1825	83.8	67.6	4.9	84.7
1829	59.4	86.4	5.1	99.8
1833	7.0	97.3	9.7	110.0
1837	1.9	88.0	48.5	142.0
1841	6.5	64.0	20.2	127.3

Source: Jonathan Elliott, *The Funding System of the United States and Great Britain*, p. 18 (28 Congress, 1 Session, House Document 15, 1845). Compiled from Treasury Reports. The total includes the proceeds of loans and Treasury note issues during the war years. The peak of the debt was 132 millions in 1815. This table does not agree in all details with that of *Historical Statistics of the United States*, pp. 712, 721.

tion in 1809 but was more than doubled by the end of his second term; it was twenty years before it reached so low a point again. Table 1 gives the amount of the public debt outstanding at the close of each administration, with the total revenues from the principal sources during each four-year period.

Spanish milled dollar

CHAPTER 5

PUBLIC AND PRIVATE ENTERPRISE BEFORE THE CIVIL WAR

BOTH public and private enterprise were hampered by a shortage of investment capital in the early stages of United States industrial development. This shortage was made more acute by the relative scarcity of labor and the high level of wages which exerted constant pressure on business enterprisers to use as much mechanical equipment as possible. Although in the long run this resulted in high productivity, in the short run it created many problems.

The inadequate amount of investment capital was matched by the inadequate organization of the market for funds. A small investor, with one thousand dollars or less at the time of the Revolution, had little choice but to buy a share in a ship or voyage—not a share of stock, but a fractional share in the net earnings or profits of the voyage—or a share in a land company on a partnership basis. The ill-fated Yazoo Land Company of Georgia, for example, was organized in 1795 with several partners who put in as little as £200, and with only one who put in more than £2000. After the funding of the United States debt an investor could buy government "stock," as it was then called, or bank stock issues which became gradually available in the larger cities. Mortgages were always available as investment but were usually handled on a person-to-person basis.

Business Corporations

This situation changed gradually as the corporate form of business organization became more widespread. Before the Revolution the formation of business corporations had been hampered by the British Bubble Act.* After the Revolution this was no longer in force, but there was still a strong suspicion among the general public that the corporation was associated with monopoly and privilege and therefore not an appropriate form for private business. An anonymous pamphleteer of 1827, discussing "The Use and Abuse of Incorporations," put it in these words:

every act of incorporation for the purpose of pecuniary profit, carries with it such privilege, as in the nature of things, the great mass of the people cannot exercise. . . . Under the abuses of this system of corporations and monopolies, where the means of corruption are absolutely created by the act which calls them into existence . . . [it] bestows on them a privilege to prey upon society.

As a result of this attitude, each company had to make special application for its charter of incorporation. Madison had proposed that the new Constitution give Congress the right to charter business corporations, but he had been overruled. It was therefore only the state legislatures which could grant such charters. Not until 1795 was any general incorporation law enacted by a state, and this law of North Carolina applied only to canal companies. New York passed a somewhat more general law in 1811 and, in 1838, a Free Banking Act for bank charters. Finally in 1848 New York began to incorporate any kind of business without a special act of the Legislature. Other states followed this lead grudgingly but not until 1875 can special charters be considered a thing of the past.[1]

The separate applications for charters of incorporation were not only time-consuming for the legislature, but also uncertain for the applicant. If he were not of the same political faith as the majority of the legislature the charter might not be granted at all, or might be granted hypocritically

---

* See pp. 11, 15.

as in the case of a Pennsylvania charter authorizing the company to do business anywhere except in Pennsylvania. Although companies could, and many did, operate as partnerships, this denied them the advantage of limited liability for the owners. As the industrial enterprise increased in size and more capital was needed, the partnership became a less suitable form. Yet the proprietorship and the partnership continued to be the dominant type of business enterprise since the majority of firms were still small.

The merchant who had long been the business leader in his community began gradually to lose to the industrialist his position of prestige. Some merchants became industrialists or bankers as the capital which had been acquired through profits of mercantile activity began to be shifted into manufacture. In New England, for example, profits of the China trade went into the great textile factories. Without such previous accumulation of capital it was difficult to set up a manufacturing establishment. Unless the entrepreneur owned real estate which could be mortgaged, his promissory note was not considered adequate security for a loan even if the conventional limit of 60 days could be extended by renewal. Benjamin Franklin had been concerned about this problem even before the Revolution, and when he died had left a fund to provide aid for honest and industrious mechanics.* Another attempt to help young men get a start was made by the Pennsylvania legislature in 1790 when at the urging of Tench Coxe it subscribed £1000 to a Society for the Encouragement of Useful Arts, which among other things established its own calico factory. In 1806 the Philadelphia Domestic Society was incorporated to help weavers obtain raw materials and market their products. These efforts had some success even before the war.

The embargo of the war years gave still stronger impetus to domestic industry by cutting off the supply of foreign goods and raising the price of domestic. In 1810 Secretary of the Treasury Gallatin stated in his Report that a good start had been made in the United States in the manufacture of cotton, woolen and linen fabrics, hats and straw bonnets, paper, printing types, gunpowder, window glass, jewelry, clocks, and liquors. In other lines it was already self-sufficient—wood and leather manufactures, soap and candles, refined sugar, coarse earthenware, snuff,

---

* See p. 63ff. *n.*

chocolate, mustard, and hair powder. The annual sum of all these manufactures he placed at about 120 million dollars. Much of this development was ascribed to the effect of the embargo. At the end of the war, when British imports arrived in enormous volume to be sold through auctions, many of the new firms did not survive.[2]

When the new manufacturing enterprises were organized as corporations, they often found it difficult to sell their stock. In many cases the subscriber to a new issue paid in only a fraction of the par value, and then became subject to calls from the promoter for further funds as the company got under way. This had long been standard practice in relation to bank shares, where it had been facilitated by the new bank's willingness to lend to the stockholder the funds needed to finish paying for his shares. Industrial companies were unable to oblige their subscribers in this way, and many were able to complete their capital funds only by determined nagging of the stockholders. The Rhode Island Aquidneck Coal Mine offered, through an advertisement in the New York *Evening Post* of February 8, 1811, 400 shares at 150 dollars each, for which only one-fourth had to be paid in cash, and the rest in notes at 6, 12, and 18 months. In 1812 the Utica Glass Company obtained its capital only after making more than eighteen calls on its subscribers.

Companies organized to construct roads and canals had a more difficult time in raising capital, particularly for canals. Many of the subscribers to their stocks were local residents anxious to benefit by the improved transportation, but blessed with very small incomes. The New York *Evening Post* on April 17, 1804, for example, carried an advertisement to the effect that "The Proprietors of Stock in the Morris Turnpike Company are hereby notified and required to pay . . . . Two Dollars on each share of stock." A similar call on a shareholder in the Dutchess County Turnpike Company brought a sharply worded protest to Gilbert Livingston in December 1804:

By pressing the stockholders when not absolutely necessary they are put to great trouble for no adequate benefit—I find it quite inconvenient to complete the payment demanded—If therefore it can be postponed till spring I shall be much accommodated . . . . The call you have made has a very unpropitious effect on the stock. I believe it may be purchased at 5 p^r c^t under par.

The Chesapeake and Delaware Canal Company, which had been

chartered in 1799 with a capital of 400,000 dollars, easily obtained subscriptions for most of the amount, but collecting the funds was a more difficult matter. Nearly 100,000 dollars had been spent on the purchase of water rights and land, and construction had begun, when the Board of Directors reported in 1805 that it was impossible to proceed without more money. "The chief difficulty . . . is the despondency of the private subscribers, many of whom are persons of small or moderate fortunes, to whom the amount of their subscription is of considerable consequence." The Board was therefore left "with no alternative but the prosecution of suits against the deficient parties, and suspension of the work until legal justice should furnish the funds which the defection of individuals has retained." The Canal was not completed until a decade later, and then only with the help of public funds from Maryland, Delaware and the United States.[3]

The Federal Period of Internal Improvements

Although the wealth of the country was increasing, and the growing use of the corporate form for business enterprise made somewhat easier the task of raising funds, the local communities and even the state governments were not able to provide all the new transportation facilities which were needed. They built bridges and roads to bring farmers to local markets, but it became increasingly clear in the early part of the nineteenth century that only the national government could raise sufficient funds, and had sufficient interest, to plan and build an adequate system of transportation connecting western territories with the seaboard.

The real impetus to federal participation in internal improvements came from the great anti-federalist Thomas Jefferson, when he announced happily if somewhat prematurely in his second Inaugural address in 1805 that the end of the public debt was in sight, and that "the revenue thereby liberated, may . . . be applied, *in time of peace,* to rivers, canals, roads, arts, manufactures, education, and other great objects within each State." He recommended a constitutional amendment in order to remove any doubt about the power of the federal government to do this. Albert Gallatin, his Secretary of the Treasury, was in full agreement with this plan, and had indeed already embodied a provision for construction of the Cumberland Road, the famous Na-

Delaware and Hudson Canal and Banking Company.

Pursuant to the provisions of an Act of the Legislature of the State of New York, entitled "An act to incorporate the President, Managers, and Company of the Delaware and Hudson Canal Company", books will be opened at 12. O'clock on Friday the seventh day of January next, at the Tontine Coffee House, in the City of New York, for the purpose of receiving subscriptions to the stock of the said Company.

The shares are one hundred dollars each, and five dollars is to be paid upon each share at the time of subscribing. —

New York December 2d. 1824.

Philip Hone —

Lynde Catlin

Jeremiah Thompson

G. B. Abeel

tional Pike, in the 1802 Enabling Act governing the sale of public lands in Ohio, still a territory. The report of the Commissioners appointed to lay out the road was presented to Congress five years later, and within a month a first appropriation of 50,000 dollars had been made for the formal survey. It was quite in line with this interest that Gallatin was requested by the Senate to prepare a general scheme for internal improvements.

The plan which he presented after a year's study was a grand design estimated to cost 20 million dollars over a period of 10 years. A system of four short canals parallel to the eastern coast would connect existing waterways and provide an internal waterway from Boston to Georgia. A turnpike road from Maine to Georgia would provide land transportation through the same area. To join east and west, a system of canals would link eight rivers, with roads over the mountains where canals were impossible. In addition to these great highways by land and water, a number of smaller canals and roads were proposed, some of them designed to bring traffic from the Great Lakes and the St. Lawrence to the Atlantic seaboard. It is a tribute to the perspicacity of Gallatin that almost every part of his plan was eventually carried out. The Cumberland Road was the first to be opened, in 1818, and the last was the Cape Cod Canal, nearly one hundred years later, in 1913. By that time some of the older canals, after years of useful service, had been abandoned for the more modern railroads, as some of the railroads were later, unhappily, abandoned for the still more modern superhighways.

The reduction in federal revenues during the embargo and the war made it impossible to proceed rapidly with Gallatin's plan. The depression of 1819 further delayed the construction of any large-scale internal improvements. Although the question of constitutionality had not yet been resolved, President John Quincy Adams advocated internal improvements "in a more enlarged extent" in his first annual message to Congress in December 1825.[4]

There was by this time a House Committee on Roads and Canals. Now a Civil Engineer Corps was set up within the Army Engineers, and Congress was to be kept informed of all projects. Grants of 5 percent of the proceeds of public land sales were made to new states like Ohio to encourage them to build roads and canals. Bills for the improvement of rivers and harbors by the federal government were passed in 1824, and in 1826 Congress passed the first of the combined "Rivers and Harbors" appropriations which were to become notorious as "pork barrels" into which Congressmen dipped to ingratiate themselves with their constituents back home.

Another method of providing federal aid for local improvements was that of subscriptions to capital stock. This was believed to be less costly for the central government, and was supposed to combine the advantages of private and of public enterprise. Under an Act of 1828, for example, the United States acquired 1 million dollars worth of stock in the Chesapeake and Ohio Canal. The city of Washington subscribed another million, and Alexandria and Georgetown each subscribed a quarter million. By 1829 the various forms of federal expenditures on internal improvements amounted to 2 million dollars on four of the canals proposed by Gallatin and another 2 million on the Cumberland Road. With smaller amounts invested in various projects, the central government had an impressive list of accomplishments to its credit. However, the Jacksonian Democrats took office in that year on a platform which included opposition to all such expenditures. The era in which the federal government took the initiative in planning and carrying out internal improvements came to an abrupt end with the veto by President Jackson of the Act to permit a federal government subscription to the stock of the Maysville and Washington Turnpike Road on May 27, 1830. This left the task to state and local government authorities, many of whom were ill-equipped financially and technically to undertake it.

Internal Improvements by the States

Of course, many roads, bridges, and canals had already been built by local governments, and local bodies had provided aid by direct investment or subsidy to private undertakings. The pattern varied over the country. In New England the turnpike companies received little help from their legislatures; Connecticut gave no aid except tax exemption.

Southern states frequently gave aid to private companies for internal improvements, following the pattern which had been established for aid to banks early in the century. Maryland in 1810 purchased 250 shares in the Baltimore and Frederick-town Turnpike Company; in 1822 the state refused to renew the charters of several Baltimore banks unless they provided funds for the ten miles of road still to be constructed between Baltimore and Wheeling. Georgia authorized a lottery to raise capital for river improvement and, when the lottery failed, made an outright appropriation of the money. Virginia bought nearly half of the stock of the Potomac Company, which was to build a canal, and took some shares in the James River Company. The state invested also in the Dismal Swamp Company in which George Washington had long been interested. The swamp included a part of his Virginia estate, and the land was very fertile when properly drained. Although he helped to survey the land and sent some of his own slaves to work on the project, little was accomplished before the Revolution, and it was not until 1828 that the Dismal Swamp Canal from the Chesapeake Bay to Albermarle Sound was opened.

The most ambitious of all the state undertakings was the Erie Canal in New York, begun in 1817 under Governor DeWitt Clinton. An earlier attempt by the Western Inland Lock Navigation Company, chartered in 1792, to build a canal had met with very limited success and had eventually been subsidized by the state. This example, and the general prejudice against private monopoly, created an atmosphere in which Clinton's carefully reasoned "Memorial" convinced businessmen like William Bayard in New York City and landholders and farmers upstate that the canal should be built by the state. It was an ambitious and, to many, a foolhardy undertaking; it committed the state, with a population of only 1 million, to an expenditure of 5 or 6 million dollars. The final total was of course much larger than the original estimates—between 7 and 11 million, depending on how the costs of administration were allocated.

There was very little difficulty in raising the funds. Big land speculators in the northern part of the state contributed thousands of acres to the right of way. The first loan of 200,000 dollars at 6 percent for 20 years was placed with the help of two British "assurance" companies who took one-third of it, and, of two banks in New York City in which the state owned stock, the New York State Bank and the Mechanics and Farmers Bank. These banks offered a higher price for the canal bonds, and thus outbid their competitors, on condition that their notes be used to pay the wages of the laborers employed in the construction of the canal. The loans were to be financed by salt and auction taxes and, if necessary, by lotteries until the revenue from tolls became sufficient to meet all charges.

After the success of the first issue, it became easier to sell succeeding issues, and the bonds were widely held by small investors and by savings banks. When the canal was opened in 1825 its earning power soon became evident, and foreigners began to invest in it. By 1829 more than half the stock was held abroad; by 1833 it was selling at a 20 percent premium.

The success of the New York canal was viewed with justifiable alarm by other states on the seaboard who wanted to share in the growing trade with the west. Pennsylvania had the most at stake. It had already subsidized private companies in the construction of 1800 miles of east-west turnpikes and feeder roads during the first two decades of the century. By 1816 its appropriations for roads and bridges had reached a total of 2.4 million dollars, and by 1823 the total of state and private expenditure amounted to 10.5 million. The state had also, in 1821, guaranteed the 6 percent interest on 450,000 dollars in 25-year bonds issued by the Schuylkill and Susquehannah Canal Company which had been chartered in 1815. But much more had to be done if western trade was to be enticed away from the Erie Canal and drawn through Pennsylvania to the coast. A great debate began between the proponents of canals and those of railroads. Mathew Carey, the Philadelphia publisher who had already come into prominence as champion of the "American System" of high tariffs, sponsored the Philadelphia Society for the Promotion of Internal Improvements in the Commonwealth, which in 1824 issued a series of objective, technical papers on the relative merits of the two forms of transportation.

After lengthy debate a combination of the two was decided on, and the legislature authorized a loan (with quite inadequate provision for servicing it) for the construction of the first canal. By 1834 a railroad between Philadelphia and Columbia completed the mainline system, consisting of canals, railroads, and portages, constructed at a cost of more than 12 million dollars. The system was never a successful competitor to the Erie Canal. The delays at the points of transshipment from canal to rail and back again caused loss and annoyance to shippers, and in spite of constant changes and improvements the revenues barely covered expenses. By 1843 the net result to the state was a debt of 40 million, and in 1857 the whole system was sold to the Pennsylvania railroad for 7.5 million.

Ohio was another state which undertook an extensive program of canal construction, not to compete with New York or Pennsylvania but to enable its farmers to use the facilities of the other states. Ohio had already invested heavily in the stock of turnpike companies, as it was later to invest in railroad companies. During the decade after 1825 the state concentrated on canals, borrowing through its Canal Commissioners nearly 4 million dollars on state "stock" at 5 and 6 percent, repayable after 1850. Prime, Ward and King and the Bank of the Manhattan Company acted as agents for these issues in New York and negotiated the sale of a large part of them to foreigners. Indiana and Illinois also built canals with public funds, but on a much smaller scale than Ohio. The federal government aided some of the projects with grants of public lands.[5]

Canal building in the United States fell into three cycles. The first one produced the Erie Canal and its early rivals up to 1834; the second was concerned largely with feeder lines and reached a peak in 1840. A third cycle spread over the years to the Civil War, and brought the total investment in canals before 1860 to an estimated 188 million dollars, of which nearly three-fourths was raised by state and city governments. Nearly one-third of all the funds used in canal construction by both private and government agencies came from foreign investors, mostly between 1825 and 1840.

Canals were not financed with public funds in all states. New Jersey, with extensive coastline and river boundaries, did not require an elaborate system of canals, and the legislature of that state showed a strong reluctance to go into debt. Moreover New York financiers were eager to supply funds for a private enterprise which they hoped would be as profitable as the state-owned Erie Canal. In spite of the usual fear of monopoly, and a sentiment that so important a project as a canal should not "become the sport of speculation or the avenue to a paltry spirit of jobbing" as Niles' *Register* reported, the legislature passed two bills in 1824. One provided for the construction of a Raritan Canal by the New Jersey Canal Company, which was to give a bonus of 100,000 dollars to the state in return for its charter. The other bill chartered the Morris Canal and Banking Company with a capital of 1 million for canal construction and another million for banking. The capital was heavily oversubscribed when the books were opened; shares were soon at a premium and the object of speculation. At least nine of the fifteen directors were from New York, and four of them were eventually indicted for fraud in the manipulation of the stock. The investment banking business of the company was paramount from the start, and the company was active in the handling of state securities during the lush days of the 1830s. Under the terms of the charter a canal had to be constructed, but it was far more expensive than had been anticipated. It was leased to the Little Schuylkill and Susquehanna Railroad in 1836. The company failed in 1841 and the canal was sold to a new group which, by carrying coal east and iron ore west, earned a profit until the railroads took over the carrying trade. New Jersey was one of the few states which, by refusing to finance its internal improvements, avoided carrying a heavy debt into the 1840s.[6]

Railroad Financing Before the Civil War

Railroads entered the financial scene much later than canals. Their construction was far more expensive and far more demanding of technical skill. Although the first railroad charter in the United States, that for the New Jersey Railroad Company, was granted as early as 1815, very few others were undertaken until the 1830s.

In New England the financing of railroads met fewer obstacles than elsewhere in the United States. Since the rocky terrain and rugged hills had made canals impossible in most of its territory, the New England states were relatively free from debt, and were eager to try this new mode of transportation. Moreover, the profits of shipping and industry were already producing a surplus of private capital available for investment, and there was little pressure on the states to provide funds for railroads. In granting railroad charters the state of Massachusetts sometimes reserved the right to purchase the road after a period of years— a right never exercised—but did not usually make any subscription to the stock. One of the earliest of the Massachusetts railroads, the Boston and Lowell, chartered in 1830, was able to raise most of its original capital of half a million dollars among the proprietors of the manufacturing establishments of Lowell. In the case of the Boston and Worcester, the businessmen of the community who needed a route to the Hudson River took a large part of the capital stock. Exceptions were the Boston and Portland Rail Road which in 1833 received a loan from the state of 150,000 dollars and the Nashua and Lowell which in 1836 got 50,000. Both of these loans were repaid in a few years. The state also aided the Western Railroad to connect Boston with Albany in the hope of obtaining some of the trade with the west. Most of the Massachusetts railroads were profitable from the beginning and were able to increase their capital once they went into operation.

The success of New England railroads in raising funds at home is shown by a report of a Massachusetts Senate Committee in 1841. Twenty thousand shares of stock in the Western Railroad, which had initially received some aid from the state, were held by 1949 stockholders in 80 towns and cities; 1766 of these holders had been original subscribers in 1835. A similar situation was revealed by the report of the Northern Railroad in 1850; nearly 2000 shareholders in New England held about 25,000 shares, and only 10 percent of the stock was held in other states or in foreign countries. The Old Colony Railroad reported in 1849 that most of its shares were held in small lots in New England. The Boston and Maine Railroad in the same year had two-thirds of its stock in the hands of 1164 shareholders in 92 towns of Massachusetts, and only 2000 of the total 35,500 shares were held outside of New England.

Residents in other New England states seem to have been less eager to invest in railroad stocks. Connecticut in 1832, for example, chartered the Boston, Norwich and New London Railroad Company, but at the same time, in order to assure it an adequate initial capital, chartered the Quinebaug Bank on condition that it subscribe to one-fifth of the 500,000-dollar capital of the railroad, and a second fifth if needed; the bank was not to go into operation until at least 150,000 dollars had been actually expended on construction of the road. The plan was successful, and the road eventually became a part of the Norwich and Worcester Railroad.

New York state already had a heavy investment in canals, and hesitated to put public funds into railroads which might well reduce the earning power of the canals. It was easy under the general incorporation law, however, for a railroad company to secure a charter, and by the end of the 1830s the New York *Evening Post* was able to catalogue

113 railroad companies in the state, of which 44 had been chartered in "that magnificent year, 1836." The authorized capital of these companies totaled nearly 55 million dollars, but only a fraction of that amount had been paid in, and many of the projected roads were never constructed.

The Erie Railroad began its long and checkered career* with a New York charter in 1832. The authorized capital was 10 million dollars, but the slow sale of its stock delayed the beginning of construction until 1835. It became increasingly difficult to obtain capital from private investors and, after public enthusiasm had been whipped up by a series of mass meetings, the state loaned the company 3 million. Two million more were loaned to other railroads in difficulties.

In the southern states, one of the most important of the early railroads was the Baltimore and Ohio, started in 1828. Both the city of Baltimore and the state of Maryland subscribed half a million to its stock, and individuals took the rest of the capital of 4 million dollars. Many landowners along the right-of-way contributed strips of land. After 8 years when over 3 million had been spent on 82 miles of road, the final million of the subscriptions had not yet been paid in, and would not have been sufficient to complete the line in any case. The company therefore turned to London and borrowed on the security of Maryland state bonds; it is credited with being the first railroad to tap that source of funds.

Other southern states soon followed the lead of Maryland. In the south where the terrain was unsuitable for canals, the states had little hesitation in selling their own bonds to raise funds and lend them to private railroad companies, and many cities did likewise. Macon and Savannah each took 2500 shares of the Central Railroad of Georgia. This company was unusually attractive to investors because it applied for and received banking privileges in 1835, two years after the original railroad charter; it became the Georgia Railroad and Banking Company. A similar combination was made by the Southeastern Railroad Bank, associated with the Cincinnati and Charleston Railroad Company. In some cases the railroad charter included a canal rather than a bank, like that of the South Carolina Canal and Railroad Company.

The difficulties of raising capital in these states far from the financial centers led to the use of some ingenious devices. In South Carolina, when

---

* See p. 185.

the Charlestown and Hamburg Railroad had used up the 100,000-dollar loan from the state as well as the payments made by individuals for stock subscriptions, it took the 1187 shares which remained unsold and pledged them, along with the income of the road when completed, as security for a new loan at 7 percent. The directors reported that they had experienced no difficulty in raising funds in this way. In Maryland, the Governor in his Annual Message for 1839 reported that both railroad and canal companies were issuing their own paper money to keep the construction going. In other cases, the workers were paid in scrip issued by the state or by the railroad—scrip that was sometimes so unacceptable to the workers that strikes and riots resulted.

The state of Virginia floated bonds during the 1820s and 1830s to finance an elaborate system of railroads and canals connecting the area west of the Blue Ridge Mountains with the sea. Although only the Richmond, Fredericksburg and Potomac railroad survived the Civil War, Virginia never repudiated the debt. With the help of West Virginia (granted unwillingly under court order) which had separated from Virginia during the war, the bonds were finally paid off in full in 1966.

The Central Ohio Railroad, although chartered in 1847, was still trying to raise its capital in the "dark period of 1853–4." It had hoped to get the funds from local residents but, as the financial agent reported,

The obtainment of stock subscriptions from a community chiefly agricultural—who, although the most to be benefitted, are sometimes the slowest to acknowledge the value of such enterprises—proved to be a work of peculiar difficulty. The authorization of county and town subscriptions, under a special law, by diffusing the burden, made the matter less objectionable to most; but even in such cases, all the appliances of newspaper and pamphlet publications, and stump-speeches throughout most of the territory interested, had to be available to carry even public subscriptions, against the reluctance of the taxpayers.

Even after such efforts, individuals subscribed less than half of the total of 1,627,000 dollars; the rest was made up by counties and towns in subscriptions ranging from 10,000 to 250,000 dollars of the stock.

Nevertheless, with the combined efforts of private enterprise and public funds, the building of railroads proceeded at a rapid pace. In 1835 there had been slightly more than 1000 miles of road in actual operation. The total nearly doubled in every five-year period up to the war, bringing it to more than 30,000 miles by 1860. By the end of the war a contemporary writer estimated that 1.5 billion dollars had been invested in railroad construction. Unfortunately the rapid changes in prices during the war make his figures difficult to evaluate.[7]

The rapid extension of railroads over the country undoubtedly contributed to accelerating its rate of growth. Highways and canals could never have brought products to market and taken consumer goods back to the farms as rapidly. The opening up of new territory, the stimulus to immigration, and the widening of the market, would all help to encourage investment, increase productivity, and raise the standard of living. Whether a rapid rate of change in all these factors was better than a more leisurely growth is still an open question.

Foreign Capital in the United States

In spite of the strenuous efforts made to raise funds at home, it was inevitable that American development should rely heavily on foreign investors. Stocks and bonds which went into the hands of foreigners reached them by various routes. Some were sold in the first instance to individual foreigners, others to foreign bankers for their own or customer accounts, or to agents of foreign firms.

Holland, which had aided America materially during the Revolution, continued to buy state and federal securities although in much smaller amounts than England. In 1829, 2 million dollars of canal loans guaranteed by the cities of Washington, Georgetown, and Alexandria were taken by Dutch investors within three hours after the subscription books were opened. Hope and Company of Amsterdam and Hottinguer of Paris continued their interest in American securities, and the Rothschilds, with wide connections on the Continent as well as in London, had an agent in New York from 1835 on.

England continued to be the best market for American securities. Its early start on industrialization, combined with the great reduction in British taxes after Napoleon was finally vanquished, made available for investment annually an amount estimated at 40 to 50 million pounds. The Barings of London, who had been active speculators in American land and merchants for American cotton as early as 1795, expanded their interest to the placing of American securities. They continued such financial transactions even during the War of 1812, and after the war they became the leading agents in London for American bankers, businessmen, and government agencies. During the 1820s when the federal debt was being rapidly reduced, the Barings handled New York, Pennsylvania, Louisiana, and Virginia state issues. They had close and friendly relations with the private bank of Girard in Philadelphia and with the Second Bank of the United States. During the 1830s and the 1840s they acted as agents and underwriters for canal and railroad companies.

The firm with which the Barings were most closely associated in the United States was that of the Bayards. Under various firm names, the Bayards of New York were active in land and security speculation from the early part of the century, and were being used as financial advisors to the state of Ohio in the 1820s. Another firm often associated with the Barings was that of Prime, Ward and Sands, later and perhaps better known as Prime, Ward and King. This firm helped to distribute the Erie Canal stock, and continued to float many other state issues for internal improvements.

The Bank of the United States in its later years also functioned as an investment banker and used its wide European connections to further the placement of American issues. Other banking houses which in the period before the Civil War began to specialize in what is now known as investment banking were Astor and Sons, Brown Brothers and Company, Winslow, Lanier and Company, and Nevins, Townsend and Company in New York; Lee Higginson in Boston; Thomas Biddle and E. W. Clark in Philadelphia. Interlocking directorates were common among all these firms, which were usually organized as partnerships rather than as corporations; some of them had foreign branches or offices.

The states would have found it impossible to finance their internal improvements without the purchase by foreigners of an estimated 80 million of state bonds by 1838;* this was in addition to the 30 million of bank and railroad bonds held abroad by that year. The federal bonds issued during the Mexican War went abroad in large amounts, and in 1849 one-third of the total federal debt was in foreign hands. In 1853 the Secretary of the Treasury obtained from corporations and govern-

---

* This influx of funds provided the basis for the business boom and price inflation of 1835–1838. See pp. 94, 99.

ment officials, reports on the basis of which he estimated the total of American securities held abroad at 222 million, about 18 percent of all the American securities then outstanding. Of this amount, nearly one-half consisted of state bonds, and one-fourth of railroad stocks and bonds; the remaining one-fourth included bank, insurance company, and canal issues, and other government obligations. By 1860 the total foreign holdings, according to the Secretary of the Treasury, had increased to 400 million.

As they had done in the troubled period 1837–45, foreign investors stopped purchasing American securities and even sold some of their existing holdings when the Civil War started. By the end of the war the total was down to about the level of a decade earlier but rose rapidly thereafter.* None of these estimates included the direct investment of foreigners in business enterprises in the United States.[8]

Securities Markets

Specialized financial markets developed very slowly during the ante-bellum period. Merchants bought and sold commercial paper for a commission, and drew on their correspondents abroad and sold the drafts, this in addition to their regular business of handling commodities for their own account or on a commission basis. Mortgages were usually held by private individuals, especially widows or retired persons who did not wish to engage in active business. Even commercial banks, the most specialized institutions of the period, often became involved in the marketing of security issues, a function which later became the specialty of the investment banker.

The early brokers also carried on a wide range of activities, and only gradually sorted themselves out into commodity, commercial paper, or security brokers. The security dealers in New York made a tentative agreement among themselves as to fees as early as 1792, but it was not until 1817 that they became more formally organized into a Stock Exchange. Philadelphia had a Board of Brokers from about 1800 on. In both of these cities the exchange operated with little protocol, and little specialization. There were no requirements for listing. The names

---

* See p. 148.

of the securities were read off daily at specified hours, and offers to buy or sell determined the prices. Brokers in New York were subject to a fine of 6 cents if they were absent from the session. It was not until after 1830 that as many as 1000 shares a day were traded, but the total increased rapidly with the speculative boom in railroad shares of the middle 1830s. The daily turnover reached 8700 on one peak day in 1834; it declined again and sank as low as 2000 in the early 1840s. Some transactions were also carried on after the regular session, in the offices adjoining the Exchange or even in the street outside.

Even in the middle 1830s the list of securities was short. In addition to reporting various federal, state, and local government obligations, the New York *Evening Post* gave quotations during 1835 for 22 New York City banks, 14 banks outside New York, 21 railroads, 32 insurance companies, and 7 gas, coal, or canal companies. There were no manufacturing companies among them. By 1856 the railroad issues outnumbered the banks, 42 against 35; insurance issues had been reduced to 9, and there were 20 industrials on the list, although most of them were not manufacturing companies but were engaged in mining, transportation, or real estate.

It should be noted that the terminology with respect to stocks and bonds was very vague in these early years. Government obligations, federal or state, were frequently referred to as stocks rather than as bonds, and even corporate issues were not always defined correctly by modern standards. When the New York *Herald* discussed the financing of railroads in its issue of December 23, 1845, it took pains to refer to railroad bonds as "debt" and to stocks as "capital stock," but that was rather unusual precision. Foreign investors, it pointed out, however they might name them, preferred to buy bonds since the rate of return was presumably assured. Domestic speculators usually operated in stocks, and even a few foreign capitalists were attracted into that highly volatile class.

The technique of trading in those days encouraged speculative manipulation. A By-law of the New York Board of Brokers in 1817 had required that, in the absence of an agreement to the contrary, settlement for stock purchases should be made on the following day—"the regular way." Many contracts, however, provided for payment only after 6 or even 12 months, so that a broker could operate with very little capital of his own. The limit was reduced to 60 days after Jacob Little in one of his Erie stock manipulations of 1840 took advantage of his option for a 12-month settlement. Another wave of reform swept the Board of Brokers after the panic of 1857 and caused the limit to be further reduced to 30 days, but this was repealed several weeks later.

Gradually the proportion of time settlements declined, and the regular way of payment became customary. The introduction of telegraphic quotations facilitated this change, and even more important was the growth of the call loan market in New York.* The close connection which developed between the New York banks and the stock market through the call loan market gave the New York securities market a character which differed markedly from that of other money markets; it played an unfortunate role in every panic for nearly a century, and was not broken until restrictive legislation was finally enacted after the crash of 1929. It also facilitated the manipulations of such dramatic figures of antebellum finance as Jacob Little, Joseph Barker, and Daniel Drew, who made and lost fortunes, usually in railroad issues, giving the New York Stock Exchange a reputation from which it never quite recovered.[9]

Banking before the Civil War

The demise of the Second Bank of the United States left the banking system of the country without any coordinating agency, if indeed it was any longer possible to speak of a banking *system*. The state banks were left to operate under inadequate state legislation, without the supervision and control which their usually inexperienced administrators sadly needed. The country had a currency consisting largely of bank notes so subject to depreciation that no merchant could safely accept them before consulting his "Banknote Detector" to determine their probable value. Depositors had even less protection than note holders; failed banks often were able to save nothing from the wreckage. Had the Bank of the United States been allowed to survive and develop, the state banks need never have lost their note issue power, and the National Bank note would have been unnecessary.

---

* See p. 125.

One section of the country which was successful in controlling the quality of its bank notes was New England. The Suffolk Bank of Boston, after 1818, offered to redeem notes of any country bank which would maintain with it a balance of 5000 dollars; if the country bank refused, the Suffolk Bank regularly took the notes back to the counter of the issuing bank and demanded specie redemption on the spot. Until 1857 it had a practical monopoly of the redemption business, and on occasion not only cleared the notes of its 500 correspondents, but offered them unsolicited advice on the prudent management of their affairs. It was obliged to suspend during the panic of 1857 and gradually after that shifted to conventional banking.

Through the 1830s most state banks continued to be chartered by special act of their legislatures. After that the states one by one enacted general banking laws which followed the pattern of general incorporation laws. These laws made it possible, by applicants fulfilling the requirements regarding stock subscription, specie payment, and the like, for a charter to be secured almost automatically from the state officer in charge of banking, regardless of the political affiliation of the organizers. The advantages of removing bank charters from the political arena were obvious, but the disadvantages of opening the business of banking to anyone who could meet a few minimal conditions were not at first so evident. It became much easier for persons without ability or training or adequate capital to enter the field, and it opened the way for the bank promoter who had no interest except in starting a bank and then selling it at a profit. The ease of obtaining charters in many states and the inadequate restrictions in many charters were important factors in the unsatisfactory performance of the American banking system during much of the nineteenth century.

State banking laws only gradually began to include measures to ensure more conservative and less inflationary note issue practices. New York, which after the closing of the Second Bank of the United States was the undisputed financial and commercial center of the country, had found that its Safety Fund system established in 1829* was not adequate to protect the creditors of banks which had failed during the depression. In 1838 therefore the state passed a Free Banking Act which became

---

* See p. 91*n*.

a model for many other states (and eventually for the National Bank Act of 1863). Anyone who could raise the capital might obtain a charter which granted "the necessary powers to carry on the business of banking—by discounting bills, notes, and other evidences of debt; by receiving deposits; by buying gold and silver bullion, and foreign coins, by buying and selling bills of exchange, and by issuing bills, notes, and other evidence of debt; . . . and no other powers whatever, except such as are expressly granted by this act." The charter required the bank to hold against its notes the full amount in collateral security in the form of mortgages or state bonds, and an additional 12.5 percent of specie for the redemption of its notes. This specie reserve requirement was repealed 2 years later, but the main provisions of the Act were in operation until state banks ceased to issue notes. Ohio had a law similar to that of New York, with a still higher reserve requirement of 30 percent against notes; however, one-half of this might be in the form of deposits in banks in New York, Boston, Philadelphia or Baltimore. Louisiana also had high reserve requirements of 33⅓ percent against all demand liabilities, deposits as well as notes.

In many states with a general banking law, the charter required a certain ratio of capital to notes or deposits or both, and some requirement for regular reports. To enforce all these requirements special officers were necessary, and the bank examiner appeared on the American scene. His function was to visit the bank without warning and to verify its accounts and its assets. The protection thus afforded the note holders and depositors of the bank was often more apparent than real; the tales of the bank examiner trotting along the main highway in his buggy from one bank to the next, while an Indian runner raced through the woods bearing the just-counted gold to the next bank on the examiner's list, are probably not completely apocryphal.

Instead of enacting a general banking law, several states established a state bank to issue notes and to handle state financial operations. A second Bank of Indiana, organized in 1834 with half of its capital subscribed by the state, was very successful under the careful management of Hugh McCulloch, who later served as Comptroller of the Currency and Secretary of the Treasury. With its network of branches the Bank provided a good note circulation and increased credit facilities for the people of the state, and was one of the few banks which remained open during the panic of 1857. The Bank of Missouri, to which the state subscribed two-thirds of the capital when it was organized in 1837, had an equally good record. On the other hand, the Bank of Illinois, organized in 1835, went bankrupt in 1842. The Mississippi Union Bank, organized in 1838 with a capital of 15 million dollars derived from the sale of state bonds for that amount, lost all its capital within a few years.

In spite of the stricter regulation of banks which was gradually being provided over the country, there was great fear and dislike of banks, especially after the unhappy experience of the late 1830s. This was reflected in some of the state constitutions. Texas, in its constitution of 1845, prohibited banking altogether, Iowa and Arkansas followed suit in 1846, and by 1857 four other states had done the same. They could not, however, prevent the notes of banks of neighboring states from circulating within their borders. The total number of banks elsewhere increased. By 1860 it was estimated that there were 1600 banks in the country, some operating without charters. The total banking capital was judged to be more than 400 million dollars, and the bank note circulation more than 200 million.

Even in the states where banking had been outlawed, there were many private unincorporated banks which could not issue notes but could carry on the business of loaning on long as well as on short term. The lists in *The Merchant's and Banker's Almanac* indicate that their number had increased rapidly in the 1850s, and that the total was more than a thousand by the time of the Civil War.[10]

Banks and the Securities Market

Even the banks which were relatively well managed in this period were subject to hazards over which they had little control. Country banks were almost obliged, by the direction of trade and the demands of their customers, to keep deposits with banks in New York City on which they could sell drafts. The banks of New York paid interest on these as well as on other demand deposits, and then loaned the funds to brokers on the New York Stock Exchange on call, in order to earn enough to offset the interest they paid.* This situation had built up gradually over the

---

* See Chapter 8.

years; it had been observed in the 1820s and condemned by pamphleteers and bank investigators in the 1830s, but without effect. As the Dutchess County Bank explained in 1828, it "kept an account in the North River Bank, in the City of New York, in order to have its bills receivable and current in New York, so that such bills might pass in the state and elsewhere, without discount. . . ."

Bankers in other parts of the country found it equally advantageous to send balances to New York, the commercial center of the country. Banks in the opening states of the Middle West chose New York without question as the keeper of their balances. Even the New England banks, although the redemption of their notes after 1818 was at the Suffolk Bank in Boston, were gradually drawn toward the New York banks, and some of the New England state laws were changed to permit New York balances as well as Boston balances to count as legal reserve. After 1840, banks in the South also increased their deposits in New York. By 1850 a writer in the *Bankers Magazine* estimated that probably 600 banks throughout the country had balances of 17 million dollars in New York, and that out-of-town brokers, private banks, and individuals had an equal amount on deposit there.[11]

One result of the concentration of bankers' balances in New York was to exaggerate the seasonal rhythm already implicit in an economy so largely dependent on agriculture. William Stanley Jevons observed this in England in 1866 when he wrote of "The Autumnal Pressure in the Money Market." In the United States the need of the farmers for cash with which to pay off their farm hands and meet their other obligations at the end of summer created a tremendous demand for currency in the interior and a withdrawal of funds from New York just when imports were heaviest and payments had to be made abroad. The New York banks thereupon ceased to make call loans to brokers, and the brokers had to curtail their activities. Stock prices fell as interest rates on stock loans rose.

The banks whose notes were best protected by security collateral were precisely those least able to expand their circulation in response to the seasonal need. Bank notes could not meet the demand for funds to export abroad. A central bank might have been able to provide control before, and assistance during, an autumnal crisis, but there was no longer such a bank in the United States. The Independent Treasury in spite of the honest concern of some (but not all) of the Secretaries for the good of the community, was worse than useless, since its hoard of specie was quite unrelated to the seasonal or any other fluctuations of business activity. "What a comfort to business men to have such a regulator as the Bank of England, and managed with such judgment!" wrote James Brown of New York to a banker friend in England in the middle of the crisis of 1857.[12]

The Crisis of 1857

The lack of effective organization of the banking system combined with a number of factors in the securities market to make the crisis in the autumn of 1857 a very serious one. There had been a short period of financial difficulty in 1851, and in 1853 a somewhat more serious one, both aggravated by Treasury policy.* American railroads which had been selling their securities abroad found the market reduced by the outbreak of the Crimean War. Several states felt obliged to come to the aid of half-finished railroads, and this action weakened the state bonds which were held as collateral for bank notes. Some banks in Ohio, Indiana, and Illinois were forced to suspend specie payments in May 1854. The situation was not improved by the news that fraudulent stock had been issued by the New York, New Haven and Hartford Railroad, and that 3000 shares of the New York and Harlem Railroad had been forged; there were also rumors of irregularities in Illinois Central issues. Since most Stock Exchange collateral consisted of railroad securities, the Exchange was badly hit, and call loans became almost impossible to obtain. Even the railroads which were untouched by these activities were in precarious condition; with a capital of 491 million dollars, they had run up a debt of 417 million; and against an income of 48 million in 1856–57 they had interest charges of 25 million. All of these factors created a highly inflammable situation in the money market.

The immediate spark to the crisis of 1857 was the failure of the Ohio Life Insurance and Trust Company, which had its head office in Cincinnati and an agent in New York. It had never done much insurance business in spite of its name, but received a few deposits, made loans, and

---

* See p. 138.

acted as transfer agent for the state of Ohio. The company had a reputation for conservative banking, and at the head office in Cincinnati no note could be discounted without the approval of the directors. But its agent in New York had unlimited powers, and his speculations in railroad securities resulted in losses greater than the capital and surplus. It became known that the New York office had been obliged to close its doors on August 24. Most of the New York banks were holders of its drafts, and they were immediately called on by their nervous correspondents in the country to remit their balances; New York bank deposits fell from 64 to 43 million dollars during the next two months.

Security prices fell rapidly, especially for the railroads, making it almost impossible for brokers to borrow on their collateral. The banks had little to lend on call as their balances from the interior were drawn down. Call loan rates were at 5 percent per month in September, and after that the New York *Journal of Commerce* simply published no rates at all. During September the banks in Philadelphia and Baltimore suspended specie payments, and western banks, except in Kentucky and Indiana, followed their example. New York banks held out until October 12, when all but the Chemical were forced to stop redemption of their notes.

In this emergency when the Treasury was powerless to help them, the New York banks began timidly to use the Clearing House which had fortunately been organized in 1853. A Loan Committee was appointed as the basis for concerted action. In spite of their inclination to reduce their loans in order to protect their declining specie reserves, the banks agreed that all would increase their loans proportionately so that the Clearing House balances would cancel out. A few weeks later they went a step further and permitted the member banks to settle balances with Clearing House loan certificates issued by the central committee against the notes of the banks instead of against specie. This made it possible for the city banks to continue to redeem the notes of country banks, even before they were able to resume specie payments of their own notes in mid-December.

After the worst of the panic was over, the Clearing House appointed a committee to recommend improvements in the management of the banks. Its report showed a clear understanding that deposits were as important a liability of the banks as the notes, and that reserve requirements should apply to both; it recommended for its members a 20 percent specie reserve against deposits and notes. It recommended also that no interest be paid on demand deposits, and 40 of its 46 members agreed to abandon the practice (although they did not do so). The New York State Superintendent of Banks made the same recommendations and emphasized the central position of the New York banks in the financial structure of the nation. These points were recognized when in 1863 the National Currency Act was passed.[13]

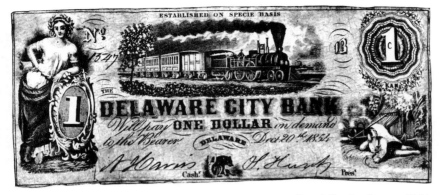

One dollar bank note, 1854

CHAPTER 6

FEDERAL, STATE, AND LOCAL FINANCE BEFORE THE CIVIL WAR

The Independent Treasury

THE financial follies of the Jackson period—the destruction of the Bank, the scattering of the Treasury deposits among the pet banks, the specie circular, and the distribution of the surplus—affected revenues and expenditures at all levels of government, but created the most serious problems for the federal government. The depression of 1837 had already begun when Van Buren succeeded Jackson and found the Treasury facing default. One of his first actions was to call a special session of Congress to cope with the emergency.

Van Buren proposed to Congress four financial measures. One was postponement of payment of the fourth installment of the "surplus"; it had long since turned into a deficit* but Congress debated the measure bitterly before passing it. Another proposal would have made the suspension of specie payments by a bank tantamount to bankruptcy, and would have destroyed nearly every bank in the country; fortunately it

---

* See p. 94.

was not passed. A third proposal authorized the issue of Treasury notes with which to meet current expenditures. Larger denominations were to bear interest at 6 percent, but the smaller ones bore no interest and were designed to circulate as currency. This measure was enacted because there seemed to be no alternative, and further issues were approved by several succeeding Congresses. They were not, however, made legal tender.

The fourth and most important of Van Buren's recommendations to Congress was the establishment of an Independent Treasury. The Treasury had of course been "independent" ever since the suspension of specie payments had made it impossible to use the banks as depositaries or to accept depreciated bank notes. In sponsoring this legislation, Van Buren repudiated the powerful Albany Regency, the group of banks whose support had been largely responsible for putting him into office. He took instead the position of the Loco-Focos who were the antibank extremists of his party. Both sides had eloquent advocates in and out of Congress, and they carried on the controversy in speeches and pamphlets.

William Gouge, a minor Treasury official under Jackson, supported the plan for an Independent Treasury in his pamphlet, "An Inquiry into the Expediency of Dispensing with Bank Agency and Bank Paper in the Fiscal Concerns of the United States." He gave particular attention to the recent difficulties of the Treasury in its attempt to use state banks as depositaries, ignoring the fact that the problem had been created largely by the failure of his own party to recharter the Bank of the United States. In his opinion, separation of Treasury financial operations from those of the rest of the country was quite feasible, and would solve all of its problems.

Daniel Webster, speaking against the plan, believed that it was impossible to separate government finance from the rest, since the government was not only the largest income receiver but also the largest spender and the largest borrower in the economy. He stressed also the advantages of credit over cash in making payments. Albert Gallatin, whose experience as Secretary of the Treasury and as banker made him well qualified to judge, was another opponent. He emphasized the practical difficulties for New York bankers in providing importers with specie to pay customs duties, if the Treasury were hoarding large amounts.

Secretary of the Treasury Levi Woodbury was not in a position to oppose Van Buren's plan, but he was quite aware of its absurdity. In his Annual Report for 1837 he suggested a number of changes which would make the scheme less inflexible and more workable: some public officer should have authority to invest any surplus which might arise in order to avoid the hoarding of specie by the Treasury; the Secretary should be authorized to issue a limited amount of notes in case of deficit; payment for public lands should be accepted in advance of the actual purchase to make it unnecessary to carry specie to the west; and customs duties should be made payable as goods were withdrawn from government warehouses, rather than at the moment of arrival. None of his recommendations was incorporated into the original bill, but most of them were eventually either written into the law or adopted in practice.

Although it had a small Democratic majority, Congress showed little enthusiasm for the idea of an independent treasury. The first time the bill came to a vote, in June 1838, it was rejected by a narrow margin. Six months later it was introduced again in the regular session, and was finally passed in June 1839, to go into effect on July 4, 1840. It had not yet got into full operation when the election of 1840 put the Whigs in power; the death of Harrison after a few months as President left the erratic Tyler head of the government.

One of the first acts of the new Whig Congress was to repeal the law creating the Independent Treasury. Henry Clay, who introduced the bill for repeal, said that banks, in spite of the law, were still being used as depositaries, and bank notes were still being accepted by the Treasury. In New York City the Treasury agent was using the vaults and offices of the Bank of America. Senator Benton, one of the original sponsors of the system, described its actual operation as "humbug."[1]

After the repeal, banks were again legally used as depositaries; thirty-nine held government deposits in 1844, but by that time government revenues were so small that the deposits were of little advantage to the banks. As was to be expected, the Whig Congress introduced a bill to establish a new national bank under the title, "Fiscal Bank of the United States." President Tyler, much to the dismay of his party, vetoed the bill because he disapproved of a national bank. In an attempt to overcome his opposition, they changed the title to "Fiscal Corporation" and passed the bill again. Tyler was adamant, and vetoed this also. The majority of the Cabinet resigned in protest, and Henry Clay resigned from the Senate a few months later.

When the Democrats returned to office in 1845 with Polk as President, the hard-money Loco-Foco branch of the party was in full control. They soon introduced a bill for what its sponsors liked to call a "constitutional Treasury." Few new ideas came out of the debate on the bill. Secretary of the Treasury Walker tried in vain to ameliorate some of the more extreme sections of the measure, but was thwarted by Senator Benton, who was still waging the hard-money battle to which he had devoted his life. The principal provisions of the bill required all officers of the government "to keep safely, without loaning, using, depositing in banks, or exchanging for other funds than as allowed by this act, all the public moneys collected by them, or otherwise at any time placed in their possession or custody, till the same is ordered . . . to be transferred or paid out." The bill did, however, include one of the recommendations made by Secretary Woodbury nine years earlier; it established government warehouses for imports so that duties could be paid gradually as goods were withdrawn.

The regulations issued by Secretary Walker to implement "the great and beneficial purpose of Congress . . . to enlarge the circulation of gold and silver and to prevent Treasury drafts becoming a paper currency" instructed all government officers, from January 1, 1847, to accept only gold and silver coin (including the foreign coins still in circulation) and Treasury notes; after April 1, they were to pay out only the same. In passing the bill, Congress had neglected to make appropriation for the additional clerical expenses of the Treasury, or for the construction of adequate vaults in which to keep the coin, or for the cost of transporting the coin from New York, where two-thirds of the revenue was collected, to other parts of the country, where it had to be paid out. The Treasury therefore, even in the first days of enthusiasm for the new plan, was still obliged to rely on bankers for the safekeeping and transfer of its funds. It was a decade before proper vaults were constructed for all the Treasury offices; as late as 1854, one strong room in Indiana was a wooden barricade opening off a tavern barroom, compared by an inspector to the fortification of Robinson Crusoe.[2]

Currency Difficulties

The financial problems created by the Independent Treasury were aggravated by the recurring shortages of coin. The original ratio of gold to silver, 15 to 1, established when bimetallism was adopted in 1792, had been close to the market ratio, with silver only slightly overvalued, so both metals remained in circulation for several decades. When England adopted the gold standard in 1819 the market value of gold increased, and gold left the United States where it was undervalued by the Mint. In 1834, to stop this drain, Congress changed the ratio to 16.002 to 1, compared with a market ratio of about 15.75 to 1. This did bring back gold but it drove out silver. The slight change in the ratio in 1837 to 15.988 to 1 was made to satisfy the states in the south where a small amount of gold was being mined. They hoped that overvaluing it would increase its circulation. The Mint price of gold became 20.67 dollars per ounce and that of silver, 1.29 per ounce. Neither metal was coined in large amount and the country still depended on foreign coins for most of its metallic circulation.*

In his Report for 1847 Secretary Walker congratulated himself and the country on the fact that under the new regime, 24 million dollars worth of specie had been imported, most of it foreign gold coins, and 21 million of it recoined into American gold pieces. He added fatuously that at this

rate we would soon supply our own people with our own coin, and in time, also, with our augmenting commerce, Americanize, to a great extent, the coin of the world; and thus introduce our simple and beautiful decimal currency gradually throughout all nations, substituting it for the complex system of pounds, shillings and pence, or of doubloons, ducats, and rupees, which retards business and complicates accounts.

His optimism was premature. In spite of California gold discoveries, coins of full weight had almost entirely disappeared by 1852, and the small channels of circulation were occupied with the silver Spanish fractions—sixteenths, eighths, fifths, and quarters—while dollars and upwards were supplied by bank notes; gold was rarely seen, and was used only in the foreign exchanges.

---

* See p. 97.

In 1853 the coinage law was changed to reduce the amount of fine silver in the subsidiary coins. Because this action made it unprofitable to melt them down and export them, they gradually replaced the foreign coins in circulation. After 1857, foreign coins were no longer legal tender, and the supply of American small coins increased until the outbreak of the Civil War again sent them into hiding.

No mention was made of the silver dollar in the Act of 1853. It had practically disappeared from circulation. Only 2.5 million silver dollars had been minted since 1793, compared with 79 million of subsidiary silver coins and more than 200 million in gold coins of larger denominations. For 30 years, from 1806 to 1836, no silver dollars had been coined at all.[3] The debates in Congress show quite clearly that the intention of the Act of 1853 was abandonment of the bimetallic standard. Congressman Dunham, who was in charge of the measure, reported that the Committee on Ways and Means "desire to have the standard currency to consist of gold only, and that these silver coins shall be entirely subservient to it, and that they shall be used rather as tokens than as standard currency. . . . We have had but a single standard for the last three or four years. That has been, and now is, gold. We propose to let it remain so, and to adapt silver to it, to regulate by it." The real demonetization of silver occurred twenty years before the "Crime of '73."*

Federal Revenues: The Tariff

The flurry of public land buying during the Jackson administration subsided during the long depression which followed, and left the federal government again dependent on import duties for most of its revenue. Since tariff legislation was more often motivated by the desire to protect favored groups than to provide income for the government, the Treasury had to make difficult adjustments. Periods of surplus alternated with periods of penury, and the successive Secretaries, hampered by the straitjacket of "independence," were hard put to avoid calamity for the government or for the money market.

The Tariff of Abominations of 1828, which had not really been approved by either party, had helped to create the surplus so troublesome

---

* See Chapter 9.

to Jackson. Its worst defects were in part corrected in 1832, and tea and coffee were again put on the free list. In 1833 the Compromise Tariff provided that the rates on dutiable articles should be reduced gradually from their average of 33 percent to a uniform rate of 20 percent by 1842. All rates were to be *ad valorem,* and little consideration was given to infant industries which might need special, temporary protection. Protectionists tried to claim later that all the economic difficulties of the 1830s were ascribable to the declining tariff rates. The lowest scale of rates was never put into effect, however, since the Whigs came into office in 1840 and immediately revised the rates upward, although not to the heights of 1828.

These rates were superseded by a more systematic revision in 1846. Secretary of the Treasury Walker, a Democrat with free trade principles, outlined a series of general propositions and was able to have most of them embodied in the legislation. He thought that tariff income should be adjusted to the government budget; that the rate should be set at a level to bring in the maximum total, which would not necessarily be a maximum rate; that luxuries should pay higher rates than necessities; and that *ad valorem* duties on home market values should be used in place of the elaborate system of specific duties and nominal minimum valuations.

One practical improvement in tariff administration was made by dividing all dutiable commodities into groups. Those under Schedule A paid 100 percent duty; under Schedule B, 50 percent. Schedule C, with 30 percent duty, included most of the articles on which the manufacturers had demanded protection, such as manufactured metal, wool, leather, paper, and glass. Schedule D, on which the rate was 25 percent, included cotton. Tea and coffee were on the free list as they had usually been. Although neither the northern manufacturers who wanted protection nor the southern planters who wanted free trade were satisfied by this tariff, the rates remained in force until 1857, when they were further reduced to the lowest levels since 1816 in order to reduce the Treasury surplus.

The total amount of revenue produced by customs duties, on which the federal government depended for most of its income in these decades before the Civil War, varied widely from year to year. The chief factor in this fluctuation was the state of business. The low point was the year

1843, when duties amounted to only 7 million dollars; the high point was 1854 when the total reached 64 million. The effect of such wide swings in customs income was that the government in nine of the years between 1840 and 1860 had deficits which ranged from 3 to 30 million dollars. Internal revenues during these decades were minimal, and the receipts from sales of public lands from 1839 to 1869 never amounted to as much as 4 million dollars except in 1854, 1855, and 1856, when they were 8, 11, and 9 million, respectively.

The resulting irregularity in the income, expenditure, and borrowing of the federal government was a highly disturbing element in all phases of financial life. Even if the national funds had been managed with great discretion and concern for the general welfare, their unpredictable fluctuations would have created difficulties. But when, in addition to the irregularity of operations, the artificial restriction of the so-called Independent Treasury was added, the problems were compounded.[4]

Financing of the War with Mexico

The war with Mexico, which was officially declared on May 12, 1846, found government finances in poor condition to support the additional expense. The Treasury had been relying on issues of Treasury notes to maintain its solvency, since long-term bonds could be sold only at a heavy discount. Even Congressmen had received their pay in Treasury notes rather than coin until Senator Benton protested in January 1842. Some of the outstanding notes were refunded in 1843 into 10-year bonds at 5 percent, but in the same year more were issued in the denomination of 50 dollars, redeemable in specie at any land office or customhouse. By 1843 the total debt had gone beyond 25 million.

After that year business conditions began to improve and with them the government revenue from import duties. It was not in time, however, to meet the needs of war financing, and in July 1846, on the recommendation of President Polk, Congress authorized another 10 million dollars of Treasury notes or 20-year bonds, at not more than 6 percent in either case. Six months later, in January 1847, another loan of 23 million was authorized, either in the form of negotiable 50-dollar notes or as long-term bonds. When the loan was offered to the public, bids were received for more than twice the amount, at or above par. From

Check signed by Millard Fillmore, 1849

this time on a business revival brought increased imports and customs revenues, and the credit of the government improved, a happy circumstance ascribed by Senator Benton entirely to the "hard-money system" which had just gone into operation. The expenses of the Mexican war were calculated by the Secretary of the Treasury at about 64 million dollars, on the basis of expenditures by the army and navy compared with a similar period of peace. Since the debt increased by 49 million during the war, it would appear that three-fourths of the cost had been met by borrowing and only one-fourth from revenue. Congress had steadfastly refused to increase excise or import duties in order to meet war costs, or even to restore the duties on tea and coffee. Nevertheless the debt was reduced rapidly after the war and was down to 29 million by 1857. The Mexican war indemnity of 15 million was also paid off during those years.[5]

Although the tariff rates of 1846 were not high in comparison with earlier tariffs, they produced very large amounts of revenue. Once the Mexican war was over, funds accumulated in the Treasury, representing not only a loss of interest to the government but also an embarrassment to the money market. The law permitted the Treasury to repurchase bonds before maturity only if they were at or below their par value, and it did not permit (after a disastrous experiment with Arkansas and Michigan state bonds in the 1830s) purchase of any other securities. The Secretary therefore asked permission from Congress to purchase bonds at the market price. Since the alternative would have been a reduction in import duties, Congress granted the request and large amounts of the public debt were taken off the market during the next two years. In February 1849, Treasury notes as well as bonds were redeemed in order to dishoard funds from the Treasury, and 1 million dollars of the Mexican indemnity was paid in advance in March of that year.

The Treasury and the Money Market

The money market stringencies which occurred nearly every autumn in these years were a cause of great embarrassment to the Treasury, which was supposed to act quite independently of the money market. The purchase of bonds was sufficient to relieve the pressure in 1851, but in 1853 that device was not enough. Specie in the Treasury was at a peak of 22 million dollars, and a delegation went from New York to Washington to ask for a further release of funds. The Secretary was sympathetic, but powerless under the law. Fortunately the normal disbursements of the Treasury during the latter months of the year eased the tension. Much the same pattern was followed in the next few years. In December 1856 the New York subtreasury balance was so large that the New York *Times* seriously suggested distributing the fourth installment of the 1837 surplus as a relief measure. By March of the next year the total balance of the Treasury was more than 21 million, and in the New York subtreasury alone the balance was 15 million; specie reserves of the New York banks had fallen to 8 million, a reduction of more than 50 percent in two years.

When the financial crisis began in August 1857, the revenue of the government was sharply reduced. Not only did the volume of imports decline, but also, under the Act of July 1857, the rates of duty had just been lowered. When in October all the New York banks except the Chemical were obliged to suspend, the Treasury had to issue 20 million dollars of its own short-term notes to make up for the loss of customs revenue.*

From this time until after the Civil War the problem of the Treasury was one of deficit rather than of surplus. Import duties did not cover government expenditures, and borrowing became more difficult as the impending conflict cast its shadow over the country. Twenty million

---

* See p. 127.

Wall Street in the panic of 1857

dollars of bonds were issued in June 1858 and the Treasury notes of 1857 were renewed until 1860. By June of that year the funded debt was 45 million, and 20 million of notes were outstanding in addition. When the cotton export trade collapsed late in 1860, it became impossible to borrow on long term either at home or abroad and the rate on short notes had to be raised to 6 percent. The independence of the Treasury was effectually ended and it became more and more dependent on the aid of the banks.[6]

State and Local Finance before the Civil War

The picture of state and local finance in the years before the Civil War continued to be one of confusion. The thirteen original states had organized their local governments under many different forms, with counties in some states, towns in others, as the principal subdivisions, and below those, townships, villages, cities, with a wide range of privileges and responsibilities. As new states were formed from the territories of the west, still greater variety was introduced into the structure of local government.

The collection and administration of revenues reflected this situation. In some states the tax collectors were employed by the state and responsible to it; in others, state taxes were levied on the towns or counties, which were left to collect them in any way they could devise. Few states, and even fewer counties and towns, made budgets for future expenditures and required disbursing officers to remain within their limits. There was overlapping of tax sources and double taxation. Borrowing in some periods was easy and a tempting way to avoid the political unpopularity of heavy taxes; in other periods it was impossible to sell state or local bonds at home or abroad except at substantial discount. Governmental agencies at all levels found it hard to raise the funds needed to meet the widening demands of their rapidly growing population.

The property tax was the chief reliance of most governmental units in the northern and western areas, and was used to a lesser extent in the south. The definition of property was far from being uniform. It always included the value of land, but that value was sometimes estimated from original cost, sometimes from market value or income, and the tax base or assessed valuation was a varying fraction of the estimated value. The problem of equitable assessment became even more complicated when to the value of the land was added the value of such improvements as fencing, draining, and clearing as well as buildings.

In some areas personal property was included in the assessment. The taxpayer was sometimes required to file a list of his personal possessions, but it was difficult for such a list to be checked. Jewelry and cash were easy to conceal, as were also the securities which began to be important elements in personal property. Farmers, especially, complained of inequity since their personal property was apt to take the quite visible forms of machinery and equipment.

The New England states for the most part still found the property tax adequate for their needs in this period because they avoided heavy expenditures for internal improvements. Massachusetts was the exception, and it used an income tax from 1821 to 1849.

New York had earlier derived large revenues from the sale of her public lands,* but as the lands were sold off the state used taxes on real and personal property. The valuation was left to locally elected officials, and the state tax, set by the Legislature at so many mils for each dollar of assessed valuation, was added to the amount to be collected in the counties. It was not a satisfactory system; to the usual problems of assessment and valuation were added the efforts of the neighboring states of Connecticut, New Jersey, and Pennsylvania to lure industry away from New York by exempting from taxation all personal property and mortgages. Connecticut and New Jersey had very small state debts and could manage without the tax on personal property. Pennsylvania, like New York, had a large debt in this period and turned to the taxation of bank dividends in 1835 as a way of supplementing the property tax.

As the western territories were organized into states—and all of them east of the Mississippi had become states by 1860—they continued to rely on the property tax for most of the state and local revenues. Ohio, which became a state in 1803, included only land in the tax base for the first quarter-century, but in 1825 added buildings and personal property. By 1841 the enumerated personal property amounted to one-fourth the value of the real estate, and by 1856, to 40 percent. Two-

---

* See p. 65.

thirds of the revenue went to the state, and one-third to the county; administration of the tax was in the hands of county commissioners.

Wisconsin did not become a state until 1848, but had used the property tax, with the permission of Congress, long before that date. The first tax law passed after it became a state gave a definition of property which excluded improvements to land (in order to encourage them) but included merchandise inventory and paid-in stock of corporations.

In the southern states the property tax was unpopular because of the political power of the large landholders. Once the period of internal improvement was over, these states had little occasion to increase expenditures since they provided few such services as public education for their citizens. Most of them continued to find the poll tax and license fees adequate for revenue.

New sources of revenue were made possible in many areas by the shift from agriculture to commerce and industry of a large part of the working population. Many states resorted early to taxation of corporations. The historical dislike of monopolies and distrust of corporations made such taxes popular, and the attitude that a corporation charter was a privilege granted by the state made these taxes seem appropriate. As early as 1811 some of the bank charters in Massachusetts had provided for a tax of one-half of 1 percent per annum on the outstanding stock. Other states soon followed this example, taxing sometimes the stock, sometimes the dividends, of banks. Ohio found it difficult to collect the tax on bank stock, and in 1831 levied a tax of 5 percent on the dividends of banks, insurance companies, and bridge companies. The attempt made in some states to include bank capital and surplus in the definition of property so that banks could be assessed for the property tax was not usually successful. A property tax on railroads was more easily levied since the railroads possessed large amounts of tangible assets which could not easily be concealed from the assessor. However, many states were so anxious to have railroads built that, instead of taxing them, they exempted them from all taxes for long periods, and often loaned them funds, or granted them stretches of land along the right of way.

When the tax on corporations took the form of taxing dividends, it began to resemble the modern income tax. If wages and profits were taxed, the phrasing was reminiscent of the old "faculty" taxes which had been used in some of the colonies. Six states in addition to Massachusetts introduced some form of income tax during the difficult years of the 1840s. Several of the state constitutions adopted during that period provided for the levying of income taxes if necessary. In spite of all the devices for increasing their revenues, most states and some territories by the 1840s faced serious financial problems.

State Debts

The total amount of bonded indebtedness incurred by the states in each 5-year period after 1820 had increased rapidly, and the state "stocks" which had been so enthusiastically issued during the boom years of the early thirties had carried their combined debt to nearly 175 million dollars by 1838. Table 2 gives the amounts for each period.

TABLE 2. OUTSTANDING DEBT INCURRED IN EACH FIVE-YEAR PERIOD FROM 1820 TO 1838 (*in millions of dollars*)

1820–25	12.8 by 7 states
1825–30	13.7 by 6 states
1830–35	40.0 by 12 states
1835–38	108.4 by 16 states
Total	174.9 by 18 states

Source: Tenth Census of the United States, 1880, Volume VII page 523.

Only eight of the twenty-six states of the Union at that time were free of long-term debt: New Hampshire, Vermont, Connecticut, Rhode Island, New Jersey, Delaware, North Carolina, and Georgia. Maine and Missouri had very small debts. Florida had a debt of 5 million dollars, large in proportion to her population, but was not yet a state. Michigan also had accumulated a debt of 5 million while still a territory; she demanded and received admission into the Union in 1837 and immediately increased her borrowings in order to embark on a program of internal improvements which included three canals and three railroad lines.

Most of the state debt had been issued to pay for public improvements after the federal government ceased to finance them. Of the total state debt of 175 million dollars in 1838, canal shares accounted for 60 million, railroads for 42 million, banking for 52 million; turnpikes and miscellaneous purposes made up the remaining 20 million.[7]

By 1840, additional issues had raised the total indebtedness of all the states to an estimated 200 million dollars, a large portion of which was held abroad, mostly in England. When the depression years began, and especially after the failure of the Bank of the United States of Pennsylvania,* it became increasingly difficult to dispose of American issues either at home or abroad. Daniel Webster was able to sell £40,000 of Massachusetts bonds in London in May of 1839, and New York was able to borrow half a million dollars from the Manhattan Company in order to enlarge the Erie Canal. But later in the summer, Pennsylvania was unable to obtain a single bid for its loan of 1.5 million. The 5 percents of Indiana were sold in New York during the summer of 1839 at 50 cents on the dollar, those of Illinois at 60 cents on the dollar, and very few could be disposed of even at those prices.[8]

Since the internal improvements financed by the borrowed funds were slow to bring in any income, the states had great difficulty in meeting their interest obligations, not to mention the repayment of principal. Pennsylvania, Maryland, Michigan, Indiana, Illinois, and Mississippi fell behind in their payments, and Missouri passed a stay law which temporarily postponed the date of payment. Pennsylvania, which had been the last of the states to suspend payments, in 1842, was among the first to resume, in 1845, out of her regular income. Maryland paid no interest from 1841 to 1848, but eventually levied a special tax of 20 cents on each hundred dollars of assessed valuation of real and personal property; in addition the state sold its stock in the Chesapeake and Ohio Canal Company, the Baltimore and Ohio Railroad Company, and several others, and was thus able to raise the needed funds. Illinois paid no interest from 1842 to 1847, and finally settled with its creditors by deeding to them its canal stock. Other states issued due bills or interest certificates which were eventually paid.

Only Mississippi and Florida completely repudiated their debts in this period.[9] Mississippi became a symbol of irresponsibility throughout the financial world, for she deliberately repudiated her outstanding bonds and never paid them. The bonds had been given to the Union Bank in 1838 in payment for the state subscription to its stock; the Bank had been unable to sell the bonds at par, as the law required, and had sold

---

* See p. 98.

them to Nicholas Biddle at a discount. He took them abroad and used them as security for borrowing by the Bank of the United States. The Union Bank became insolvent within two years of its establishment, and by that time the Bank of the United States had already suspended. When the governor reported these facts to the Legislature, he claimed that the issue had been illegal and that the state was therefore under no obligation to pay the bonds. The courts failed to sustain this claim, but the state persisted in its refusal and compounded its disgrace by refusing also to pay the bonds issued in 1830 when the state had borrowed to pay for its stock in the Planters Bank. The Legislature of 1848 refused to pay either the accumulated interest or the principal. A popular referendum of 1852 confirmed the refusal, and in 1875 a new constitution forbade the state ever to "assume, redeem, secure, or pay" any such indebtedness. The face value of these bonds was 7 million dollars.[10]

The case of Florida was less complicated but equally disastrous for its creditors. When it became a state it refused to pay the principal of the bonds issued while it was a territory on the grounds that it had had no power to issue such bonds in the first place. Another 5 million dollars of railroad bonds issued after she became a state in 1845 were also repudiated.

It was only to be expected that the states which were most heavily in debt should call on the federal government to help them as it had already done on two previous occasions. Whig journals began to agitate for assumption of the state debts, and it became an issue in the Presidential campaign of 1840. The pressure from the states was augmented by pressure from the foreign bondholders, who were showing reluctance to purchase federal bonds while so many state bonds were in default. To foreigners unfamiliar with the relationship between states and federal government, all bonds from this side of the Atlantic were American bonds, and equally tainted by the behavior of Mississippi and Florida.

The Whigs won the election with Harrison, and a bill for assumption was introduced into the House and passed; it failed in the Senate. It would have forced the solvent and thrifty states to bear much of the burden undertaken by the less provident. After President Harrison's death, President Tyler opposed assumption of state debts in his first Message, but recommended that the states receive the revenue from the public land sales so that they could meet their obligations. This would have given them an estimated 3 million dollars per year. In spite of lobbying by foreign bondholders, this proposal also failed.[11]

The inability of state governments to foist on the national treasury the debts which had been so incautiously incurred ended this phase of internal improvements by the states. They might encourage the building of railroads by granting generous charters and even by tax exemption, but after this period the states themselves were unwilling to undertake such projects. Indeed in many states, as in Tennessee after 1840, the government was specifically prohibited from subscribing to the stock of any company organized for internal improvements. In New York the new constitution of 1846 forbade the state to incur any debt, for any purpose, without specific provision for taxes with which to repay that debt. The constitution adopted by Wisconsin when it was admitted to the Union in 1848 limited the total amount of the state debt to 100,000 dollars except in an emergency, and provided in addition that the credit of the state was never to be loaned in aid of any individual, association, or corporation. The revision of the Kentucky constitution in 1850 forbade the Legislature to create any bonded debt of more than 500,000 dollars without a vote of the people.

These strict limitations on the borrowing power of the states had two important results in addition to keeping the states on the path of financial sobriety. The first was a transfer to counties, towns, and municipalities of some of the pressure for aid to railroads and roads. The first annual report of the Susquehanna Railroad Company, for example, in 1854, lists subscriptions of four counties for 300,000 dollars of the total of 1,305,000. Unfortunately these subscriptions were paid in bonds of the counties, which the company was not able to sell at par. The city of Nashville made a similar subscription to the Nashville and Chattanooga Railroad in 6 percent bonds which bankers in New York, Philadelphia, and Washington would take only at a price of 88⅜ for resale in Europe. Baltimore, Richmond, Pittsburgh, Philadelphia, Cincinnati, and Toledo were among the cities reported in the financial press as borrowing, between 1847 and 1852, and many others were named in the reports of the railroad companies of that period. In 1840 Henry C. Adams estimated that the total debts of cities amounted to about 25 million dollars; by 1860 the debts of the cities had doubled to about 51 million, and the debts of other minor civil divisions stood at about 100 million additional. This was the 20-year period during which cities in the United States reached a new high in their rate of growth.[12] The demands of their growing population were the basic cause of much of the increase in debt which occurred.

Another result of the termination of internal improvements by the states was the encouragement which this gave to corporate enterprise. Citizens were becoming disillusioned about the merits of public enterprise, and were ready to entrust even large-scale projects like railroads to monopolies organized as corporations, of which they had formerly been so fearful.

CHAPTER 7

"Greenback," 1862

FINANCIAL ASPECTS OF THE CIVIL WAR

The Crisis of 1860

THE country was still recovering from the crisis of 1857 when it was struck by a new crisis in the autumn of 1860. This time the difficulty was as much political as economic. Specie had been going out in large amounts throughout 1860 as European investors, concerned about the danger of conflict, prudently divested themselves of American securities. They also withdrew 30 million dollars of call loans which they had placed in the New York market. Another 50 million of call loans had been made on American account by the New York banks, and these also were reduced in the autumn as interior banks recalled their deposits. Stock prices declined, and after the election of Lincoln in November the withdrawal of funds was still more rapid, forcing banks to reduce their loans at just the season when normally they would have been expanding. The collapse of the cotton export trade demoralized the foreign exchange market. Southern banks suspended specie payments in November, and the bonds of the southern states lost much of their value. Western banks which had used them as collateral for their note issues were soon in difficulties.

In New York the Clearing House banks resorted to the technique developed in 1857 and issued loan certificates against security collateral for use in the daily settlements. This enabled them to increase their loans and to avoid suspension of specie payments. They were even able to support the foreign exchange market.

The Treasury was in worse plight than the banks, and the outlook for government financing was not propitious.* The debt had doubled, from less than 30 million dollars in 1857 to 60 million in 1860. By the middle of that year the balance in the Treasury was down to 3.6 million; Congressmen had not received their salaries for several weeks. Treasury notes which had been issued to tide over the period of low tariff revenues had to be reissued as they matured, but the new offering of 10 million at 1 year could be sold only at a discount. The rapid turnover in the office of Secretary of the Treasury during the last days of the Buchanan administration did not improve the credit of the government. Howell Cobb of Georgia was replaced on December 10 by Philip F. Thomas of Maryland, who after barely a month gave way to General John A. Dix. Borrowing abroad was out of the question, since many foreign governments were in sympathy with the position of the south and expected it to win any armed conflict.

Treasury Borrowing

In the last days of the session, in February 1861, as an emergency measure Congress authorized an issue of 25 million dollars in 20-year bonds at 6 percent. The Secretary of the Treasury was able to sell 18 million of them at a discount of 11 percent and was thus able to refund most of the outstanding notes. Another loan of 10 million was authorized on March 2, but with the unrealistic proviso that no more than 6 percent interest might be paid and that the long-term portion might not be sold below par; if this were not possible, only short notes might be issued, and so they were.

When President Lincoln took office on March 4, 1861, he immediately appointed, as Secretary of the Treasury, Senator Salmon Portland Chase, a lawyer of high reputation without any financial experience except that

---

* See p. 140.

which he had gained by observation as governor of Ohio during the crisis of 1857. It had made him a hard-money man, as suspicious of bank paper as Jackson and Benton had been, and as devoted to the principle of the Independent Treasury. The situation which faced him would have daunted the most experienced financier. During his first three months in office, Treasury receipts were less than 6 million dollars, while its expenses were 24 million. Borrowing in some form was essential, and at a special session in July the new Congress had passed a more realistic Act than the previous one; it authorized a bond issue of 250 million at 7 percent, or Treasury notes in denominations of 50 dollars or more at 7.3 percent, or non-interest-bearing notes in smaller denominations up to a total of 50 million.

The Secretary had to make an immediate decision about this loan; should it be in the form of long-term bonds or short-term notes? The short non-interest-bearing notes offered the quickest and cheapest method of raising funds, but the Secretary was under no illusion about the danger inherent in this method of financing. "The greatest care will, however, be requisite to prevent the degradation of such issues into an irredeemable paper currency, than which no more certainly fatal expedient for impoverishing the masses and discrediting the government of any country can well be devised."[1] Long bonds, on the other hand, presented serious difficulties in the existing state of the money market. The fall of Fort Sumter in April and the reverses of the northern armies during the summer had shown that the war could not be won quickly and that heavy expenditures would be required.

Chase was well aware that the success of government financing would depend largely on the attitude of the bankers, and he very wisely turned to them for advice and cooperation. They had already been of assistance in placing the loans offered during March and April, although even with their aid it had been impossible to sell the bonds at par. At the beginning of July, before the special session of Congress, the banks of New York had again come to the rescue of the Treasury by advancing 5 million dollars for 60 days against the security of Treasury notes.

In the middle of August the Secretary went to New York to meet representatives of the banks of New York, Boston, and Philadelphia. At this time the banks were in a strong technical position, since heavy grain exports and reduced imports had increased their gold reserves, and the decline in business activity at home had left them with funds available for investment. They agreed that they would subscribe at once a Treasury loan of 50 million dollars, to be shared among them in proportion to their capitals. The Treasury would issue the same amount of 3-year notes at 7.3 percent interest, to be sold to the public if possible; if the notes were not sold, they would be retained by the banks. A second and a third loan would be made on the same terms in October and December.

Congress had already, on August 5, authorized this borrowing and had specifically repealed part of the Independent Treasury Act of 1846 in order

to allow the Secretary of the Treasury to deposit any of the moneys obtained on any of the loans now authorized by law, to the credit of the Treasurer of the United States, in such solvent specie-paying banks as he may select; and the said moneys, so deposited, may be withdrawn from such deposit for deposit with the regular authorized depositaries, or for the payment of public dues, or paid in redemption of the notes authorized to be issued under this act. . . . [2]

Even with this specific authorization of Congress and in spite of the fact that he had already violated the spirit of the Independent Treasury Act by calling on the bankers, the Secretary was not willing to go any further. To the great dismay of the bankers, who had not understood his intention, Chase insisted that the banks pay the Treasury in specie, and that the specie might not be redeposited in any bank. This put a heavy burden on the banks. There was probably not more than 250 million specie in all the northern states in the latter part of 1861. State bank notes provided another 150 million for circulation, but they were not acceptable to the Treasury. In New York City the associated banks held about 50 million in specie when the loan agreement was made. By pooling their reserves through the Clearing House Loan Committee they were able to meet the first two of the three payments to the Treasury.

In normal times the gold would have returned to the banks as it was paid out by the Treasury, but now the public was losing confidence in the outcome of the war and had begun to hoard gold. Sales of Treasury notes were proceeding very slowly; hence the assets of the banks were increasingly tied up in this nonliquid form. Moreover, the Treasury had

Fractional currency

begun to meet its obligations by issuing its own demand notes, which still further reduced the credit of the government. The bankers who had agreed to loan 150 million dollars had understood that Chase would not make such issues; Chase claimed that the bankers had discussed and approved his action. James Gallatin, son of the former Secretary of the Treasury and president of one of the leading banks of New York, protested in vain. He pointed out that, with the continuing drain of specie, it was only a matter of time before specie payments would have to be suspended. When his protests went unheeded, he urged the New York banks to take the step at once, before all their gold was gone. They hesitated for several weeks, but by the end of December their specie reserves had been cut in half and were declining so rapidly that they could no longer maintain the 25 percent reserve ratio against liabilities. They suspended on December 30. Banks in other cities soon followed the lead of New York. The Treasury was therefore deprived of any more income receipts in specie, and it too was obliged to suspend. The rest of the loan of 150 million, like all the later loans to the Treasury, had to be made in bank paper or in Treasury paper. The well-intentioned but misguided effort of Secretary Chase to secure specie for the Treasury by insisting on terms of the Independent Treasury Act which had already been repealed, resulted in depriving not only the Treasury but also the whole country of the advantages of specie. Suspension of specie payments would probably have resulted from the war eventually in any case, but to have it happen so early was a serious handicap to the war effort.

When Secretary Chase made his official report to Congress at the end of 1861, he was still far from comprehending the financial burden which the war would create. He believed that taxes could be made to cover ordinary expenditures of the government as well as interest and amortization of the debt. Since, according to the census of 1860, the northern states had real property of about 7.5 billion dollars, and personal property of 3.5 billion, a tax of 4 dollars per thousand would bring in 44 million. Another 20 million might be raised by a direct tax on the states in proportion to population, and 30 million by income and internal revenue taxes, making a total of 94 million. Even if import duties could be counted on for 30 million, an additional 200 million would have to be borrowed for that year, to bring the total up to the needed 324 million.

In his first annual report, the Secretary suggested that sales of government bonds might be stimulated by some provision for a bond-secured currency similar to that issued by New York banks under the Free Banking Act of 1838. This recommendation, like those for increased taxes, fell on deaf ears. Congress, absorbed in urgent military problems, had no time to consider any but the most immediate financial measures.

The Greenbacks

To Secretary Chase, a convinced sound-money man, the suspension of specie payments by the banks in December 1861, although largely the result of his own intransigence, was an unexpected blow. The Treasury stock of gold was already so low that it was certain gold would soon disappear from circulation altogether. Indeed the Treasury had been paying out its own demand notes since August to reluctant government clerks and merchants; banks would take them only on special deposit.

The House Committee on Ways and Means, following the suggestion of Secretary Chase, had begun to work on a bill for a national bank system, but it was clear that this could provide no immediate relief for the desperate state of the Treasury. A measure for the issue of legal tender notes in denominations of 5 dollars or more for temporary purposes was therefore introduced into Congress on December 30. It was debated at length during January and February. Its advocates, like Senator John Sherman, who had replaced Chase as Senator from Ohio, stressed the need which was daily becoming more acute. Its opponents based their case principally on the question of constitutionality, although Attorney General Bates had given an unofficial opinion that, since the Constitution contained no specific prohibition of such issues by the federal government, the notes were probably not unconstitutional.

The bankers, who had been doing their utmost to support the government, were greatly disturbed by the proposal to issue fiat paper, and sent a delegation to Washington to confer with the Secretary and the Congressional Committee. They presented a plan for financing the war which would avoid the necessity for legal tenders by heavily increasing taxation, using banks as government depositaries (as had already been authorized by Congress), abandoning the issue of demand notes by the Treasury, and selling long-term bonds at their market value, which also had been authorized by Congress.

The last point, which meant in effect that the government would have to increase the yield of its bonds, either by raising interest rates or by selling them below par, was strongly opposed, not only by the Secretary but also by many members of Congress. Mr. Spaulding of New York, who had drafted the legal tender bill, argued that it would mean "the knocking down of Government stocks to seventy-five or sixty cents on the dollar" and "damaging the credit of the Government to the extent of sending it to 'shin' through the shaving shops of New York, Boston and Philadelphia."[3] To him, selling bonds below par, with its open admission that government credit was not good enough to entitle it to interest rates below those of the market, was far more objectionable than issuing paper money which was bound to depreciate. Secretary Chase was equally adamant on this point, and in a letter to Spaulding he wrote that "solicitous to regulate his action by the spirit as well as the letter of the legislation of Congress, [he] did not consider himself at liberty to make sales of the 5-20 bonds below the market value; and sales except below were impracticable."[4]

There was probably no question that the Treasury would have to issue more short-term or demand notes in order to meet its current bills, as it had already been doing for several months. The real question was, should this paper, issued as fiat money with no metallic backing, now be made a legal tender? A declaration that a money must be accepted as a legal tender in payment of all debts is almost always the signal that it is no longer worth its face value. If government paper had been issued without the legal tender quality, it would probably have been accepted only on special deposit by the banks, but for other purposes it would have been no worse than the greenbacks, which rapidly depreciated in terms of gold and which were handled in separate accounts by everybody, including the banks. Most of the arguments for the "necessity" of the legal tender notes were relevant to the need of the Treasury for funds but irrelevant to the legal tender quality of the notes. Had they been issued without that quality, an enormous number of legal and political problems would have been avoided.

Secretary Chase, who only six months earlier had warned against the danger of irredeemable paper, now took the position of "regretting exceedingly" the "necessity," and accepting it as "the mode most useful and least hurtful" to the general interest.[5] He did not abandon his scheme for a national currency, but knew that it could not be put into operation without a long delay.

The Act as it was finally passed on February 25, 1862, provided for an issue of notes to be "lawful money and a legal tender in payment of all debts public and private," except duties on imports and interest on the public debt. The total was set at 150 million, but 50 million merely took the place of the old demand notes which were now to be withdrawn from circulation. The gold coin received for import duties was to be earmarked for payment of interest on the public debt.

The Treasury was authorized at the same time to accept deposits of the new notes in units of 50 dollars, which could be exchanged for 6 percent bonds redeemable after 5 years and payable after 20 years. This provision was considered an extremely important anti-inflationary device. Mr. Spaulding wrote in 1864,

the right to exchange these notes at par for six per cent. bonds . . . was in the nature of a contract made by the Government with the holders of the notes. . . . It also had a tendency to prevent any great inflation, for the reason that as soon as this currency became redundant in the hands of the people, and not bearing interest, they would invest it in the six per cent. bonds to prevent any loss of interest.

The second legal tender act retained this conversion privilege, but the third, passed in 1863, omitted it at the express request of the Secretary of the Treasury, because he wished to reduce the interest rate on future bond issues to 5 percent. The omission was severely criticized by Senator John Sherman in 1870 and he added, "It is a grave question whether this measure was not a breach of public faith." This it certainly was, but the mere retention of the conversion privilege would not have prevented inflation and depreciation of the greenbacks. It would have prevented the reduction of the interest rate on bonds, however, and this would have made it easier to place them in the hands of private investors.[6]

The first legal tender law also included a provision that deposits of the United States notes might be made with the Treasury, repayable at 10 days' notice, with interest at 5 percent, up to a grand total of 25 million. Both the interest rate and the total were increased by subsequent legislation. These deposits provided a steady if modest flow of funds through the Treasury, reaching at their maximum point a total of more than 120 million.

The new currency could not be made ready for circulation before April 1862. In the meantime, by an Act of March 1, 1862, the Treasury was authorized to pay to creditors willing to receive them certificates of indebtedness payable in 1 year with interest at 6 percent. They helped to tide the Treasury over its immediate difficulties. By the time the greenbacks were actually in circulation it was clear that larger amounts would be needed very soon. Bond sales were going very slowly, and other revenues were inadequate.

At the request of the Secretary, therefore, a bill was introduced to authorize a second 150 million of greenbacks. It was passed on July 11, less than 6 months after the first. In the debate on this bill its supporters emphasized the need for more currency for general circulation, and urged that 35 million of the new issue should be in denominations of 1 to 5 dollars. The currency shortage was genuine, but it was not met by the provisions of this act. A separate law a few days later provided for the use of stamps as fractional currency and made it illegal for any unauthorized person to issue paper money of less than 1 dollar.

The Treasury continued to fall behind in meeting its bills, and especial indignation was caused by its failure to pay the soldiers promptly. A third issue of greenbacks was therefore approved, at first by a resolution of Congress in January 1863, for 100 million; later by the Act of March 3 which not only increased the authorized greenbacks to 150 million, but gave the Secretary the right to borrow up to 900 million dollars during the next two fiscal years. There was less discussion than before about the necessity for the greenbacks. The supporters of the increased issue claimed that any rise in prices was due to speculation, not to currency increase or, if it was caused by currency increase, it was the fault of overissue by the banks. A tax of 2 percent on state bank notes was included. The Treasury was authorized to issue 50 million of fractional currency to take the place of the flimsy and sticky stamps and the "shin-plasters" issued by many corporations.

Although there had been great reluctance to admit the danger of the irredeemable paper, the feeling was growing both in Congress and in the country that further issues would be unwise. Moreover, the "necessity" which had been urged as justification was somewhat less pressing, since tax returns had finally begun to increase and bond sales had improved. In his report at the end of 1863 Secretary Chase declared that it was inexpedient to increase the amount of the greenbacks; without his approval, Congress was not likely to press the matter. It even set a limit, in the revenue law of June 30, 1864, to the total issue at the already authorized figure of 450 million.

There were no more issues of the legal tender demand notes, but there was resort on several occasions to legal tender notes in denominations of 10 dollars or more, which bore interest either in the form of coupons, or in the form of compound interest to be paid at the end of 3 years maturity. In October 1865, government officials estimated that 10 to 30 million was in actual circulation and another 75 million was held by national banks.

Taxation during the Civil War; the Income Tax

Congress approached the subject of internal taxes with great reluctance at the outbreak of the war. The only new source of revenue provided during its first session in 1861 was a revival of the direct tax on the states, which had not been used since 1815. According to the Constitution, such a tax could be levied only in proportion to population. Following the recommendation of Secretary Chase in his first report to Congress, a total of 20 million dollars was divided among the states, 15 million among the loyal and 5 million among the seceding. The states were given the option of collecting it themselves (in which case they obtained a rebate of 15 percent), or of having it collected by federal revenue officers. Western states particularly resented this levy because their average income was low. The only states which showed much zeal in collecting the tax were those to which the federal government owed money for enlisting and equipping troops. The seceding states paid only about one-half of the assessment, and that usually by selling lands, with considerable hardship for the luckless owners. The net revenue to the Treasury was negligible, and no further assessments were made after 1864.*

Internal revenue taxes were not levied until the middle of 1862, although Secretary Chase had included them in his first recommendations to Congress. They had been used during the War of 1812 but not by the federal government after that period. The first of the internal revenue measures put a specific tax on iron, tobacco, whiskey, kerosene, leather, and many luxury goods. *Ad valorem* taxes were levied on many manufactured goods at 3 percent, and the same rate was applied to railroad receipts and dividend payments; the latter were deducted at the source. Stamp duties were levied on many commercial and legal documents and on advertisements. Succeeding Congresses added to the list of taxable articles until, as the Special Commissioner of the Revenue reported in 1868:

At the close of the war, taxation under the system of internal revenue had been extended . . . and with the exception of land and the direct products of agriculture—other than cotton and sugar—had been made, so far as domestic production was concerned, all but universal. In the case of manufactured products, furthermore, the system had been made to embrace not only the finished and marketable product, but very generally also every constituent which entered into the composition of such product. But burdensome and complicated as the system was, its incep-

---

* What had been collected was returned to the states in the 1890s to reduce the Treasury surplus and thus reduce the demand for lower tariff rates. See p. 234.

tion and origin must be regarded as one of the wisest and most successful measures of the war; and it is only to be regretted that recourse was not earlier had to so effectual a method of raising revenue, rather than to the expedients at first exclusively resorted to, of loans at a heavy discount and an irredeemable paper money."[7]

The proceeds of this tax increased in each of the war years, and by 1868 had reached a peak of 1.1 billion dollars. Even after the expenses of collection were deducted, this amounted to a large proportion of the total cost of the war. It was not a popular method of taxation, and the public objection to it (the popular complaint was that "everything is taxed except coffins") caused most of it to be repealed after the war.

In addition to the direct tax on the states and the internal revenue tax, Congress levied a tax on incomes during the Civil War. It was first included in the Revenue Act of August 5, 1861 (Sec. 49); it set the rate at 3 percent on all income above the exemption of 800 dollars; income from United States securities, however, was taxable at only half that rate. The tax was to be collected by the same Commissioner who was responsible for other internal revenues.

The law was changed before it could go into effect; the exemption was reduced to 600 dollars, and the basic rate remained 3 percent, but on income above 10,000 dollars the rate was raised to 5 percent. The office of Commissioner of Internal Revenue was created by this Act. Two years later the Act of June 30, 1864 (Sec. 116) again increased the rates and made them more progressive. Income between 600 and 5000 dollars was taxed at 5 percent, that between 5000 and 10,000 dollars at 7.5 percent, and the excess above 10,000 at 10 percent. No special rate was granted to income from United States securities, but householders might deduct from their taxable income the amount of other taxes paid and the value of their annual rental, whether they owned the house or not. On March 3, 1865, the 10 percent rate was applied to all income in excess of 5000 dollars. The tax continued to be levied until 1872, but with increasing exemptions and declining rates.* It brought in far less than the internal revenue taxes, only 194 million dollars from 1863 to 1867 inclusive.

---

* See p. 182.

Tariff Revenue during the War

The Tariff Act of 1857 which had reduced rates to the lowest levels since 1815—less than 20 percent on the average for dutiable articles—had come at an unfortunate moment for the federal treasury. In 1860, just before the election of Lincoln, Congress retreated from the liberal trade policy and raised rates, changing them in many cases from *ad valorem* to specific. The rates on iron and wool in particular were increased in the hope of winning support for the Republican party in Pennsylvania and some of the western states.

The new duties of the Morrill Act went into effect in April 1861, the month in which the war began. It was soon evident that far greater revenues would be needed. Rates were raised and new commodities were included in the list of dutiable articles in nearly every session of Congress from the extra session of the summer of 1861 until the end of the war. By 1865 the average rate on dutiable imports had risen from 20 to 48 percent. Some of the increases, like those on tea and coffee, were primarily for revenue, others for protection to domestic manufactures, and still others to compensate for the excise taxes levied on articles of home production. Since the total of imports did not regain its prewar level during the war, the revenue from duties was less than had been expected and was exceeded by the revenue from income and internal revenue taxes. Indeed, import duties never regained their position as the most important source of federal income.

Further Borrowing; Jay Cooke

That first loan of 150 million dollars from the bankers, which had been followed shortly by the suspension of specie payments and the issue of legal tender notes, did not long meet the needs of the Treasury. Both the Secretary and the Congress were slow to recognize that the war would be a long one. They were willing to use taxation to pay the ordinary expenses of the government, but Congress agreed with the Secretary that

so long as it seemed highly probable that the war would be speedily brought to a successful close, . . . it was wisest to obtain the means for nearly the whole of the extraordinary expenditures by loans, and thus avoid the necessity of any considerable increase of burdens of the people at a time when the sudden outbreak of flagitious rebellion had deranged their business and temporarily diminished their incomes.[8]

To implement this policy, Secretary Chase in February 1862 requested and obtained the permission of Congress to issue, in addition to the legal tender notes, 500 million bonds at 6 percent, callable in 5 and redeemable in 20 years, to be sold "at any time, at the market value thereof," for coin or for Treasury notes. It was difficult and almost impossible to place these bonds at par; by October only a small part of them had been sold, but the Secretary was unwilling to use his privilege of selling them at the market value below par.

He turned for assistance to his banker friend from Ohio, Jay Cooke, who had been very successful in selling an issue of state bonds in Pennsylvania a few years earlier. Cooke had recently opened an office in Washington and had already been used as agent for the Treasury in several small financial transactions; he undertook his new assignment with enthusiasm. As an Ohio Abolitionist, he was genuinely concerned with the successful conclusion of the war, and as a banker he was delighted with this opportunity for his newly established firm. His commissions were to be one-half of 1 percent on the first 10 million of bonds sold, and three-eighths on the rest; out of this he had to pay all expenses.

Cooke knew that bankers in the United States could not take many more government obligations, and that foreign investors would not be interested. He therefore directed his efforts toward the great mass of small investors who had never before purchased government or any other securities. They could be reached by appeals to their patriotism, and they were not so apt as the bankers to go in and out of the market. He also recognized what Alexander Hamilton had earlier pointed out, that owners of government bonds would have a deeper concern for the welfare of their country.

He set up an elaborate organization with 2500 agents throughout the country, aided and supervised by traveling representatives. Advertisements were put in local newspapers, and at a time when this was still unusual for financial offers. Papers which had been handsomely paid for carrying advertisements were glad to print the news articles sent out from the Cooke offices describing the rush of activity and the clamor for the bonds, with the daily totals of sales. His methods were very successful. By the end of 1863 the issue of 5-20's had been oversubscribed, and most of the bonds were in the hands of individuals. With the 6 percent interest payable in gold, the bonds were a good hedge against inflation.

The continuing need for funds resulted in the Act of March 1863 authorizing loans of 300 million dollars during the current fiscal year, and 600 million the following year. These bonds, unlike the previous 5-20's, were callable in 10 years and repayable in 40 years, and were known as the 10-40's. The interest rate was left to the discretion of the Secretary but was not to exceed 10 percent. Half of the amount might be issued as 3-year Treasury notes with interest up to 6 percent. Representative Spaulding commented that this

conferred more discretionary power on the Secretary of the Treasury than was ever granted to any other Finance Minister in the world; and which ultimately led to a dangerous expansion of credit circulation in various forms . . . and to an enormous inflation of prices, caused by the over-issuing of paper money which came very near proving fatal to the finances of the government and the legitimate business of the country.[9]

Much of this unfortunate result arose from the fact that the Secretary chose to set the interest rate at only 5 percent. It was impossible to sell the bonds at that rate, even with the methods of Jay Cooke, and the ill-advised effort to save 1 percent per year in interest turned out to be an expensive mistake for the country as well as a serious embarrassment to the Treasury. More short-term Treasury notes and certificates of indebtedness had to be issued in order to pay the troops and meet other expenses. Only 73 million of the 900 million issued was sold during 5 months, and most of them were purchased by bankers who could use them as security for the new national bank notes.

The National Bank Act

Although Secretary Chase had consented with reluctance to the issuance of the greenbacks, he had not considered them a substitute for the national currency which he had advocated in his first annual report. He returned to the subject a year later, after the suspension of specie payments. During the interval a bill had been drafted and presented to the House, but it had received very little attention and had been permitted to perish. It had followed closely the form of the New York Free Banking Act of 1838.

There had been opposition to any such legislation from many parts of the country, especially from bankers in western states whose profits came largely from their note issue. Hugh McCulloch made a special trip to Washington to work against the bill, which he viewed as a menace to the Bank of Indiana, of which he was then president. Note issue was less important to bankers in the large cities of the east, but they also showed little enthusiasm for the proposed system. Jay Cooke, who was interested in increasing the sale of bonds, carried on a newspaper campaign which succeeded in arousing some popular support for the idea of a national bank.

However, it was not until President Lincoln, at the insistence of Chase, had sent a special message to Congress urging the bill as a necessary part of the war finance program that the Senate began to consider a new draft of the bill. After only three days of discussion it was approved and sent to the House. There it was considered briefly, with very inadequate debate, and passed within a week. It was signed by the President on February 25, 1863. It was only in the midst of such a war that such a bill could have been passed.

Although the National Bank Act had won the approval of Congress primarily because it created a new market for government bonds, its long-run benefits to the country were quite different. For once and for all, it provided a uniform paper currency and made possible the elimination of the motley array of state bank paper which had so long plagued the economy. This was eliminated gradually, not by the Act, but by taxation. A 2 percent tax had been levied on state bank notes by the internal revenue legislation of 1862. In 1866, in order to give the national banks a monopoly of note issue and increase the market for government bonds, the tax was increased to 10 percent; at such a rate there was no more profit in the issue of state bank notes. Only notes of national banks therefore remained in circulation, and it was no longer necessary for merchants to consult the Bank Note Detector to learn the value of the money their customers were offering. In spite of its inflexibility, the national bank note gave the country for the first time a note issue which was uniform in value and this, it should be observed, in spite of the fact that it was not a legal tender.

The revision of the Act in 1864 adjusted reserve requirements more closely to the ratios of cash which the banks had been accustomed to keep before the war. The eighteen large cities named as redemption centers were permitted to keep one-half of their 25 percent reserve on deposit with New York banks; the country banks were now required to keep reserves of only 15 percent, and three-fifths of this might be on deposit in one of the redemption centers. New York thus became recognized as the reserve center as well as the trade center of the country. These new requirements did not greatly raise the total reserves of the banks of the country, but they did tend to equalize their distribution. Nor did they change the pyramiding of reserves in New York which was so often criticized before the establishment of the Federal Reserve System. They did, however, improve the banking structure by raising standards and gradually forcing state banks to improve their operations.

An important aspect of the National Bank Act was the recognition it gave to deposits as liabilities of equal standing with notes, and in equal need of protection to keep innocent customers from being injured. In the days when most deposits were taken to the bank in the form of coin or paper money, a deposit was assumed to be made at the risk of the depositor, since he was under no compulsion to make a deposit at all. But, as loans came more and more to be made in the form of deposit credit at the bank rather than in currency to be carried away by the borrower, the use of checks, frequently found in the larger cities as early as the 1790s, became the customary form of settlement among business firms, and the depositor became as helpless as the note holder, with the same need for legal protection.

In requiring reserves to be held against deposits as well as against notes, the National Bank Act recognized the change in business practice. The example was followed only slowly by the states, and as late as 1879 only six states required banks under their charter to keep such reserves; in only three of the six were the requirements for reserves against deposits as high as those for national banks.

In spite of the stricter reserve requirements, the national bank charter was attractive because of its note issue privilege. The number of national banks increased rapidly after the revision of the Act in 1864. Many new banks were organized, and an even larger number of state banks changed to the national charter. By the end of 1865 there were 1601 in all, with 171 million notes outstanding, backed by government bonds.

The number of state banks declined sharply during the war years. Many of them failed as a result of the war. In Illinois, for example, with 110 banks in 1861, there were 13 million dollars of notes in circulation. Unfortunately 9 million were backed by bonds of southern states and, when it became evident that these states were about to secede, a run on the banks to obtain specie forced 37 of them to close at once, and 52 more to close by the end of the year. Much the same situation in Indiana was responsible for the closing of 27 banks, and in Wisconsin, of 39 banks.

With the inauguration of the national banking system, the decline of the state banks continued. In 1863 there had been 1466 incorporated banks in the northern states, with 239 million notes outstanding. By 1865 the number was down to 349. However, the trend was eventually reversed as notes became less important than deposits. Several decades later the number of state banks became equal to that of the national banks.*

The improvement in the note issue was not the only innovation made by the national bank legislation. One change, which was apparently inadvertent, was the failure to authorize national banks to have branches. This was brought about by the dropping of the plural ending "s" from the word "office" in the revision of the Act in 1864; it had been included in the Act of 1863. Since many state banks were permitted to have branches, this became one of their prized advantages over the national banks, and efforts to change the national charters in the same direction were unsuccessfully carried on for many years. This was a handicap to the development of the banking system; branches of strong banks would have been far more useful and less dangerous in small communities than the inadequately capitalized state banks which were the alternative.

One other feature of the national banking legislation affected the financial market—that which prohibited loans on real estate mortgages of the type that state banks had been accustomed to make, and con-

---

* See Chapter 9.

tinued to make but the gap was not filled. Mortgage banks attempted to supply the demand for such long-term funds, but many of them failed during the 1890s. It was not until decades later that efforts to meet this need began to achieve success.

In spite of its obvious imperfections, the national banking system made an important contribution to the economy. It created a sound currency, albeit inflexible, and put an end to the era of wildcat banking, an era which seems from a distant point of view dynamic and even romantic, but which caused serious hardship to many who had to cope with it.

Financing the Confederacy

The Confederate government in the south faced far more difficulties in financing the war than did the federal government of the north. It was the least industrialized part of the country, and the small population, only one-third of the total in 1860 (and only one-fourth of the white) was widely scattered and largely dependent on agriculture for its livelihood. According to Jefferson Davis, the Confederate president, two-thirds of the entire taxable property of the area at the outbreak of the war was in land and slaves. Tariff duties could not be counted on for revenue since the volume of imports into southern ports had never been large and became even smaller as war embargoes closed one port after another. Even if imports had increased, it would have been difficult to raise duties, since the south had always been opposed on principle to tariff levies. Moreover, one of the basic sources of conflict in the war was the question of states' rights, and the southern states could hardly be expected to react kindly to the levying of any kind of tax by a central government, even the new one which they themselves had just established.

The Secretary of the Confederate Treasury, Christopher G. Memminger, recommended a property tax as early as May 1861 in the hope that it would yield 15 million dollars, but it was not until August that such a measure was passed. This levied a flat rate of one-half of 1 percent on real estate, slaves, cattle, personal possessions and securities (except Confederate bonds). Since the central government was not yet fully organized, the assessment and collection of taxes was urged on

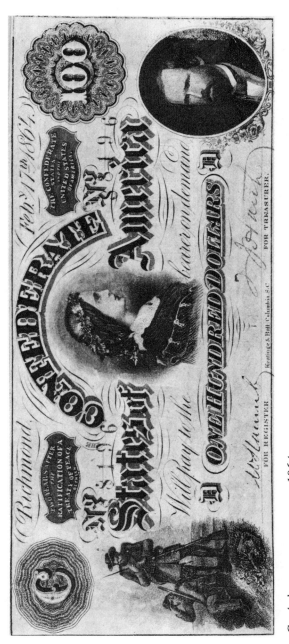

Confederate paper money, 1864

the individual states, which might obtain a 10 percent reduction of their quota by this service. Few states viewed the task with enthusiasm, and only South Carolina actually collected the tax. Other states borrowed on their own bond issues, or borrowed from the state bank, or, as in Texas, confiscated the Texas property of persons living in the north. By the end of the war the property tax had contributed less than 2 percent of the total revenue of the Confederate government.

The failure of the property tax and the unpopularity of internal revenue and excise taxes led Secretary Memminger to propose a tax on incomes. This was levied in April 1863, with an exemption of 500 dollars and progressive rates up to 15 percent on income over 10,000 dollars. At the same time most of the other tax rates were increased, and a tax in kind was levied in the hope of increasing supplies for the army. As the economic condition of the country deteriorated under the pressure of the invading armies, it became less and less possible to collect any kind of tax; not only the taxpayers, but in many cases the collectors also, fled from their homes as the northern armies advanced. In 1863 the government was driven to resort to impressment and, in spite of public protests, seized food and property in order to supply the army.

Like the government of the north, the Confederacy tried to tide itself over the first months of the war by borrowing. England seemed a likely source of funds, since it was desperately in need of cotton, but it gave encouragement to the southern cause only as long as that cause seemed to be winning, and the encouragement did not include financial aid. One loan of £2,200,000 (over 10 million dollars), secured by bales of cotton in storage, was floated in England, but the cotton was seized by northern armies and no more loans could be obtained abroad.

The alternative was borrowing at home, but this also was not easy as the war continued. An issue of 10-year bonds at 8 percent interest was offered in May 1862, to be paid in specie, in military stores, or in proceeds of sales of raw produce or manufactured articles. The loan was well subscribed, but many of the subscriptions were never paid up. Later issues were offered, to be paid in either currency or cotton, but none of the devices for attracting investors could counteract the effect of rising prices for commodities and declining prospects for victory. Only 23 percent of the total revenue of the Confederacy during the war came from sales of bonds, and another 9 percent from the sale of Treasury call certificates. Although the total debt of the southern government had risen to 1148 million dollars by the end of the war, this provided only one-third of the funds expended for the war.

Debts of the southern states also increased during the war, but not so much as the debt of the central government. The total in 1860 estimated by Special Commissioner of the Revenue, David Wells, in his report for 1867, had been about 84 million dollars, and by 1866 had risen to 116 million.

Inevitably the southern government turned to the issue of paper money in order to pay its expenses. Some of the notes bore interest and were redeemable within 1 year; others were issued without interest but were convertible into bonds at varying rates of interest. The effort to reduce the total by refunding proved to be futile. By the end of 1862, 400 million was already in circulation, and by the end of 1863, the total was 600 million. By that time 50 million was being issued each month because other revenues had practically ceased. States and cities also issued notes with which to meet their obligations, and they issued fractional paper currency as well; some corporations followed their example. Banks in the southern states increased their note issue during the war as prices advanced. Specie disappeared early from circulation, as it had done in the north, but the total of money in circulation, consisting of many different kinds of paper, had increased about elevenfold by January 1864.

The effect of the increasing paper circulation was a rapid increase in prices. During 1863 the price of a gold dollar rose from 3 dollars in paper to 20 in paper. The general price index rose about 10 percent a month and eventually reached a height of about 28 times the starting level. The increase in prices was greater than the increase in the monetary circulation, since there was an increasing scarcity of goods as production declined and hoarding increased. There was also an increasing velocity of circulation as confidence in the eventual outcome of the war gave way to despair. The most cruel effect of the inflation was the high price of food. Farmers were exhorted to plant grain rather than the customary cotton and tobacco for which markets could no longer be found, but food shortages persisted, and the civilian population suffered along with the military. There is certainly a wide margin of error in the price index, but it is clear that the Confederacy was suffering from hyperinflation with all it entailed of want and misery.

The Cost of the War

The real cost of such a war to north and to south can of course never be measured. The lives lost or ruined, the property destroyed, the goods never produced, are beyond calculation. As part of his final report in 1869, Mr. David Wells, the Special Commissioner of Revenue, included an estimate of the cost of the war up to that time. Table 3 shows how he itemized it.

TABLE 3. ESTIMATED COST OF THE CIVIL WAR (*in millions of dollars*)

4996	total loans and receipts April 1, 1861, to June 30, 1869
825	estimated normal expenditures for that period
4171	cost of the war to the northern government
200	capitalized cost of pensions
123	increase of state debts
200	increase of local government debts
600	war expenditures of state and local governments
1200	loss to industry and shipping
2700	expenditures and loss of Confederate states
9194	estimated total cost

Source: Fourth Report of Special Commissioner of the Revenue, 1869, Vol. V.

A decade later, in 1879, Congress ordered another summary of all war costs to be prepared. This report classified the expenditures into direct military and naval expenses and indirect costs of interest on the debt, pensions, cemeteries, and Freedmen's Bureau, but did not give the totals for each year. It is therefore impossible to eliminate the effect of inflation. The grand total of 6.2 billion dollars does not differ greatly from that of Mr. Wells, since it does not include the Confederate costs. Nor could it include the costs of the war which continued after 1879 in the form of interest on the debt, and pensions to veterans and their families.

This total of 1879 excludes also the nearly half a billion dollars which states had expended for supplies and war materials. Toward the end of the war many of the loyal states had given bounties to volunteers in order to encourage enlistment, and this added another quarter of a billion to the war expenditures of the states. Several efforts were made after the war to persuade Congress to reimburse the states for their outlays, but without success. No reliable estimate exists for the amount of food, clothing, and blankets donated by patriotic groups to aid the soldiers; at some periods of the war the total was considerable.

The greatest difficulty in estimating the monetary cost of the Civil War, as of the Revolution, arises from the changing price levels of the period. Any military operation is likely to cause some increase in consumer prices because it diverts production from consumer goods to war goods without reducing the purchasing power of consumers—unless of course consumers are heavily taxed or can be persuaded to invest the difference in government bonds, and this seldom happens. When to this reduction in consumer goods is added the factor of increased monetary circulation, the effect is doubly inflationary.

In the Civil War, prices began to rise in the north as soon as specie payments were suspended at the end of 1861. When the greenbacks went into circulation in April 1862, gold coins were already at a premium and wholesale prices had risen about 10 percent, according to Mitchell's careful calculation. The peak in the wholesale price index was reached early in 1865 when it stood at more than double the level of 1860. However, this figure cannot be taken as a measure of the change in consumer prices or of the changes in the cost of the military supplies purchased by state and national governments. The estimates of how much the inflation added to the cost of the war range from half a billion dollars, about one-fifth of the debt, up to one billion or two-fifths of the debt. These figures do not include the additional costs to local and state governments of their ordinary and extraordinary expenses during the war, or the enormous losses of many individuals.

Although the use of fiat money as a way of financing the Civil War was less justifiable than the Continental money of the Revolution, when the central government had no effective taxing power, the greenbacks alone cannot be held responsible for the war inflation. The total issues, 450 million, were only one-sixth the amount of the increase in the federal debt, and their impact was concentrated in the first two years of the war. That was a period when Congress and the nation were still unconvinced that the war required every effort. For this reason Senator John Sherman, in his autobiography written many years later, defended the issue of the greenbacks as "the turning point of our physical and financial history" and believed that "It would be difficult to measure the beneficial results that rapidly followed the passage of this bill."[10]

From the vantage point of a century later, it can be seen that the greenbacks were necessary only because adequate taxation and borrowing could not be achieved promptly enough to meet the sudden increase in government expenses. The London *Economist* in 1862, drawing on the British experience of the Crimean War, thought that "a heavy direct tax on property or income, payable *at once*" and "imposed *at once* at the beginning of the war" would have maintained the government credit, increased its income, and made it possible to borrow abroad, without inflating the currency at home.[11]

Perhaps even more serious than the issue of greenbacks was the mistake made in not permitting interest rates to rise sufficiently to attract investors in the early days of the war. Chase believed that to sell a 6 percent bond at a price below par, in order to yield more than 6 percent, was a kind of disgrace, an admission that the credit of the government was not good. It certainly was not good at that time, and the mere refusal to admit the fact did not improve the situation. The same mistake was made in the financing of World Wars I and II.

As a result of the inflation, fixed incomes dependent on pensions and dividends suffered severely, yet business profits in some lines were high and gave an illusion of prosperity. The situation in various parts of the country was summarized by Auguste Laugel, a young French engineer who traveled widely in the northern states during the war. He wrote in 1865:

Financially, the whole weight of the gigantic struggle in which the Union was involved bore upon the Atlantic States. So far from being impoverished, the West is enriched. . . . The farmer was thus enabled to pay back in paper what he had received in specie. The increase of prices not only allowed him to free himself very rapidly [from debt]; he has also been able to lay up and invest money, in land, or in the Federal loans.[12]

Agriculture in the west benefited not only from the demand at home, but also from three successive crop failures in Great Britain. Exports of wheat which had formerly gone down the Mississippi now went eastward on the great railroad lines which had been constructed during the 1850s with generous government subsidies. In spite of bank failures in western states at the outbreak of war and high freight rates as railroads took advantage of the increased demand for service, farmers were able to buy new machinery, and even sewing machines for their wives. New lands were opened throughout the war, as the Homestead Act of 1862 encouraged migration.

In the eastern states there was frequent complaint about the extravagance and speculation of war profiteers. Luxury industries expanded. However, for many kinds of activity the war was a repressive rather an expansive force. Half of the cotton mills had to close down for lack of raw material. Workers in other industries found that wages did not increase so rapidly as prices. There was little actual unemployment, in part because the army was absorbing so many men.

Although the cost of the war was enormous—it was not until 1869–73 that the annual national product averaged 6.7 billion dollars—the inflation would undoubtedly have been more severe, with a corresponding increase in the cost and the debt, had not a large part of the later bond issues been purchased by individual investors. This absorbed some of the purchasing power which would otherwise have bid up the prices of goods. It also made it unnecessary for banks to buy the bonds with newly created credit which would have increased the volume of purchasing power.

This fortunate circumstance can be attributed in part to the imaginative and ingenious methods of Jay Cooke in selling the bonds, but his success was made possible by the higher interest rate (6 percent instead of 5) offered by the Treasury, and by the improved position of the northern armies after early disasters. The inflation was never entirely out of control and, in comparison with modern wars, was not abnormal. Very few wars have been fought on a pay-as-you-go basis; the Civil War was no exception.[13]

CHAPTER 8

FROM THE CIVIL WAR TO RESUMPTION

Growth after the War

THE end of the war made it possible for industrial production to turn toward normal activity, and the next few years were marked by rapid expansion in many lines. In spite of a temporary setback in 1866 which reflected the Overend-Gurney banking crisis in England,[1] the economy forged ahead. The Atlantic cable was laid in 1866, and the first transcontinental railroad was opened in 1869. The miles of railroad in operation increased by 50 percent between 1865 and 1870, and the freight ton-miles carried by thirteen railroads more than doubled. The production of steel ingots and castings, thanks to the Bessemer process, provided a basis for the industrial expansion by tripling the annual output between 1868 and 1871. The steel industry shifted from the eastern seaboard toward the west and south; great new mills were constructed to take advantage of the technical advances in refining and smelting. The new petroleum industry also developed in the early years after the war, spreading steadily from the Pittsburgh area southwestward. Immigration increased again after the war and continued high until the depression of 1873 gave it pause.

Much of the capital for this postwar business expansion came from abroad. Even before the end of the war, when it became clear that the northern government would be victorious, European investors returned to the American market. By 1866, the Secretary of the Treasury estimated in his annual report, foreigners were holding one-eighth of the federal debt, about 350 million dollars, in addition to 150 million of state and municipal obligations, and 100 million of railroad and other corporate securities, a total of 600 million. During the Overend-Gurney crisis of 1866, English investors returned some of their American holdings, but by 1869 the total had increased to a new high of about 1500 million, of which nearly two-thirds was in United States bonds.

The depression years following the crisis of 1873 caused another temporary halt in the flow of foreign capital to the United States, and withdrawal of about one-fifth of previously invested funds. After this time there was also a shift away from federal securities, since their price at home was rising and the yield was falling; national banks were buying them to serve as a basis for note issue, and many state banks and insurance companies also held them. The foreign demand therefore turned to railroad issues of both stocks and bonds. For example, the Atlantic and Great Western Railroad, built during the Civil War, was almost entirely owned in England, and foreign shareholders held about three-fourths of the stock of the Illinois Central. Railroad issues were the backbone of the Stock Exchange and were largely bought and sold by domestic as well as by foreign investors. Relatively few industrial issues were traded on the Exchanges, and they were less acceptable as collateral than the rails.

The Currency Problem

The question which overshadowed all economic and political life in the first decade after the war, in times of prosperity as in times of depression, was that of the resumption of specie payments. It was almost universally assumed that resumption could not take place without contraction of the currency, and this prospect was exceedingly painful to the many groups for whom the high prices of the war had meant prosperity. They presented arguments to justify high prices as the basis of economic health, and they opposed any action which would reduce the amount of currency in order to bring the greenbacks back to the level of gold.

Secretary Chase himself was still convinced that the premium on gold was the result, not of Treasury policy, but of the mainpulations of speculators. His remedy was to bring the price of gold down by forbidding time contracts for it, and thus destroying the futures market. Congress passed such an Act which went into effect on June 17, 1864, when the price was about 190 in paper currency. Within a few days the price had advanced to 285. Even Chase had to admit that the gold bill had "failed to produce anything but mischief." Its repeal after nineteen days provided a tragi-comic footnote to Chase's career as Secretary of the Treasury, for by that time he had resigned petulantly in a dispute over a minor political appointment.

After a brief interlude under Secretary Fessenden, the Treasury was put into the strong and capable hands of Hugh McCulloch in March 1865. He had been head of the Bank of Indiana for many years and had then served as Comptroller of the Currency for the new national banking system.

The premium on gold was not the only problem facing the new Secretary. The debt was still rising, and it did not pass its peak until August 1865 when it stood at 2.8 billion dollars. Even more disturbing than its magnitude was the fact that only two-fifths of it was in the form of long-term bonds. Another two-fifths was in short obligations maturing within 3 years, and the rest was in greenbacks for which no redemption had yet been provided. The cash reserve of the Treasury at its low point was only 88 million, and the annual interest charges amounted to 97 million.

Secretary McCulloch was committed to a policy of contraction and debt repayment, and he began at once to carry out this task. He requested and received from Congress in April 1866 wide discretionary powers to convert short obligations into funded debt, and to sell bonds at home or abroad, at any rate and in any amount that he found necessary. The only restriction was that no more than 10 million of greenbacks might be retired during the next 6 months, and no more than 4 million in each month thereafter. The Secretary continued to urge greenback contraction in each of his annual reports, reiterating the statement he had made in 1866, that he regarded "a redundant legal-tender currency as the prime cause of our financial difficulties, and a curtailment thereof indispensable to an increase of labor and a reduction of prices, and augmentation of exports and a diminution of imports."[2] In spite of his firm conviction that contraction was the right policy, he was unable to keep the support of Congress. Businessmen feared the effect of deflation on their profits, exporters knew that a premium on gold encouraged exports, and farmers who had benefited by high prices were resentful of the fact that agricultural prices were falling more rapidly than industrial. Both groups put pressure on their Congressmen, and the contraction law was repealed in 1868, when only 48 million greenbacks had been retired—not enough to account for the decline in prices.

The total amount of money in circulation was still very large—far more than could be justified by the needs of business now that prices were falling. Coin was at a premium of 40 percent over paper, and the ratio of gold and gold certificates to the total had dropped from nearly one-half to just over one-tenth, as shown in Table 4.

TABLE 4. CURRENCY IN CIRCULATION OUTSIDE THE TREASURY IN 1860 AND 1867 (*in millions of dollars*)

	1860	1867
Gold and gold certificates	207	91
State bank notes	207	4
United States notes (greenbacks)	—	319
National bank notes	—	287
All other	21	158
Total	435	859

Source: *Historical Statistics of the United States*, p. 649. New York, Horizon Press, 1965.

Although he was unable to carry out his plan for contraction of the currency, Secretary McCulloch was successful in funding the debt. He was too knowledgeable a financier to believe, as Chase and Fessenden had believed, that the short-term nature of so much of the debt was an advantage; he knew that each maturity date would in effect be a vote of confidence in the credit of the government, a vote which might not always be affirmative. Moreover, the great variety in interest rates, maturity dates, and other provisions created confusion in the mind of the public and greatly magnified the task of the Treasury in meeting its obligations.

During his first six months of office more than 500 million of 3-year notes bearing 7.3 percent interest were sold to meet unpaid bills of the government, and 100 million of the short-term certificates of indebtedness were paid off. Some of the compound interest notes were refunded into tax-exempt 6 percent bonds maturing in 5 to 20 years, a type of obligation which became the principal instrument of the conversion operation. With the increased powers granted him under the Act of April 1866 the Secretary was able to proceed more rapidly, and by the middle of 1868 he reported that the task of converting 1 billion of temporary obligations into a funded debt was practically completed. The long-term portion of the debt had been increased, but the total had been reduced, and the cash reserve of the Treasury, as well as its gold holdings, had increased.

All of this had been carried out in close cooperation with the money and securities markets, and the Secretary defended his policy.[3]

He could not be indifferent to the condition of the market, nor avoid connection with it, for it was, in fact, with the market he had to deal. He would have been happy had it been otherwise. . . . The task of converting a thousand millions of temporary obligations into a funded debt, on a market constantly subject to natural and artificial fluctuations, without depressing the price of bonds, and without disturbing the business of the country, however it may be regarded now, when the work has been accomplished, was, while it was being performed, an exceedingly delicate one.

Secretary McCulloch did not allow the ghost of the Independent Treasury to frighten him away from doing what he regarded as essential to the welfare of the economy. His success in repaying part of the debt and refunding the remainder laid a foundation for the next step, which was to reduce the interest cost of the debt, a step made possible by the improvement he had effected in the credit of the government. A part of this improvement can be ascribed to the passage on March 18, 1869, of "An act to strengthen the public credit." Its objective was to "remove any doubt as to the purpose of the Government to discharge all just obligations to the public creditors, and to settle conflicting questions and interpretations of the laws" by declaring "that the faith of the United States is solemnly pledged to the payment in coin or its equivalent of all the obligations of the United States not bearing interest, known as United States notes, and of all the interest-bearing obligations of the United States, except in cases where the law authorizing the issue . . . has expressly provided that the same may be paid in lawful money or other currency than gold and silver."[4] This bill had been one of the last passed by the

Congress of President Johnson's administration. Johnson refused to sign it, and it was introduced again into the new Congress; it became the first bill to be signed by President Grant. It represented a compromise among the many factions, since it was in effect a "no contraction, no repudiation" measure.

The new Secretary, George S. Boutwell, carried on McCulloch's policy of refunding the debt at lower rates of interest. In July 1870 he persuaded Congress to authorize bond issues for the refunding of the wartime 5-20's which carried a 6 percent dividend. These new bonds were to be exchanged par for par with the old, or sold and the funds used for redeeming the old. The new issues were of

> 200 million at 5   percent, redeemable in 10 years
> 300 million at 4.5 percent, redeemable in 15 years
> 1 billion at 4   percent, redeemable in 30 years

The lower rate on the longer bonds was defended on the grounds that interest rates in Europe, where it was hoped to sell many of them, were already at 3 percent, and that market rates in the United States were already falling and would go still lower as resumption of specie payments approached. In spite of their exemption from federal taxation, the bonds sold slowly at first. The outbreak of the Franco-Prussian war in 1870 hampered the sale abroad, and the panic of 1873 made it difficult to sell them at home. It was not until 1879, after resumption, that the last of them were disposed of and the bank consortium which was handling them was able to complete its contract. Since market rates of interest fell still lower in the next few decades, the bonds turned out to be an excellent investment.

Black Friday

Although the Treasury was successful in its debt management policy, it had not yet been able to obtain Congressional permission to resume specie payments. Gold was paid in for customs duties, and paid out for principal and interest of the debt, but other transactions were carried on in greenbacks or national bank notes, at varying discounts with gold. The Treasury, like the banks and the merchants, continued to keep accounts in two media.

When gold from customs duties accumulated in the Treasury, it had to be sold again if it was not paid out, because the portion of the Independent Treasury Act which was still in force made it impossible to deposit it in banks. The Treasury sales of gold thus became an important factor in the money market, and the reserves of the New York banks (gold and greenbacks) varied inversely with the Treasury balance. Not only bankers but also businessmen had to keep a watchful eye on sales of gold by the Treasury. At first they were made secretly, but this created so much apprehension in the market that after October 1868 the sales were made publicly, in amounts announced in advance.

The absurdity and inherent danger in this system were thrown into sharp relief by the events of September 24, 1869, which became known as "Black Friday." During the preceding summer several speculators, of whom Jay Gould and Jim Fisk* were the leaders, attempted to convince President Grant and Secretary Boutwell that no gold should be sold during the crop-exporting period, as this would increase Treasury holdings of greenbacks and might lower prices received by farmers. While the President was away on a short vacation trip the speculators, certain that the Treasury would remain aloof, bought up all the available gold, cornered the market, and trapped those who had sold short. The frantic short interests pushed the price of gold higher and higher, amid disgraceful scenes of hysteria at the Gold Exchange. The President and the Secretary were alerted; and the Treasury finally released enough gold to ruin the corner and those who were involved in it. For the rest of the year, 2 million of gold was sold each week.[5]

Although there was not another such dramatic incident as that of Black Friday, there was continuing difficulty for the business community, the securities and commodity markets, and the Treasury until the final resumption of specie payments in 1879. It required the most delicate balancing of one type of operation against another to prevent serious stringency. Sometimes the Treasury was obliged to offset a sale of gold by a purchase of bonds in order to prevent a shortage of greenbacks. Had the Treasury been permitted to place gold customs receipts on special deposit with the banks, as private individuals were doing in this period, this absurd and artificial situation could have been avoided.

---

* See p. 186.

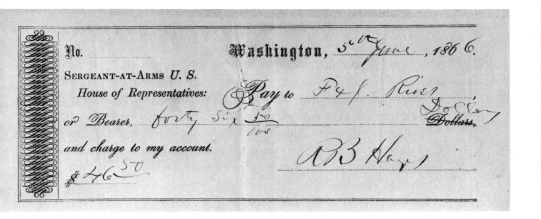

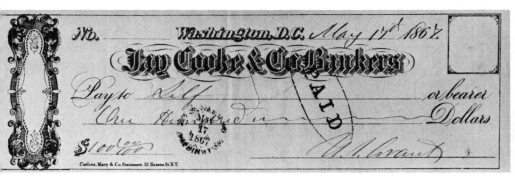

Checks signed by Presidents Hayes and Grant

Federal Revenue

In spite of the problems created by the delay in bringing the value of paper currency up to that of gold, the postwar period was one of general prosperity and business expansion, and government revenues were large, both from internal taxes and from customs receipts. The extraordinary taxes which had been levied on domestic trade and on personal and corporate incomes during the war were yielding more than tariff duties. Popular protest against them increased when the war was over, because military expenses were falling off sharply as armies were disbanded and the revenue was no longer needed. Moreover, the disclosure of frauds in the collection of taxes on liquor, tobacco, and kerosene made it imperative to reconsider the whole system.

Early in 1865 Congress authorized a review of federal revenues. Mr. David A. Wells, an experienced economist, was made a Special Commissioner to study the effect of the various forms of taxation on industry and commerce. In a series of four reports he made recommendations for changes in the tax structure and improvements in tax collection. Although his advocacy of lower tariffs went largely unheeded, his more popular proposals for reduction of excise and internal revenue taxes were adopted by Congress. Within four years the number of articles subject to taxation was reduced from nearly 300 to 55, and direct taxes were retained only on such luxury items as alcoholic beverages, cigars, perfumes, cosmetics, and playing cards.

Income taxes, although very unpopular, were continued for a number of years after the war. Farmers found the tax especially burdensome because it required them to compute and report "income and gains derived from the increased value of live stock, whether sold or on hand, and the amount of sugar, wool, butter, cheese, pork, beef, mutton, or other meats, hay, grain, or other productions" sold by the farm. City dwellers found the tax equally iniquitous, and their attitude was probably fairly represented by George Templeton Strong, a respected New York lawyer, who referred to it in his diary in May 1872 as "odious, inquisitorial, unequal, unconstitutional.[6]

There was generally admitted evasion of the tax, and in 1868, out of a total population of nearly 40 million, only 250,000 returns were filed, representing perhaps 2.5 percent of the population. In 1870, only 9500 of all the persons filing returns admitted to incomes of 5000 dollars or more. Inaccurate reporting was actually encouraged by the number of items which might be deducted, such as house rent, wages, interest, and repairs. The most successful provision of the law was that which provided collection at the source for taxes on dividends; in 1865 nearly 40 percent of the total was collected from banks, canal companies, railroads, insurance and turnpike companies, and federal employees. The revenue from the income tax steadily declined, and it was finally abandoned in 1872.

The reduction in excise and income taxes after the war greatly reduced the burden of direct taxes on individuals and on business firms. Tariff rates, however, remained high. They had been hastily enacted in a desperate effort to increase revenues during the war, and they resulted in many inequalities among producers. One of the tasks assigned to the Special Commissioner of the Revenue was the study of the existing rates and their effect on the economy. Mr. Wells in his reports from 1866 to 1869 recommended that duties on producer's goods be reduced in order to lower costs, that protection by means of tariffs be limited to genuine "infant industries," and that no duty be charged on goods not produced in the United States. His evidence regarding the burden of high tariff rates to both producers and consumers indicated that war tariffs should be reduced, but the bill which embodied his recommendations was disregarded by Congress.

Tariff legislation during the following years was piecemeal. The Act of 1870 lowered the duties on tea, coffee, wines, and molasses. More important was its reduction of the duty on pig-iron from 9 to 7 dollars per ton, although this was partially offset by an increase of the duty on steel rails and some other manufactured articles. It was not until 1872, when the government surplus was so large that high rates could no longer be justified by the need for revenue, that popular agitation for tariff reduction became effective. Western farmers were those most injured by the high prices of protected manufactured articles, especially machinery and textiles, which they had to buy, while the products they sold did not benefit from tariff protection. Western Congressmen of both parties therefore supported the move for tariff reduction. The protectionist group, particularly the manufacturers of cotton, wool, iron, steel, metals, paper, glass, and leather, in order to prevent more sweeping changes agreed on a flat reduction of 10 percent on most articles. Tea and coffee were again put on the free list, and salt and coal duties were cut nearly in half in a move to pacify consumers.

Unfortunately the business depression of 1873 reduced the revenue from imports so much that the 10 percent cut was repealed, and many rates were back at substantially their wartime levels. Wool fiber, for example, paid a combination of specific and *ad valorem* duties, with higher rates for the more valuable grades. In order to compensate the manufacturer of wool for the high cost of his raw material, a higher duty was laid on woolen fabrics under an elaborate system of specific and *ad valorem* rates which enormously increased the cost of clothing, blankets, and carpets to the consumer. Some other commodities on which rates remained particularly high, such as copper and steel rails, had a less immediate and visible effect on consumer costs because they were concealed in the earlier stages of production; the cost was of course increased many times before the finished product finally reached the retail purchaser. The farmers' discontent was well publicized by their organizations, but the plight of the unorganized, low-income, urban consumer seems seldom to have been considered either in the Congressional hearings or in the public press.

Banks and the Securities Markets

Although the National Bank Act had greatly improved the banking system, it had not affected one banking practice which closely linked the banks to the securities market and accentuated the panics which so frequently occurred. This practice was the payment of interest on deposits by banks in New York, which attracted to New York far larger sums than were needed there for commercial business. The practice had been noted, usually with expressions of disapproval, as early as 1804 and had been strongly condemned in 1857.* By the war period it had become quite frequent, especially among the larger city banks. Some of the state banking commissioners had long opposed the practice because they believed that it enticed funds away from the areas under their jurisdiction to the central money market in New York. When the Comptroller of the Currency was given responsibility for the national banks, he shifted the

---

* See p. 125.

objection to a wider base and pointed out the link between interest on deposits and call loans on Stock Exchange collateral.

This link had developed in the United States out of the method of settling accounts among brokers. In most of the money markets of the world such accounts had been settled once or twice a month, so that brokers need borrow only over the settlement days. In the United States, however, and particularly in New York, where the bulk of security trading was carried on, the presence of a large volume of demand deposits available for call loans made it easy for brokers to settle their accounts every day. Proposals for the adoption of a system of term settlements were never seriously considered, although successive Comptrollers of the Currency and Secretaries of the Treasury as well as responsible bankers themselves inveighed against the dangerous association of banking and security speculation.

Not only did the banks of New York in some periods lend up to half of their resources on call with security collateral, they also certified the checks of their customers for large amounts, in advance of the actual deposit of the amounts certified. It was understood that the deposit would be made before the end of the banking day, but in a period of rapidly changing security prices there was danger that the broker might not be able to cover his loan before the banks closed. Moreover, the availability of this easy source of credit tended to encourage speculation and make the securities markets even more "feverish and fluctuating."[7] This practice of overcertification was forbidden by the Act of March 3, 1869, but the law was ineffective; it was not until further legislation in 1882 that it ceased. The payment of interest on deposits was not eliminated until many decades later, under the Federal Reserve system, when the Stock Exchange also became subject to regulation.*

Since this was the period in which railroad expansion was the dominant factor in the capital market, it was inevitable that much of the speculative activity which was rife in this period should have been in railroad issues. The "bulls" and the "bears," manipulating prices up or down in their raids on the market, created an unfortunate public image of Wall Street.

One of the railroads which thus achieved a dubious fame was the Erie. Chartered in 1832, it was not opened until 1851, and then only after

* See p. 333.

successive rescues from its financial difficulties by the state of New York.*
By the end of the war the road had been through a receivership and a
reorganization and was operating 773 miles of track with an annual
income of 16.5 million dollars. During the early 1850s Mr. Daniel Drew
had become a member of the Board of Directors, and for many years
he was treasurer of the company. "Shrewd, unscrupulous and very illit-
erate—a strange combination of superstition and faithlessness, of daring
and timidity,—often good-natured and sometimes generous," as he was
described by Charles Francis Adams, Jr., in his *Chapters of Erie,*[8] Drew
was a notorious speculator in the stock of his own company. In 1866,
for example, he had sold far more of its stock than had been issued, but
had fulfilled his contracts by exercising the right (which had been quite
overlooked by his adversaries) to convert 3 million of bonds into stock.
Since this operation netted him an enormous profit, it was viewed with
admiration by much of the public opinion of the time.

Shortly after this, a contest developed between the Erie, which operated
on the west side of the Hudson River, and the road on the east side.
This was the Harlem, which became the nucleus of the New York Central,
under the guidance of "Commodore" Vanderbilt whose title derived
from a Staten Island ferry boat and a Hudson River steamship line.
Vanderbilt wanted control of the Erie in order to have a monopoly of
traffic on both sides of the river with its lucrative grain shipments from
the west. After a bitter fight involving legislators and judges as well as
financiers, a compromise was reached between Drew and Vanderbilt in
1868 which amounted to a division of the spoils. The Erie was again
almost bankrupted by the manipulations its stock had undergone and
eventually fell into the hands of two others, Jim Fisk and Jay Gould.
They carried on the tradition of despoiling the road for their own profit
and left it in such bad financial shape that the Erie paid no dividends
to its stockholders for three-quarters of a century, until 1942. Gould was
finally driven out of the Erie management and turned his attention to the
new railroads of the west, applying many of the same methods to the
manipulation of their stocks. Fisk was shot by a jealous rival on the steps
of the opera house he had built for a well-known actress; he did not live

---

* See p. 115.

to witness the panic of 1873 to which his activities had undoubtedly contributed.

Another railroad scandal which came to light early in 1873 involved federal government officers. The need of the army for better transportation during the war had lead the government to aid railroad building in the west by the purchase of 64 million of bonds in six companies, and by grants of enormous areas of land as well. The Union Pacific road, for example, was given a right-of-way through the public domain, with 20 square miles of land along each mile of road and loans up to 48,000 dollars per mile, secured by second mortgages. The railroad in return gave lower rates for troop fares and mail. For no reason except that of financial chicanery, a new corporation, the Credit Mobilier, was organized under a Pennsylvania charter to take over the stock of the Union Pacific and to carry on the actual construction. Congressmen were bribed to approve the plan by offers of stock at low prices, and at least one of the government commissioners was persuaded with cash to declare completed a section of the road not yet built, so that payment could be collected from the government. This was revealed to Congress in February 1873, but the full loss to the government was impossible to ascertain. The official report stated that "Your committee have earnestly endeavored to get the exact cost of the road to the company and to the contractors. . . . The books have been kept in such a way, and the transactions have been of such a character, as that their true nature has been very much disguised."[9]

Crisis of 1873

The climax of this investigation in the early months of 1873 added to the uneasiness of the business and financial community. The disastrous fire in Chicago in October 1871 had caused the failure of an important insurance company, and another fire in Boston a year later had weakened other companies. The usual autumn stringency of 1872 had continued into the following spring, with high interest rates especially on call loans. It became increasingly difficult to place or to carry new issues of securities, and the demand for bank loans was heavy in spite of the high interest rates. Gold exports increased, since securities were no longer being sold abroad in amounts sufficient to pay for the imports of manufactured goods.

The immediate occasion for the crisis was a succession of business failures associated with railroad financing. The building of new railroads, which between 1869 and 1873 had increased the total capital invested in railroads from 2 to nearly 4 billion dollars, had finally overreached itself and the top-heavy credit structure collapsed. Many of the new roads had expanded into areas which for a long time would not provide enough traffic to cover their costs, and they had borrowed heavily from banks and insurance companies when they could not sell their stock. By the end of 1873, fifty-five railroads were in default and the banks which had loaned to them were in difficulty.

The first serious warning of the impending crisis was the failure not of a bank, but of the New York Warehouse and Security Company, on Monday, September 8. Although it had been organized to finance grain and other agricultural products, it had become involved in the Missouri, Kansas and Texas Railroad. Two smaller firms had to suspend on the same day. On Saturday of that week the banking house in which Daniel Drew was a partner, Kenyon, Cox and Company, failed; it had indorsed 1.5 million of paper for the Canada Southern Railroad. On the following Thursday, September 18, the highly respected firm of Jay Cooke and Company was obliged to close when the leading banks in New York found themselves unable to extend it any more credit. Hugh McCulloch, who after leaving the Treasury had become the London partner in this firm, was greeted as he stepped off the ship from England on his return to the United States with this "astounding intelligence" which he found "absolutely stunning."[10]

Another less reputable brokerage firm, that of Fisk and Hatch, failed on the following day. Runs on the banks began, and a bank and a trust company were obliged to close on Saturday, September 20; the trust company had loaned heavily to the Lake Shore and Michigan Southern Railroad. The Stock Exchange was thereupon closed for ten days because the system of settling by certified checks had broken down completely. Sixty million of call loans secured by Stock Exchange collateral were still outstanding; the banks did not dare sell them before the Exchange closed, and could not sell them thereafter. In the meantime the country correspondent banks were recalling their funds, and New York bank reserves declined *pari passu* with the country deposits.

During this crisis the Treasury was quite willing to assist the money market by releasing funds through bond purchases, but unfortunately its cash reserve was smaller than usual because of the decline in imports. After purchase of 13 million of bonds during the early days of the crisis, it could buy no more and was obliged to withdraw from the market. It did, however, reissue 26 million of the greenbacks which had previously been taken out of circulation. The only other device which might have been used, the purchase of foreign exchange with Treasury funds, would certainly have been extralegal if not actually illegal, and the Secretary was not willing to go so far.

This situation left the banks of New York under the necessity of organizing their own relief, and they turned to the device which they had used in previous emergencies, the issue of Clearing House loan certificates. The committee of the Clearing House issued the certificates either against the full value of bonds offered as collateral, or against 75 percent of the value of commercial bills receivable. The total reached nearly 27 million by the end of November. The committee also equalized reserve funds among the members of the Clearing House, and suppressed its weekly reports so that no one could tell which banks had resorted to the committee for aid. This was an admirable arrangement, although in effect it amounted to a partial suspension of specie payments. The final report of the Clearing House committee showed that the New York banks were fully conscious of their responsibility as holders of the final reserve of the country, "in the absence of any important central institution such as exists in other commercial nations."[11]

Resumption of Specie Payments

When the first Legal Tender Act was passed, on the grounds of urgent need, it was taken for granted by members of Congress as well as by government officials that this was a temporary expedient and that, as soon as the war was over, there would be a return to specie payments. The sincerity of this intention was evidenced by the inclusion in the Act itself of a provision for converting greenbacks into 6 percent bonds or for taking them on deposit at the Treasury at 6 percent interest.

The problem of resumption was made more difficult by the judicial wavering as to the constitutionality of the legal tender notes. The first decision on the subject had been made by the New York Supreme Court in 1863; it upheld the right of the government, on the grounds of war necessity, to make its notes a legal tender. All the state courts except that of Pennsylvania followed the lead of New York.

When, however, the famous case of Hepburn v. Griswold reached the Supreme Court of the United States, it was argued and reargued, and the decision was finally rendered in the negative. By that time, the December term of 1869, the Chief Justice of the court was the same Mr. Chase who as Secretary of the Treasury had affirmed the constitutionality of the legal tender notes. He now reversed his position and was upheld by his colleagues in a four to three decision. The motives of the Chief Justice have been subjected to severe scrutiny by historians, and there seems to be little doubt that his hope of obtaining the presidential nomination of his party played a role in this change of opinion.

Shortly after this decision two new judges were appointed to the court, one to fill the place of Justice Grier who had resigned, and the other to occupy a new place just created by Congress. Since both of the new judges were known to favor constitutionality of the legal tender acts, the case was reopened and five judges against four reversed the previous judgment. This decision in May 1871 (Parker v. Davis) relied heavily on the argument of war necessity, and there still remained the question whether Congress had the power to pass such an act in time of peace. This was settled in the affirmative by an eight to one decision in 1884 in the case of Juilliard v. Greenman.

Although the legal question was finally settled, the problem of future policy continued to agitate the country, and it was inevitable that it should become embroiled in politics. The issue of resumption was never clear-cut along party or class or sectional lines. Both parties did their best to straddle the issue and confuse it with contraction and debt repudiation. The Democrats, although they had tended to view the original issuance of greenbacks as an example of Republican dishonesty, were by 1868 including in their platform a plank favoring the payment of interest on the national debt in "lawful money," including greenbacks and silver as well as gold, on the plausible principle that what was good enough for the plough holder was good enough for the bond holder. Their platform also opposed contraction of the currency. In that year the National Union Republican party handled the financial question very gingerly in an effort to please eastern manufacturers without antagonizing western farmers. Repudiation of the national debt, their platform declared, would be "a national crime," but the rate of interest on the debt should be reduced.

The Republican victory and the election of Grant in 1868 made possible the passage of the Public Credit Act of March 1869.* With the general prosperity of these years and rising real income after 1870 in spite of the falling price level, the controversy died down temporarily. Secretary Boutwell was busy with his refunding operations and had little interest in resumption. The party platforms of 1872 were again ambiguous on the question. The Republicans denounced repudiation of the debt, but praised the greenbacks, and implied that resumption would come about without further currency contraction, through economic growth. The Democrats and Liberal Republicans favored speedy resumption, but their candidate for the presidency was Horace Greeley whose slogan, "The way to resume is to resume" could hardly be taken seriously. Both parties were more concerned with grants of free land to the railroads than with the currency. In spite of railroad and gold scandals, the Republicans were able to reelect Grant as president.

The panic of 1873 brought a temporary end to the period of expansion and increased the inflationist sentiment in many parts of the country. Some agricultural areas, traditionally antibank and pro-hard-money in their attitude, began to waver toward greenbackism, and even some of the eastern business and financial leaders began to favor plenty of money as a guarantee of low interest rates and prosperity.

On the other hand, many bankers and businessmen in the industrial areas of the northeast, and especially those who had international interests, were in favor of resumption. With all the important industrial nations on the gold standard, it was becoming more important than ever for the United States to be rid of a paper currency with a varying discount from gold. Foreign capital was still essential to the expanding industry of the United States, and American securities could not be sold

---

* See p. 178.

abroad unless they contained a firm commitment for repayment in gold. Federal and state securities were as dependent on this factor as were those of corporations.

When the new Congress met late in 1873, it was immediately faced with a great variety of finance bills ranging from immediate resumption to outright inflation by the issuance of more fiat money. The debate went on for months, and eventually it filled more than 1700 columns of the *Congressional Record.* Abolition of the national banking system, bonds interconvertible with greenbacks, repayment of the national debt in greenbacks rather than in coin, were among the remedies offered in these first months of the depression as unemployment mounted and rioting occurred in some areas.

The bill which finally emerged from the Senate Finance Committee was surprisingly moderate in view of the violent tone of the debate, but it did not include resumption. It provided for an increase of 46 million national bank notes in order to give new banks a share in note issue. The total of greenbacks in circulation was to be increased by 18 million to 400 million. On the other hand, it limited the amount of reserves which country banks might keep on deposit with New York banks, requiring them to hold three-fourths in their own vaults. In spite of its moderation, the bill represented to sound-money and resumptionist groups a dangerous beginning for inflation, and they rallied all their forces against it, but in vain. It was passed on April 6 by a vote of 29 to 24 in the Senate, and on April 14 by a vote of 140 to 102 in the House.

President Grant was generally believed to be in favor of the bill, and his cavalier treatment of delegations who went to urge its veto did not change the impression. It was a surprise to both factions when after a few days he sent the bill back with a veto message. The bill was reintroduced but failed to obtain the two-thirds vote necessary to override a veto.

A few months later, in June, another finance bill was passed by a bipartisan majority; it made a few changes in the total of greenbacks and the requirement for reserves against national bank notes. This gesture of conciliation was not enough to save the Republican candidates from defeat in the Congressional elections of late 1874. They lost control of the House and saw their majority in the Senate reduced. Since they had nothing more to lose, they used the rump session of Congress, meeting in early 1875 before the newly elected members took their seats on March 4, to pass a Resumption Act. Some observers called this a form of deathbed repentance; others saw in it a promise of party peace. It was in any case a middle-of-the-road measure, disliked by the extremists of both factions.

The Resumption Act which thus became law on January 14, 1875, was drawn up by the Senate Finance Committee, introduced by its chairman, Senator John Sherman of Ohio, and passed after very limited debate. In the House the debate was also limited, and in both House and Senate the vote was partisan. The Act contained three sections, each carefully designed to appeal to a special group. The first two were concessions to the mining interests and other advocates of inflation, and provided that the fractional paper for 10, 25, and 50 cents should be replaced by silver coins. The second section repealed the seigniorage charge for the coining of gold.

The third section of the Act was the longest and the most important. It first removed all limitations on the volume of national bank notes and repealed the silly and probably unenforceable redistribution of the notes which had been required under the Act of June 1874. Thereafter new banks might be organized, and notes issued, up to the limit of each bank's reserve, without regard to any limitation on the total. This was in response to the popular demand for what was called "free banking" after the usage of the New York law of 1838. As new bank notes were issued, the Secretary of the Treasury was to retire greenbacks up to 80 percent of the amount of the increase, until the total of the greenbacks was down to 300 million.

Finally, the Act took up the really important matter. After January 1, 1879, greenbacks were to be redeemed in coin (which everyone understood to mean gold coin), if they were presented to the Assistant Treasurer at New York in sums of not less than 50 dollars. In order to prepare for resumption the Secretary of the Treasury was empowered "to use any surplus revenues, from time to time, in the Treasury not otherwise appropriated, and to issue, sell and dispose of, at not less than par, in coin" any of the bonds previously authorized by the 1870 legislation.

Many of the conservatives who voted for the bill believed that resumption could not be successfully carried out without a positive contraction of the greenback circulation, a contraction which the Resumption Act did not require. Their pessimism arose from the assumption that holders of greenbacks would rush to exchange them for gold at the first possible moment, and that the Treasury would be unable to amass enough gold to meet the demand. Several factors helped to prove their pessimism unjustified—the economic growth of the country, the favorable balance of payments, and the unexpected and voluntary reduction of their own note circulation by the national banks because it was no longer profitable to them.

It was fortunate for the process of resumption under this Act that Hayes was declared to be President in 1876, after the bitter controversy about whether he had actually won the election over Tilden. As Secretary of the Treasury, Hayes appointed Senator John Sherman of Ohio, who had served as Chairman, first of the House Committee on Ways and Means, and then of the Senate Committee on Finance, and had been one of the sponsors of the Act. The Republican majority in Congress was very narrow, and many obstacles were placed in the way of the Secretary in his efforts to carry out the mandate of the law. A bill to repeal the Resumption Act was nearly successful in the early months of 1878, and the clause of the Act which had provided for further retirement of greenbacks was actually repealed, leaving the total of greenbacks in circulation at 346 million for the indefinite future, instead of the 300 million originally specified in the Act.

The passage of the Bland-Allison Silver Purchase Act in February 1878 considerably reduced the political opposition to resumption, and the elections of late 1878 increased the voting strength of the financial conservatives. Secretary Sherman therefore proceeded with his preparations for resumption. He built up the gold reserve of the Treasury until it amounted to 114 million dollars, a ratio of 40 percent to the greenbacks; this was the ratio which the Bank of England considered adequate reserve for its notes, and Secretary Sherman accepted it as appropriate. The favorable balance of payments after 1876, arising from increasing merchandise exports as prices fell, made the accumulation of gold less difficult, but it was still necessary for the Treasury to sell bonds.

The Secretary was particularly anxious to place the bonds in the hands of investors at home. He offered the 4 percents of 1877 in denominations of 50 and 100 dollars, to be paid in installments if desired, before the general subscription to larger bonds was opened. More than 75 million was sold in this way, an advantage to the small investor as well as to the Treasury. Another 100 million in larger units was sold before the date of resumption, mainly through the national banks. There were several attempts by antiresumptionists to revoke the right of the Secretary to sell bonds for resumption purposes, but they failed in this as well as in the attempt to require payment of called bonds in greenbacks rather than in gold coin. Sherman, who in his earlier years had sometimes wavered on financial questions, stood firm on his plans for resumption.

In addition to building up the gold reserve of the Treasury, Secretary Sherman in November 1878 took the important step of making the Treasury a member of the New York Clearing House Association. This made unnecessary the paying out and collecting of large amounts of specie and permitted the government to settle only its net balances with the New York banks. The New York banks agreed to accept gold henceforth as regular deposits, not special, and the Treasury agreed to permit customs duties to be paid in greenbacks as well as in gold or silver. The banks still refused, however, to take silver dollars and certificates except on special deposit, since they could not use them in the settlement of international balances (although technically they were "lawful money" and could serve as bank reserves).

With the situation so firmly under control the premium on gold steadily declined, and disappeared entirely on December 17, two weeks before the official date for resumption. When the actual date arrived, Thursday, January 2, some of the Wall Street buildings had flags flying in honor of the occasion, but there was little concern in the financial community. The anxious Secretary telegraphed from Washington to inquire, and learned that only 135,000 dollars in notes had been presented for exchange into gold coin, while 400,000 dollars in gold coin had been brought in to exchange for the more convenient notes.

Although the New York *Daily Tribune's* editorial of January 3, 1879, describing this as "the grandest page in the history of the United States" was a rather absurd exaggeration, there is no doubt that under the circumstances resumption was a great accomplishment. It was facilitated by the expansion of business which gradually grew up to the monetary circulation and thus helped to reduce American prices to a competitive level in foreign trade. Moreover, the rate of increase in real saving was at a peak during this period, and it provided a basis for economic growth. The country was therefore able to rid itself of the burden of the gold-premium system. Resumption of specie payments also improved the public credit so that it became possible to refund the public debt into bonds bearing only 4 percent interest. Secretary Sherman reported that "it was impossible to keep up the subscriptions for bonds pouring in from all parts of the United States and Europe. Over sixty million were subscribed for in the first two weeks of January."[12]

Resumption did not however put an end to the artificial Independent Treasury system which was still technically in existence, although national banks were now permitted to be used as depositaries for any public moneys other than customs receipts. The currency held by the Treasury, especially that in the New York office, was still a factor in the financial situation, and was watched anxiously by bankers whose reserves were affected by it. Not until 1888 might customs duties be paid by check.

In the absence of a central bank to watch over the money market and protect the gold reserve, the Treasury had a heavy responsibility. This was changed but not reduced by the resumption of specie payments. The silver legislation, which from the political point of view had made possible the resumption, now became from the economic point of view a threat to the stability of the financial community and the country.

CHAPTER 9

THE STRUGGLE OVER
THE STANDARD

Gold versus Silver

THE resumption of specie payments in 1879 after so many years of controversy was not a definitive solution to the currency question, but it did change the emphasis. Emboldened by their initial victory of the Bland-Allison Silver Purchase Act of 1878, the cheap-money advocates concentrated their attack on the gold monometallism which had been tacitly, although not explicitly, adopted in 1873. In this action the United States had not been alone.

The adoption of gold as the standard by Germany in 1871, by the Scandinavian countries in 1873, and by the Latin Monetary Union in 1874, followed the example set by England in 1821. The monetary demand for silver was greatly reduced by these changes, and even India, which for two decades had been a heavy importer of silver, suddenly began to take smaller amounts.

The reduced demand unfortunately coincided with increased production of the metal in the United States. Opening of new mines in the west doubled the output between 1870 and 1873, and doubled it again by 1893. Inevitably the price of silver fell; from the statutory price of 1.29 dollars the market price declined to 1.16 in 1876 and continued downward. By 1893 it was 78 cents and still declining. There was consternation among the mining groups of the west; some of the mines were forced to close. The country was still torn with dissension over resumption and the status of the greenbacks. Into this confusion of political thinking, the plight of silver injected a new factor.

Background of the Silver Controversy

The quarter-century following the panic of 1873 was a troubled one.[1] It was marked by widespread unemployment and frequent violence among industrial workers. Labor unions were beginning to organize on a national rather than a local basis and strikes began to cover a wider area. When, for example, several railroads, after cutting wages 10 percent in 1873, reduced them by another 10 percent in 1877, the first general strike in the country brought out an estimated 100,000 workers who seized not only the trains, but also railroad yards and towns. State militia were called out in six states and were augmented by federal troops sent by President Hayes. The strike failed and workers' resentment soared; they knew very well that by 1870 the same federal government had given four western railroads as much land as Ohio, Indiana, Michigan, and Wisconsin together, in addition to millions of dollars in loans or outright subsidies.

In the coal industry the blacklist system used by many employers led to secret violent organizations like "The Molly Maguires" who were not finally crushed until 1876. The Haymarket Riot in Chicago in 1886 with its aftermath of terror and judicial murder, the Homestead strike of 1892, and the Pullman strike of 1894 were desperate but unsuccessful attempts by the workers to lessen the hardships of this era of *laissez-faire*, hardships which political action seemed incapable of alleviating.

Farmers in many parts of the country felt as frustrated and helpless as the industrial workers. They had taken up land in the newly opened territories and with enormous labor had cleared and cultivated it. At the same time they had gone heavily into debt for the machinery and equipment which even in that horse-drawn era was indispensable and expensive. Since capital was scarce, interest rates were high. On the frontiers of Kansas and Minnesota, agents of lending banks and other institutions were offering loans at 10 percent in 1877, but demanding also a 10 percent commission; one-fifth of the loan might be used up by such charges before the farmer obtained any cash.

In the south the farmers were trapped by the system under which a factor provided seed, fertilizer, and even food during the crop season; at the end of the season the farmer was obliged to sell his cotton to the factor at the factor's price, with little net return to tide him over until the next year. Since cotton was the most profitable crop, farmers were practically forced into concentrating on that commodity rather than diversifying and becoming less dependent on the factor.

Prices of agricultural products were also declining rapidly in most areas. Wheat, which had sold for 2.95 dollars per bushel in 1866, was down to 1.40 in 1875, and the decline continued for another twenty years to a low point of 56 cents in 1894. Cotton was worth 43 cents per pound in 1866 and reached a low of 6 cents in the 1890s.

Although the trend of all prices was downward in the two decades before 1890 and farm prices declined less on the average than others, the movement of farm prices was more erratic. As has been frequently pointed out, the demand for farm products is inelastic so that prices received by farmers were heavily influenced by weather conditions beyond their control. Moreover, grain prices depended on conditions in other countries such as Australia, Argentina, and Russia which were becoming competitors in the grain markets of the world.

Railroad rates also declined during this period, on the average, but this did not help farmers dependent on one line, which with its local monopoly could discriminate among shippers and alter its rates in ways which seemed unfair. The same sort of inequity appeared to exist in interest rates; with limited mobility of capital among sections of the country, the farmers in newly opened areas suffered from the lack of local savings. And the great increase in new acreage created more demand for mortgage credit which could not be met locally.

To the farmers and the workers whose incomes were falling either absolutely or relatively in these years it seemed self-evident that what was needed was more money. It is so clearly a matter of common sense that more money is good for the individual that it seems to follow as a matter of logic that more currency is good for the country. One rebuff after another from the old-line parties turned the hopes of the disaffected toward political action under their own auspices, and they were ready to endorse any program which promised relief.

The clamor for more money ignored the fact that an increasing proportion of payments in the United States was being made by bank check rather than by currency. Even in 1869 the ratio of demand deposits to currency in circulation was 1.2. In New York City at the end of the war, 95 percent of all payments were said to be made by check, and even outside the metropolis, in one group of cities studied in 1871, seven-eighths of all payments were made by check. The trend toward checking accounts continued. While coin and paper money increased from 820 million to 1430 million between 1878 and 1890, or less than a doubling, the demand deposits in commercial banks nearly tripled, rising from 1026 million to 3020 million. Another factor in the declining importance of currency was the more rapid velocity of circulation of bank deposits. Although rather difficult to measure in this period, it must certainly have been increasing since it was in the cities, where velocity of circulation is always highest, that the use of checks was most common. By 1890 over 90 percent of all transactions in the United States were being settled by check, and currency was used primarily for the small retail payments which were large in number but insignificant in total.[2] This situation made irrelevant the comparisons with the higher per capita circulation in several European countries.

The Bland-Allison Act of 1878

In spite of these well-known facts, every session of Congress from 1876 on, after the passage of the Resumption Act, was besieged by advocates of bills aiming to raise the falling price of silver by increasing its use as money. Some would have restored the coinage of the old silver dollar without regard to the market price of silver bullion. Others would have achieved their aim by giving full legal tender to a silver dollar of larger size to offset the lower value of silver. There were many variations of these proposals, and the bills in the House were sometimes introduced by the Committee on Mines and Mining, sometimes by the Committee on Coinage, Weights, and Measures. In the Senate the fight for silver was led by Senator Jones of Nevada, "a half-taught speculator who had great quantities of silver to sell," in the unkind words of the New York *Nation*.[3] Congress spent so much time discussing silver during these years, as evidenced by the pages of the *Congressional Record*, that it is a wonder any other business was transacted.

It is in these debates that the "crime of '73" developed into a full-fledged myth. Senator Jones, for example, spoke of "the sinister legislation of 1873." Representative Fort of Illinois declared that "This little mischievous law repealing the legal-tender quality of silver dollars was stolen through Congress, as I believe, by being hidden in the body of a long bill professing only to modify the coinage laws, and was not discovered by the good men who were on guard here then."[4]

When it was clear that no silver legislation could be rushed through Congress, a Commission was set up under a Joint Resolution of August 15, 1876, to inquire into the cause of the change in the gold-silver price ratio and its effect on the economy of this and other countries; into the policy of restoring the double standard, and the legal relation of the two metals; into the effect of continuing the legal tender notes, and finally into the best means of facilitating the resumption of specie payments under the Act of 1875.

The majority report of the Commission was written by Senator Jones and concurred in by three of the six other members. It opened with the bland statement that "The question of the desirability and utility of using both gold and silver as monetary metals has been decided in the affirmative by the general judgment and practice in all historical times." A single standard was ruinous to debtors and eventually to creditors also, since "If the proportion of silver and gold in the money of the world be assumed to be equal, the total discarding of either metal would diminish the amount of money one-half and double the pressure of debts." No statistical verification of the equal proportions of gold and silver was even attempted, since of course the assumption of equal proportions was far from the truth. The report concluded that the "true and only cause of the stagnation in industry and commerce now everywhere felt is . . . a shrinkage in the volume of money" and that "the remonetization of silver in this country will have a powerful influence in preventing and probably will prevent the demonetization of silver in France and in other European countries in which the double standard is still legally and theoretically maintained."

Three other members of the committee, including Senator Boutwell, former Secretary of the Treasury, and Professor Francis Bowen of Bowdoin College, filed a minority report which characterized the double standard as "an illusion and an impossibility," and they opposed the free coinage of silver by the United States alone; silver in their opinion was unfitted for monetary use except in subsidiary coins because of its increasing production and changing value.[5]

The report of the minority made little impression on Congress, and a bill for free coinage of silver was passed by the House but did not reach the Senate. In the new session, under the Hayes administration, a similar bill was introduced by Representative Bland of Missouri and passed by the House. In the Senate under the guidance of Senator William B. Allison of Iowa, it was amended so that instead of free coinage of unlimited amounts of silver, only 2 to 4 million dollars worth were to be coined each month. The full legal tender quality of silver was maintained and the weight of the dollar was to be 412.5 grains as in 1837, a ratio of 15.5 to gold. Other amendments provided for the issuance of paper certificates for 10 dollars or more, since it would be difficult to keep the heavy coins in actual circulation; forbade the use of silver dollars to redeem gold certificates; and called for an international conference on silver.

The bill was passed by both houses early in 1878 but was vetoed by President Hayes, largely on the ground that the price of silver had fallen so much that dollar coins would not be of full value and would drive the gold currency out of circulation. The veto was overruled, and the Bland-Allison Act became law on February 28, 1878, ten months before resumption.

The "Crime of '73"

Since the "Crime of '73" has become a part of American folklore, it should be examined with some care. The original coinage law of 1792 had provided for bimetallism, with the dollar defined in both gold and silver. The ratio of 15 to 1 had proved unsatisfactory and had been changed several times in unsuccessful efforts to approximate the market ratio and keep both metals in circulation. By 1860 the only full-value coins in circulation were the gold pieces; the silver content of the half-dollar, quarter-dollar, dime, and half-dime had been reduced after 1853 so that they would not be melted down and exported.* State bank notes made up nearly half of the total currency supply. During the war the metal pieces disappeared altogether; greenbacks and "shin-plasters," and, later, national bank notes, took their place.

The end of the war made possible a return to metallic subsidiary coins. It was an appropriate time to codify and harmonize the sixty or more conflicting laws which governed operations of the United States mint, and in 1869 the Comptroller of the Currency, John Jay Knox, was requested to prepare a plan. After consulting many experts in the United States and abroad and obtaining the advice of mint officials and metallurgists, he drafted a bill which incorporated their recommendations. His report and the bill were published as a Senate document and was available to anyone who wished to see it.[6]

For the first time the mints of the country were to be placed under one director responsible to the Secretary of the Treasury. Details of organization, bonding of officials, purchase and coinage of bullion, technical instructions for minting, and salaries to be paid were spelled out in detail.

In discussing the list of coins to be minted under his plan, Mr. Knox called particular attention to the fact that it provided for "discontinuing the coinage of the silver dollar." He devoted a separate paragraph to the subject and headed it with the caption, in capital letters, SILVER DOLLAR—ITS DISCONTINUANCE AS A STANDARD.

He pointed out that the silver dollar had practically disappeared from circulation. Fewer than a million and a half had been coined down to 1805, and none at all from 1806 to 1836. After that year, until 1870, about 160,000 dollars had been minted annually, but most of them had been sent abroad and very few were in circulation in the United States. During the Senate debate, Senator Sherman of Ohio declared that in all his years of active business he had never seen one.

In view of the charge made later that the legislation of 1873 was enacted through a secret conspiracy against the silver dollar for the benefit of gold merchants and speculators, it is worthwhile to follow in some detail its course through Congress. It was introduced in the Senate by

---

* See p. 133.

Senator Sherman, Chairman of the Committee on Finance, in April 1870. The debate there occupied forty-four columns of the Congressional Globe; of these, forty-two columns were devoted to the seigniorage charge for minting gold coins, which the bill proposed to reduce from one-half of 1 percent to one-fifth. This charge was retained in the Act of 1873, but was eliminated by the Resumption Act of 1875.* The question of silver coinage was mentioned only incidentally, and the bill passed the Senate on January 10, 1871, by a vote of 36 to 14.

It then went to the House Committee on Coinage, Weights, and Measures and was reported out by the committee in January 1872 after "as careful attention as I have ever known a committee to bestow on any measure" according to Chairman Kelley of Pennsylvania (who declared a few years later that he "did not know that the bill omitted the silver dollar"). The House considered the bill section by section. There was animated debate over the salaries to be paid to mint employees. There were acrimonious charges against the nickel miners who would benefit by the change in the alloy of silver coins, and against the silver bullion dealers who wanted a higher silver content in the coins.

When the House reached Section 14, about which the later controversy centered, there was less discussion and most of it was favorable. Mr. Hooper of Massachusetts was so explicit in presenting the section that the Committee recommended the gold dollar as the unit of value,

gold practically having been in this country for many years the standard or measure of value, as it is legally in Great Britain and most of the European countries. The silver dollar, which by law is now the legally declared unit of value, does not bear a correct proportion to the gold dollar. Being worth intrinsically about one dollar and three cents in gold it cannot circulate concurrently with the gold coins . . . the value of the silver dollar depends on the market price of silver. . . . The committee, after careful consideration, concluded that twenty-five and eight tenths grains of standard gold, constituting the gold dollar, should be declared the money unit or metallic representative of the dollar of account.

Even Senator Stewart of Nevada, one of the "silver Senators" voted for this.[7]

As a result of the debate in the House, the silver dollar was retained,

---

* See p. 193.

not as the standard of value, but as one of the subsidiary coins, of the same proportional weight and fineness as the half-dollar, quarter, and dime. The bill was passed on May 27, 1872, by a vote of 110 to 13. By the time it was through the conference committee, the dollar had been changed again, this time to a larger coin (420 grains as compared to the former 412.5 grains) designed to be used in competition with the Mexican dollar in the trade with South America and the Orient. Such a dollar had been suggested originally by Comptroller Knox in the hope that it would create a demand for the silver which was being produced in increasing quantity by the mines of the western states. Senator Sherman declared that it would benefit mainly the people of California and those engaged in trade with China. Its legal tender quality was limited to 5 dollars, but no limit was put on the amount which might be coined. The discussion as reported in the Senate was concerned only with the propriety of dropping the eagle from the reverse side of the dollar as from the other silver coins. It should be noted that this oversize dollar was never able to gain general acceptance in foreign trade and at home it was no more popular than the old silver dollar had been. Only 36 million were minted after 1873, and the demand for them fell off as the price of silver declined. The Secretary of the Treasury ordered coinage to be stopped in 1877, and the law which authorized them was repealed in 1887.[8]

The substitution of the trade dollar for the former standard silver dollar may have been debated in the conference committee, for which no minutes were published, but it created little interest on the floor of Congress. The bill had been back and forth between the House and Senate and their respective committees for several years, and every legislator had had ample opportunity to become familiar with it. Senator Sherman in his *Recollections* said of it, "There never was a bill . . . so publicly and openly presented and agitated. I know of no bill in my experience which was printed, as this was, thirteen times, in order to invite attention to it." He pointed out that during these years the Pacific coast states had six Senators all of whom voted for the bill. They "would have carefully looked out for the interest of silver, if the bill affected them injuriously. . . . But the silver dollar at that time was worth more than the gold dollar. California and Nevada were on the gold standard."[9] When the Coinage Act of 1873 finally became law on February 12,

1873, it was hardly noticed by the public. The *New York Times,* for example, made no mention of the Act when it was passed, and two months later carried only a brief news item regarding the coinage of the trade dollar.

In his report published at the end of the year 1873 the Secretary of the Treasury was preoccupied with the financial crisis of the autumn, and he mentioned only technical features of the law. In the same volume the Director of the Mint, Mr. H. R. Linderman, explained the changes in organization of the mints now under his direction, and gave a history of United States coinage. He added that the Act of 1873 "thus legally established gold as the sole standard or measure of value" in the United States, and he summarized the steps by which the principal countries of Europe had also arrived at the gold standard.[10] There was no attempt at secrecy or evasion in either of these reports.

The International Position of Silver

Most Americans knew little and cared less about what was happening in European countries. Technical intricacies of exchange rates, mint par, and the like were of small concern to sturdy Americans who tended to distrust foreigners even if their own ancestors had come from abroad a generation or two earlier. Fortunately the financial officers of the government, as well as some members of Congress, were aware of the importance for United States policy of foreign developments. They were able to insert in the Bland-Allison Act a provision for an international silver conference to be called by the United States.

As a nation in need of foreign funds with which to develop its rich resources, the United States had long depended on a good credit rating in the international money markets. To improve its standing, just after the war, in June 1867, the United States had sent a delegate to a conference in Paris called by the Latin Monetary Union. Mr. Samuel B. Ruggles, a New York lawyer who had made a special study of currency, met with representatives of eighteen other western powers to discuss the possibility of extending the Latin Monetary Union. This Union had agreed in 1865 on a common value for the coins of France, Italy, Switzerland, and Belgium (and later Greece and Rumania) with a standard silver coin worth 19.3 cents, a ratio of silver to gold of 15.5

to 1, and a limit on the coinage of each country of 6 francs per capita (about 1.158 dollars). The Paris conference of 1867, however, after several weeks of discussion, failed to approve an extension of the Latin Monetary Union, and recommended almost unanimously the adoption of a common currency based on a single standard, gold, with a common unit based on a multiple of the French 5-franc piece, then worth two United States half-dollars or four quarters. Nothing came of these recommendations, for Germany refused to agree, and events in most of the nations were moving rapidly toward the adoption of individual gold standards.

A second international currency conference, called by the United States to carry out the instructions of the Bland-Allison Act, was scheduled like the first one to meet in Paris. Representatives of twelve governments attended for two weeks in August 1878 but the results were very disappointing to their American hosts. Germany refused even to send a delegate. The Swiss and Belgians advocated a single gold standard. The representatives of the other nations, while approving bimetallism in principle, believed that the general use of silver was not advisable until Germany had disposed of the 75 million dollars worth of silver which her adoption of the gold standard in 1871 had released; the adoption of a common ratio for the two metals was therefore impracticable for the time being. Since by the time of the conference the market ratio of silver to gold had fallen to 17.5 to 1, the Latin Monetary Union itself had been obliged to suspend the coinage of silver francs. The United States had already embarked on the policy of limited coinage of silver; it would have been disastrous to open its mints to free coinage at the ratio of 15.5 to 1. The American delegates therefore had nothing to offer as a basis for bargaining, and the conference ended in frustration.

The continuing fall in the price of silver proved the impotence of the United States to change the trend, acting alone through its silver purchase program. Another international conference was therefore called, by France and the United States, to meet in Paris in April 1881. England and Germany agreed to send delegates if the meetings were for discussion only, not action. Fourteen nations altogether were represented, and thirteen sessions were held. There was unanimity in "acknowledging the state of discomfort" with regard to monetary standards, but it was impossible to obtain any agreement for joint action to restore the monetary position of silver. The Congress adjourned until the following year, but never met again. An American mission was sent to Great Britain, France, and Germany in 1885; they reported unhappily that there had been no change in foreign opinion since 1881 and that a conference on the subject would be useless.

No further international meetings on the subject of silver were held until a decade later when, in November 1892, again on the invitation of the United States, nineteen nations sent representatives to Brussels to discuss "what measures can be taken to increase the use of that metal in the currency systems of the world." After ten sessions this conference also adjourned until the following year, "reserving its final judgment upon the subjects proposed for examination"; it never met again.[11]

The situation in the United States with respect to silver had so seriously deteriorated by that time that no further attempts were made to invoke international aid. France remained nominally on the bimetallic standard until 1925, but most of the industrial nations of the world followed the example of England and Germany in adopting the gold standard, as did the United States in 1900.

Banks and Silver

The national banks came under attack periodically during this period of agitation for more money. At first it was the limitation of the total issue to 300 million on which the opposition focused.* This had given an advantage to the banks in the northeast which had been first to take out national charters. When the limit on the total issue was removed in 1875, criticism shifted to the profits the national banks were making on their note issues. It was true that between 1864 and 1880, when the bonds serving as collateral for notes were selling at par or just above, there was a handsome return on bank capital tied up in notes, even when the 1 percent tax and other expenses were eliminated. In the smaller towns where currency was still used for many payments this gave an advantage to the national banks. In the large cities, however, where checking accounts were widely used, many of the banks had abandoned their note issue. During the 1880s the price of bonds rose,

---

* See p. 194.

and the return on note issues fell below that of loans and discounts. The total of national bank notes outstanding fell from 300 to 126 million during that decade. State banks, in spite of their inability to issue notes, found that they were now able to compete with the national banks, and their number increased until by 1887 it was equal to that of banks under national charter. Even opponents of the national banking system and the national bank notes did not propose that the right to issue notes should be restored to the state banks; the troubles they had caused were still too fresh in popular memory.

When the silver agitation was at its height, national banks opposed any change in the status of silver which might lower the value of the bonds they held as backing for their notes. Their stand increased the resentment of western and southern soft-money advocates toward a banking system which they regarded as a monopoly and a tool of Wall Street. The refusal of the New York Clearing House banks to accept silver dollars except on special deposit was also cited against them, although Comptroller of the Currency Knox in 1880 defended their action; with silver declining in value and with international payments to be made, they could not afford to build up large holdings of that metal.

The distrust of silver evinced by the banks was shown to be justified by the panic of early 1884. European investors began to sell their American securities early in that year, as American business declined and silver issues increased. Security prices fell rapidly, and gold was exported in enormous amounts during March and April. The actual panic was precipitated on May 8 by the failure of the prominent brokerage firm of Grant and Ward; this was followed during the next weeks by the suspension of two of the large banks of New York.

The New York Clearing House arranged for the issue of loan certificates, and the banks were tided over the crisis without seriously involving the rest of the country. There was no shortage of funds in the market, and interest rates showed little change, for the market was glutted with silver certificates. The New York banks, by refusing to accept silver in settlement of the Clearing House balances, were protecting themselves against the drain of gold, and were in a position to provide the Treasury with gold in the months after the crisis when it might otherwise have been forced to suspend gold payments.

Treasury note of 1890

The Sherman Silver Act of 1890

The price of silver continued to fall, and the Treasury, in order to meet the legal requirement of at least 2 million dollars worth monthly, was obliged to purchase increasing amounts. The coinage of the bullion was a heavy expense, and the storage of the coins was a problem. Secretary Windom, in his annual report for 1889, described the continuing coinage of silver as "a disturbing element in the otherwise excellent financial condition of the country," and the coinage policy as one that was approved by no one.

These facts did not discourage the silver interests. A Silver Convention was called in St. Louis in November 1889 by mining investors and by the Miners' Stock Exchange of that city. Representative Bland of Missouri addressed the 150 delegates with his usual claim that in 1873 "It was not more than six months after we demonetized silver* till we found our country in the throes of a financial panic, the most disastrous in our whole history." Thirty thousand copies of the 300-page report of the convention were distributed over the country to serve as the basis for a new silver campaign.[12]

With a Republican President in the White House after 1888, elected on a sound-money platform, and a Republican-controlled Congress, there seemed to be little probability that anything more could be done for silver. But four new western mining states had been admitted to the Union by 1890, and this changed the balance in favor of silver. Moreover, the advocates of higher tariffs saw the necessity of winning support for their measure by assisting the western silver bloc.

A new silver bill was therefore introduced into Congress and debated during the first six months of 1890. An amendment to provide free and unlimited coinage of silver was defeated, as was also a proposal for the continuation of full legal tender for silver dollars. When finally passed in July 1890, the Act merely increased the amount which the Treasury was required to purchase monthly. Instead of 2 to 4 million dollars worth, 4 million ounces were to be bought each month at the market price, as long as that did not exceed 1.29 dollars, the statutory price set in 1837. No silver dollars had actually to be coined under this

---

* The actual demonetization had of course occurred twenty years earlier. See p. 134.

law, since it had been found impossible to keep them in circulation. Instead, Treasury notes of full legal tender value were to be issued up to the cost of the bullion; they were "redeemable on demand, in coin." Although Senator Sherman did not approve of the measure, he voted for it in order to prevent the worse alternative of free coinage of silver; the Act took its name from him because of his position as Chairman of the Senate Finance Committee.

The silver lobby had worked quite openly and effectively with the silver Senators, headed by Jones and Stewart of Nevada, in securing the passage of the Sherman Act. Representative Edwin A. Conger of Iowa, Chairman of the House Committee on Coinage, Weights, and Measures, who was in favor of limited but not free coinage of silver, characterized the efforts of the silver advocates as "the most persistent, courageous and audacious lobby upon this question that I have ever seen since my term of service began here."

There were also rumors that a less open "Silver Pool" had enabled a dozen Senators and at least a dozen Representatives to make a profit from the rise in the price of silver when the Act was passed. Direct evidence was hard to obtain, but certainly the price of silver which had fallen to 93 cents in 1889 rose to 1.05 dollars on July 1, 1890, and by September 3 was at 1.21 dollars; in December it was down again to 97 cents. Representative Dockery of Missouri made determined efforts to obtain an investigation after the St. Louis *Globe-Democrat* charged in an article on September 20, 1890, that a million dollars profit had been made by members of Congress. After two months of proceedings, during which witnesses were arrested for not testifying, then forbidden to gives names when they did testify, the Congressional committee appointed to look into the charges disbanded without bringing in a report.[13]

The obligation to purchase silver under the Acts of 1878 and 1890 seriously curtailed the freedom of action of the Treasury, which was still hobbled also by vestiges of the Independent Treasury Act of 1846. Successive Secretaries protested in vain against the expensive and futile policy. Any profit from the coinage of silver was eaten up by the expense of transporting it to the areas where it was hoped it might remain in circulation. Disbursing officers were required to pay out silver for salaries and other expenses, but two-thirds of it returned quickly and accumulated in the vaults of the Treasury.

After the resumption of specie payments in 1879 the Treasury accepted gold, silver, or greenbacks in payment of all dues including customs duties, and exchanged one for the other as the public wished. The New York Subtreasury reported that there was little demand for silver, and that notes were usually preferred to either gold or silver because more convenient to carry. In response to a request from Secretary Sherman in 1879 that "the utmost efforts should be made to cause the general distribution and circulation of silver dollars" the harassed Assistant Treasurer in New York replied "I can only regret that my ability to carry out the wishes of the Secretary is so much less than my desire. I was never of the opinion that the people could hanker much after silver, so long at least as there was a plentiful supply of small notes redeemable at any time in gold, but the utter neglect of it, both in city and country, so far as my observation extends, is more than could have been reasonably expected." The Secretary himself wrote, in answer to a complaint from Chicago that silver dollars were not being put into circulation, that "every effort is being made to distribute them by sending them free of expense. . . . The preference for paper money is so strong that neither silver nor gold is demanded in place of it."[14]

Successive Secretaries struggled with the rising tide of silver dollars. In 1883 Secretary Folger complained of the increasing cost of storing the coin. Four years later Secretary Fairchild urged that silver certificates be issued directly against bullion to save the cost of minting; this change was made in 1890. Secretary Windom in 1888 was courageous enough to reinterpret the Independent Treasury Act, and allow the Treasury to accept checks instead of coin. Within a month two-thirds of the customs collections were being made in this modern manner. Even when paid by check, however, the proceeds had to be drawn by the Treasury in currency, since the check merely transferred deposits made each morning in his bank by the importer. In 1889 Secretary Windom was struggling with the same problem. "No proper effort has been spared by the Treasury Department to put in circulation the dollars coined under this law. They have been shipped, upon demand, from the mints and subtreasuries, free of charge, to the nearest and most distant localities in the United States, only to find their way back into Treasury vaults in payment of Government dues and taxes."[15]

The increased purchases of silver under the Sherman Act amounted to about 50 million Troy ounces annually, but could not counteract the depressing effect on price of increasing world production. From 63 million ounces per year in 1873 this had risen by 1892 to 152 million, and the price continued to fall. In 1893 it was down to 65 cents, and the silver interests were agitating for free coinage of silver without any such limitations on the amount as had been imposed by the Bland-Allison and Sherman acts. Every session of Congress was bombarded with bills for silver.

The silver agitation, combined with a crisis in London in 1890 when the important firm of Baring Brothers defaulted, had caused European investors to return some of their American securities. Gold exports increased, and the money market became so tight that on August 22, 1890, the *New York Times* reported call loan rates touching 200 percent. Good crops in the United States and crop failures in Europe helped to reverse the gold outflow for a time, but by the end of 1890 the net drain of gold had amounted to 54 million dollars. During 1891, good crops again turned the balance in favor of the United States. By April 1892, however, the gold reserve of the Treasury had fallen below the 100 million dollars which the Secretary regarded as a minimum, and gold receipts were falling off.

Cleveland had been elected in 1892 for a second time, after an interlude of four years, on a Democratic platform which advocated bimetallism but only if an international agreement could be obtained for the ratio between gold and silver. The Republican platform had advocated the use of both metals, but "under restrictions" to maintain the parity of gold, silver, and paper. The Populist party had drawn a million votes for its candidate on a platform which included among other provisions free and unlimited coinage of gold and silver, at the old ratio of 16 to 1, and an increase in the per capita circulation.

The President declared firmly that gold payments would be maintained, but the Treasury was paying out as little as possible. In May 1893 there was a panic on the Stock Exchange, and New York banks began to hoard what little gold they could get, refusing to discount the notes of southern and western banks. Some banks closed, and there were unemployment and distress in many parts of the country. A Silver Convention held in Denver in July charged that all the trouble was due to an international conspiracy to demonetize silver. In Chicago a few weeks later the American Bimetallic League held a convention with 800 delegates who demanded bimetallism at the old ratio of 16 to 1.

Repeal of the Sherman Act

A special session of Congress was called for August 7; by that time the situation had worsened, and the President demanded repeal of the Sherman Act in strong phrases which made no effort to save face for those who had passed the Act three years earlier. The debate in the House went on for three weeks. Among the notable speeches was that of young William Jennings Bryan of Nebraska, who for three hours charmed the House with the eloquence which he brought to the subject. Nevertheless the repeal bill passed by a vote of better than 2 to 1, and the Senate took up the struggle. There the silver states had a much higher proportion of votes, since the population of the state made no difference to the number of Senators. Two months went by while the silver adherents filibustered. It was only the stubborn refusal of President Cleveland to accept any compromise that finally convinced them that their cause was doomed, and on October 30 the repeal bill passed the Senate. It was signed by the President on November 1. The cleavage in both Houses was along sectional lines rather than on party lines, and both parties were badly split.

The repeal of the silver purchase law removed one source of strain on the Treasury, but it did not settle the question of the monetary standard, and the advocates of free and unlimited coinage of silver continued their agitation. The uncertainty which was created in the world money markets over the future policy of the United States, known to be erratic and unpredictable, caused prudent investors abroad as well as at home to take out gold while they could. By the beginning of 1894 the Treasury gold reserve was below 66 million dollars, and its other available funds were only 18 million. Secretary Carlisle felt obliged to sell bonds, under the old Resumption Act of 1875, but was unsuccessful in placing them until New York bankers came to the rescue and took most of the issue, paying in gold which had come in part from the Treasury. Another bond issue later in the year was paid for in the same way.

The domestic situation continued to deteriorate. Nearly one-fourth of the total railroad capitalization passed through bankruptcy courts within two years. Smaller firms suffered equally and the number of failures among them rose. Wheat and cotton prices collapsed. The total number of unemployed was estimated at more than 3 million; many of them roamed the country in desperate search for work, and in March 1894 "Coxey's Army" invaded Washington, demanding immediate issue of half a billion in paper money.

The stubborn illusion that more money in circulation was the remedy for all economic difficulties should have been dispelled by the fact that the monetary circulation had increased by about 8 percent (125 million dollars in gold and national bank notes) in the four months after the repeal of the silver purchase legislation, without any improvement in the situation of farmers, unemployed, or debtors.

Although the total money in circulation reached new heights in 1895, gold exports soon began again and climbed to record levels. Cautious European investors were reluctant to have their money in American securities. By February, when the Treasury reserve was only 41 million dollars, daily withdrawals by foreign and domestic groups were 2 million. Since further sales of bonds on the same basis as before would be of no help, President Cleveland took matters into his own hands and arranged with a consortium of New York bankers, headed by J. P. Morgan, for a bond sale of 65 million, to be paid in gold imported from Europe. The bankers agreed to stop the export of gold by controlling the exchange rate. They made a handsome profit of 5 million dollars (some estimates placed it as high as 7 million) when they resold the bonds. Cleveland was bitterly criticized for making the deal; it was a hard one, but it saved the Treasury from bankruptcy. That the President had fought to get easier terms from the bankers was not generally known. If Congress had been willing to make express provision for repayment of the bonds in gold, the bankers would have been willing to take a smaller return. But the risk they were taking was considerable, and they lived up to their contract to prevent exports. By May 1895 foreign investors were back in the market for American securities, and by the end of the year the Treasury reserve was again above 100 million.

Silver certificate of 1896

The Bryan Campaigns

The repeal of the Sherman Act only aroused to a higher pitch of activity the advocates of silver. They were able to draw into their movement additional support because of the recent decisions of the Supreme Court. Not only had the income tax been declared unconstitutional, but also prosecution of the great trusts under the Sherman Antitrust Act of 1890 had been blocked by the decision for the E. C. Knight Company.* To make the situation worse, labor union action had been restricted by the decision of the Supreme Court in 1895 in the Debs case, which sanctioned the use of injunctions in labor disputes.

To debt-burdened farmers and unemployed industrial workers, the government under the Democratic administration seemed as subservient to the interests of the trusts and monopolies as under that of the Republicans. The Populist party had not been enough of a success to encourage its continuance, and the best alternative seemed to be a Populist campaign to take over the Democratic party. It would be pledged to free silver first of all, with other reform planks to be taken up later.

During 1894 and 1895 an active campaign for free silver was carried on throughout the west and the south. Representative Bryan went on an extensive speaking tour. He was subsidized by the American Bimetallic League, organized by such mine owners as Marcus Daly of Anaconda Mines, J. Augustus Heinze, and William Randolph Hearst, the heir of the gold-mining Senator from California. Bryan also received a regular salary for his editorials in the Omaha *World-Herald* which was supported by western mine owners.

Among the colorful aspects of the campaign for silver was the publication of a little book by William Hope Harvey called *Coin's Financial School.* Harvey was the son of a West Virginia farmer, and had been schoolteacher and lawyer before going into the real estate business in Denver. He had great success while the silver boom lasted, but when it collapsed his business was ruined and he decided to devote himself to the cause of silver. His book purported to be a series of class discussions in which the teacher effectively demolished all the arguments of students opposed to free coinage of silver. Since he gave actual names to the students—Professor Laurence Laughlin of the University of Chi-

* See p. 231.

cago, Marshall Field the merchant, and the like—many readers believed that the debates had really taken place. Thousands of copies of the book were sold, and it had enormous influence. A number of books were written in answer to Harvey. Probably the most effective was *Coin at School in Finance* by George E. Roberts of Iowa, who later became Director of the Mint. Another was *Coin's Financial Fool* written by Horace White, the financial historian.

By the time the Democratic convention was held in Chicago in July 1896, the silver movement had become so strong that the nomination of Bryan for president was inevitable. The "cross of gold and crown of thorns" speech, which had been carefully rehearsed at several previous gatherings, roused the convention to the customary pitch of hysterical enthusiasm, but Bryan would have been nominated even without it. The convention was bitterly critical of President Cleveland and the gold loans he had negotiated; it opposed the McKinley tariff, and approved the income tax in spite of the Supreme Court decision. Bryan himself, who had formerly opposed high tariffs because he thought prices were too high, was now supporting free silver on the grounds that prices were too low. In this dilemma, he simply avoided discussing the "tariff for revenue" plank in his platform.

The Republican platform was "unreservedly for sound money," and it opposed the free coinage of silver except by international agreement. Of the six other parties, one platform followed the Republicans, three followed the Democrats, and two were silent on the issue.

The campaign of 1896 was violent and vituperative on both sides. Bryan was supported by the Hearst newspapers, the New York *Journal,* and the San Francisco *Examiner.* The influential Cincinnati *Enquirer* followed this lead, as had the Omaha *World-Herald* earlier. In New York the daily *Post* and the weekly *Nation,* both edited by Henry Villard, led the campaign for McKinley and sound money. With his European background and his close connection with international bankers and investors in American railroads, Villard was very conscious of the importance to the United States of a monometallic gold standard. Joseph Pulitzer's *World* and the *Times* in New York also opposed Bryan. The backers of McKinley were reported to have raised a campaign fund of more than 3 million dollars, which was undoubtedly far more than the Bryan forces could muster.

Bryan and the silver interests were in the end defeated, more by the reviving prosperity of the country than by the theoretical arguments for the gold standard. Both the south and the west were losing confidence in silver as the solution to their problems. Even Bryan, when he ran again in 1900, soft-pedaled the silver question and emphasized other issues.

The Gold Standard

The election of McKinley did not of itself provide a positive decision on the currency. The business interests of the middle western states had finally come to see the importance of settling the matter. They agreed with the statement which had been made by Secretary of the Treasury Carlisle in 1894:

We cannot therefore preserve our trade relations with the best customers for our surplus products unless we maintain a monetary system substantially in accord with theirs: and until they manifest a disposition to cooperate with us in effecting a change upon terms just and fair to all interests, we ought to continue our adhesion to the gold standard of value with as large a use of silver as is consistent with the strict maintenance of that policy.

The western group therefore took the initiative in calling a monetary conference. The Boards of Trade in seventeen cities west of Ohio and north of Missouri issued a call for a conference in Indianapolis in January 1897. Twenty-six of the forty-five states were represented in the roster of 500 delegates, and after several days of discussion they agreed almost unanimously to set up a Commission "to make a thorough investigation of the monetary affairs and needs of this country, in all relations and aspects, and to make appropriate suggestions as to any evils found to exist and the remedies therefor, and no limit is placed on the scope of such inquiry. . . ."

The actual work of the Commission was done largely by Professor J. Laurence Laughlin of the University of Chicago and two young assistants who later achieved distinction as economists, L. Carroll Root and H. Parker Willis. They issued a report of nearly four hundred pages describing and evaluating the monetary measures throughout the history of the United States, and also drafted a bill embodying their proposals for reform. Although it was not adopted in all its details, it exercised enormous influence on the thinking of the country.

The report of the Indianapolis Monetary Commission appeared at a fortunate moment. After the revision of 1897 the tariff had ceased to be a political issue.* The prestige of the new Republican administration under President McKinley was high, and the country was prosperous. The silver Senators who had counted on a war with Spain to force remonetization of silver had been gravely disappointed. All of these factors helped to pave the way for enactment of the Gold Standard Act. When the bill for the gold standard was introduced into the House in December 1899, it was passed with a majority of 50 votes after a debate of only a few weeks, and went to the Senate, where it was slightly amended and sent to a conference committee. By March 14, 1900, it was ready for the signature of the President.

The Act confirmed the gold dollar as the standard of value; all other forms of money were to be kept at a parity with it. The gold redemption fund for the legal tender greenbacks was increased from 100 to 150 million, and the Treasury notes of 1890 were to be canceled as they were paid into the Treasury. Many small changes were made in the denominations of the various paper and metal issues. Special bonds at 2 percent were to be issued by the Treasury for use by national banks as reserve against their notes.

A final section of the Act declared that it was "not intended to preclude the accomplishment of international bimetallism whenever conditions shall make it expedient and practicable to secure the same by concurrent action of the leading commercial nations of the world and at a ratio which shall insure permanence of relative value between gold and silver." Since three commissioners had just returned from France and England with the report that no one would even discuss this matter seriously with them, the clause offered little hope.

The Gold Standard Act left a number of important financial problems still unsolved. Inelasticity of national bank notes, inability of the Independent Treasury to function in financial crises except in extralegal if not illegal ways, differential interest rates over the country, would not be tackled until a decade later. But the question of the standard was

---

* See p. 241.

settled. The increased production of gold after the discoveries in South Africa and Alaska made it possible for the Treasury to maintain its reserves without difficulty, since the balance of payments was again favorable to the United States.

The new supplies of gold also meant rising prices over the world, and effectively put an end to the cheap money movement in the United States. The United States thus became a member in good standing of the international financial community. To have adopted the silver standard when the other great industrial powers were on the gold standard would have hampered her development and isolated her from the modern world.

CHAPTER 10   *United States $2.50 gold coin, 1868*

TRUSTS AND TARIFFS
BEFORE 1900

Changes in the Structure of Business

THE last quarter of the nineteenth century, in spite of the confusion and turmoil of the long-drawn-out controversy over the standard, the labor riots, and the agricultural unrest, was marked by flamboyant expansion in many lines, with corporation mergers, high profits, and high government revenues. It was a period in which growing population and widening markets stimulated or even forced changes in the organization of business enterprise.

Before the Civil War very few firms had been operating outside their local area. The Second Bank of the United States with its many branches had been one of the first, but it did not long survive. Most manufacturing plants were able to handle their affairs with several officers and a plant superintendent. The Erie Canal in New York and the longer railroad lines were among the few enterprises of sufficient size to require new methods of management and financing. There was some consolidation of railroad lines even in this early period, and some pooling of services.

During the war the shortage of labor encouraged the increased use of machinery in manufacturing, and many enterprises expanded to offset the higher overhead costs. Sewing machines, shoe machinery, and agricultural machines like reapers were among the new developments of this period. The market for them was waiting, and there was little or no need for special financing or for special management skills.

In the decade after the war the industrial expansion took the form of an increase in the number of firms, without much change in their size. The resulting competition for markets soon produced combinations in the form of rather simple agreements to limit production or selling. Whiskey distillers, pig and bar iron manufacturers, nail and stove producers were among the industries which resorted early to such devices. The agreements were easy to make but hard to maintain or enforce, and were better suited to regional than to nationwide enterprises. They did not require any marked change in management or in financing.

By the mid-1870s many of the agreements were being replaced by the type of pools which had been in use among railroads, especially among the coal-carrying roads. They allotted definite shares of production or markets to each firm, which was obliged to sacrifice a part of its independence and adopt more careful accounting methods. The Michigan Salt Association, for example, formed by the salt producers of the Saginaw River valley, was by 1876 able to force its members to deliver all their salt to the association by levying a fine of 10 cents per barrel for private sales. Wallpaper, pig iron, steel rail and nail manufacturers also attempted to limit competition by forming pools. These pools or syndicates, like the simple agreements, seldom required outside financing.

The inadequacies of agreements and pools led during the 1880s to the development of a new type of combination, the trust, which was particularly adapted to larger industries where control was more difficult to achieve. Since the trust agreement did not involve any new incorporation, it did not come under any legal surveillance or requirement for publicity. The first industrial trust was that of the Standard Oil Company of 1879; its revised trust agreement of 1882 served as a model for many other industries. All the stockholders of the participating corporations, and the partners of participating partnerships, gave up their stocks or rights of control and received in return trust certificates with a proportionate right to earnings, and the right to vote for nine trustees who had complete control of the management of the business. Trust certificates might be bought and sold, and in 1889 they were more actively traded than shares. By that year there were six large industrial trusts, all in processing industries: cotton oil, linseed oil, whiskey, sugar, and lead, as well as petroleum. As in the case of industrial agreements and pools, many of which remained in existence, the formation of trusts seldom involved any new capitalization, since the stock was simply exchanged for trust certificates.

Although the word "trust" continued to be used in popular discussion, the true trust agreement gradually gave way to another form of combination, the merger, facilitated by the change in the New Jersey incorporation law permitting a corporation to hold the stock of another corporation. The merger movement which was so conspicuous a feature of the 1890s resulted in the disappearance of hundreds of corporations by consolidation or acquisition, with corresponding changes in the size and financial requirements of the resulting enterprises. Management could be effectively centralized with economies of scale and standardization of materials and processes. Specialization of production was also facilitated. These horizontal changes in turn created a need for vertical integration in order to control supply of materials and distribution of finished goods.

Before 1889 the largest corporations had been railroad companies. The Pennsylvania line headed the list with net worth of more than 200 million dollars, and there were ten roads with net worth of 100 million or more. Among industrial enterprises very few were over 10 million; a great many had a net worth of less than 2 million; many were partnerships and many were still family enterprises. The big distributors like Macy, Marshall Field, and Wanamaker were all partnerships in the 1880s. Few industrial securities were listed on the stock exchanges— textile company stocks in Boston were an exception—and there was little demand for outside capital or the services of the investment bankers who had been active in railroad financing and government bond sales.

This situation changed rapidly during the 1890s. A number of factors were operating at this time, in addition to the legal changes, to encourage the formation of mergers. The rapid growth of the market for manufactured goods provided a strong, possibly the strongest, incentive to gain control of the market, and the relative ease and cheapness of transportation were an important contributing element. New sources of power made the use of heavy machinery practical, but economical only if large-scale production could reduce the unit fixed costs.

The financial structure had grown to the point where, if it was not actually an inducement to mergers, it was no longer an impediment. Outside financing could be obtained quite easily by large companies in the growth sector of the economy. About half of the mergers between 1890 and 1893 raised funds by issuing preferred stock, since this was more attractive to investors. The merger movement was interrupted briefly by the depression of 1894* but in a few years it was again in full swing. In 1899 it reached a peak marked by the legal disappearance of more than a thousand corporations, mostly in manufacturing.[1]

This development could not proceed unnoticed, and the traditional American fear of monopoly caused it to be viewed with suspicion and even alarm. Public officials, politicians, economists, newspaper editors, even clergymen, joined in the debate, while labor and farm groups attempted to organize in order to attack the problem more effectively.

The Interstate Commerce Act of 1887

The most obvious point of attack were the railroads, since their services directly affected a larger group than any other. The relationship between the sugar monopoly, for example, and the high cost of living was not so simple as the railroad freight rate paid by the farmer to his local freight agent. It was not only the amount of the charges which created resentment, but also the inequalities among areas and the favoritism shown to large and influential shippers. Even where competition existed among the roads, it often took the form of rate wars which ended in pools and combinations to maintain high rates, rather than in reduced rates. Small businessmen as well as farmers were determined to get legislative control over these evils.

Since all railroad corporations were chartered by states, the obvious remedy seemed to lie with state legislatures. In the western farm states the Granger movement, organized in 1869 as The Patrons of Husbandry, was able to force regulatory legislation through some state legislatures. An Illinois law for example ordered that railroad rates should be "just, reasonable and uniform" and later established a board of railway and warehouse commissioners to define the terms and enforce their rulings.

---

* See p. 216.

It was a difficult task. Even when such laws were placed on the statute books, the courts which were supposed to enforce them were often under the influence of the railroads.[2]

The futility of state legislation became evident when a series of federal court decisions stated that no state could regulate commerce which was interstate, and that such efforts violated the "due process" clause of the fourteenth amendment to the Constitution. There had been efforts even before these court decisions to obtain federal regulation, but to no avail. After the Crédit Mobilier scandal* of 1874, Senator Windom presented a report from the Select Committee on Transportation Routes to the Seaboard. The committee, after taking nearly five hundred pages of evidence, presented a report of nearly equal length in which the principal evils were said to be combination and consolidation of lines and stock watering of their securities. The committee recommended publicity of rates and fares rather than regulation, advocated the establishment of a Bureau of Commerce, and made the rather startling observation that the only effective competition would have to come from railroads owned by state or federal government.

It was not until a decade later, after the Cullom Committee report of 1886, that Congress took up the question of railroad regulation seriously. By this time, in addition to the earlier complaints, there were charges that the anthracite coal companies had formed a combination, that Pacific railroads were charging extortionate rates on short hauls, that shippers of dressed beef were being unfairly treated at the behest of the stockyard rings, and that the "water" in the common stocks of railroads was about equal to their actual cost, or half of their nominal value.[3] Since western and southern Congressmen of both parties were under pressure from their constituents to pass some kind of regulatory legislation, a bill was finally agreed on and passed.

The Interstate Commerce Act of 1887 followed the example of legislation which had already been tried in several states with respect to the prohibition of pooling and traffic agreements, the prohibition of higher rates for short hauls than for long, and its requirement of equal rates for all classes of shippers, thus outlawing the whole system of rebates which had grown up. Actual enforcement would still be left to the courts,

* See p. 187.

on complaint of the five-man Commission appointed by the President, if its "cease and desist" orders were not obeyed by the carrier. Penalties of 5000 dollars for each offense might be imposed for failure to carry out the orders of the Commission; two years later possible imprisonment was added to the penalties. The weakest feature of the Act was its failure to define adequately such terms as "reasonable," "just," and "substantially similar circumstances."

The new Commission was very successful in getting from the railroads reports of their rates and operations and in setting up principles for determining what was permitted under the act and what was prohibited. The enforcement of the Commission's ruling was more difficult; the Commission first had to hear the case against the railroad and make a decision; if the road failed to comply, the Commission had to apply for an injunction; the road might appeal from the court order, and so the case might drag on interminably. In 1896, in a series of decisions culminating in that of the Maximum Freight Rate case, the Supreme Court denied altogether the rate-making power of the Commission. Thereafter the Commission had to rely heavily on publicity to correct railroad abuses.

Not until 1906, with the passage of the Hepburn Act, was the Interstate Commerce Commission strengthened. In that year, after the usual Congressional battles, a number of amendments were made to the original act. The Commission might set maximum rates, and court review was limited. Full reports in standardized form had to be submitted by the railroads to the Commission annually, and also monthly or oftener if required; standardized cost accounting was also required. These technical accounting changes were extremely important. They would benefit existing stockholders and employees, and be reflected in all future financing. Property valuation, depreciation and maintenance charges, were thus brought under control, and a foundation was finally laid for effective regulation, although many problems remained.

The Sherman Antitrust Act of 1890

The relative failure of public regulation of the railroads had the effect of increasing public demand for more effective legislation to control industrial monopolies, which were in many ways similar to the railroads.

As in the case of the railroads, the first attempt at regulation had been made by the states. Some of this action was in the state courts. Louisiana, for example, in 1887 filed a suit against the Cotton Oil trust on the grounds that it was doing business in the state although it had not been incorporated by the state; the court granted an injunction against any further activity. Other states brought cases against other trusts on various grounds, using in some suits the common law principles which made monopoly illegal. Fourteen states by 1890 had attempted to solve the problem by constitutional prohibition of monopolies, trusts, price fixing, or other restriction of competition. Thirteen other states had legislative prohibitions, and a few states had both.

By the late 1880s the traditional American dislike of monopoly, and the unfavorable publicity surrounding the operations of some of the trusts, made it impossible for Congress to ignore the subject. The possible link between trusts and tariffs was also a matter of public concern. In 1888 the House of Representatives ordered a special investigation into the Standard Oil and sugar trusts and "their effect upon the prices of any of the necessaries of life" and upon import duties.[4] Other studies disclosed the fact that there were twenty-seven industries carried on by trusts or other combination agreements for the purpose of controlling production and prices. They ranged from the steel rail trust, protected by a tariff of 17 dollars per ton, through metals, bags, cordage, and cottonseed oil, down to the slate pencils used by every child in school, which paid a duty of 30 percent.

The Democratic platform of 1888 contained a plank in opposition to trusts. Even the Republicans included "opposition to all combinations of capital organized into trusts or otherwise," with a recommendation for federal and state legislation. The chief spokesman for the party during the campaign, however, James G. Blaine, said that trusts were "largely private affairs, with which neither President Cleveland nor any private citizen has any particular right to interfere."[5]

In spite of this attitude, the Republicans, after they had won the election, realized that they could not ignore the trust problem if they wanted to raise tariff rates once again. Senator Sherman understood this very clearly and, in discussing the relation between them, he commented "The great danger of this tariff . . . is that the beneficiaries themselves . . . will combine and confederate to cheat the people of that which they have a right to enjoy. This protective policy must not degenerate into monopoly, —into trusts or combinations to raise prices against the spirit of the common law." His concern was justified, for of all the trusts in existence at that time only Standard Oil and the Whiskey trust were not protected by the tariff. This did not prevent the protectionists from pressing on with the increase in rates to which they were committed. It did however, influence them to legislate against trusts by the Sherman Antitrust Act of July 2, 1890—"a lightning-rod to prevent the popular feeling against the trusts from striking the tariff," as Carl Schurz described it.[6]

Whatever the motivations of those who voted for it, their combined votes were sufficient to get the Sherman Antitrust Act ready for President Harrison's signature in the same month, July of 1890, as the Sherman Silver Purchase Act. The farm and labor groups accepted Sherman's assurance that the act could not be used against them and that railroad monopolies as well as industrial could be attacked through the new legislation. There was to be no regulatory commission like the Interstate Commerce Commission, but the Act was in effect a codification of the common law principle which proscribed monopoly and restraint of trade.

The first of the Act's eight sections declared illegal "every contract, combination in the form of trust or otherwise, or conspiracy, in restraint of trade or commerce," interstate or foreign. The penalty for violation was a fine of up to 5000 dollars or imprisonment up to one year, or both. The next two sections extended the definitions to include "monopolizing." The last four sections dealt with judicial procedures. Any injured party was authorized to sue, for triple damages and costs, any person or corporation that had violated the law. It was expected that this would make the law self-enforcing.

The effectiveness of the law may be judged by the fact that in the next decade the number of corporation mergers reached a peak, quite uninhibited by the legislation or the judicial actions attempted under it. The weakness of the Act soon became apparent. Its phrases were difficult to define, and the courts almost immediately began to deprive it of the little force it had. The enforcement provisions were so weak that for many violations it was less costly to pay the fine than to cease the illegal activity.

Although Harrison had signed the Act, he showed little interest in its enforcement. In the three last years of his administration only seven cases were initiated; three of them were concluded, with one victory for the government in the Tennessee coal case. The notorious Whiskey trust case was quashed for lack of sufficient evidence. President Cleveland was well known as an opponent of trusts, but during much of his second term, he was so preoccupied with monetary problems that he took little positive action against the trusts. In his last message to Congress he questioned the power of the federal authority in this sphere and suggested that the states take stronger action. This feeling had been engendered by the Supreme Court decision in the Sugar trust case (United States v. E. C. Knight Co. et al.) in 1895, the first case to reach the high court of the seven which had been initiated during President Harrison's term. The undoubted power of the trust to control the manufacture of sugar through its refining plants was declared to be no proof that the trust controlled commerce in sugar. It should be noted that, even at this early stage, Justice Harlan wrote a strong dissenting opinion, declaring that the majority opinion had defeated the main objective for which the Act had been passed.

It was during the term of President McKinley that the merger movement reached the peak which was earlier described, yet, after quoting the Republican platform statement on trusts in his inaugural address, he gave no attention for several years to the growing problem. The Spanish-American war demanded much of his attention, but it seems more likely that he did not wish to emphasize the issue. He had after all been largely responsible for the "McKinley tariff" of 1890 which had been vigorously fought by the antimonopolists. His last two messages to Congress mentioned the subject, but seemed to agree with President Cleveland that the states should enact more effective legislation and bring their laws into conformity with each other. Only three suits were instituted during his term, but several cases started earlier were decided by the court.

In two of these cases the decisions in favor of the government confirmed the power of Congress to regulate interstate commerce. They were the Joint Traffic Association case of 1898 and the Addyston Pipe and Steel Company case of 1899. The latter was the first unanimous decision of the Supreme Court in a Sherman Act case; it was based on their finding that the sale and delivery of the pipe was the basis for the restraining contract, and that it was therefore interstate commerce. It was not until Theodore Roosevelt became president in 1901 that the Sherman Act was utilized more effectively.*

The Treasury Surplus

Growing realization that high tariff rates were contributing to the high profits of the trusts, and that both were making life harder and more expensive for the consumer, was not enough to force reform in these areas until another group began to be concerned—the bankers and businessmen, especially in the north and east, who found the government surplus resulting from high tariff rates to be a serious disturbing factor in the money markets.

From the modern point of view a Treasury surplus appears as a great advantage. Even in the days of the Independent Treasury it might have been so had government revenues been approximately balanced by month-to-month expenditures, the surplus being used to redeem government debt. Unfortunately about half of the revenue was obtained from tariff duties which were heaviest in spring and summer, and which until 1879 had to be paid in gold or in greenbacks and could not be deposited in banks. The expenditures of the Treasury, on the other hand, were heaviest at the beginning of the two half-year dates when interest on the government debt fell due. For several months at a time, therefore, the Treasury might be in physical possession of large amounts of currency which would be suddenly released when interest payments were made.

After 1879 when all forms of currency became interconvertible, Secretary Sherman ruled that customs duties might be paid in silver coin or certificates as well as in gold or greenbacks; checks, however, were still not acceptable even if certified. And the New York Clearing House, of which the New York Subtreasury had become a member, refused to accept the silver dollars which by this time were being coined in large amount. Relatively little could be kept in circulation, so that the vaults of the Treasury were increasingly filled with the new coin.†

---

* See p. 256.
† See p. 213.

More serious than the problem of physical storage of coin was the effect on the business community of large balances held in the Treasury when receipts exceeded expenditures. Only internal revenue and miscellaneous tax receipts could be deposited by the Treasury in banks, and these only to 90 percent of the par value of bonds put up as collateral, with a maximum of half a million to any bank. After 1882, government bonds were well above par in the market, and banks were unwilling to use them in so unprofitable a manner. The rule was changed in 1887 to permit bonds to serve as collateral up to their full par value, and to permit any bank to receive 1 million dollars in deposits. Thereafter the volume of Treasury deposits in national banks increased rapidly and helped to alleviate the stringency caused by Treasury hoarding.

Bankers and businessmen still watched the weekly Treasury statements with anxiety, since they gave the only clue as to whether bank reserves would be low or high, with money correspondingly tight or easy. Even these statements were not an entirely reliable indicator of the money market position, because they often recorded fictions of bookkeeping rather than actual changes in the cash position of the Treasury; bonds purchased before maturity, for example, were not recorded until their maturity date. It was not until 1903 that the statements were finally put into such a form that the change in the Treasury balance could be calculated from the figures for income and expenditure.

The redemption or refunding of bonds before maturity in order to release funds was permitted under the law, even when the bonds were selling above par in the market, but private holders were no more anxious to sell than were the banks; consequently, the efforts of the Treasury to buy sometimes served only to raise prices still further. Nevertheless the debt was reduced from 2 to 1 billion dollars between 1881 and 1891.

It was of course always possible for the troublesome Treasury surplus to be disposed of by increased governmental spending. Congress was generous in its pensions to war veterans, and not finicky in its definition of the term during these years. Although the Pensions Bureau had been established to handle all claims, Congress was asked to deal with thousands of special bills for payments to men who claimed to have disabilities resulting from war service. President Cleveland aroused the ire of Congress when he vetoed bills based on the more preposterous of the claims. During the following four years under the more open-handed President Harrison, the outlay for pensions rose from 88 to 160 million dollars.

Another device for putting the Treasury surplus back into circulation was the annual Rivers and Harbors bill, popularly known as the "pork barrel." Enormous amounts were appropriated for the improvement of navigation on streams which could hardly float a rowboat, or for harbors where no ships ever docked. An appropriation of 18.7 million dollars for such purposes was vetoed by President Arthur in 1882 but was passed over his veto. In 1887 it was suggested quite seriously by James G. Blaine, the unsuccessful Republican contender for the presidency, that the surplus might be spent on coastal fortifications or, following the unhappy precedent of 1837, that it might be divided among the states.

The Treasury surplus reached a high point in the middle of the year 1888 and began to decline when a short depression reduced imports and customs revenues. Treasury deposits in national banks were gradually drawn down and bond redemptions were discontinued. When serious stringency developed in the money market in August 1890, the Treasury was able to prepay some interest on its bonds and during the next four months redeemed nearly 100 million dollars worth of bonds in order to assist the money market. This so depleted the Treasury that during the Baring crisis in London in the middle of November no further aid could be given. The banks in New York survived the crisis by issuing Clearing House certificates and avoided suspension, but there were several occasions when the call loan rate went above 180 percent.

The dependence of bank reserves on the fluctuations of the Treasury balance became even more dangerous when the surplus turned into a deficit during the last quarter of 1891. For reasons largely connected with the currency controversy the proportion of gold paid into the Treasury for customs duties was declining at the same time that gold exports were increasing. When a series of railroad and bank failures began in May 1893, and bank loans contracted by 15 percent in the next five months, the Treasury was impotent to assist; indeed it had to call on the banks for aid in one of the most humiliating episodes in the chronicles of the national government.*

---

* See p. 215.

Tariff Legislation; Income Tax Provision

In spite of the problems created by the excessive tariff revenues, few changes of importance had been made in the rates during the two decades following the war, and there was little direct attack on the high duties. The tariff was mentioned in nearly every political platform of these years, but usually in terms too ambiguous to serve as a real campaign issue. The Democrats in 1876, for example, denounced the high tariff which had "impoverished many industries to subsidize a few" and which "costs the people five times more than it produces to the treasury"; they demanded that "all custom-house taxation shall be only for revenue." The Independent Greenback and the Prohibition parties that year concentrated on their own special reform proposals and ignored the tariff. The Republicans declared that the tariff "should be so adjusted as to promote the interests of American labor and advance the prosperity of the whole country." Campaign speeches of all parties took for granted that some protection was necessary in order to maintain employment.

In 1880 the Democrats came out even more explicitly for a tariff for revenue only. Again the radical parties were silent on the tariff, while the Republicans claimed credit for the favorable balance of trade and insisted that "duties levied for the purpose of revenue should so discriminate as to favor American labor."

During these years the ratio of duties collected to the value of dutiable imports remained almost constant—at a few points above or below 45 percent. The ratio of duties to all imports declined somewhat because certain commodities were no longer dutiable; coffee, tea, cocoa, and quinine had been put back on the free list where they had usually been before the war. Since they were not produced in this country, there was no group to demand their protection. The great industries of the country, however, which had long since passed the infant stage, had succeeded not only in maintaining the tariff walls which protected them, but even in raising them.

Rising protests against the high tariffs led Congress in 1882 to appoint a Tariff Commission to report at the next session what changes it considered desirable, in order to establish "a judicious tariff or a revision of the existing tariff upon a scale of justice to all interests." Six of the nine members were frankly representatives of protected industries, and the chairman was Secretary of the Wool Manufacturers' Association. They listened to 604 witnesses in 29 cities, and presented a two-volume report of 2600 pages which began with the statement, unexpected from such a group, that "a substantial reduction of the tariff is demanded, not by a mere indiscriminate popular clamor, but by the best conservative opinion of the country."[7] The Commission declared that it had sought to present recommendations which would result in reductions averaging 20 to 25 percent.

The rest of the report did not bear out this statement. Quinine was left on the free list, but very few reductions were proposed for articles imported in large amount. On steel rails, which were among the more important of these, the rates were raised in effect by changes in classification. The lowered rates on wool imports applied only to grades which were seldom imported; on dress goods the rates were substantially increased. When Congress took up the report, acting in haste because Democrats would be in control in March 1883, there had been so much juggling of the rates that nobody knew exactly what the changes would amount to, and the actual reduction, instead of 20 percent, was estimated at 4 percent. The Tariff Act of 1883 was summarized as "a half-hearted attempt on the part of those wishing to maintain a system of high protection, to make some concession to a public demand for a more moderate tariff system."[8]

In the elections of the next year the Republicans lost not only control of the House but also the presidency. The victory of Cleveland over Blaine was due to a variety of factors and could not be credited entirely to his advocacy of freer trade. It did, however, give new vigor to the campaign for tariff reduction. A National Tariff Reform League was organized late in 1885, headed by David A. Wells* who had been Special Commissioner of the Revenue for several years after the war. His arguments for lowering the tariff had gone unheeded at that time; now he had another opportunity to plead his cause. In his report for 1885 Secretary of the Treasury Manning also urged reform of the customs laws, "a chaos rather than a system" inherited from the war, stressing the burden of the existing high rates on workers and producers.

---

* See p. 182.

The tariff became a more important issue than silver in the Congressional elections of 1886, but the results were inconclusive. It seemed impossible to force Congress to take any action on the tariff which would solve the problem of the surplus. Almost in desperation, President Cleveland decided to take the unprecedented step of devoting his entire message of December 1887 to the subject of the tariff. He described it as a "vicious, inequitable and illogical source of unnecessary taxation." He demonstrated the burden to the consumer, the workingman, and the farmer of the high prices it caused, and stressed the relationship between the tariff and the trusts it protected. The argument of the protectionists that the tariff was necessary in order to maintain employment and provide high wages for workers was demolished by the facts he cited: that only 15 percent of all workers were in the protected industries; and that the wages they received were not the highest. He might have added that, even under the existing high tariff rates, there had been 1 million unemployed workers in the country in the year ending July 1885 out of a labor force of about 20 million.

This straightforward attack on the mystique of protection cleared the air for the campaign of 1888. The Democratic platform endorsed the President's position on the tariff, but supinely added "with due allowance for the difference between the wages of American and foreign labor." The Republicans concentrated their campaign attacks on the danger of free trade and declared themselves "Uncompromisingly in favor of the American system of protection." They were willing to reduce internal revenue taxes on tobacco and on spirits used in the arts, but they opposed the "surrender of any part of our protective system at the joint behests of the whiskey trusts and the agents of foreign manufacturers." This appeal to the virtuous and the patriotic, aided by financial support from manufacturers and big business, won the election for the Republicans.

They had not, however, stilled the demand for tariff reform, which from this time on was closely tied to the demand for regulation of the trusts. In his last message before leaving office, in December 1888, Cleveland again called attention to the tariff and the resulting Treasury surplus, as well as to the responsibility of the high tariff for the "trusts, combinations, and monopolies" which were "largely built upon undue exactions from the masses of our people."

Although Cleveland received a majority of the popular vote in 1888, the Republican candidate had a majority in the Electoral College, and Harrison became President. This was hardly evidence that the voters approved the policy of protection, but the Republicans hastened to take advantage of the change in administration. The result was the McKinley tariff, named for the chairman of the House Committee on Ways and Means who later became President.

The general effect of the Act which went into effect in October 1890 was in the upward direction, in spite of a few reductions. Tea, coffee, and cocoa remained on the free list. Raw sugar was put on the free list, but a duty of one-half cent per pound was levied on refined sugar in order to protect the influential sugar refiners; at the same time a bounty of 2 cents a pound (the rate of the former duty) was granted to domestic producers who contributed only one-eighth of the total. The stock of the American Sugar Refining Company tripled in price in the next three years.

The wool and woolens schedule was again one of the most sharply debated. On carpet wool, almost all of which came from abroad, a complicated set of *ad valorem* duties combined with ambiguous specifications effectively increased the burden to the consumer of carpeting for his home. Wool manufacturers opposed the tariff on wool because it increased their costs. In order to compensate them, the rates on woolen cloth were increased by a reclassification which put the cheaper grades under the same duty as had formerly been levied on the higher grades. An elaborate combination of specific and *ad valorem* rates made it more difficult than ever to compute the final effect, but many fabrics paid more than 100 percent of their foreign value in duties. Similar manipulation of the rates on cotton cloth and knit goods increased and sometimes doubled the tariff formerly levied.

No change was made in the duty on pig iron, and on steel rails the rate was reduced by a small amount. On tin plate, however, a duty of 2.2 cents per pound was levied, about double the previous rate; the provision was added that the duty would be abolished in 1897 if domestic production had not in the meantime increased to one-third of the average imports. This was one of the few genuine cases of protection for an infant industry, and the domestic production did increase.

The complaints of farmers about the high cost of farm machinery were met, not by reducing the high duties on machinery, but by increasing the duties on agricultural products. Since most farm produce was exported rather than imported, this protection was illusory. Wheat farmers did not succeed in getting binder twine on the free list, and southern cotton growers continued to pay duty on the cotton bagging they used. Hides were kept on the free list in order to encourage South American countries to buy in the United States. Farmers paid far more in the extra cost of their woolen clothing than they received in higher prices for their protected wool clip.

The best feature of the law was probably the provision for reciprocity treaties, which for almost the first time in American tariff debates admitted that foreign trade might be advantageous to both parties, and that certain details of the tariff might be entrusted to the Executive rather than to the lengthy bargaining in Congress. Under this section of the law, treaties were concluded with a number of Central and South American countries which resulted in the lowering of import duties on their products; on the other hand, duties were imposed on sugar, tea, coffee, and hides from Venezuela, Columbia, and Haiti because they were considered to have imposed unjust or unreasonable duties on some American products. The total effect of the reciprocity clauses was very small, and they were repealed in the Tariff Act of 1894, but the idea was picked up in later legislation and became important in 1934. Only the reciprocity arrangement with respect to Hawaiian sugar, which had been separately enacted in 1876, remained in force throughout the period; its motivation had been political rather than economic, and it resulted in enormous profits for the American sugar producers in Hawaii without benefiting American consumers at home.

In spite of the reciprocity features and the slightly longer free list, the bill as a whole was regarded as the most protective tariff that had ever been enacted. It even for the first time levied a duty on goods brought back by travelers if the total value exceeded 500 dollars.

The vote on the bill was on strictly party lines, western Republicans supporting the higher tariff in return for eastern support of silver legislation. It was passed only after the Sherman Silver Purchase Act and the Sherman Antitrust Act had become laws. *Harper's Weekly* referred to the fact that "the possible and alleged bargains between friends of free silver and friends of the McKinley tariff naturally disturb the public mind," and the *New York Times* editorialized that the "Sherman Silver-Purchase act of 1890 was supported by the Republican Party and passed as the price of the votes of the Republican silver highwaymen for the McKinley tariff."[9]

The effect of the higher duties became apparent very quickly. Even before the rates went into operation, storekeepers were urging their customers to stock up while prices were still low. Cloth and clothing and household furnishings increased in price. Although sugar was slightly cheaper, flour and meat and coal were more expensive. Canned fruits and vegetables cost more because of the increased tariff on tin plate.

Two years later Cleveland was returned to the presidency, and the Democrats came into control of the Senate as well as of the House. Unfortunately for the prospects of tariff reform, the silver problem had by this time become so acute, and the accompanying commercial crisis so severe, that the first efforts of the administration had to be concentrated on legislation to correct that situation. By the time the silver purchase law was repealed the Democratic party was deeply divided and no thoroughgoing reform of the tariff was possible.

In 1894 a few changes were made in the tariff, and raw wool was put on the free list for the first time in decades. The really surprising feature was the inclusion of an income tax, which had been an unpopular measure for Civil War financing and had been advocated occasionally in campaign platforms during the 1870s and 1880s by Democrats and reform parties. No serious attempt to revive it was made until the return of Cleveland to the presidency. When it became clear that not much tariff reform could be expected from Congress, several income tax amendments were brought in. The only one to obtain approval was supported by Bryan and other westerners. It provided for a tax on all personal and corporate income over 4000 dollars at a flat rate of 2 percent, with an exemption for income from United States bonds. In spite of the six and one-half columns of fine print text of the bill in the Congressional Record, the bill was badly drawn and would have been difficult to enforce.

The tax on incomes might have helped to allay the discontent of the agricultural and Populist groups. However, the Supreme Court declared it unconstitutional, by a vote of 5 to 4, on the grounds that it was neither a direct tax based on population nor an excise tax.* The closeness of the decision, and the class consciousness evidenced by the lawyers arguing against the bill, created dreadful excitement and convinced the Populist groups more than ever that the federal government was run by and for the rich and privileged.

Although the tariff of 1894 was so unsatisfactory to the majority of Democrats that Cleveland refused to sign it and it became law without his name, it was equally unsatisfactory to the Republicans. President McKinley called an extra session of Congress in March 1897 to legislate only on the revenue and the tariff, ignoring the currency question which had been the principal issue of the campaign. The approaching war with Spain made the reduction in federal income a matter of concern, and the failure of the income tax as a resource seemed to point inevitably to an increase in tariff rates as the solution. Within three days the House was presented with a bill, and within two weeks it was passed. The Senate did not act quite so hastily, but passed the bill with 872 amendments early in July. By the 24th of that month the conference committee had completed its work and the bill became law. Its passage had been assured, according to the *New York Times,* by the successful negotiation of a treaty with a sufficient number of free-silver Senators from the west, since the Republicans had only an exact half of the Senate.[10]

The general trend of the Dingley tariff was upward, as was to be expected. From the free list were removed salt, cotton bagging, hides, and, most important of all, wool, and rates on woolen cloth were increased. Combinations of specific and *ad valorem* duties were levied on such manufactured goods as pocket knives, guns, and razors. The 1894 duty on raw sugar was increased, and a compensating increase made for refined sugar. Taking wool and hides off the free list had been aimed at satisfying the farmer. A similar desire to satisfy the silver interests of the western states accounted for the increased duty on lead.

One of the few good features of the Dingley tariff was restoration of the provisions for reciprocity, which had been omitted from the Act of 1894. The law of 1890 permitted the President to impose duties under certain conditions; the new law permitted him to reduce duties on certain

---

* See p. 218.

commodities, in return for concessions by the foreign country. This tariff remained in force through a series of Republican administrations, until 1909, a longer period than any previous tariff had survived. Although it raised many rates, the country was so preoccupied with the currency contest and the Spanish war, and so lulled by the increasing prosperity after the war, that the agitation for tariff reform was quiescent for a time.

CHAPTER 11

FINANCIAL REFORM BEFORE WORLD WAR I

THE financial era which followed the passage of the Gold Standard Act of 1900 might be viewed in many respects as a golden age. The successful functioning of the gold standard was assured by the gold discoveries in Alaska, South Africa, and Colorado, and by the technical improvements in mining, so that the monetary gold stock of the world was doubled by 1914. This laid the foundation for rising prices in all the industrial countries, and in the United States wholesale prices rose 50 percent between 1897 and 1914, a peacetime record for a period of that length. Except for the short reactions of 1903 and 1907 this was a period of unusual prosperity, with rapid industrial growth and heavy agricultural production. In each of the years 1905, 1906, and 1907, more than a million immigrants came to the country.

The Treasury versus the Money Market

Although the question of the standard had been settled, many financial problems were still unsolved. Among the more persistent was that of the handling of federal government funds. The antiquated laws which still governed many operations of the Treasury became even more of a menace to orderly financial functioning as the country became more industrial and less agricultural. Successive Secretaries wrestled with the situation, and evaded, circumvented, or reinterpreted the law in valiant efforts to prevent complete collapse of the monetary and credit mechanism. The spectacle would have been amusing if it had not had overtones of tragedy in the crises which affected not only the speculators of Wall Street but also the marginal workers in factories and on farms.

Once the Gold Standard Act of 1900 had become law, the receipts of the Treasury began to exceed its expenditures, and the absurd problem of the surplus again raised its head. Even when imports increased relative to exports and the balance of trade shifted adversely, Treasury income based on customs duties increased. The need to restore surplus Treasury funds to general circulation therefore became increasingly urgent.

Secretary Gage, Secretary Shaw, Secretary Cortelyou, and Secretary MacVeagh in turn demonstrated that they had a far larger conception of their office than one of mere watchdog, and they evidenced varying degrees of ingenuity in coming to the aid of the money market when it seemed necessary. Secretary Shaw was particularly imaginative in his operations. When he retired in 1906 after five years in office, he summarized with some satisfaction the devices by which he had aided the financial community, devices which he considered superior to anything a central bank could have used, since a bank, he thought, would have been motivated primarily by the desire for high earnings. In addition to the prepayment of interest and early redemption of bonds, which had become routine, Secretary Shaw had announced that he would not prosecute national banks which did not maintain the required reserve against government deposits; and he accepted nongovernment bonds as collateral for them. He held apart from the general funds certain revenue and miscellaneous receipts until they were needed for deposit in banks in order to relieve a crisis; the law forbade redepositing such funds, but by this technicality the Secretary circumvented the prohibition. When 50 million dollars had to be paid for the Panama Canal in 1904, the Secretary called on J. P. Morgan (as Cleveland had done on an earlier occasion) to handle the disbursement in order to avoid disturbance of the money market. On several occasions the banks were permitted to count as collateral for Treasury deposits the gold which had been engaged for import but had not yet actually arrived. In sum, the Secretary stated flatly that "The money of the country belongs to the people, and Treasury operations must be made subordinate to the business interests of the country."[1]

Several of the innovations of this Secretary were enacted into law by Congress on March 4, 1907. The Secretary was given discretion as to collateral required of depositary banks, and all government funds might henceforth be deposited in banks; for the first time since 1846 customs receipts were no longer set apart. The currency situation was also eased; greenbacks might be issued in 5 dollar denominations, and gold certificates in denominations of 10 dollars.

Crisis of 1907

These changes were made just in time to assist Treasury operations during the crisis of 1907. As in earlier crises, the causes were multiple: the San Francisco fire of April 1906, which had caused enormous losses to many insurance companies; the heavy crops of that year and the resulting shortage of freight cars and currency; and the inability of the railroads to raise capital which forced them to borrow on short-term notes in order to increase their equipment. To make matters worse, London at the end of 1906 refused to discount any more American finance bills, and this necessitated the contraction of loans by the New York banks.

As in previous crises, it was the lack of organization within the financial system which was the most serious aspect. The New York banks were holding not only the reserves of the country banks, but also large amounts of deposits of state banks and trust companies, many of which had quite inadequate reserves against their own customers' liabilities. Since these institutions in New York City had large amounts outstanding as call loans, any pressure on them resulted in pressure on the commercial banks of the city. These banks had in turn no recourse except to the Treasury.

The failure of the Knickerbocker Trust Company on October 22, after a run, precipitated the panic, since it was the third largest in the city, and not a Clearing House member. Within a few days the Trust Company of America, second largest of the trust companies, followed. The Clearing House banks had to meet the drain of currency to their trust company depositors, and to the interior banks, as well as to their own local customers. The Secretary of the Treasury, now Mr. George B. Cortelyou, deposited 36 million dollars in New York banks during the last two weeks of October. J. P. Morgan organized a pool of banks and financiers to prevent further stock price declines; the savings banks refused to pay out funds to depositors without the 60 days legal notice; the Clearing House on October 26 resorted to the certificates which probably should have been used earlier. Even with all these measures the New York banks felt obliged to restrict withdrawals of deposits by the end of the month. Their example was soon followed by banks in many parts of the country. It was not until the beginning of 1908 that restrictions on cash payments disappeared.

In his final summary of the panic of 1907, made for the National Monetary Commission report of 1910, Professor O. M. W. Sprague concluded that the banking situation of that year was handled "less skillfully and boldly than in 1893, and far less so than in 1873. . . . A situation which was certainly less serious than in 1873 or 1893 and probably less serious than in 1884 was allowed to drift into the most complete interruption of its banking facilities that the country has experienced since the civil war."[2] The one good aspect of the panic of 1907 was that it put into such strong relief the faults of the financial system that remedial action had finally to be undertaken by both state and federal governments.

The need for reforms in the American financial situation was made more urgent by the changing international position of the country. During the first decade of the twentieth century there was a gradual shift from capital importing to capital exporting. The heavy investment by foreigners which had been indispensable in building American canals and railroads and equipping American industry slowed down in several periods after the Civil War and was even reversed in some years by the distrust arising from currency controversies and Treasury deficits.

In the meantime American investors were tentatively beginning to invest abroad. By the end of the nineteenth century, loans to China, Sweden, and Germany had been floated in the United States, as well as to Canada and South America. When the Boer War occupied the attention of the London money market from 1899 to 1902, New York investment bankers were able to take advantage of the opportunity. The United States was gaining experience for handling the creditor position it would assume during World War I, but it could not become a world financial center until it had set its own house in order.

The "Inelasticity" of the Currency

The frequent crises in the financial markets which caused the United States to be regarded as an international financial nuisance were aggravated by the inadequacies of the currency. The very prosperity of the country in most of these years created a shortage of hand-to-hand currency, especially in the agricultural districts where bank checking accounts were not customarily used. The situation in many areas became critical every autumn when farmers had to pay the full summer's wages to the "hands" in cash after the crops were harvested. Country banks had to provide this currency by calling in their balances from city correspondents, thus reducing reserves of the city banks at the very time that funds were needed for foreign payments and for security trading. The result was that financial crises continued to occur as they had done before the passage of the National Bank Act and the Gold Standard Act.

The inflexibility of the currency was usually blamed on the legal restrictions for the national bank notes, but there were other antiquated provisions in the monetary laws which contributed to the difficulty. Greenbacks were limited in amount to their 1878 circulation of 346 million and were also limited as to denomination; until 1907 only one-third of them might be for 5 dollars, and none might be for less than 5. The total of subsidiary silver coins from March 1900 to March 1903 was set at 100 million, in spite of the great demand for them, and in spite of the fact that the Treasury would have made a handsome profit by coining some of the bullion accumulated in its vaults under earlier silver purchase legislation. Silver dollars were coined at the rate of 1.5 million monthly as a sop to the defeated silver interests, and went into circulation in the form of certificates, but this amount was inadequate to meet the demand for small bills. Gold imports and exports varied with the balance of payments but had little relation to the currency needs of the country. Gold was an important component of bank reserves and made up a large share of Treasury balances, but it was not responsive to seasonal changes in circulation.

The total currency in circulation outside the Treasury increased by fits and starts between 1900 and 1913 more than 60 percent, with only the Treasury notes of 1890 showing an absolute decline as they were withdrawn. Only the national bank notes, however, could be increased or decreased when the bankers wished, and this caused the demand for currency improvement to be concentrated largely on the national bank notes. Their elasticity was often of an inverse type, since the laws which protected their value often acted to reduce their volume at the very time when more were needed in circulation. In a period of business expansion, the price of bonds rose, and banks tended to sell the bonds which they had been using as note collateral, thus reducing the circulation. Treasury efforts to increase the circulation often had the same result. If the Treasury offered to buy back its obligations before maturity in order to put funds into the money market, that also increased their price and encouraged the banks to sell, which again reduced the note circulation.

During the first decade of the new century the successive Comptrollers of the Currency made many recommendations for improving the system. Comptroller Charles G. Dawes pointed out that it had required twenty-five days to get out new notes during the crisis of 1893, and urged that emergency notes, unsecured by bonds, be authorized, subject to a tax heavy enough to ensure their withdrawal when the emergency was past. The Currency Act of March 14, 1900, incorporated some of his proposals. It permitted national banks to issue notes up to the full par value of bond collateral, and reduced the capital required for banks in towns of less than 3000 population from 50,000 to 25,000 dollars.

Weakness of the Banking System

This change in the law, although it slightly improved the currency situation, weakened rather than strengthened the banking system as a whole. It produced a rapid increase in the number of small national banks during the next three years—805 with capital of 50,000 dollars or less, and 407 with more. Most of these banks were in the south, middle west, and west, and they provided service for many communities where none had been previously available, but they did not greatly increase the amount of national bank notes outstanding.

The reduction in capital requirements for national banks put them on a basis comparable to that of state banks in many areas. Even as late as 1910 only three states, Maryland, Massachusetts, and New Jersey, required capital of more than 25,000 dollars for banks under their charters. State banks also had lower requirements for reserves against deposits. By 1910 there were still 10 states and territories which required no reserve, and in the 33 states which had a requirement, bonds and balances with other banks were often included. The supervision over state banks was usually less effective than that of the Comptroller of the Currency over national banks, and their rate of failure was higher than that of national banks. The small banks, state or national, were too weak to survive a serious strain and a large proportion of them failed during the 1930s.

In the larger cities the inadequacies of state supervision were partially offset by restrictions imposed by local clearing houses. In New York, for example, Clearing House members ever since the panic of 1857 had been expected to maintain a reserve of 20 percent against deposits. Other banks in the city could, however, obtain clearing service through a correspondent member bank without maintaining the required reserve; many state banks subject only to the state requirement of 15 percent adopted this device. After 1909 the state requirement was increased, and the situation of state and national banks in New York City was more nearly equal.

Growth of Trust Companies

There was one group of financial institutions which for many years escaped regulation and control because they were not technically commercial banks. These were the trust companies, organized originally, often in connection with insurance companies, to handle investment funds. Gradually they took on a commercial banking character, making short-term loans and accepting demand as well as time deposits. They were all under state charter but were not subject to even the limited supervision exercised over state commercial banks. It was the failure of the Ohio Life Insurance and Trust Company which had precipitated the panic of 1857, and trust company failures had been a conspicuous part of the panic of 1873.

Commercial bankers, especially those operating under national charters, began to complain about the competition from trust companies as their fiduciary activities shifted to lending. Not only were trust companies in most states free of reserve requirements and supervision, but also in many places they had a tax advantage over commercial banks and were able to attract deposits away from banks by offering higher rates of interest on deposits. They were also able to make loans against mortgage security, which were prohibited to national banks. The Superintendent of Banks in New York advocated their control as early as the middle 1880s, but without result. New York State had required annual reports from them after 1874 and in 1887 had passed a general incorporation act designed to limit the number of new trust companies. It failed of its purpose, as did similar acts passed in other states about the same time.

Trust companies increased rapidly in number and resources during the boom period over the turn of the century. In the decade before 1904 the number of trust companies in New York City had nearly doubled until they outnumbered the national banks, although the total of their capital and deposits was less. In Chicago the deposits of trust companies had increased fifteenfold, while those of the national banks had little more than doubled. Secretary Shaw proposed (without result) that these companies, at least the larger ones in the large cities, be permitted to incorporate under a national charter; this would achieve national regulation of their activities.

The New York Clearing House banks were concerned not only about the competition offered them by the trust companies but also about the failure of the trust companies to accept any responsibility when there was a stringency in the money market, since many of them were not members of the Clearing House. It was not until 1899 that the New York Clearing House began to require from nonmembers who cleared through members the same kind of weekly report which had long been required of members. In 1903 a still more stringent rule was passed which required a trust company clearing through a member bank to maintain a cash reserve of 10 percent of deposits; the state law required only a 5 percent reserve. Within a few months most of the nonmember trust companies had severed their connection with the Clearing House members through which they had formerly cleared, and the banks had to employ runners in order to cash checks drawn on the trust companies.

The Clearing House had failed in its effort to enforce adequate reserves for the trust companies, but the New York State Superintendent of Banks was more successful. Under the 1906 law he pushed through the legislature, trust companies in large cities, like state banks, were required to maintain a 15 percent reserve against all deposits, time as well as demand, although only one-third of this had to be cash in their own vaults. In the smaller cities the reserve was 10 percent, one-third in cash. After the panic of 1907 all reserves of trust companies had to be kept in cash in their own vaults. In other states the regulation of trust companies was gradually tightened until they were for the most part under the same control as state-chartered commercial banks.[3]

Life Insurance Companies

Closely associated with the trust companies were the big life insurance companies. Their assets had increased rapidly after the Civil War, giving them enormous power in the investment market, a power often used in ways which made them subject to criticism. Some officers of insurance companies were closely involved with investment banking syndicates, and investments were made in securities which offered profit to the syndicate rather than safety to the insured. The companies expended large amounts in competing with other companies for policyholders, and sold to many individuals desiring insurance protection more than they could carry; the policies which lapsed were a total loss to the holder and, of course, a net profit to the company.

The largest companies were in New York, and the three which led the field were the New York Life, the Equitable, and the Mutual. In 1905 the New York legislature authorized an investigation into the conduct of these and other companies on the ground that "the interests of policy holders and their beneficiaries in life insurance companies doing business in the state of New York are not properly safeguarded by existing laws." A committee headed by Senator William W. Armstrong was to look into the investments, costs, expenses, and any other phase of the business. Charles Evans Hughes, who had won a reputation by his investigation of the cost of gas in New York City, was chief counsel for the committee, and he patiently extracted seven large volumes of testimony from some-times reluctant witnesses.

The result of the investigation was a series of laws which set limits to the investment in real estate and common stock by insurance companies, forbade them to underwrite security issues or participate in security syndicates, made it illegal for them to contribute to political campaigns, and required them to hold adequate cash reserves against outstanding policies. Any policy which had been in force for three years or more was to have a surrender value for the holder. Since any life insurance company which wished to sell its policies in New York had to live up to these standards, even if it was incorporated in another state, the law had far-reaching effects.[4]

The Hughes Commission in New York State

When Charles Evans Hughes became governor of New York, a post achieved in no small measure by his success in the insurance investigation, he continued his efforts for reform of the financial structure. One of these was the appointment of a commission to look into changes which might be advisable in the laws "bearing upon speculation in securities and commodities." The commission held hearings during six months. Its report of June 1909[5] was quite specific in recommending that no stock be listed on an Exchange by a corporation that did not make frequent public reports of balance sheets and income and expense, that stock trading be done on a margin of at least 20 percent paid in cash, and that the Board of Governors of the Exchange have power to settle a "corner" in any stock. It did not suggest that the Exchange be incorporated.

Many of the recommendations of the Hughes Committee were adopted by the New York Stock Exchange. It abolished its unlisted department and strengthened the conditions for listing, but did not set any margin requirements. No legislation was enacted to carry out the recommendations of the Committee but, after the publication of the Pujo Report of the Congressional Committee, the New York State Legislature passed laws making it a crime to operate a bucket shop,* to make fictitious sales, and to operate as a broker after insolvency—activities which had previously been immune to legal prosecution.

---

* A bucket shop is ostensibly a brokerage office, but customers' orders are not actually executed; the transaction is closed by the payment of gains or losses as determined by price quotations. In other words, they are merely places for the registration of bets or wagers.

The Money Trust

Another evidence of popular discontent with the financial situation in the country was the investigation carried out by one section of the House Committee on Banking and Currency under its chairman, Mr. Arsene Pujo of Louisiana. The resolution authorizing this study was passed in February 1912, and it mentioned many points which had been raised in earlier years—interlocking directorates of railroads and financial institutions, misuse of funds by insurance companies, relation of banks and securities markets, and "management of the finances of the great industrial and railroad corporations of the country."[6]

The committee did not really get under way until after the election of late 1912. During the following months the hearings, under the direction of Mr. Samuel Untermyer, the Committee's legal counsel from New York, were carried on in a glare of publicity. The reluctance of some of the witnesses to testify regarding their own actions and their power to control the actions of others reinforced the effect of their actual testimony and created an image of "Wall Street" as arbiter of industrial and financial corporations throughout the country.

The intricate organization of the American financial structure was exposed to public view in these hearings. A few investment banking houses, with J. P. Morgan as leader, dominated the field and controlled the distribution of securities. In New York City the Morgan firm owned a large part of the stock of the First National Bank and the National City Bank; together or separately they owned stock of other large banks and trust companies, and through interlocking directorates with insurance companies and savings banks they were able to control in large measure the allocation of capital funds to the principal industries. Companies borrowing through these bankers were often obliged to have them represented on their boards of directors.

In Boston the investment banking houses of Lee, Higginson and Company and Kidder, Peabody and Company were closely linked with the Morgan interests in New York and with Boston banks and trust companies representing most of the banking resources of the city. In Philadelphia the firm of Drexel and Company was only another name for Morgan interests. In Chicago the three largest banks were tied closely to the Morgan directorate. It would have been almost impossible for a railroad, a steel mill, a coal company, a public utility, to sell its securities without the approval of this group, which collected a handsome commission for underwriting the issue. Even the strongest companies, whose securities needed no underwriting in order to gain public acceptance, had to pay tribute or run the awful risk of incurring their displeasure and forfeiting their assistance when future issues were needed. No genuine competition among these interests existed; it was prevented by "gentlemen's agreements" or by "codes of ethics" designed for the purpose.

The power exercised through this network of financial institutions had been strengthened by the corporation mergers which the bankers had helped to achieve during the years around the turn of the century.* The Morgan group was conspicuous in this field. It had begun with railroads during the 1890s when frequent bankruptcies offered many opportunities for lucrative reorganization and interlocking directorates. The growth of manufacturing companies opened other possibilities. Among the more important results was the creation of the United States Steel Company out of what had originally been 228 smaller enterprises. The assets of the combined companies in 1901 were valued at 676 million dollars, but the new company was capitalized for 1400 million. Eventually the company grew up to its capital and was able to earn dividends on it, but in the meantime the bankers had pocketed an underwriting fee of 12.5 million and a profit of 50 million from support of the price during the distribution period. The American Tobacco Company was formed in 1904 out of a number of manufacturing units and soon controlled more than three-fourths of all types of tobacco products except the cigars, which were still handmade; the company also had large interests in foreign companies. The International Harvester Company controlled many types of farm machinery, fitting neatly into the banker-steel producer-manufacturer complex. Another successful merger in this period was that of the General Electric Company, which started out by controlling waterpower plants in eighteen states and gradually extended its operations into many foreign countries.

Not all the attempts at combination were successful. The United States Shipbuilding Company fell apart in 1904 after several years of effort,

---

* See p. 225.

because its bonds could not be marketed. The International Mercantile Marine, in spite of the prestige of the Morgan backing, was another failure. Nevertheless, by 1901, more than 200 industrial combinations had been formed, with a total capitalization of 10 billion dollars.

These corporation mergers produced a flood of new security issues and greatly increased the volume of trading on the stock exchanges of the country. In New York the number of industrial shares listed by 1913 was 191, a thirteenfold increase since the Civil War, while the number of listed rails had only doubled in the same years and was below the industrials, at 147. Banks, insurance companies and a few canals and mining companies made up the rest of the list. There was also a long list of "unlisted" stocks deemed unworthy to be listed, although the Exchange permitted them to be traded on its floor. Some of the less reputable issues were traded on the curb, outside the Exchange itself; not until 1921 was a Curb Exchange given a roof over its head. Rival exchanges were occasionally organized in competition with the "Big Board" but usually were short-lived. Exchanges in Chicago, Philadelphia, and Boston followed the pattern of New York, although they were not so closely associated with banks through the call loan market.

All of such facts and more were brought to the attention of the public in the hearings before the Pujo Committee. Recommendations for corrective legislation were included in its report: clearing houses should be incorporated, interstate commerce should be illegal between stock exchanges unless they were incorporated and subject to requirements of margins for stock purchases, regular reports of their activities, and the like. Interlocking directorates among banks should be prohibited, and commercial banks should not engage in underwriting. No new legislation resulted directly from the work of the committee, but the groundwork was laid for the Federal Reserve legislation which was being prepared at the same time by another section of the House Banking and Currency Committee.

"Trust Busting"

Another phase of the zeal for financial reform during the first decade of the new century was the renewed attack on the great industrial combinations, with new interpretations of the law. When Theodore Roosevelt succeeded President McKinley in 1901, he was already committed to a policy of "trust busting" but his was not a narrow, purely legalistic point of view. He stressed many times the prerequisite for adequate control— detailed knowledge, facts, and publicity. Without that, much of the anti- trust legislation "is not one whit more intelligent than the mediaeval bull against the comet." The books of the corporations should be subject to examination, like the books of the banks, and the results published if the public good demanded it. This alone, he believed, would remedy some of the abuses of monopoly.

He did not stop with publicity, however. The Sherman Antitrust Act had become practically moribund, and the Interstate Commerce Com- mission had been unable to limit the power of the great railroad systems. The Supreme Court had done little more than rule that the Act was constitutional, but had taken such a narrow view of its jurisdiction that little could be accomplished by it.

Announcement was made early in 1902 that the Attorney General was bringing suit against the Northern Securities Company on the grounds that it was a combination in restraint of trade. The company had been organized to hold the stock of the Northern Pacific Railroad controlled by J. P. Morgan, and that of the Great Northern controlled by James J. Hill, and to buy up the stock of the Chicago, Burlington and Quincy in order to form one great western line and incidentally prevent E. H. Harriman from controlling it. After several years of litigation, the case was won by the government on the grounds that, since the two railroads operated parallel lines, a combination would actually restrain compe- tition, and that the principal object of establishing the holding company had been for that purpose. A second important case of this period was the suit against the "Beef trust" in 1902 (United States v. Swift and Company et al.) which forced the leading meat packers to refrain from practices which had given them control of about 60 percent of the trade in fresh meat. There were not required to dissolve, only to desist, but the Supreme Court had gone far beyond the narrow interpretation of the law which had guided it in deciding for the sugar trust in the E. C. Knight case of 1895.*

In a later case, that of the Standard Oil of New Jersey in 1911, the

---

* See p. 231.
* See p. 231.

Check signed by Theodore Roosevelt

court ordered that the holding company be dissolved and the stock of the component companies be redistributed to the owners of holding company stock. This left the control where it had been. The same year the court ordered that the American Tobacco Company reorganize into smaller companies, which it did by setting up individual units for snuff, chewing tobacco, and the like, and three companies for cigarettes. The latter competed vociferously through advertising but usually charged the same price for cigarettes.

Although the court decisions in these two important cases were evidence of stronger determination to protect competition, they also introduced a new factor into the controversy—the "rule of reason," which implied that there might be good or at least innocuous trusts as well as bad trusts. This gave encouragement to the formation of trade associations in many industries, which gathered and exchanged information but avoided the appearance of control of prices or markets.

The difficulties faced by the courts in applying antitrust legislation, and the fear that such legislation might be used against labor and farm organizations, caused Congress in 1914 to pass the Clayton Act and to establish the Federal Trade Commission. To allay their fears, nonprofit organizations of workers and farmers were specifically excluded from the Sherman Act provisions. Unfair *methods* of competition were made illegal, as well as unfair competition itself. Such methods included discrimination among purchasers as to price, service, or facilities, as well as a wide range of other activities. The Federal Trade Commission of five members appointed by the President was to interpret and enforce these prohibitions, and was empowered to initiate investigation of any suspected violation.

Another very important power was given the Commission—to gather and compile information and to require corporations to file regular and special reports on their organization, business practices, and relation to other business enterprises.

The Aldrich-Vreeland Act

The first effort at improvement in the banking situation had been made in 1907 while the Republicans were still in control of Congress. Their innocuous proposal in the Aldrich-Vreeland Act of May 1908 carefully avoided introducing any institution even faintly resembling a central bank. It was designed for action during emergencies, but no provision was made for preventing emergencies. National banks of each city or district were permitted to form "national currency associations." Banks which were members of such an association might, after satisfying a number of conditions as to their own solvency and previous bond-secured note issues, use commercial paper as collateral for more notes. No single bank might have an amount of notes greater than its unimpaired capital and surplus, and the aggregate for all national banks might not exceed 500 million at any one time. Both the issue and the retirement of notes were speeded up under this plan, and it would have provided some of the elasticity which was so urgently needed. It was utilized only briefly under the stimulus of the European war's outbreak in the summer of 1914. At the end of that year the Federal Reserve system went into operation and there was no need for Aldrich-Vreeland notes. The act expired on June 30, 1915.

The National Monetary Commission

By far the most important part of the Aldrich-Vreeland Act had been tacked on in the three final paragraphs. They created a National Monetary Commission of nine Senators and nine Representatives appointed by their respective presiding officers. Senator Nelson Aldrich of Rhode Island was chairman. Their mandate was "to inquire into and report to Congress at the earliest date practicable, what changes are necessary or desirable in the monetary system of the United States or in the laws relating to banking and currency." They were empowered to send for persons and papers, summon and compel the attendance of witnesses, and travel abroad when necessary to obtain information.

The result of this investigation was a series of forty-two reports covering every phase of financial operations at home and abroad, from the First Bank of the United States to the latest central bank in Europe, from the reserves maintained by state banks and trust companies to the seasonal variations in exchange rates of foreign currencies. Much of this material had never before been available to legislators or financial historians.

The National Monetary Commission sent its final report to Congress in March 1912. It included a bill embodying several reform measures which went well beyond the national currency associations of the 1908 Act. A National Reserve Association with a capitalization of at least 100 million dollars would be organized with stock subscriptions from state banks and trust companies as well as from national banks. Directors would be elected from each of fifteen districts to represent banking and business groups. Actual control would be in a committee of seven members, mostly Cabinet officers, at a head office in Washington; fifteen branches would be located about the country.

All notes would be issued by the Association, with provision for increased issues in emergencies. To make membership more attractive, member banks would be permitted to make loans on real estate and accept bills and drafts. Their commercial paper might be rediscounted by the association, in proportion to their capital. It was hoped that discount rates could thus be made more nearly uniform over the whole country.

This Aldrich Plan was favored by bankers in the large cities. It would have made some slight improvements in the existing system, but it would have done nothing to correct such obvious evils as the high cost of collecting checks, the pyramiding of reserve balances in New York, or the connection between the banks and the securities markets. The Aldrich bill was never seriously considered by Congress, since there was a change of administration after the election of 1912 and banking reform took another direction. Some of the technical provisions of the Aldrich plan were, however, taken over into the new legislation.[7]

One other small change was enacted during 1911, the creation of a postal savings system, which had long been advocated by reformers and labor leaders. They pointed to similar systems in European countries, where they were usually efficient and inexpensive and served individuals who did not have checking accounts. American bankers were strongly opposed to this legislation; although they did not succeed in preventing it entirely, they were able to keep interest on postal savings deposits so low that they were unattractive to most individuals. It was not until the depression years of the 1930s, when many commercial and savings banks failed, that the postal savings system began to grow. After that it declined again (and was abandoned in 1966).

The Federal Reserve Act

A subcommittee of the House Committee on Banking and Currency began to work on the draft of a new law as soon as the Democratic victory made Woodrow Wilson the next President. Public hearings were held during January and February of 1913 even before Congress met in March. Bankers representing small as well as large banks in many different parts of the country appeared before the Committee, and financial and economic experts prepared suggestions and even drafts of legislation. Businessmen and labor leaders were invited to testify, but few of them showed any interest.

As a result of this preliminary work, the general plan was ready for presentation to Congressional committees a few weeks after the inauguration in March. Instead of a European type of central bank with branches, it created a group of reserve banks located in the principal cities of the country. They would centralize reserves and provide credit and currency as needed. The maintenance of the gold standard was not questioned, and gold was to serve not only as the basis for the currency, but also as the final reserve for the deposits in the Reserve banks which were the reserves of the member banks in the system. If member banks increased their loans in response to the needs of business, they would be able to rediscount their commercial paper at the Reserve banks, thus providing elasticity of deposits and of currency. At the same time, the power of Wall Street, which had so recently been exposed in the Pujo Committee hearings, would be broken or at least reduced by the fact that there would be a number of the new reserve banks, not just one, and that the Federal

Reserve Board, the coordinating agency, would be located in Washington.

The new proposals were threatened from two sides. On the one hand, bankers in large cities preferred the Aldrich plan of associations with little control or centralization of reserves. They would have accepted a central bank of the European type with power to rediscount commercial paper in an emergency; they were, however, opposed to the system of branch banking which prevailed in most European countries, and they clung to their privilege of holding reserves of country banks. The chief result of their intransigence was the provision in the Act for an Advisory Council with one member elected from each district by its Reserve Bank, to consult with the Board appointed by the government. The small country bankers for their part objected to the enforced segregation of savings deposits from demand deposits but were even more strongly opposed to the provisions for par collection of checks; this opposition continued for many years, even after the establishment of the system.

On the other hand, the Bryan faction in the Democratic party, strengthened by the naming of Mr. Bryan as Secretary of State, still clung to its greenback principles, and demanded that the new system be operated by the government. The new notes should be in effect greenbacks, and be substituted for national bank notes. A compromise was reached by making the notes of a Federal Reserve bank an obligation of the Treasury as well as a first lien on the assets of the bank. They were to be issued against 100 percent of commercial paper with an additional reserve of 40 percent in gold. The Treasury was to be custodian of a 5 percent redemption fund and responsible for the ultimate redemption of the notes. Mr. Bryan also insisted that the coordinating body of the system, the Federal Reserve Board, be appointed by the government, and that three of the nine directors at each of the Reserve banks be government representatives with one of them to serve both as Chairman of its Board and as Federal Reserve Agent in charge of its note issue.

After all of these preliminary hearings and discussions, the bill was brought to the House by Mr. Carter Glass of Virginia, the new chairman of the Committee on Banking and Currency. With only a week of debate there, it passed on September 18 by a vote of 287 to 85. In the Senate the battle was far more difficult; the President himself felt obliged to put on pressure. It was nearly a month before the bill was passed, by a much smaller margin of 54 to 34. There still remained the work of the Conference Committee, since in the course of its passage through the two houses it had been amended more than five hundred times.

The Conference Committee made a number of important decisions but did not change the basic plan of the new system. The Secretary of Agriculture was eliminated from the Board. The number of Reserve banks was set at not over twelve. Government funds were to be deposited with the Reserve banks at the option of the Secretary of the Treasury; the Independent Treasury was not even yet completely abolished. Government guarantee of bank deposits was unfortunately eliminated (and not restored until twenty years later). Slight changes were made in the requirement for reserves against deposits of both Reserve and member banks. An inconspicuous provision which proved to be very important was that which empowered the Board to meet its expenses by assessing the twelve Federal Reserve banks, thus freeing it of political control by Congress. Earnings over 6 percent were to go to the Treasury. The bill was signed by President Wilson on December 23, 1913, and is generally recognized as one of the greatest achievements of his administration.[8]

The Act which was thus passed had as its purpose "to provide for the establishment of Federal reserve banks, to furnish an elastic currency, to afford means of rediscounting commercial paper, to establish a more effective supervision of banking in the United States, and for other purposes." Some coordination was to be achieved by the creation of a Federal Reserve Board of five members appointed by the President for terms of ten years, with not more than one from any Federal Reserve district; the Secretary of the Treasury and the Comptroller of the Currency were *ex officio* members.

All national banks were required, and state banks and trust companies were permitted, to become members and to subscribe 6 percent of their capital stock and surplus to the capital stock of the Reserve bank of their district (only half of this was actually called in). These member banks were required to keep reserves of 12, 15, or 18 percent of their demand deposits (depending on their location in country, Reserve city, or central Reserve city) and 5 percent of their time deposits, to be transferred gradually to the Federal Reserve bank.

Offsetting these new requirements, member banks were given the privilege of electing six of the nine Directors of their district Reserve bank and, more importantly, the privilege of rediscounting their commercial paper if it met the eligibility requirements established by the Board. Some American bankers who had had experience with European banking systems hoped that the domestic trade acceptance would again become a popular credit instrument, as it had been in the days of Nicholas Biddle, but the American tradition of the promissory note was too strong to be changed.

Indeed there were many features of the new banking system which grew out of the country's history and were therefore unique. The Populist influence was strong in the decision to have many district banks instead of one bank with branches, as well as in the failure to abolish the Independent Treasury. The inflexibility of the national bank notes and the instability of the old state bank notes were responsible for the reserve requirements of the new Federal Reserve notes. The power of the President to appoint members of the Board reflected the age-old fear of Wall Street and monopoly. The banking system of the United States, a country which is so self-consciously a "free enterprise" economy, is one of the most tightly knit and closely controlled in the world.

A provision of the Act which became very important in the development of the system was that authorizing the Reserve banks to take the initiative in buying and selling federal government securities and bankers' acceptances in the open market. This provided a powerful weapon for the control of credit, even when the discount rate was ineffective. The sale of such instruments was a device for "mopping up" excess reserves of member banks and tightening credit, while purchases could be used to pump funds into the market to stimulate economic activity by lowering interest rates.

In a few respects the new Reserve legislation did not accomplish all that had been hoped from it. It did not provide for uniform lending rates throughout the country, as did the Bank of France in its much smaller and more homogeneous territory.

Nor did it meet the needs for farm mortgage credit. This had been a problem of special concern ever since the failure of many mortgage loan associations during the 1890's. President Theodore Roosevelt's Country Life Commission in 1908 had included among its recommendations that of better credit facilities for farmers. The National Monetary Commission also studied the problem. The Reserve Act took only one step toward providing more long term loans to agriculture; it gave member banks the right to loan against farm mortgages for five years up to 50 percent of their appraised value. Many state banks already had this power, but it was new for national banks.

Tariff Revision

The banking system was not the only target of the reformers in this period. The general disillusionment which followed the panic of 1907 eventually touched also the tariff, which had not been changed during the years of Republican administration since the Dingley tariff of 1897. The Republican platform statement on the tariff in 1908 was quite different from the truculent protectionist attitudes of former years. They declared "unequivocally for a revision of the tariff by a special session of Congress immediately following the inauguration" and reiterated their belief that "the true principle of protection is best maintained by the imposition of such duties as will equal the difference between the cost of production at home and abroad, together with a reasonable profit to American industries." This moderate-sounding principle would of course have justified enormous duties on tropical fruits, had any American decided to grow them in hothouses, but it fitted in with the popular belief among all parties that high wages could not be paid without high prices, and that, if tariff protection were not granted to maintain high prices, wages would inevitably fall. The fact that in highly mechanized industry low *unit* costs of production are frequently associated with high rates of wages has been very hard for politicians and voters alike to grasp. Political speeches through the years have made much of the lower wage rates abroad, and the necessity for protecting the American worker from this "unfair" competition. One glance at the wages of "protected" workers in such American industries as steel and iron, cotton and wool, should have been enough to dispel this illusion.

President Taft had promised, if elected, to reduce tariff rates and, to the dismay of his party, he used his influence to carry out his promise. Hides, the most hotly debated of all the rates because of their importance in trade with South America, were again put on the free list where they had been until 1897. Coal, iron ore, and lumber duties were reduced; little change was made in the rates on wool, woolens, and sugar. In spite of his effort, there were heavy increases on finer cotton textiles and silks, with elaborate schedules of specific duties for goods of various values.

In several other respects the Payne-Aldrich tariff was a retrogression. The reciprocity provisions of 1897 were repealed. The President was given the right to raise tariff rates by 25 percent of the value of the article, if the exporting country were found to have "unduly" discriminated against the United States in any way. President Taft was opposed to this whole idea and was able, by the end of the allotted period, to state that no country had discriminated unduly and that no rates should be raised. The Tariff Board, appointed in 1909 under one of the clauses of this Act, was useful in providing information for such decisions, but it was allowed to expire for lack of funds in 1912.

The rising cost of living, although it could certainly not be ascribed to the high tariff alone, continued to arouse a public resentment which the modest reductions of the Payne-Aldrich tariff did little to alleviate. The Republicans lost ground in the Congressional elections of 1910, and the House had a majority of Democrats in the 62nd Congress; the Senate was still safely Republican, and little change could be made in the tariff. Two years later the Democrats won control of both houses as well as the presidency, and started immediately to put into effect their platform promises to reduce tariff rates.

Even this Underwood tariff was still far from one of genuine free trade. It aimed to be a tariff for revenue only which would "not injure or destroy legitimate industry." Just how these terms were to be defined was not clear, but their purport was clearly in the direction of lower import duties. Sugar and wool were again put on the free list. Woolen and cotton cloth, as well as silk, were to pay lower duties, and the elaborate schedules of specific rates were abandoned in favor of simple *ad valorem* duties. Agricultural implements, coal and lumber were put on the free list, as well as iron ore, pig iron, barbed wire, and steel rails. Other iron and steel products were given lower rates. On the average, tariff rates were reduced from 37 percent of the value of all imports to 27 percent. The reduction was about two-thirds on woolen clothing, about one-third on cotton clothing, and about one-half on farm products and foodstuffs; the general effect was to reduce prices for consumers and especially for farmers. Tariff revenue was also reduced by the new rates, from an estimated 305 million to 249 million dollars, but the loss was more than made up by the new income taxes on corporations and individuals. The Republicans complained that this new tariff was not "scientific" in their peculiar sense of the word, but it was greeted with approval by the public. The feature which created the greatest sensation, as the new rates were put into operation overnight, was the prohibition on importation of egrets. Outraged society ladies returning from Europe complained loudly and publicly when feathers were stripped from their Paris hats by conscientious customs officials.[9]

The Federal Income Tax

The federal income tax was another reform measure enacted by the new Democratic administration, but it was possible only because the Republican Congress of the Taft administration had, surprisingly, adopted the 16th amendment to the Constitution and had started it on its rounds among the state legislatures for ratification. The Supreme Court in 1895 had decided that only states had power to levy an income tax, since it could not be made proportional to population, as the Constitution required. A few states had made use of this power after the Civil War, and their experience had been only mildly successful. Nevertheless the federal income tax was a favorite reform measure, especially among western radical groups.

The Republican Congress during 1909 was chiefly concerned with the tariff and was willing to accept almost any proposal which would prevent tariff reduction. Even conservative eastern legislators were willing to accept the 16th amendment as the price of their tariff, since they believed that it would never be ratified by the states. Moreover, it seemed a less dangerous measure than the inheritance tax which President Taft had suggested. The Republicans had also to accept a tax on corporate dividends; it was called an excise, not an income, tax, although the rate was set at 1 percent of the net income above 5000 dollars.

In spite of the Republican prophecy, the income tax amendment was ratified by the necessary thirty-six states, just as the Democrats came into office in 1913. They immediately took advantage of the opportunity, and an income tax law was made Section II of the Tariff Law of 1913. It was modest enough in the light of later levies. Exemptions of 3000 dollars were granted to an individual, 4000 to a married couple, but no exemptions were made for children. Income above the exemption level was taxed at 1 percent, income from 20,000 to 50,000 dollars paid an additional 1 percent, and the rates gradually increased until income over 500,000 dollars paid 6 percent. Income from federal, state, and municipal bonds was exempt. Gifts were taxed, but not inheritances. The corporation income tax was left at 1 percent of net income with no exemption.

The income tax was levied for the first time on the last ten months of 1913, since it could not be retroactive. From a population of about 100 million, returns were filed by 368,000 individuals or families; only 44 of them reported incomes of more than 1 million dollars. The yield of the tax for this period was 28 million, far below the estimate of 70 million made so optimistically when the law was passed. The administrative machinery was soon working more smoothly, and the revenue increased rapidly. By 1916, the last prewar year, it amounted to 68 million, well above the 57 million yield from the tax on corporations.

The adoption of the personal income tax was an important milestone for federal financial policy. The customs duties which for so long had been the mainstay of the central government's revenue had, even in peacetime, become inadequate to pay for all the new services which an industrialized, growing population required; transcontinental highways, for example, could not be left to the whims of state legislatures. In the second place, the income tax made possible the financing of the war in much higher proportion by taxation than by inflationary borrowing. And thirdly and most importantly, the income tax for the first time made possible the use of fiscal policy as a stabilizing device to counteract inflation or depression. Up to this time central government spending, taxing, and hoarding had been subject to arbitrary and outmoded regulation with little or no regard to its effect on the economy. With this new tool at its disposal the Congress could no longer ignore its responsibility.

State and Local Government Finances

The expenditures of the federal government always attract more attention than those of state and local bodies, but the total of the latter makes up a significant part of the tax burden. In 1900 about three-fourths of all workers employed in any governmental service were with state and local units, and these figures do not include the hundreds of thousands of teachers and administrators engaged in public education. By 1910 the percentage on federal payrolls had increased slightly, but state and local units were still the principal employers. It was only the increase in the armed forces during World War I which changed the ratios perceptibly. Purchases of capital assets and other assets followed the same pattern, state and local governmental units spending two or three times as much as the central government in both 1900 and 1910.

During this period the expenses of state and local governments were increasing rapidly, and they doubled between 1902 and 1913. The state governments, which except in Delaware and Pennsylvania had relied heavily on property taxes during the post-Civil War decades, had gradually moved toward other sources of taxation. The growing importance of industry as compared with agriculture, and the increase of intangible property such as stocks and bonds, made it possible for a large amount of property to evade any share in the tax burden. Moreover, the administration of the general property tax gave rise to serious inequalities of assessment, and the extension of business beyond local and state lines raised difficult questions of jurisdiction. Taxes on corporations and public utilities, either on earnings or dividends or capital, franchise taxes, special assessments for improvements, taxes on inheritances, were variously used in many areas to supplement the property tax.

There was a strong movement toward the abandonment of the property tax by state governments, to leave it in the hands of the local authorities who were in a better position to assess values. Local government units still relied primarily on the real estate tax for their income, and efforts to supplement this with taxes on personal property were unsuccessful.

The struggle to obtain adequate revenue was reflected in the heavy debt burden of the local governments. In 1913 the federal debt was only 1193 million dollars and the state debts only 379 million. But the local units had a total debt outstanding of 4035 million, with an annual interest charge of 159 million.

State and local financial administration lagged far behind that of the central government in adjusting to the changing requirements of increasing population and its rapid urbanization. The corruption which pervaded so many state and municipal authorities can be ascribed, not to unusual wickedness among politicians, but to ignorance and lethargy among citizens, and to inadequate techniques for controlling the collection and expenditure of local revenues.

The reforms which were introduced during the decade before World War I were long overdue in all sections of the financial structure. They occurred just in time to make it possible for the United States to carry the new responsibilities which fell on its inexperienced shoulders at the outbreak of war.

CHAPTER 12

World War I and Its Aftermath

T HE outbreak of war in Europe in the summer of 1914 prematurely opened a new stage in the financial history of the United States. During the next five years the country shifted from its former net debtor position and became a net creditor to the world. At the same time the war brought to the United States a flood of gold which pushed the dollar into the foreground of international finance, changed the direction of Federal Reserve development, and provided the basis for eventual inflation, stock market speculation, and collapse.

By the end of the war, foreign holdings of American securities had declined from the 5.4 billion of 1914 to 1.6 billion, and the direct investment in American companies from 1.3 to .9 billion. Great Britain, which had held about 63 percent of all foreign-owned American securities, sold back about three-fourths of them. France had owned only one-tenth as much as Britain, but sold back an even larger proportion. When their securities had been liquidated, the Allies had to borrow, and by the end of 1920 Great Britain owed the United States 4.2 billion dollars, France owed 3 billion, and Italy 1.6 billion.

Great Britain was the country which suffered most. The total debt, 5.5 billion dollars, accumulated during the war, hastened the deterioration in her position as a world financial power. The even greater sum owed to her was repaid only in part after the war. Her share of world trade had been declining since the turn of the century, when German competition in iron and steel and chemicals, and Japanese competition in textiles, began to make serious inroads in her former preeminence. This was made more serious by the worsening terms of trade; prices of the goods Britain sold were relatively lower and the prices of goods purchased were higher, so that repayment of her debts became increasingly difficult. The combined force of these factors left the pound sterling after the war in a weak position compared to that which it had held during the nineteenth century.

The Panic of 1914

The immediate impact of the war on the United States, still recovering from the mild depression of 1913, was a trade and financial panic. For several weeks, European investors had been selling their American securities, and gold had been moving out. Stock prices fell with such rapidity during the last days of July that the New York Stock Exchange was closed on July 31. Although some unofficial trading went on around the corner on New Street, it was not until December 15 that the Exchange was officially reopened. During this period, banks were unable to call their "call" loans because the securities held as collateral were no longer equal in value to the loans. Sterling exchange fluctuated wildly as Americans tried to settle their accounts abroad; at one moment on August 1 the rate touched 7 dollars for cable transfers, far above the par of 4.8665. A gold exchange fund provided by state and national banks sold 10 million dollars worth of gold for export, and the premium disappeared in November. By April the pound sterling was down to 4.76 dollars.

There had been the usual panic hoarding of currency by individuals and banks. Since the new Federal Reserve notes were not yet ready, the Aldrich-Vreeland Act of 1908 was hastily amended in order to increase the issue of National Currency Association notes.* About 380 million were actually put into circulation, but the possibility of obtaining them was in itself a reassuring factor; all but 100 million had been withdrawn from circulation by the end of the year. Clearing Houses in the larger

---

* See p. 258.

cities resorted to certificates, as they had done in previous crises, to settle balances among their members; this also relieved the tension and helped to bring interest rates back to normal.

There was grave danger that Europe might not be able to take the customary amounts of grain and of cotton, and commodity prices collapsed. Since the Secretary of the Treasury was Chairman of the new Federal Reserve Board, the two agencies were able to cooperate in organizing a cotton loan fund of 100 million dollars to make advances to farmers caught by price declines. This fund, like the gold exchange fund, was actually provided by the big commercial banks, and in this case, as with the Aldrich-Vreeland notes, the possibility of aid was more important than the amount of aid granted. To encourage exports in spite of the submarine menace to shipping, the Treasury set up a war-risk insurance plan under the Act of September 2, 1914.

The need for these emergency measures soon passed. It was not many months before the submarines were practically vanquished and the heavy flow of American exports to Europe began. By April 1917 when the United States entered the war, the Allied powers had purchased 7 billion dollars worth of food and supplies. During the war years 1914 through 1918, the value of American exports nearly tripled, and that of imports doubled. Even with the effect of rising prices eliminated, the increases were large. Employment rapidly increased, unemployment was almost eliminated, and new workers were added to the labor force. The increased buying power of the workers, and the smaller volume of consumer goods in the market, as production was shifted from consumer to war goods, were significant factors in the price increases which soon appeared.

The First Years of the Federal Reserve System

The commencement of European hostilities just when the new banking system had to be set up made the task far more difficult, and there were some who proposed that it be postponed until the war was over. Fortunately this counsel of despair was ignored. Instead, by an enormous effort, the opening of the twelve Federal Reserve banks was speeded up and they began to transact business on November 16, less than a year after the system was authorized. The transfer of reserve balances from member banks to Reserve banks proceeded smoothly; the change was eased by the fact that under the new system the total of required reserves was 465 million less than under the previous system. Moreover the disruption of correspondent relations among banks, which had been so feared by the large city banks, never occurred. To the surprise of all concerned, country banks continued to maintain, and even increase, their working balances with city banks although they were no longer counted as part of the legal reserve.

In addition to all the details of organization and procedure, the Federal Reserve authorities had to determine the larger questions of policy. The only specific directive in the Act was that the system should operate "with a view of accommodating commerce and business"—a passive rather than an active concept of its function. The first report of the Federal Reserve Board, issued in January 1915, discussed the question and took an intermediate position. The duty of the Board, it declared, was "not to await emergencies but by anticipation, to do what it can to prevent them," adding, "It should at all times be a steadying influence, leading when and where leadership is requisite."[1]

This leadership, it had been taken for granted by the framers of the Reserve system, would be exercised principally through the discount rate. At the Bank of England this Bank Rate, as it was called, was usually set slightly above the market rate on bankers' acceptances, which were the prime paper in the London market. In the United States, however, there was no real market for bankers' acceptances, since national banks had not been permitted to accept such drafts. Moreover dollar drafts had not been widely used in the financing of foreign trade. The banking structure of the United States, with its thousands of small independent banks, was quite different from that in England or on the continent, and the principal form of business paper was the promissory note.*

Nevertheless a serious effort was now made to develop a market in the United States for the bankers' acceptance. Member banks were given the right to accept bills of exchange drawn in dollars (they had always had the right to invest in bills drawn in dollars), and it was hoped that banks might thus be weaned away from their dependence on the call loan market as an outlet for surplus funds. This would tend to make the bill of exchange drawn in dollars a more attractive instrument for the financing of

---

* See p. 89.

international trade, and such bills might even compete with the sterling bills which had been the preferred medium for so long. Acceptances were given a preferential rate of discount at the Reserve banks; at first this rate applied only to bankers' bills, but later it was extended to acceptances used in domestic trade as well.

In addition to the preferential rate of discount, bankers' acceptances had another important advantage; they might be purchased by the Reserve banks in the open market, on their own initiative without waiting for an offer from dealers. These open-market purchases were the real support of the acceptance market during the early years of the Reserve system. Even after the war, commercial banks showed little inclination to abandon their long-entrenched habit of financing customers by means of the promissory note. The Reserve banks steadily increased their open-market purchases of acceptances in order to support the market, since only small amounts were offered for rediscount by dealers or banks. After 1920 the business depression and the decline in foreign trade caused a reduction in the volume of both types of acceptance in the market. The bankers' acceptance drawn in dollars gradually became important, but the domestic trade acceptance was never able to gain status in the United States; it was used principally as a device for forcing collection of slow accounts or for financing installment sales.

Closely related to the question of preferential rates on certain types of paper was that of "eligibility" of paper offered for rediscount. The Federal Reserve Board was given the entire responsibility for determining qualifications since Section 13 of the Federal Reserve Act specified only that the paper to be discounted should consist of notes, drafts, and bills of exchange drawn for agricultural, industrial, or commercial purposes, or of bankers' and trade acceptances. Much of the time of the Board during its first years was devoted to the detailing of eligibility requirements. By 1917 an elaborate structure had been set up, with thirteen classes of paper, each with its own rate of discount. "Short-term, self-liquidating paper growing out of commercial, industrial and agricultural operations" was the preferred type, and was given a lower rate of discount than long-term paper or paper arising out of speculative transactions.

When the United States entered the war, the thirteen classes of paper were reduced to eight, but the whole question of eligibility on which so much time and energy had been expended became purely academic.

Another question of policy occupied the attention of the Board, although less urgently than that of eligibility—the uniformity of rates in the twelve districts. The higher cost of credit, both short-term and long-term, in the west and south had always been a source of resentment in those areas. The Reserve Act had empowered the district banks "to establish from time to time, subject to review and determination of the Federal reserve board, rates of discount . . . for each class of paper." This was interpreted to mean that the Board could not take the initiative in setting rates. It did, however, exercise considerable influence on the district banks in the direction of equalizing rates over the country. During the first months of operation the three important northeastern districts set their rates on 30-day commercial paper at 5.5 percent, and all the other districts set it at 6 percent. Two years later all the districts had rates of 4 or 4.5 percent. In its second annual report in December 1915 the Board stated its conviction that although "it may not be practicable to maintain uniform rates throughout the twelve districts . . . they should unquestionably bear a consistent relation one to another, while a very much greater adherence to uniformity than before the enactment of the Federal Reserve Act will undoubtedly be secured."[2] Even the new resources of the Reserve system were not able to eliminate entirely the sectional differences based on different economic conditions.

Since the discount rates in all districts were set primarily for the purpose of accommodating business, they did not always provide an income adequate to cover the expenses of the Reserve banks. Fortunately, from this point of view, the Act permitted the Reserve banks to buy government securities and municipal warrants in the open market. In the early years of the system these purchases were more important in volume than either the rediscount of commercial paper or the open-market purchases of acceptances. During 1915 total open-market purchases amounted to nearly one-half of the earning assets of the Reserve banks, and in 1916 to nearly three-fourths. It was not until later that such operations were viewed primarily as a device for credit control.

All the questions regarding eligibility, uniformity, and earnings faded into insignificance when the United States entered the war in April 1917. Henceforth top priority had to be given to aiding the Treasury in financing the Allies as well as the United States. To facilitate this, member banks were given the privilege of discounting their own notes with government securities as collateral; in a Board ruling of May 1919 this privilege was extended also to nonmember banks if their paper had the endorsement of a member bank. Banks had always regarded the rediscounting of customers' paper as a confession of weakness, and they eagerly accepted this alternative. Since these notes were secured by government obligations, they were given a preferential rate of discount, and banks could borrow at a low rate and lend at a higher rate, a strong inducement to participate in the "Borrow and Buy" campaigns for selling Liberty and Victory bonds.

Although the Independent Treasury was not legally abolished until May 1920, the Federal Reserve system had been made the fiscal agent of the Treasury in November 1915, and after January 1916 the Treasury kept its working balance in the Reserve banks. When the United States entered the war, the Reserve banks were given the task of handling issues of certificates of indebtedness, and redeeming or reissuing them at maturity, as well as issuing bonds. This placed a heavy burden on the new system, and a large clerical staff had to be added to handle the work, especially at the New York bank. Moreover, if an issue was not promptly taken by the market, the Reserve banks themselves were expected to purchase any remainder.

Still other chores were entrusted to the Reserve system during the war. Until a Capital Issues Committee was set up in April 1918, the Federal Reserve Board had to approve all issues of industrial and public utility securities of 100,000 dollars or more in order to ensure that their amount and timing would not interfere with government offerings. The Reserve Board also exercised informal control over stock exchange loans and the call money market. When, under authority of the Espionage Act, President Wilson issued a proclamation forbidding unlicensed exports of coin, bullion, and currency, the issuing of licenses also was entrusted to the Board.

Production of gold, in spite of miners' priorities for obtaining supplies and materials, declined during the war as rising costs made it unprofitable. It was considered necessary therefore to consolidate existing gold and gold reserves in the hands of the Reserve banks. By an amendment to the Reserve Act on June 21, 1917, member bank reserve requirements were reduced from the original 12-15-18 percent against demand deposits to 7-10-13 percent, and from 5 to 3 percent against time deposits. However, only deposits with Reserve banks might be included in calculating legal reserve; cash in vault no longer counted as part of reserve. Another change in the law reduced the requirement for reserves against Federal Reserve notes from 140 to 100 percent, so that Reserve banks might pay out notes, rather than gold, as currency demand increased. The result of these changes was to increase the share of the monetary gold stock held by the Reserve banks from 26 to 55 percent of the total, an addition of about 200 million by the end of the year when the new requirements were in effect.

Little gold was left in the vaults of the commercial banks, and it could no longer be paid out to individuals on request. The Treasury was still under legal obligation to buy and sell gold at the price of 20.67 dollars per ounce, plus or minus handling charges, the dollar was still defined in terms of gold, and gold was the basis for reserves against currency and bank deposits. Paper money, however, could no longer be redeemed in gold, and the full gold standard was therefore not in operation. By 1918 the monetary gold stock of the United States was 2.87 billion dollars, about one-third of the world total.

Another step toward centralizing gold holdings was the campaign to bring more state banks into the Reserve system. As a result the number of state member banks increased from 53 to 936 between June 1917 and June 1919. This was still only 11 percent of the total number, but they were the more important ones and they held 54 percent of all state bank assets. Several amendments to the Reserve Act had made membership more attractive to them: they were assured of their right to withdraw from the system when they wished; and they were permitted to retain their original charter and statutory rights. Their membership in the System not only aided in the concentration of gold, but also gave the Reserve authorities a more direct channel of communication with them.

One of the few occasions on which Federal Reserve *bank* notes (as contrasted with Federal Reserve *notes*) were issued occurred during the war. England was in need of silver with which to meet war expenses in India. An appeal to the United States, which had enormous idle stocks of silver, resulted in permission to purchase 350 million ounces (although only 260 million were actually taken, at 1 dollar per ounce). Federal

Reserve bank notes, with gold certificates or Treasury certificates of indebtedness as collateral were issued to take the place of the silver withdrawn from circulation. On the insistence of Senator Pittman of Nevada, Chairman of the Committee on Banking and Currency, all the bullion exported had to be replaced after the war, and standard silver dollars coined to the full amount. The total of 260 million was an insignificant fraction of the total monetary circulation of 5 billion, and the whole episode was a tribute to the lingering power of the free silver mythology.

Treasury Policy during World War I

When the war began in Europe, the United States Treasury was in a relatively strong position. The national debt was only 1.2 billion dollars, about one-half of which served as collateral for national bank notes. The budget was in balance for the fiscal year 1914; there was a slight deficit the following year, but the war-engendered prosperity created a Treasury surplus for fiscal 1916 and made possible a reduction of the national debt. This fortunate situation did not continue for long. Income tax receipts increased rapidly, but much more slowly than expenditures. Import duties were no longer an important source of revenue, and federal income from excise taxes on liquor and tobacco was reduced by the action of many states in adopting prohibition of alcohol and regulation of cigarettes, although the national prohibition amendment did not go into effect until January 1919.

The troubled situation in Mexico added to the national concern about involvement with the war in Europe and made an increase in defense expenditures inevitable. The obvious resource was an increase in the income tax on individuals and corporations. For the first time, Congress passed, as the Revenue Act of September 8, 1916, an income tax measure which was not a mere appendage to a tariff bill. The Act left exemptions unchanged, but rates were approximately doubled and the normal tax was increased to 2 percent for both individuals and corporations. The surtax for individuals was raised from the previous maximum of 6 percent on the income over 500,000 dollars to a maximum of 13 percent on the income over 2 million. Corporations had to pay a new tax of 50 cents per thousand on the total of capital, surplus, and undivided profits; munitions manufacturers had to pay an additional tax of 12.5 percent on their net profits. Another innovation was the progressive inheritance tax on estates larger than 50,000 dollars, starting at 1 percent and rising to a maximum of 10 percent on any amount over 5 million.

Even before this Act could take effect on September 9, it had become clear that still more revenue would be necessary. A new Act, hastily pushed through both Houses of Congress, raised the schedule of taxes on estates, and introduced a tax of 8 percent on the profits of all corporations, above the exemption of 5000 dollars. The bill was signed on March 3, 1917, but again events moved more quickly than the lawmakers. Before this Act could take effect, Congress had been called into special session and had declared war on April 6, 1917.

A second set of amendments to the Revenue Act of 1916 was added with unusual unanimity on the part of Congress in October 1917. Exemptions were reduced to 1000 dollars for individuals whether married or single, but an additional exemption of 200 dollars was granted for each dependent. Normal tax rates went up to 4 percent for individuals and 6 percent for corporations, and the surtax rates went up to 63 percent on individual incomes above 1 million. A complicated schedule for the taxation of excess profits of corporations was included in the law in spite of the recognized difficulty of defining and administering such a tax; it replaced the special tax on munitions manufacturers and, with many amendments, remained a part of the income tax system until 1921.

Tax receipts under this Act were larger than had been estimated, but war expenditures were still outrunning them and were expected to be 33.5 billion for the fiscal year 1918–19. The end of the war in November 1918 did not greatly reduce the need for revenue, since many expenses would decline only gradually as armies were brought home and allies were aided. The Revenue Act of 1918 (actually not passed until February 24, 1919) therefore increased normal rates again, to 6 percent for individuals and 12 percent for corporations on 1918 income, but for later years 4 and 10 percent, respectively, for individuals and corporations. Excess profits and war profits were treated in much the same way, with higher rates for 1918 and lower rates thereafter. This Act also attempted to correct some of the inequities of previous legislation, but many details of interpretation had to be left to the judgment of revenue administrators. The gap between war revenue and expenditures can be seen in Table 5.

TABLE 5. UNITED STATES GOVERNMENT REVENUES AND EXPENDITURES FOR YEARS ENDING JUNE 30, 1917 TO 1920 (*in millions of dollars*)

	1917	1918	1919	1920
		Revenues		
Customs	226	180	184	323
Internal revenue	809	3,186	4,315	5,405
Other	89	299	653	967
Total	1,124	3,665	5,152	6,695
		Expenditures		
War expenditures	1,455	11,802	16,981	4,380
Civil expenditures	498	705	915	1,003
Interest on debt	25	190	619	1,020
Total	1,978	12,697	18,515	6,403

Note: War expenditures include Army and Navy expenses, purchase of obligations of foreign governments, and supplementary war expenditures. Civil expenditures include Panama Canal. Figures from the annual reports of the Secretary of the Treasury.

President Wilson and many of his advisors had hoped to raise a large part of the war expenses by taxation to avoid heavy borrowing. In opening the special session of Congress on April 2, 1917, the President urged somewhat pedantically that Congress should "protect our people so far as we may against the very serious hardships and evils which would be likely to arise out of the inflation which would be produced by vast loans." A year later in his Message of May 27, urging Congress to provide more adequate resources for the Treasury, he reiterated that "It would be a most unsound policy to raise too large a proportion of them by loans. . . ."[3] In spite of his admonitions, Congress found it impossible or impolitic to raise more than 35 percent of war costs from taxes; even if the war loans to the Allies are excluded, the ratio was only 55 percent. It was nevertheless considerably better than the Civil War ratio of 35 percent.

The special war session of Congress authorized the issue of 2 billion of short-term obligations, and up to 5 billion of long-term bonds. Interest on them was limited to 3.5 percent and none were to be sold at less

Check signed by Woodrow Wilson

than par, but maturity and other details were left to the Treasury. Under this authorization, the first Liberty Loan was offered to the public in May 1917 in the form of 2 billion 30-year bonds bearing interest at 3.5 percent, with attractive conversion features, and exemption from all taxes except those on estates and inheritance. Although the yield on good railroad bonds at that time was 4.75 percent, the loan was heavily oversubscribed because of exemption from the income tax, which was expected to go much higher. A great popular campaign reminiscent of Jay Cooke's Civil War methods urged the public to Borrow and Buy, which the public was delighted to do. Five months later a second Liberty Loan was offered, with fewer exemptions and conversion privileges, but with 4 percent interest; it too was heavily oversubscribed for about 4 billion dollars. The third and fourth Liberty Loans in April and September 1918 bore 4.25 percent interest, and were similar in most of their features to the second loan; they were oversubscribed and raised about 4 and 7 billion, respectively. A final Victory Loan in April 1919 offered 4.5 billion of 1- to 5-year notes, those which were tax exempt at 3.75 percent, and those with fewer exemption privileges at 4.75 percent.

In addition to these large-scale offerings, over 1 billion dollars was raised during the war by the continuous sale of thrift stamps, war savings certificates, and small bonds in schools, post offices, offices, and factories. The return on the certificates was lower, about 3 percent, and they carried no exemption features.

The initial mistake in Treasury policy was the effort to keep interest rates low—a misguided attempt to reduce the cost of borrowing. In his report for 1917, Secretary of the Treasury McAdoo stated his position thus: "In my judgment, an increase in the rate of interest on such bonds would be extremely unwise and hurtful. The higher the rate on Government bonds, the greater the cost to the American people of carrying on the war and the greater will be the depreciation in all other forms of investment securities." The result was that the Treasury felt obliged to use tax exemption in order to make more acceptable to the market the low rate of interest. The introduction of tax exemption into war borrowing had very unfortunate results. It gave large investors a decided advantage over small ones and seriously undermined the progressive character of the income tax. Once introduced, it became extremely difficult to dislodge.

Since market rates were well above the rates offered by the Treasury, the tax exemption was not sufficient to make up the difference, and Liberty Loans sold below par in the market almost as soon as they were issued. Just before the third Liberty Loan campaign in the spring of 1918 the Treasury became so concerned over this situation that it established a Bond Purchase Fund, under the War Finance Corporation, to support the price of bonds by buying for its own account in the open market. The 1.7 billion in funds for such purchases were obtained by selling short-term certificates of indebtedness, a financial robbing-of-Peter-to-pay-Paul which was not only expensive but also ineffective, since only the fully tax exempt first Liberty Loan was ever brought up to par in the period before 1920.

Certificates of indebtedness were used also to tide the Treasury over periods between bond issues, and to relieve strain on the market at the time of the bond issues. They were introduced in 1917 and became an important instrument of Treasury policy. The certificates were issued with varying rates of interest and varying maturities up to 1 year. They were usually sold in the first instance to the Federal Reserve banks, which invited or indeed insisted on subscriptions by the member banks in proportion to their resources. When the certificates bore relatively high rates of interest, they were taken by individual investors and there was less pressure on the banks to buy them. Since the certificates could be used in payment for Liberty Loan bonds, they helped to spread the transfers of funds over a longer period of time, as did also the frequent issues of Treasury bills and notes.

Other devices for smoothing out the disruptive effect on the money market of the large bond offerings were the provisions for installment payments of bond subscriptions, and the use of depositary banks to hold proceeds of bond issues for a time until they were needed by the Treasury. Since at this time government deposits were not subject to reserve requirements, banks were glad to have these "War Loan Deposit Accounts," and the net transfers of cash were greatly reduced. This arrangement had the added advantage of shifting fluctuations in Treasury balances from the Reserve banks and spreading them over a large number of commercial banks.

The Treasury and the Reserve System

The Federal Reserve Board, newly organized and inexperienced, was ambivalent in its attitude toward the financing policies of the Treasury during the war. In all countries, central banks were bending to the exigencies of their governments. The Reserve authorities, even if they had dared risk the charge of lack of patriotism, were in a weak position. The Secretary of the Treasury was Chairman of the Federal Reserve Board, and the offices of the Board were located in rooms of the Treasury. There is little evidence that members of the Board disapproved of Treasury policy at the time, although Reserve officials were very critical of it later, when the inflationary effects had become apparent. In its annual report for 1917 the Board had stated its opinion that "Banking expansion . . . is an unavoidable incident of war finance." However, the Board considered that it was "one of its most important duties to prevent, as far as practicable, expansion of banking credit from running an uncontrolled course."

Even after the war, during 1919, the Reserve banks continued an easy-money policy and bought large amounts of bankers' acceptances. In spite of the heavy stock market speculation, the discount rate was not raised until November, after successful flotation of the Victory Loan. The Board, however, had issued warnings to member banks not to encourage speculation in commodities and farmlands, and advised them to reduce their lines of credit for speculative and nonessential uses.

By January 1920 the Treasury had decided to issue its obligations at market rates, and the Reserve banks were no longer under pressure to keep their discount rates low. From the 4.75 percent rate of November 1919 the New York Federal Reserve Bank jumped its rate to 6 percent in January 1920 and to 7 percent on June 1 of that year. Other districts followed at varying intervals. The break in commodity prices in mid-1920 was blamed on this sudden tightening of the money market, and a Joint Commission of Agricultural Inquiry was set up by Congress to investigate. In his testimony before the Commission, Governor Benjamin Strong of the New York bank stated his conviction that rates should have been raised early in 1919, but that Treasury policy prevented. (One of the results of having twelve districts in the Reserve system was that the other eleven were far outweighed by the importance of New York as a financial center. Governor Strong had enormous prestige, and acted as an unofficial spokesman for the system, to the annoyance of the Board in Washington. This was changed by the Banking Act of 1935.*)

Controls during the War

Since the Treasury was borrowing heavily, it became important to limit the borrowing of private corporations to purposes essential for war production. A Capital Issues Committee was set up in May 1918 to take over from the Federal Reserve Board the supervision of new securities issues. It functioned until August 1919 and received during that time 3309 applications totalling 3.8 billion; only .9 billion were disapproved. A War Finance Corporation was also established to ensure that essential war industries could obtain adequate funds. In 1919 its authority was enlarged, as a way of encouraging revival of normal trade among nations, to lend up to 1 billion to exporters or to banks which were financing exports.

The Treasury also became responsible for the operation of the railroads. They had been in critical shape even before the war, with car shortages and traffic congestion at ports. A Railroads' War Board was set up in April 1917 as a voluntary organization and was able to improve operation of the roads in many respects. However, the Sherman Anti-

---

* See p. 319.

trust Act and the antipooling provisions of the Interstate Commerce Act were still operative and made effective unification of the lines impossible. In the face of a threatened strike for an eight-hour day and higher wages, the government took control at the end of 1917, with Secretary of the Treasury William McAdoo as Director-General. He cooperated closely with the War Industries Board and other agencies. The railroads were returned to private management in March 1920.[4]

The government attempted also to control prices during the war, in spite of the fact that the principal factor in the inflation was the Treasury policy of insisting on low interest rates for its borrowing, and of encouraging investment in its issues by the device of "Borrow and Buy." The ease in the money market encouraged bank lending. Total demand deposits increased from 16 to 24 billion between mid-1917 and mid-1920, and currency rose from 4.1 to a peak of 5.5 billion.

Even before the United States entered the war the index of wholesale prices had risen by 60 percent above the 1914 level. Prices of metals and metal products, not surprisingly, led the increase and more than doubled. Farm products and food nearly doubled in price, and building materials as a group had an increase of 14 percent. When the United States became a belligerent, the rate of increase of wholesale prices leveled off, in part because of the controls which were exercised.

There were eight separate agencies which at one time or another had price control functions. The Food Administration had power to control prices of many staple foods, wheat, livestock, and poultry. The Fuel Administration controlled coal and coke prices. The War Industries Board controlled many basic raw materials; its Price-Fixing Committee set prices for certain commodities purchased by the government. The War Trade Board had specific powers over imports and exports and controlled their prices. The Army and the Navy were given power to set prices of some of the articles they purchased. The Federal Trade Commission controlled the price of paper. The Department of Agriculture had limited powers over some farm products.

The control devices were various; in a few cases, as with foods and fuels, prices were controlled directly, in others prices were influenced by the setting of profit margins, and for a few commodities the control was directed toward stabilizing supply and demand. In addition to the price controls, a system of centralized buying for the Allies and their government agencies prevented competition among them from raising prices.

The objectives of these controls were as various as their techniques. Some were designed to reduce the cost to the government of its purchases; others aimed at keeping down the cost of living. Professor Taussig of Harvard University, who had been one of the "price fixers," gave it as his judgment that

government price fixing during the war was not uniform in its objects, and was little guided by principles or deliberate policies. In the main it was opportunist, feeling its way from case to case. So far as the experiment went, and so long as it lasted the outcome seems to me to have been good. The rise of prices to be expected from inflation of the circulating medium was not prevented; but then no endeavor was made to achieve this sweeping object. . . . Food and fuel prices were prevented from fluctuating as widely and soaring as high as they would have done in the absence of regulation.[5]

The price controls during the war undoubtedly helped to slow down the increase in many lines. After controls went into effect, prices of 78 commodities under control actually declined while for 193 uncontrolled prices the rise continued. But, for consumers, prices of essential commodities were noticeably higher. Bread, for example, had doubled in price by the middle of 1918; sugar stood occasionally at four times its prewar price, and seldom at less than double. Clothing had nearly doubled by the middle of 1918, and the cost of living for working class families was estimated to have increased by two-thirds.[6]

Wages had increased in many lines, but the increases were very unevenly distributed. Shipyard workers profited most by the sudden demand for their skilled services and were receiving double their earlier rates; electricians were also among the beneficiaries of rising wages. The building trades lagged far behind, and agricultural workers had increases of only one-third to one-half in spite of the increased demand for food products. In some families the total income was increased by the employment of women and young people who had not previously been in the labor force. On the other hand, in order to keep two jobs, it was necessary for many families to maintain two places of residence.

Although there was outspoken resentment against the rising cost of living, there was little understanding of the factors which were producing the increase in prices. As during the Civil War and the Revolution, blame was placed on profiteers and speculators, and laws were demanded to prevent their nefarious activities. The fault was sometimes attributed to the increase in "money," and a resolution in Congress in 1919 called for a decrease in the volume of currency in circulation. In response to an inquiry from the Senate Committee on Banking and Currency, the Federal Reserve Board pointed out that an increase in currency was the result rather than the cause of increased prices, since currency was added to circulation only as banks needed it to meet demands of their customers.[7]

The unsatisfactory results of all the effort to control prices gave evidence again that price controls have to be backed up by rationing of commodities if they are to hold inflation in check and enforce relatively equitable distribution of goods. Even if rationing had been used, it could not have held off inflation indefinitely, since both monetary and fiscal policies were working in the opposite direction.

The Break in Prices and the Problem of Agricultural Credit

The postwar break in prices began in the United States in mid-1919 with livestock, hogs, bacon, and mutton. Prices of other commodities soon followed as the European demand was reduced by the ending of the war. Prices all over the world were collapsing at this time for the same reason. Wholesale prices in Great Britain, France, and Italy passed their peak in April 1920; in India, Canada, and the United States in May, Swedish prices in June, and Australian in August. The silk market in Japan had collapsed in March, and the sugar and coffee markets in South America a few months later.

Nevertheless, there was a great outcry against the Federal Reserve banks because they had raised discount rates during 1919 in a belated effort to ward off the effects of the earlier easy-money policy. It was also claimed that there had been discrimination against agricultural paper. So great was the uproar that Congress set up a Joint Committee of Agricultural Inquiry, which after lengthy hearings brought in a report in 1921. The evidence showed that the plight of the farmer in 1920–21 had been caused, not by discrimination, but by the easy credit and resulting high prices of the war period. Wheat prices had risen under the stimulus of war demand from 94 cents a bushel in 1914 to 2.30 dollars in 1917, and good wheat land had risen rapidly in value. Many farmers had gone heavily into debt to buy such land, and when the price of wheat collapsed they were unable to meet even the interest payments. The high price of meat encouraged the formation of live stock loan companies in the western states, which made loans to farmers for raising and fattening cattle. When meat prices declined, commercial banks which had bought paper endorsed by these companies suffered heavy losses.

Although the Reserve system increased its credit to member banks in the agricultural states during 1920 and early 1921, many of the country banks were not members of the system. As farm income declined, their deposits fell, and they were unable to renew loans to their farm customers. Small state banks which had loaned heavily on farm mortgages began to crumble, and the total of failures was over 500 during 1921. Commercial failures also increased and reached a peak of nearly 24,000 in 1922.

Between May and November 1921 the Federal Reserve Bank of New York reduced its discount rate from 7 to 4.5 percent, and other districts followed suit. The reduction, like the preceding increase, was ill-timed and came too late to be of much assistance. Fortunately the depression was relatively short, and industry soon shifted to peacetime production. The year 1922 brought recovery in many lines. One permanent effect was the addition of a "dirt farmer" to the Federal Reserve Board by the Act of June 3, 1922, to ensure that the interests of agriculture would be adequately represented.

There still remained the problem of long-term amortized loans to farmers, since the business of agriculture was becoming increasingly mechanized and demanding increasing capital. The Federal Farm Loan Act had been passed on July 17, 1916, just as the United States was becoming involved in the war. It set up a system of credit institutions for agriculture somewhat resembling the Federal Reserve System. A federal Farm Loan Board consisting of the Secretary of the Treasury and four members was to establish twelve districts (not the same as the Federal Reserve districts), each with a Federal Land Bank with capital of 750,000 dollars subscribed by individuals, corporations, and, in case of necessity, by the Treasury. Each Land Bank would be directed by five local residents and might borrow on its own bonds secured by the farm mortgages used as collateral for loans to the local farm loan associations. The latter were organizations of ten or more farmers who subscribed for shares of the stock at 5 dollars per share and thus obtained the right to borrow 100 dollars for each share of stock owned, with the loan amortized over periods of 5 to 40 years.

In addition to these banks, another set of joint-stock land banks was authorized under the same Federal Farm Loan Board, to be privately owned and managed. The history of these banks was an unhappy one; several failed, and they were all liquidated after 1933.

Since this elaborate system still did not meet the needs of the farmers, an Agricultural Credits Act was passed in 1923 establishing the Federal Intermediate Credit Banks, with the same districts and the same directors as the Federal Land Banks, but with separate officers and separate accounts. They were permitted to lend to banks and to agricultural co-operatives rather than to individuals and might augment their original capital of 5 million dollars subscribed by the Treasury by selling collateral trust debentures secured by agricultural and livestock paper. Some of this paper was made eligible for rediscount by the Federal Reserve banks.

The whole elaborate structure of agricultural credit failed miserably to restore the farmer to his former position in the economy. His problems were far more complicated than mere inadequacy of credit. Technological change, corporate management of increasing areas of farming, drought conditions in plains which should never have been plowed, began to phase out the independent self-sustaining farmer. Credit institutions based on the assumption that this was still the normal pattern of American farming were bound to prove inadequate. In the 1930s still another attempt was made to solve the problem, through price supports for agricultural products, with equally unsatisfactory results.*

Banks and Banking

The commercial banks of the country found their position altered in many ways by the events of this period. Not only were reserve requirements lowered for banks which were members of the new Reserve system,

---

* See p. 329.

but also the composition of their portfolios was changed. The war interrupted the normal course of business in many lines, government credit was substituted for bank credit in some important sectors of the economy, and the banks turned to government obligations as earning assets, not only to take the place of the former business loans, but also in a patriotic endeavor to assist in the distribution of Treasury issues.

TABLE 6. PORTFOLIOS OF ALL COMMERCIAL BANKS ON JUNE 30, 1913 TO 1920 (*in billions of dollars*)

June 30	Loans	U.S. Government Obligations	Demand Deposits
1913	12.8	0.8	9.2
1914	13.4	0.8	10.3
1915	13.8	0.8	10.7
1916	16.1	0.7	12.9
1917	18.6	1.3	15.1
1918	20.6	3.0	15.7
1919	22.8	4.9	19.3
1920	28.6	3.6	21.6

Source: *Banking and Monetary Statistics,* published by the Federal Reserve Board in 1945.

As Table 6 indicates, the increase in bank loans was very small during the war years, and did not show a sharp change until 1920. The investment in United States obligations, on the other hand, almost doubled in the year ending June 30, 1917, and more than doubled again in the next year. At the end of the war, commercial banks were holding one-fifth of the government debt.

Banks in the industrial areas recovered quickly from the abnormal situation of the war and their heavy involvement in government obligations. After the crisis of 1920 the proportion of commercial loans increased, and the city banks were in good position, with few failures. The country banks, however, had become so heavily involved in loans based on the high prices of produce and land during the war that many were quite unable to retain sufficient liquidity for continuing operations. It was among this group of small banks in small communities, usually organized under state charters with inadequate capital, that the greatest proportion of failures occurred in the early 1930s when the reckoning could no longer be postponed.*

Cost of World War I

The real cost of a catastrophe such as World War I is of course impossible to calculate. The cold figures of dollars borrowed and spent represent only a small part of the total losses of materials, goods never produced, lives never completed. All that can be done is to count up the actual expenditures of the nations involved and recognize that this sum represents only one aspect of the cost. Even this is not a simple task, for some of the money spent in one nation was borrowed from another. Some of these loans were never repaid, and others ran on for years with interest accumulating at various rates. Moreover, the inflation which occurred in most of the belligerent countries made it impossible to add up the expenditures year by year without taking into account the steady decline in the value of the monetary units. To make addition possible, each figure would have to be reduced to an equivalent in constant purchasing power. The fluctuating foreign exchange rates, resulting from the internal depreciation of the currencies, were another source of statistical error in any attempt to combine costs of different countries. They were also a factor making the settlement of war debts and reparation more difficult.

With all of these variables carefully evaluated, an attempt was made in 1924 to estimate the total cost from 1914 to 1920 to all the warring nations on both sides. The grand total amounted to 82 billion dollars in gold. Of this amount, the United States accounted for 17 billion, the British Empire for 23 billion, France for 9 billion, Russia for 5 billion, and the Central Powers for 25 billion. The remaining 3 billion was expended by half a dozen other allies.

On the basis of these estimates, the cost of the war was calculated as shown in the accompanying table, with 1913 dollars as the base.[8]

When the cost of the war to the United States is looked at from a different point of view, as the excess of expenditures during the war over

---

* See p. 310.

	Gross Cost per Capita	Gross Cost as Percent of National Wealth
United States	$177	8.7
Great Britain	525	34.5
France	280	19.4
Italy	125	20.6
Russia	44	13.1
Germany	293	31.6

normal peacetime expenditures, the figure arrived at is about 33 billion dollars, a sum greater than the total expenditures of the United States from 1791 to 1913, including all the wars during that period. Almost one-third of this 33 billion total had been loaned to allies, leaving a net cost of 23 billion. Another indication of the cost of the war to the United States is given by the tenfold increase of the national debt to 26 billion in a period when the whole national income never rose above 70 billion per annum. Neither of the two latter estimates takes into account the depreciation in the value of the dollar which occurred during the war. This inflation was a heavy burden to the large numbers of citizens whose incomes did not increase proportionately—the old, the widowed, the unfortunate.

In accepting this depression check, I pledge that I will use it to check the depression and will put it back in circulation as soon as possible and in no event will I hold it more than 12 hours.

LAFAYETTE POST Nº 37
AMERICAN LEGION

Holder of this check please
Tel. 5000 at 12 noon and 6 p.m.

Nº 204

POUGHKEEPSIE, N.Y. *Jan. 21* 1933

PAY TO THE ORDER OF *Bearer* $ 1/00 / XX

One Dollar no/xx DOLLARS

TO THE **Farmer's & Manufacturers National** 50-165 **Bank** POUGHKEEPSIE, N.Y.

John D. Lansing TREAS.

VITASIGN CO.

CHAPTER 13

Check used as currency during Bank Holiday

THE NEW ERA: BOOM AND CRASH

Financial Aftermath of the War: The New Position of the United States

THE enormous number of casualties and the physical destruction of the war had made impossible any speedy return to normalcy in the western world. The illusion in the victorious allied countries that reparations paid by the vanquished would compensate for their losses was rapidly dispelled. The victors came to the unhappy realization that their own prosperity would depend on the rapid return to productivity of the erstwhile enemy. It was taken for granted in all the economic discussions of this period that the first step in this direction would be a return to the gold standard, which had functioned in relatively satisfactory fashion during the previous century. Countries which had previously not had such a standard were to be aided in adopting it, either in its old form based directly on gold, or in the form of a gold exchange standard based on another gold currency.

One international conference after another wrestled with the problems of reparations, debts, and standards. The League of Nations, organized in 1919, summoned the first meeting in Brussels in 1920, with experts from thirty-nine countries, including the former enemy powers. The conference recommended the establishment of an Economic and Financial Commission of the League of Nations to advise the League on all economic questions which might be solved by international agreement. It was soon clear that this was not enough. Sixteen months later, in January 1922, the currencies of Poland and Austria had collapsed, and there had been a foreign exchange crisis in Germany. A five-power conference in Cannes accomplished little except to call another conference in Genoa. One of its recommendations was that, as a way of facilitating international financial cooperation, central banks be established in countries which lacked them.

This recommendation was followed by most of the succession states carved out of the old Austro-Hungarian empire, and also by India and countries in South America. The League of Nations used its influence to keep the central banks independent of their governments, and in general to keep them within the pattern of British central banking. This made it possible for them to arrange loans on better terms and lower rates of interest. The League itself did not make loans to either central banks or governments, but it gave direction and supervision to the expenditures of the borrowing countries.[1]

The central banks were expected also to assist in the restoration and maintenance of stable values for their currencies. An important step toward stabilization of the pound was taken when the Anglo-American debt agreement was signed in 1923, reducing England's debt burden for the immediate future. This was followed in October 1924 by the so-called Dawes Loan of 200 million dollars (800 million gold marks) for 25 years at 7 percent, which gave Germany the means to establish the Rentenmark and start the process of recovery from the collapse of the mark in 1923. More than half of the total came from investors in the United States. This loan aided England also by encouraging the return of balances from New York to London. During the next six months, more than half a billion dollars of European loans were floated in the United States. Britain, on the other hand, put an embargo on new foreign loans in London for a year in preparation for restoring the pound to its former parity of 4.8665 dollars. England also arranged for credits in the United States from a group of banks headed by J. P. Morgan and the Federal Reserve banks to support the pound sterling if necessary during the transition period. The discount rate in London was kept about 2 percent higher than that of New York during this period in order to attract gold to the London market and facilitate the maintenance of the exchange rate.

As a result of these measures, England went back to the gold standard on May 13, 1925, but on a bullion rather than on a currency basis; gold coins never again went into general circulation. More than thirty countries, in and out of the Empire, returned to gold with England, and there was much rejoicing that this long step had been taken on the road back to normalcy. France stabilized her currency *de facto* during 1926, although not legally until June 25, 1928, and then at a rate of 3.92 cents, far below the prewar rate of 19.3 cents. Italy also devalued the lira when it was stabilized at the end of 1927 at the rate of 5.2 cents.[2]

The burden placed on the United States money market by its increasing responsibility for the financial health of the world was one which it was ill-prepared to assume. Federal Reserve officials had little knowledge of the foreign field. In the United States there were few well-developed channels for the handling of foreign securities, and few experts to evaluate such offerings. The Edge Act of December 1919 (actually an amendment to the Federal Reserve Act) authorized the organization under federal law of corporations to carry on commercial banking operations abroad and to issue foreign securities. National banks were permitted to invest in these corporations as much as 5 percent of their capital and surplus, but very few Edge Act corporations were formed. On the other hand, during the 1920s many American banks opened foreign branches for the convenience of their American customers doing business abroad.

The lack of foreign banking experience and the absence of any effective controls over the issuance of securities, domestic or foreign, were factors in the stock market hysteria of the late 1920s. In the boom years the American investing public showed little restraint or discrimination in their purchase of foreign securities. Warnings were sounded by a few experienced financiers like Thomas Lamont of J. P. Morgan and Company and S. Parker Gilbert of the Reparations Commission in Germany, but little heed was paid to them.

The ease of selling foreign issues in the United States, and the high commissions paid to the promoters, resulted in ludicrous and extravagant competition among investment banking houses; some of them sent emissaries abroad to urge and even to bribe officials to borrow for their governments. Latin Americans were especially susceptible to this persuasion. The son of the president of Peru, for example, was paid nearly half a million dollars for his efforts in arranging a loan which was far in excess of the country's ability to repay, and was shortly repudiated by the succeeding government. Cuba, Bolivia, Brazil, Colombia, and the Argentine as well as Central American governments were represented in this parade of borrowers. By 1929 at the peak of the boom, total American holdings of Latin American securities had increased to 1.6 billion from the .7 billion of 1924. After the crash in 1932 some of these bonds were selling at 7 percent or less of their par value.

European securities were equally attractive to United States investors. Before the war, only France, Norway, Russia, and Sweden had borrowed in the United States. After the war, most of the countries of Europe, including the succession states set up by the Versailles Treaty, came into the American market. Many loans were made to corporations as well as to local and central governments. The European loans on the whole stood up better than those to Latin America, but some of them defaulted during the depression.

During the ten years 1920–29 the total of foreign investment by Americans, direct and portfolio, increased from 7 to 17 billion.[3] About one-tenth of this increase was in the form of short credits owed to banks and individuals in the United States. France especially became a short-term creditor, since her investors, after having lost so heavily as a result of the war and the Russian revolution, were no longer willing to buy foreign bonds. This floating mass of "hot money" greatly increased the instability of currencies because it could be shifted rapidly from one center to another as interest rates varied.

Domestic Securities Markets

The overheated security market in the United States which absorbed foreign securities so incautiously was equally hospitable to new domestic issues, and equally incautious. Many of the new stock issues did not carry voting rights, so that management could be retained firmly in the hands of a small inner group which lost none of its power in adding to its capital; this was not a form of preferred stock, but of "A" and "B" classes of stock.[4] Many corporations, moreover, found it more advantageous and less costly to raise their working capital by issuing stock than by borrowing on the usual short terms from banks, with the necessity for frequent refinancing.

The rapid increase in securities issued in the United States, and in the volume of trading on the New York Stock Exchange, can be seen in Table 7. The total market value of all the stocks listed on the New York

TABLE 7

Shares Issued in the United States Each Year
(in millions of dollars) ·

| | Total | Domestic Corporations | | | Foreign Issues | Shares Traded in New York (in millions) |
		Common Stock	Pre-ferred Stock	Bonds and Notes		
1920	2788	555	483	1750	497	228
1921	2270	200	75	1994	623	173
1922	2949	288	333	2329	764	261
1923	3165	329	407	2430	421	236
1924	3521	519	346	2655	971	284
1925	4223	610	637	2975	1083	460
1926	4574	677	543	3354	1125	452
1927	6507	684	1054	4769	1388	582
1928	6930	2094	1397	3439	1263	931
1929	9376	5062	1695	2620	673	1125
1930	4957	1105	421	3431	908	811

Data from *Banking and Monetary Statistics*, 485, 487; *Historical Statistics*, 658.

Stock Exchange reached a peak of 90 billion dollars by September 1929. After the crash the market value of the list fell to a low point of 16 billion in July 1932.[5]

Associated with this ease of selling securities was a new wave of corporate mergers. For the first time since the turn of the century, the number of manufacturing and mining corporations which legally "disappeared" within a year was more than a thousand in 1928, and in 1929 reached a peak of more than 1200. Of the 200 largest corporations 49 disappeared in the decade before 1929 through mergers. That many of these mergers were economically viable is indicated by the fact that, as late as 1955, 15 of the 100 largest manufacturing corporations had been through an important merger of some type in the 1920s.

There were many factors in this development in addition to the exuberance of the security markets and the investment bankers. The high degree of industrial concentration which had resulted from the previous peak period of mergers had declined, and the increasing size of the market made possible a reduction in unit costs when overhead expenses could be reduced by consolidation. In some cases the purpose was control of materials and parts. Henry Ford became part owner of some of his suppliers. DuPont became majority owners of General Motors, partly to protect their existing investment, partly to protect the market for some of their products. Others invested surplus funds in expansion in order to avoid paying to their stockholders dividends which would be subject to income taxes.

Corporate Structure

The device of the holding company carried this process of investment in other corporations still further. A profitable operating company such as a public utility could be controlled by ownership of 51 percent of its common stock. A corporation organized for the express purpose of ownership could then be controlled by another corporation which held 51 percent of that stock. This process could be repeated almost indefinitely until a relatively small investment in a holding company could gain control of a relatively large operating company. Such holding companies became a favorite device during the boom period. Samuel Insull quite legally became the ruler of five midwestern utility systems generating one-eighth of the nation's power, through his Insull Utilities Investments company. The Van Sweringen brothers of Cleveland, through their holding companies, the Vaness Company and the General Securities Corporation, controlled many railroads in much the same way as Insull his utilities. In these many-tiered corporate structures it was difficult to trace the lines of actual ownership, control, and earnings. Neither the Van Sweringen empire nor that of Insull survived the depression.

The merger movement of this period was subject to no effective control by the antitrust legislation. The original Sherman Act of 1890 had been buttressed by the Clayton Act and the Federal Trade Commission Act of

1914. All of these laws had been amended in efforts to strengthen them, but the financial community was able to find its way around them in order to carry out the mergers of the boom period. It was not until the banking crisis of 1933 that effective action was taken to curb the security markets; the problem of regulating monopoly and ensuring competition still remained.

Another financial device which became a prominent feature of the securities market in this period was the investment trust—not to be confused with the "trusts" of the earlier period.* Such corporations had been in existence for many years in England and in the United States, but had never been popular in the United States. The boom of the 1920s encouraged the organization of these companies, which issued their own securities, usually common stock, to purchasers who assigned any voting rights they might have to the trust. The trust invested the proceeds as it liked and paid dividends on its own stock out of the earnings from its investments; it also received a percentage of the earnings as management fees. From about forty investment trusts in 1921, the number grew rapidly until in 1929 they were being organized at the rate of one a day; by that time they had accumulated assets of more than 8 billion dollars. Many trusts were organized by stock exchange firms and investment bankers who were able to earn fees on the securities they bought and sold as well as on their management. In many cases they showed little concern for their stockholders but, as a Congressional investigating committee declared,

degenerated into a convenient medium of the dominant persons to consummate transactions permeated with ulterior motives; served to facilitate the concentration of control of the public's money; enabled the organizers to realize incredible profits; camouflaged their real purpose to acquire control of equities in other companies; and became the receptacles into which the executive heads unloaded securities which they, or corporations in which they were interested, owned.[6]

Even when they were well and honestly managed, their influence on the stock market was inevitably great because of the large blocks of stock they held. This became evident when the break in prices finally came.

Another corporate development in this period which increased the

---

* See p. 255.

hazard of a crisis was that of the security affiliate. This was an investment banking corporation organized by a commercial bank to underwrite and distribute new security issues which the bank itself was not empowered to handle. There had been such affiliates in New York ever since 1908 when the First National Bank set up the First Security Company, with all of its capital stock owned by the stockholders of the mother bank. By 1927 there were so many affiliates that they were handling one-eighth of all new security issues, and by 1930, one-half. The danger arose when an affiliate got into a difficult position and the sponsoring bank felt obliged to purchase for its own portfolio the "frozen" issues.

Public attention was aroused to the danger of such affiliates by the collapse of the Bank of United States. In spite of its name, the Bank had only a state charter and was subject only to state supervision. Its president and vice-president organized an affiliate in which they owned all the voting shares; they then organized another company, with the same directors as the bank, for the purpose of speculating in the stock of the affiliate. Examiners who scrutinized the books of the bank in July 1929 criticized the involvement of the bank with its affiliate, but made no further examination until a year later. By that time it was too late to save the bank, even with the help of some of the larger banks in the city which hoped to avoid a public scandal in their field.[7] The Banking Act of 1933 made such relationships impossible in the future.

A conspicuous feature of the securities market in the late 1920s was the increase in brokers' loans. Call loans on security collateral had long been made by New York banks for themselves and for their out-of-town correspondents, but they had never before played so large a part in the financing of security purchases. In addition to bankers' balances from the interior, New York banks were lending in the call market large amounts for corporations, on a commission basis. Other corporations bypassed the banks entirely and placed their own call loans with brokers. Even in ordinary times these corporate funds would have been an element of instability, and in the inflated situation of the late 1920s they were a constant threat to the market. At the first hint of a decline in stock prices, the corporate funds were withdrawn, and the banks were left with the responsibility of supporting their customers and preventing a panic.

The total of call loans reported by banks increased by 1 billion dollars during 1927, and by more than 1 billion in 1928. They reached a peak of 8.5 billion in October 1929 and, if the call loans made directly by corporations had been included, the total would probably have amounted to 15 billion.[8] After the collapse of the stock market on October 24, the bank loans had fallen within ten days to 3 billion, and by 1932 they were down to 242 million. Direct loans by corporations had by that time practically disappeared from the market.

Federal Reserve Policy

In facing the problems of the late 1920s, the new position of the United States in world finance and the boom which was raging at home placed the Federal Reserve authorities in a serious dilemma. They found themselves responsible not only for the economic welfare of their own country, but also for that of their former allies and in some degree for that of their former enemies as well.

By the end of 1923 the stock of gold in the United States had doubled over that of 1914, rising from 2 to 4 billion, and the United States, the principal free gold market in the world, was holding 40 percent of the world's gold monetary stock. At a time when Great Britain and France had to have more gold if they were to return to a gold standard, this was a matter of concern on both sides of the Atlantic. If a tight-money policy were adopted in the United States in order to discourage the boom which was rapidly getting out of control, the high interest rate would attract an influx of funds which would make it difficult if not impossible for countries struggling to restore the gold standard to obtain adequate reserves. On the other hand, if interest rates were allowed to remain low, the speculation would continue until the inevitable collapse would certainly harm the United States and eventually also the rest of the world.

A tight-money policy is always unpopular, and the Board had been severely criticized for its action in raising rates in 1920. Moreover raising the discount rate would be effective only if any surplus reserves of the member banks were first "mopped up" by sales of government securities in the open-market. The Reserve system was not in possession of enough government securities to make this possible.

In these circumstances, the Reserve authorities had no clear guide to the policy they should follow. In its annual report for 1923 the Board discussed the whole question of credit policy and showed more awareness than previously of its responsibilities even when the Treasury demanded subservience. In connection with open-market operations, the Board stated its conviction "that the time, manner, character and volume of open-market investments purchased by Federal reserve banks [should] be governed with primary regard to the accommodation of commerce and business and to the effect of such purchases or sales on the general credit situation."[9] The formation of an Open-Market Committee, consisting of officers of the Reserve banks, made possible a better coordination of open-market operations with the credit policy of the Reserve system as expressed in discount rates, eligibility rules, and the like.

While the speculation in the securities markets was increasing steadily, Federal Reserve credit policy seesawed, torn between its fear of injuring "legitimate" business at home by high interest rates and its fear of encouraging speculation and jeopardizing recovery abroad by low rates. A rapid growth in time deposits, produced by a transfer from demand to time accounts by corporations and other large customers in order to benefit by the smaller reserve requirements, increased member bank excess reserves, as did the gold imports. During the first half of 1925 the Reserve banks resorted to open-market sales of government securities in order to tighten the market. In part, however, these sales were offset by purchases of acceptances. By the end of 1925 all the Reserve banks except New York had raised their rates to 4 percent, which was still below the rising rates of interest in the money market. When the New York rate also was raised to 4 percent, there was a brief decline in stock prices, and in loans to brokers, but an increase in bank security loans to customers. Because the index of wholesale prices was not rising (indeed during 1926 it fell by 6 percent), it was assumed that there was no inflation which required corrective measures.

The conflict between domestic and foreign considerations in credit policy became acute during 1927. By this time the United States held half of the world's stock of monetary gold. The Bank of England was facing difficulty in maintaining sterling exchange at the old par, and the Bank of France needed additional gold if it was to restore the franc to the gold standard. A conference of central bankers in New York in July (to which

Governor Montagu Norman of the Bank of England traveled incognito) secured an agreement from Governor Strong* of the New York Reserve bank that New York would take the lead in keeping interest rates low in order to aid the foreign currencies. The Federal Reserve Board fell in line and even brought pressure to bear on the Chicago Reserve bank, forcing it against its wishes to lower its discount rate. Other districts reduced their rates without protest.

The motives of the Reserve authorities in aiding the restoration of the gold standard in the important industrial nations were in many ways commendable. Stable currencies were desperately needed in order to revive international trade. The gold standard was restored in Italy, Poland, Estonia, Denmark, India, Ecuador, and Argentina during 1927. But the conditions which were essential to the proper functioning of the gold standard were not present—free trade and free exchange. The end results of the premature return to gold were therefore probably more harmful than helpful.

The increase in production and business, which had been predicted for the United States as the result of the lower interest rates, did not occur. Instead, it was the volume of loans to brokers which rose steadily during 1927 and 1928.

During the first two months of 1928 the Reserve banks one by one raised their rates back to 4 percent. Open-market sales were also increased but not enough to force member banks to borrow at the higher rate. As stock prices and brokers' loans continued to rise, the Reserve banks began to feel more concern, and rates were raised to 4.5 percent by June 7. Although there were brief declines in both stock prices and brokers' loans after this increase, they soon began to rise again, and discount rates went to 5 percent at most of the Reserve banks. The Chicago bank was the first to raise its rate in both cases. There was great fear on the part of Reserve authorities that legitimate business might be restricted by a tight-money policy, and a belief, quite unjustified, that credit could be kept easy for business but tight for speculation.

The fear of injuring business during the autumn when currency demands were high led to an ambiguous policy in which discount rates were

---

* See p. 284.

kept high, but securities and acceptances were purchased. The net increase of 358 million dollars injected into the market made it possible for member banks not only to provide their customers with the necessary seasonal currency, but also to increase their reserve balances and reduce their borrowings from the Reserve banks, so that the discount rate was inoperative. The reporting member banks did increase their commercial loans by a small amount during the autumn, but they increased their loans on securities by seven times as much. It should be noted that the large banks in New York City did not participate in this increase of security loans during 1928 and 1929. They foresaw correctly that they would be called on to aid the market in the approaching inevitable collapse, and they were husbanding their resources. President Coolidge, however, made a number of reassuring statements about the situation, and as late as October 1928 he expressed his belief that the economy was "fundamentally sound." After each such pronouncement, stock prices rose.

The feverish atmosphere of the financial markets was intensified during the early months of 1929. Financial writers and even some economists accepted the theory that this was a "new era" and that earlier rules no longer applied. From the shoeshine parlor and the newsdealer in the morning, to the dinner party in the evening, talk was centered on "the market." The operations of the "Big Ten", a group of speculators widely believed to act together, were of more importance in determining stock prices than such minor details as yield.[10] The secret of success was to buy a security when the Big Ten did, and to sell out just before they did, a technique more appropriate to clairvoyants than to economists.

Federal Reserve discount rates were not increased during the first half of 1929, although such action was generally expected. During each meeting of the directors at the Federal Reserve Bank of New York, financial reporters clustered outside the door of the board room, prepared to wig-wag to their confreres at the end of the hall any announcement of a change, so that the news could be rushed to the nearest telephone without loss of a second. For some time, however, the Reserve authorities continued to use only the weak instrument of "moral suasion" (sometimes referred to disrespectfully as "the open-mouth policy"). The discount rate was well below market rates and member banks were able to make a profit by borrowing. Business activity was high, wholesale prices were almost stable, and the fact that some of the important business indicators had turned downward was easily ignored. Many small investors were drawing out savings deposits in order to buy securities.

Stock prices continued to advance, in spite of occasional moments of weakness. Although the call loan rate had reached 20 percent in March, it had fallen again and remained between 6 and 8 percent most of the time. The Federal Reserve Bank of New York repeatedly, as well as those of Boston, Philadelphia, Chicago, and Kansas City occasionally, requested permission of the Board to raise their rates during these months; their requests were backed up by at least two recommendations from the Federal Advisory Council. But it was not until August 9 that the central bank authorities of the United States followed the example set earlier in the year by England, Germany, the Netherlands, Austria, Hungary, and Poland by raising the discount rate from 4.5 to 5.5 percent. At the same time the rate on acceptances was lowered from 5.25 to 5.125 percent in the hope that business would not be required to pay higher rates.

For a few weeks, stock prices continued upward. The peak of the Dow-Jones averages of industrial and rail stocks was reached on September 3. Several developments started the downward movement. A number of European central banks, and the Bank of England, increased their discount rates again in order to attract funds away from New York. In the United States, in spite of brave words by professional stock market operators and economic commentators, the rate of increase in stock prices was declining, and many holders of securities were taking their profits and getting out of the market. When it was announced during the first week in October that, in spite of lower stock prices, the total of brokers' loans had reached a new high of 6.8 billion, it became clear that stocks were going into the hands of weak, thinly margined holders. For the next few weeks, stock prices went down gradually. There were occasional rallies, but on the 24th of the month a hysterical panic developed during which the volume of trading set a record of nearly 13 million shares; the previous record had been 8 million in March. The panic continued, and on October 29 more than 16 million shares were sold. Efforts of a consortium of leading bankers, who increased their loans and investments by 1.4 billion in one week, failed to stop the decline as brokers were obliged to sell their customers' collateral when the market price went below the credit based on it.

The action of the New York banks was supported by the Federal Reserve Bank of New York, which also increased its loans to member banks by 140 million, and added another 140 million of securities to its portfolio, during the crucial week of October 23. The Board reluctantly gave its approval to this action, and the Open Market Investment Committee, consisting of Governors of five Reserve Banks with Governor Harrison of the New York Bank as chairman, was able to obtain the Board's consent for purchase of an additional 200 million if it seemed necessary.

After cheery words from President Hoover, a rally began and from November 14 until the spring of 1930 stock prices rose, without, however, recovering more than a fraction of their losses. Then they declined again and by late 1932 the index of common stock prices was one-sixth of the 1929 high.

The deterioration of the situation in Europe added to the problems of the American authorities. In May 1931 the *Credit Anstalt* of Vienna was obliged to close and the German banks to which it was heavily indebted were soon in difficulties. They could not meet their short obligations to London, and this frightened other Europeans, especially the French, into withdrawing their balances from Britain. By September England had lost so much of its gold reserve that it was forced to devalue the pound, an action which set off a series of devaluations around the world. This did not solve the balance of payments problems since it left most countries in about the same position relative to others as before.

During the latter months of 1931 the United States also faced a heavy loss of gold. In an effort to stop the drain, the Federal Reserve Bank of New York raised its discount rate from 1.5 to 3.5 percent, with only temporary effect. By February 1932 the gold of the Reserve Banks was so close to the legal minimum that the Glass-Steagall Act was passed; it permitted government securities to be substituted for gold as collateral for Federal Reserve notes, above the minimum of 40 percent. This made it possible for the Reserve Banks to increase their open-market purchases and pump new funds into the market, but the flood of bank failures continued.

The Federal Reserve authorities have been severely criticized for their action, or in some cases for their inaction, during the boom and during the depression. Decades after the event it is easy to see what might have been better or better timed. But it is unreasonable to expect that inexperienced central bankers, operating without adequate legal power and without strong government support, could by their policy within their own country counteract the effects of a long war which had involved all the industrial nations and destroyed their former financial relationships.[11]

Treasury Policy and Revenue

One of the remarkable features of the boom period was the complacency of Treasury officials. It is true that Treasury policy, laid down by the millionnaire Andrew Mellon, had been successful at several points. A budget system had been finally established in 1921, ending the haphazard appropriation procedures of the past. A surplus of receipts over expenditures made it possible to reduce the debt to 16 billion in 1930. The market value of Liberty bonds rose steadily; as market rates of interest declined in the first years after the war, the low return on government securities no longer kept their price below par.

The expenses of the federal government remained high after the war and never again fell to the prewar level. Nevertheless, the improved condition of the Treasury brought increasing pressure for tax reduction from almost every group, and especially from the corporations which had been paying high taxes on war profits and excess profits. The admitted difficulty of interpreting and administering them increased the opposition to these taxes from almost all groups except the western farm bloc. Little could be done, however, until the change in administration replaced Wilson with Harding, and Secretary of the Treasury Houston with Andrew Mellon.

A new law was signed on November 23, 1921, after hasty action in Congress. It reduced the rates on surtaxes and ended the excess profits tax after 1921. Personal exemptions were increased for married persons and heads of families from 2000 to 2500 dollars, but single persons still had an exemption of only 1000 dollars; for dependents the exemption was 400 instead of 200 dollars. Normal rates remained at their former level, but the maximum surtax was reduced to 50 percent for income above 200,000 dollars. A number of technical changes were made in order to make the law clearer and more equitable, and a capital gains tax of 12.5 percent was added. The new legislation did not really satisfy anyone, and work was immediately started on a comprehensive revision.

Every session of Congress was presented with changes in the income tax laws, some of them justified as attempts to meet changing conditions in the economy, but many of them merely efforts to meet demands or complaints of pressure groups with little regard to the effect on the economy. The Act of 1924 was better than most in that it laid down rules for treating capital gains, revocable trusts, and corporate reorganization which were retained in successive revisions for a number of years; it also solved some of the more troublesome legal problems which had arisen in connection with the collection of the income tax. The Act provided also for publicity of returns. The whole table of rates was somewhat reduced, since for two years the Treasury had reported a surplus. The first 5000 dollars of an individual's income was also given a 25 percent tax reduction because it was presumed to be earned.

Both President Coolidge and Secretary Mellon were dissatisfied with this Act, especially with the surtax maximum of 40 percent, and the provisions for publicity. Congress therefore passed a new Act in 1926 which followed most of the recommendations of the Treasury. Income tax rates were lowered, exemptions slightly increased, and earned income credit with 25 percent reduction in tax was raised to a maximum of 20,000 dollars. The tax on corporation capital stock was repealed; publicity was limited to the names of taxpayers and was not to include the amount of tax paid. The most important issue was the estate tax, and the rates were reduced retroactively to a maximum of 20 percent on estates over 100,000 dollars. The retroactive feature amounted to a gift of about 250 million to twenty great estates, but there was little protest. Oil and gas wells were allowed depletion up to 27.5 percent of their gross income, a cause for great rejoicing among the oil tycoons of Texas.[12] It was on the whole a rich man's tax bill.

In spite of the reduced rates of the 1926 law, the general prosperity of the country outside the farm areas produced a surplus for the Treasury of 30 million dollars. There was little emphasis on further debt reduction, although the Secretary of the Treasury in his Report for 1925 had said that it should be continued at the existing rate of about .5 billion annually, not enough to prevent further reduction in taxes. Secretary Mellon never abandoned his effort to abolish the estate tax altogether, but never succeeded. The Revenue Act of 1928 made a few small reductions in rates but it produced more revenue than the preceding law, and a surplus of 225 million was predicted by the Treasury for 1929. Although the stock market crash occurred in October, the Secretary recommended in December a further tax reduction for one year, and both Houses of Congress quickly passed a resolution to that effect.

By the middle of 1931 the surplus had become a deficit. Income tax receipts for March 1931 were 40 percent below those of the preceding March, with government expenditures for the year 300 million dollars greater than the estimates. By this time the income tax had become the principal source of federal revenue, accounting for about two-thirds of the total. Since it was a progressive tax, its yield declined far more precipitously than did the national income. The latter had reached a peak of 89 billion in 1929; in 1933 it was at 40 billion. The personal income tax had yielded over 1 billion in 1929; in 1931 it was only one-fourth as much. The corporation income tax declined from 1.2 billion in 1929 to 285 million at its low point in 1932.

After lengthy wrangling, Congress passed a new revenue act on May 31, 1932, which raised income taxes all along the line, starting with 4 percent on the first 4000 dollars of net income, and setting surtaxes up to a maximum of 55 percent on net income over 1 million; personal exemptions were reduced. Many small changes were made to remove loopholes; estate taxes were increased and a gift tax was imposed. In spite of the increased rates, the yield of the tax was far less than had been expected. This tax measure followed the principle which was then generally accepted, that sound finance demanded a balanced budget. The effect on the economy of increased taxes at this low point of depression was given small consideration. Fiscal policy had not yet appeared on the scene.

While the income tax revision was proceeding through Congress, a new tariff act was also in process, and there was sharp division of opinion in both parties as to which should take precedence. An Emergency Tariff Act was passed early in 1921 in a futile effort to offset the sharp drop in agricultural prices. It was obviously inadequate; and work was immediately started on a comprehensive revision. The House passed a bill in July 1921, but the Senate made more than two thousand amendments and the final result did not become law until September 1922. Farmers, who wanted tax rates on war and excess profits to remain high, were also demanding protection against the dumping of agricultural commodities by countries like Argentina and Australia who had not been able to sell all they produced during the war. The result was a measure which gave "protection" to agriculture when what the farmer really needed was more markets abroad.

With the farm groups tricked into complacence, it was possible to obtain increased tariff rates on many manufactured goods, and to include in the protected list some of the industries like dyestuffs which had become important for the first time during the war. The average rate of duties on dutiable imports was increased from 29 to 38 percent, and on all imports from 11 to 15 percent, by this Fordney-McCumber Act.

Bank Failures

More than one-half of all the banks in the United States failed during the dozen years ending in 1933. About one in ten of the failed banks was eventually able to reopen, and a few of them were absorbed by larger banks. The failed banks had held 14 percent of all the bank deposits of the country at the beginning of this period; in the final settlement nearly three-fourths of the deposits were repaid, but this frequently required years. The stockholders in most cases lost all their equity, and in some cases were even required to contribute an equal amount because of the double liability clause in certain state bank charters.

The disadvantages of the traditional American banking system of small independent banks became unhappily evident during these years. Eighty percent of the failed banks had a capitalization of 25,000 dollars or less; another 10 percent had capital of 25,000 to 50,000 dollars. Only 32 failed banks, less than one-third of 1 percent, had a capital of 1 million or more. The geographic distribution of the failed banks was closely related to their size. About 70 percent of all the failures occurred in twelve agricultural states. As was to be expected, 75 percent of the failed banks were located in towns of 2500 population or less, 88 percent in towns of 10,000 or less. Since most of the small banks in small towns had been operating under state charter, five-sixths of the failed banks were state banks. The great majority of the failed banks were not members of the Federal Reserve System.

York Times.

THE WEATHER
Cloudy and continued cold today; tomorrow fair and warmer.

by The New York Times Company.

RIDAY, OCTOBER 25, 1929.

TWO CENTS In Greater New York | THREE CENTS Within 200 Miles | FOUR CENTS Elsewhere Except 7th and 8th Postal Zones

WORST STOCK CRASH STEMMED BY BANKS; 12,894,650-SHARE DAY SWAMPS MARKET; LEADERS CONFER, FIND CONDITIONS SOUND

FINANCIERS EASE TENSION

Five Wall Street Bankers Hold Two Meetings at Morgan Office.

CALL BREAK 'TECHNICAL'

Lamont Lays It to 'Air Holes' —Says Low Prices Do Not Depict Situation Fairly.

FINDS MARGINS BEING MET

Sees Market 'Susceptible of Betterment'—Mitchell, Potter, Wiggin, Prosser at Talks.

Wall Street gave credit yesterday to its banking leaders for arresting the decline on the New York Stock market at a time when the stock market was being overwhelmed by selling orders. The conference at which the steps were taken that reversed the market's trend was hurriedly called at the offices of J. P. Morgan & Co.

The five bankers who met at the headquarters of the famous private banking house at noon yesterday and again at 4.30 P. M., follow-

Wall Street Optimistic After Stormy Day; Clerical Work May Force Holiday Tomorrow

Confidence in the soundness of the stock market structure, notwithstanding the upheaval of the last few days, was voiced last night by bankers and other financial leaders. Sentiment as expressed by the heads of some of the largest banking institutions and by industrial executives as well was distinctly cheerful and the feeling was general that the worst had been seen. Wall Street ended the day in an optimistic frame of mind.

The unanimous opinion of brokers was that the selling had got out of hand not because of any inherent weakness in the market but because the public had become alarmed over the steady liquidation of the last few weeks. Over their private wires these brokers counseled their customers against further thoughtless selling at sacrifice prices.

Charles E. Mitchell, chairman of the National City Bank, declared that fundamentals remained unimpaired after the declines of the last few days. "I am still of the opinion," he added, "that this reaction has badly overrun itself."

Lewis E. Pierson, chairman of the board of the Irving Trust Company, issued last night the following statement:

"Severe disturbances in the stock market are nothing new in American experience. The pendulum always swings widely and it would seem as though the long-expected break should bring about an equilibrium.

"The position of the Federal Reserve Bank is unusually strong and the borrowings of member banks are moderate.

"Considering the record-breaking earnings in many industries, we may well remember that whenever fundamental values are lost sight of by the unthinking majority it is time for courage on the part of those investors who have a real sense of basic worth."

Because the clerical facilities of brokerage houses are overtaxed as a result of the recent phenomenally heavy trading, an agitation was started yesterday in favor of a suspension of trading on the New York Stock Exchange tomorrow.

It is thought possible that the governing committee will take action today, without waiting for a petition from the membership. In many brokerage houses the posting of books has fallen far behind and some relief will have to be afforded, according to brokers, unless the market quiets down shortly.

LOSSES RECOVERED IN PART

Upward Trend Starts With 200,000-Share Order for Steel.

TICKERS LAG FOUR HOURS

Thousands of Accounts Wiped Out, With Traders in Dark as to Events on Exchange.

SALES ON CURB 6,337,415

Prices on Markets in Other Cities Also Slump and Rally —Wheat Values Hard Hit.

The most disastrous decline in the biggest and broadest stock market of history rocked the financial district yesterday. In the very midst of the collapse five of the country's most influential bankers hurried to the office of J. P. Morgan & Co., and after a brief conference gave out word that they believe the foundations of the market to be sound, that the market smash has been caused by technical rather than fundamental considerations, and that many sound stocks are selling too

From the New York Times, *October 25, 1929*

The Depression

The stock market collapse of late 1929 was not the cause of the depression, but it was a sharp warning that the economy was in trouble. Industrial production, as measured by the Federal Reserve, had begun to turn down during that summer, but the stability of both wholesale and consumer price indices for several previous years had been reassuring, in spite of the increase in unemployment in both 1927 and 1928. Factory payrolls, freight car loadings, and department store sales did not begin to decline until autumn of 1929.

The spectacular losses in the securities markets still further reduced the demand for consumer goods. President Hoover did his best to persuade businessmen to maintain wages, keep up production, and even increase their investments in new plant and equipment, but not even the best-intentioned of them could ignore the declining demand for automobiles, housing, and durables, as well as for the consumer goods formerly regarded as necessities. The index of industrial production was down to half of its former level by the low point of the depression in late 1932 and the first quarter of 1933. The wholesale price index went from 95.3 in 1929 to a low of 64.8 in 1932 on the 1926 base. Gross National Product went from a peak of 104 billion in 1929, to a low point in 1933 of 56 billion at current prices, 74 billion at 1929 prices.

No satisfactory index of unemployment was available for the depression years, but the evidence was clearly visible wherever one turned. Whole families left the city and went back to the family farm, if they were fortunate enough to have such a refuge. City streets were dotted with men, often in veterans' uniforms, trying to sell apples to passersby. Suburban housewives were plagued by sad-faced men and women peddling shoestrings, pins, needles. Young people were forced to leave college. Older people turned to political action and joined a Townsend Club or some other organization trying to force pensions from a government which saw its own income lowered. Hundreds of schemes for "curing" the business cycle were formulated during these years, ranging from the stamped money of Silvio Gesell (a dollar bill with a one-cent stamp affixed each week, in order to encourage holders to spend it as quickly as possible) to the "Fifty dollars every Thursday" of Major Douglas, the leader of the Social

Credit movement. There were few Americans who did not bear some sort of "Invisible Scar" as a result of living through those years.[13]

The financial community as an organized institution never really recovered its prestige. It was not only the malfunctioning underlying such a collapse which destroyed public confidence; it was also the malfeasance of some of its most honored leaders. Charles E. Mitchell, president of the National City Bank and of its security affiliate, the National City Company, was found guilty in federal court of tax evasion; Albert H. Wiggin, president of the Chase National Bank, was found to have been selling the stock of his own bank short at a time when he was urging other bank officers to invest in it; Samuel Insull, head of the enormous group of 95 holding companies and 255 operating companies in the public utility field, was accused of defrauding the public of 100 million dollars although the court finally exonerated him. Many such facts were revealed during the hearings before the Senate Committee on Banking and Currency in 1931 and 1932, when preventive legislation was being considered.

One of the more dramatic failures at the end of this period was that of Ivar Kreuger, whose Swedish Match Company had obtained a monopoly of the manufacture of matches in 15 European countries, and market dominance in 24 others. His activities also included banking, real estate, telephones, iron and gold mining, and newspapers. Kreuger and Toll, the parent company, had loaned 400 million dollars to 15 countries in the years between 1926 and 1930. Much of this was financed by 250 million dollars borrowed in the United States, largely through the respectable investment banking firm of Lee, Higginson in Boston. In 1932 it was discovered that a large issue of Italian bonds which Kreuger had put up as collateral were forgeries, and that he had been juggling his accounts since 1923; his reputation was so high that little attention had been paid to such details. Rather than face his creditors, Kreuger committed suicide in Paris early in 1932.[14]

The United States was not the only country which suffered a severe depression in these years. The economic disarray which followed the world war, the collapse of the former trading arrangements, the resulting inability to maintain the gold standard, were almost inevitable results of the destruction of men and of property during the war. England had made an enormous effort to restore her prestige in international finance, but it had created hardship in the mid-1920s for the coal miners and other workers who suffered most from the accompanying deflation. France and Italy had accepted devaluation of their currencies in order to achieve a modicum of stability. The former belligerents were also in financial difficulties.

Trade Policy

Unfortunately for the whole world, the first reaction of most nations beset by balance of payments problems was to restrict imports by one device or another. Such "beggar-my-neighbour remedies"* inevitably backfire and cause more loss to the former importer, since his suppliers are no longer able to be his customers.

The United States was among the leaders in raising tariff rates at this time. Senator Smoot of Utah, chairman of the Senate Finance Committee, had, as a representative of the sugar interests of his state, always been in favor of high tariffs. The House Committee was headed by Representative Hawley of Oregon. The depression provided the opportunity for which protectionists had been waiting, and President Hoover in spite of his vaguely liberal principles did not oppose the Smoot-Hawley tariff bill. The higher rates had for many countries the effect of closing the United States market and was a serious blow to plans for settling reparations. Countries like Germany could not hope to pay their debts unless they could sell their products. Great Britain raised its tariff in 1931, and increases in some duties were enacted by Canada, Cuba, Mexico, France, Italy, Spain, and a number of smaller countries. Still other duties were raised in 1932 by countries retaliating against the first round of increases.

Even worse than the increase in tariff rates was the use of import quotas or other quantitative restrictions on trade, starting a vicious spiral as one country after another felt itself threatened by the actions of its neighbors. Many countries used exchange controls to force trade into the desired channels. Germany under the Nazi regime developed an elaborate system of import and exchange controls, with different rates

---

* This phrase was used by Joan Robinson in *Essays on the Theory of Employment* in 1947.

of exchange for each country and each commodity. Barter arrangements between countries were another serious blow to world trade. Sweden permitted Greece to pay part of its debt in tobacco and use the rest of 400,000 dollars worth of tobacco to pay for Swedish goods. Hungary exchanged its pigs and eggs for Czechoslovak wood fuel and tourist entertainment. North and South American countries made similar swap agreements. The result was of course a continuing decline in the volume of world trade, since the possibility of such swap arrangements was limited to a small number of commodities. The total of world foreign trade fell steadily until by 1933 it amounted to about one-third of the value in 1929 and about two-thirds of the quantity.

The Bank for International Settlements

During these years when the United States was experiencing the impact of the stock market crash and depression, an international financial institution was finally organized. Several of the conferences in the early 1920s had suggested such an organization, but it was not until German reparations payments broke down and the Dawes Plan of 1924 had become inoperable that the problem was taken up in earnest. At Geneva a group of representative bankers and Treasury officials agreed in September 1928 that the reparations payments had to be settled. A few months later a conference under the chairmanship of Owen D. Young of the General Electric Company discussed methods of handling transfer and exchange operations, deliveries in kind, and bond flotations.

The plan for the Bank for International Settlements, as it was developed at this conference, provided for a bank which had as its primary function the handling of payments made by Germany on reparations account, payments which were smaller in amount than those of the Dawes Plan, and spread over a limited number of years. Stock in the Bank was to be owned by treasuries and central banks of the countries involved, except that in the United States the Federal Reserve banks were not empowered to own stock and a group of private bankers was substituted. The Bank was to be located in Basel, and accounts were to be kept in gold Swiss francs. Deposits could be made only by central banks and treasuries, and could be invested in short- and long-term obligations only with the permission of the authorities of the country involved.

The Bank began operations in May 1930 and performed a useful service in arranging the issue of the Young Plan bonds into which a large part of the German reparations had been commuted. It also handled the monthly installments of the annuity payments by Germany to the United States. By the middle of 1931 most of the central banks with gold currencies had become shareholders in the Bank, and this made possible the initiation of clearing arrangements among treasuries.

Far more important than the technical services rendered by the new institution was the opportunity it provided for regular meetings of the financial leaders of the industrialized world. The international cooperation on this informal level laid the basis for the International Bank for Reconstruction and Development and the International Monetary Fund of the period after World War II. The Bank had been organized too late, however, to ward off the breakdown which began in May 1931.

CHAPTER 14

Roosevelt dime

FINANCING THE NEW DEAL

The Banking Holiday

A T THE low point of one of the most severe depressions the country had ever seen, Franklin Roosevelt was elected to the presidency of the United States. He was regarded as a mild liberal; as governor of New York he had obtained adoption of several welfare measures and relief for the unemployed. The platform of the Democratic party on which he campaigned, however, was almost as conservative as that of the Republicans, promising a balanced budget and accusing the Hoover administration of extravagance because it had not achieved this. Roosevelt did qualify his promise by saying that he would spend if necessary to aid the poor, and he refused to give Hoover the assurance he sought, a few weeks before the inauguration, that a "sound currency" would be maintained. As a Congressman remarked later, Roosevelt was for "sound currency, but lots of it."[1]

During the campaign the situation had become markedly worse. Some of the business indices reached their lowest point in late 1932; unemployment was rising and national income was falling. The increase in the number of bank failures, including many large banks in the industrial centers of the north and northeast, forced bank holidays in 38 states between October 1932, when the first holiday was declared in Nevada, and March 4, 1933, the Saturday of the inauguration. On March 4 itself, holidays were declared in New York and in Illinois, the two great financial states, and the New York Stock Exchange and the Chicago Board of Trade were closed. These were the days when banks and exchanges were normally open for business on Saturday mornings.

Previous crises in the United States had involved the currency supply; this one did not. The Federal Reserve banks had been able to provide an ample supply of notes to meet the increasing demand for circulating media in areas where banks no longer existed, and for hoarding as the public became alarmed. The volume of Federal Reserve notes in circulation had more than doubled during the previous two years, so that by March 1933 they were nearly half of the total 7.5 billion dollars in circulation outside of the Treasury and the Reserve banks. Federal Reserve credit was also at a peak at this time, since much of the currency had been obtained by member bank borrowing; in other words, one of the principal objects of the Reserve system had been achieved.

There still remained the problem of the banking crisis. The first financial measure of the new administration was taken on Sunday, March 5, in the form of a presidential edict (under the somewhat questionable authority of the Trading with the Enemy Act of 1917) declaring a national banking holiday. It included even the twelve Federal Reserve banks, although there was no question about their liquidity. No bank might accept deposits, cash checks, or even make change except under Treasury regulation; no gold or silver might be hoarded or exported. At the same time Congress was called into special session on March 9.

When Congress met, it listened to the text of a bill drawn up in five days by Secretary of the Treasury William H. Woodin and not yet printed. The bill was nevertheless passed by both houses and signed by the President the same day. This Emergency Banking Act made legal what the presidential edict had already done: authorized the issue of Federal Reserve *bank* notes, secured by government obligations or commercial paper, and provided that banks be reopened as fast as they could be examined and licensed by the Treasury. The Federal Reserve Banks had reopened on March 13, and by the heroic efforts of banking and Treasury officials working around the clock, over 5000 member banks, about three-fourths of the total, were opened three days later. Within a month, nearly three-fourths of the nonmember banks had been opened, many with the aid of additional capital provided by government agencies. Some banks were of course never able to reopen, and some large industrial cities were without banking service for many months.

The Banking Acts of 1933 and 1935

During these months Congress was preparing a more carefully drawn bill, which became the Glass-Steagall Banking Act of 1933, signed on June 21 of that year. It widened the authority of the Federal Reserve Board so that credit might be refused to a bank making too many loans for speculative purposes. A limit might be set to the amount of security loans made by member banks, through the setting of margin requirements. As a further device for discouraging the bankers' balances which provided funds for speculation, member banks were no longer permitted to pay interest on demand deposits; even the rate of interest on time deposits was to be set by the Board. Investment banking was to be separated from commercial banking, thus destroying the affiliate system and forcing each bank to choose which type of business it would conduct. To the surprise of many, J. P. Morgan and Company, the outstanding investment banking firm of the country, chose to specialize in commercial banking and leave the investment business to some of its former partners who organized Morgan, Stanley and Company.

The most important accomplishment of this Act was the creation of the Federal Deposit Insurance Corporation. One of the tragic consequences of the depression had been the loss of lifetime savings by thousands of little people who had perforce trusted their local banks, many of which closed never to reopen. There had been several earlier experiments with deposit insurance by states; most of them had eventually failed because of insufficient supervision. A national scheme based on contributions by the banks and safeguarded by careful bank examination was quite a different matter.

The FDIC was established by adding a section to the Federal Reserve Act and assessing all member banks one-half of 1 percent of their deposit liabilities. In addition, the Treasury subscribed 150 million dollars, and the Reserve banks subscribed one-half of their surplus, about 139 million. Savings banks which wished to share in the plan were permitted to join the Reserve system. By the time the legislation went into effect, the weakest banks had been weeded out and prevented from reopening; their depositors of course did not share in the insurance plan. Fears that the experiment would be extremely costly proved to be groundless, and the system was a success. Bank failures in the next decade were so few that insured bank assessments were reduced to one-twelfth of 1 percent annually, and in 1950 to a varying amount still lower.* Individual deposits which had been insured only up to the first 2500 dollars at the start were insured up to 5000 after 1935, so that 98 percent of all deposits were fully covered. This was raised again several times and by October 1966 the maximum was 15,000 dollars. Banks hastened to become members of the FDIC in order to attract depositors. State banks with average deposits of more than 1 million were required to become members of the Federal Reserve in order to join the FDIC, but small state banks were under no such obligation. Even the large state banks were freed from this requirement in 1939.

Two years later the Banking Act of 1935, in addition to changes in the FDIC legislation, further strengthened the position of the Federal Reserve Board. It was thenceforth to be known as "Board of Governors of the Federal Reserve System," with a chairman and a vice chairman. The term of office was increased to 14 years from the previous 12 years, but reappointments were not permitted; salaries were increased. The number of members was reduced to 7, appointed by the President, thus removing the Secretary of the Treasury and the Comptroller of the Currency as *ex officio* members. The authority of the Board to establish discount rates for the Reserve banks was made specific; the original Act had left the question in doubt. In addition, the Board was empowered to increase reserve requirements against member bank deposits up to twice the ratios set by the Act of 1917 if this was considered necessary in order to avoid "injurious credit expansion or contraction."

As a corollary to the upgrading of the Federal Reserve Board, the heads of the twelve Reserve banks were no longer to be known as Governors, but only as presidents. They were to be appointed by their boards of directors, but had to be approved by the Board of Governors of the Federal Reserve system. Moreover the Board was given the ex-

---

* The rate was about one thirty-second of 1 percent for 1965.

clusive right to conduct negotiations with foreign banks and bankers. There would be no more secret meetings at the Federal Reserve Bank of New York followed by courtesy calls on the Board in Washington; henceforth the business would be conducted in Washington, and the courtesy call, if the Board gave permission, would be made in New York.

All of these provisions combined to give the Board a status and an independence which were reflected in its policy during the ensuing years. During the 1920s the leadership of Governor Strong of the New York Bank had made it the most important element of the system. The change in the Reserve Act, combined with the reorganization of the open-market operations under a Policy Conference which included heads of all twelve Reserve banks, shifted the balance and increased the influence of the bankers from the south and west.

Federal Reserve Policy

Through the early years of the New Deal, Federal Reserve policy was directed toward maintaining easy money in order to stimulate recovery. Member bank reserves were further reduced during 1933 by moderate gold exports, but the banks had little need to borrow from the Reserve system because business demand for loans had still not increased. In the hope of stimulating revival, the Reserve banks pumped 600 million dollars into the money market through open-market operations during the year, as well as continuing to hold the discount rate very low.

By early 1934 the discount rate at the New York Federal Reserve bank was down again to 1.5 percent, but even this low rate did not stimulate member bank borrowing. Even if the demand for commercial loans had increased, the member banks would have had ample reserves, since gold imports had begun to flow into the United States in heavy volume. The political and financial turmoil abroad, especially in France and Ethiopia, and later in Germany, caused enormous sums to take refuge in the United States. The gold stock reached a peak of 23 billion in 1942 (in the devalued dollar). To prevent this gold from increasing member bank reserves too rapidly, the Treasury after December 1936 began a policy of "sterilizing" the imports of gold which banks were obliged to sell to the government, by placing it in an inactive account rather than in deposits with the Reserve banks where it would have been part of their reserves.

The Reserve authorities also took steps to reduce member bank excess reserves in 1936 and 1937 by doubling the previous reserve requirements against demand deposits to 14, 20, and 26 percent for the three classes of member banks, and to 6 percent against time deposits in all classes. This was the limit of increase permitted by the 1935 legislation. On the other hand, open-market sales of securities, which would have absorbed some of the member bank reserves, were not authorized by the Open Market Committee, and Federal Reserve credit outstanding increased slightly under the authority to lend directly to individuals who were unable to borrow from banks. The net result of these contradictory policies was that excess reserves of member banks reached a peak of nearly 7 billion dollars in the latter months of 1940.

Loans to business by commercial banks increased very slowly throughout the 1930s. The banks therefore invested heavily in government obligations issued to finance relief and reconstruction. Largely as a result of government borrowing, demand deposits in all banks doubled between 1934 and 1941, rising from 18 to 39 billion. Time deposits rose more slowly, but currency outside banks also doubled, from nearly 5 to nearly 10 billion. It became evident that, although an increase in the discount rate might be an effective device in fighting inflation, a mere decrease in discount rates was of little help in counteracting depression.

Government Corporations and Relief Projects

One of the most powerful agencies by which funds were pumped into the economy during the New Deal was the Reconstruction Finance Corporation, which antedated the New Deal by more than a year. Concerned by the number of bank failures, a more active Congress established the RFC in January, 1932 on the model of the War Finance Corporation of World War I. The original capital of 500 million was subscribed by the Treasury, and its borrowing authority was limited originally to 1500 million dollars; this was increased in nearly every session of Congress as additional duties were ascribed to it.

The first task of the RFC had been to make loans to banks and other financial institutions, and to railroads with permission of the Interstate

Commerce Commission, since banks owned large amounts of railroad bonds. Six months later the Emergency Relief and Construction Act and the Federal Home Loan Act gave the RFC more funds and power, to lend to states and localities for relief purposes. Nearly every state availed itself of this opportunity in the next few months. In February 1933 the RFC was authorized to make advances to the Secretary of Agriculture for aid to farmers.

A mechanism was therefore at hand when the new administration took office, and within a matter of days the functions of the RFC were expanded. It was authorized to buy from banks their preferred stock or capital notes or debentures—a type of issue which had never before been permitted for banks—thus enlarging their capital so that they might resume operations and provide service for communities which had lacked it for weeks and even months. More than 7000 banks availed themselves of this privilege. During ten months of 1933, fourteen more pieces of legislation were passed which involved the RFC in relief for real estate, farms, foreign security holders, and disasters of various kinds. In 1934 nine more laws, and in the following three years fifteen additional laws, still further expanded the duties of the RFC. Among them was the handling of dollar devaluation.*

When the Electric Home and Farm Authority ("Little Eva" in the New Deal slang) was taken over from the Tennessee Valley Authority in 1935, the RFC purchased its capital of 850 million dollars. In 1936 the RFC acquired most of the stock of 100 million of the Commodity Credit Corporation. The Federal National Mortgage Association ("Fanny May") was set up in April 1938 with capital from the RFC to help establish a normal mortgage market. Even foreign trade was financed by the ubiquitous RFC. When the first Export Import Bank was organized in 1934 to further the growing trade with Russia, all but 1 million of its 11 million capital was subscribed by the RFC.

By 1940, when the reconstruction period was over and the defense period was beginning, the total disbursements of the RFC had amounted to nearly 10 billion dollars. About one-third of this sum had gone to banks, another third to relief projects and to agriculture, and the remainder was divided among railroads, insurance and mortgage com-

---

* See p. 335.

panies, business corporations of various kinds, and self-liquidating projects. The loans made possible by these activities ranged all the way from 25 dollars to a Georgia share-cropper, to 208 million for an aqueduct from the Colorado River to southern California. Many of the loans were repaid and the net cost would be hard to estimate.

During the years of depression there were many other projects for restoring prosperity to the economy, or for keeping people alive until prosperity returned. Some of them seemed outrageously expensive at the time, but many of them were eventually self-liquidating in whole or in part.

One of the startling innovations of the New Deal was the Tennessee Valley Authority, authorized by legislation of World War I. It was to build dams in order to control the floods which periodically devastated the area, and at the same time to use the dams to generate power which could be sold to small business and consumers at "yardstick" prices and make possible many new industries. Public utilities were certain that they would be forced out of business by this competition; to their amazement their profits increased over the years as they purchased the low-cost power and resold it at a modest markup to an enormously increased body of users. Equally important was the saving to farmers and city dwellers by the prevention of floods.

The Public Works Administration was created by the same Act that in June 1933 created the National Recovery Administration, symbolized by a Blue Eagle. It was given an appropriation of 3.3 billion dollars for two years. By 1939, in spite of a slowing down during 1937, the PWA had spent about 6 billion under the sharp eyes of Harold Ickes, who made sure that there was no waste or fraud. Its projects were financed in some cases by loans and in others by grants, and ranged from a room added to a school, to the Triborough Bridge in New York. Even if the project was not technically self-liquidating, it added to the capital assets of the nation and cannot be written off as a complete financial loss.

The Civil Works Administration spent about 1 billion, mostly during the winter of 1933–34 when unemployment was heavy and many individuals were in serious want. Because it had no time to develop elaborate plans, many of its projects were less impressive than those of PWA. But parks were developed, swamps were drained, and schools were taught by four million men and women whom it employed by January 1934.

During 1935 most of the relief expenditures went through the Federal Emergency Relief Administration which had been set up in May 1933. It made grants, not loans, to the states, in amounts which varied with the relief payments of the state and local governments themselves. During its three years, the FERA spent about 3 billion dollars, supplementing the dwindling resources of state and local agencies. The central government emerged as the only unit with sufficient taxing and borrowing power to meet the needs of the emergency. After 1935 the attempt to make federal contributions depend on local and state relief expenditures had to be given up, and the relief programs became frankly those of the central government.

One of the most successful projects, although not the largest, was the Civilian Conservation Corps, modeled after the conservation camps set up by New York state while Roosevelt was governor. It took unemployed young men, most of them from city and rural slums and, besides giving them adequate food, taught them skills and acquainted them with their own country. More than two and a half million enlisted in this program, and they did enormously valuable work in the forests—clearing them, replanting them where needed, building fire towers and trails for fire fighters. In addition the project made the country conscious of the need for conservation measures to protect the national heritage.

Of all the New Deal efforts to end the depression, the Works Progress Administration probably suffered most from abuse and ridicule. It was authorized in April 1935 by one of the largest appropriation bills Congress had ever passed, 4.9 billion dollars, and it was designed to get three and a half million unemployed men and women off of relief rolls and into employment.* Undoubtedly some of the work projects were of limited value except in restoring a measure of self-respect to the workers. But others were imaginative and constructive. Hospitals, schools, playgrounds, and airports were built or improved in communities in need of such assistance. The Federal Theatre Project produced live plays in communities which had never before seen anything but moving pictures. The Writers' Project turned out a series of state handbooks and ethnic studies which surprisingly proved that they had commercial value. There was even a Federal Art Project which decorated public buildings with

---

* The unemployables were left to the FERA and then to the states.

murals and taught painting and clay modeling to adult classes. The National Youth Administration gave jobs to students so that they could remain in school.

By the time the WPA terminated in 1943 it had provided jobs for eight million persons. The high point was three million in 1939. After that the individuals trained in WPA jobs gradually found private employment, many of them in the growing defense industries. The total expenditures of this program amounted to slightly more than 10 billion dollars, to which the state and local government sponsors added 2.8 billion. These communities were richer by 650,000 miles of roads, 16,000 miles of water mains, 24,000 miles of sewers, and 125,000 public buildings, in addition to the less obvious gains from the art, music and theatre projects.

The improved economic conditions through the first part of 1937 seemed to offer an opportunity at last to bring the budget into balance. PWA was terminated, and WPA was reduced. Fear of inflation was justified, since wholesale prices had already risen by about 30 percent since devaluation. However, in the last quarter of the year there was a sudden slump with increased unemployment. The situation deteriorated so rapidly that by mid-1938 Congress was easily persuaded to authorize the revival of PWA and WPA, and in addition to provide subsidies for low-cost housing, the National Youth Administration for unemployed youth and students, and the Farm Security Administration—a total of 3.75 billion dollars. Although these measures kept many from actual starvation, there were nine million unemployed in 1939, ten years after the great crash, about one-sixth of the civilian labor force.

Social Legislation

The depression inevitably increased the demand for a more permanent system of federal assistance to the aged, the needy, and the unemployed. Long before 1930 England and many European countries had provided some kind of help, in the form either of charitable relief based on need or insurance based on previous contributions. In the United States this had been left to private organizations or to local governments whose funds were soon exhausted during the depression. The desperate situation of many old people made it easy for Dr. Francis Townsend to organize them into Old Age Revolving Pensions, Ltd., which from 1934 on became a political force to be reckoned with, especially in the western states. Its platform demanded 200 dollars monthly to all citizens over 60 years of age, the money to be raised by a transactions tax of 2 percent. At the same time Senator Huey Long of Louisiana was heading a Share the Wealth program which was rather vague in detail but had an enormous appeal.

The federal government felt obliged to take some action, and many New Dealers hoped to obtain legislation to take care of the aged, the unemployed, and the sick. The American Medical Association successfully prevented legislation to provide what it termed "socialized medicine," but there were no vested interests to object to legislation for the aged and the unemployed.

In the summer of 1934 President Roosevelt set up a cabinet Committee on Economic Security to draft a legislative plan, and the resulting bill was presented to Congress early in 1935. Months were spent in public hearings and in debating whether the help for the aged and the unemployed should be of the insurance type, based on actuarial probability, or the relief type, and whether it should be entirely federal or joint federal and state. The Social Security Act signed by the President in August 1935 was a compromise. The old age insurance program (officially entitled Old Age, Survivors and Disability Insurance) was to be federally administered, and paid for by a tax divided between employer and employee; at the age of 65, retired workers would receive a monthly stipend based on the amount of their earnings. Many classes of workers—domestics, farm laborers, the self-employed, teachers and other professional workers—were not covered by the original Act, although most of them were brought into the system later. The most serious criticism was that the tax was by its nature regressive, and that the building up of a reserve fund in the middle of the depression was deflationary and harmful to the economy. These points were less important after recovery began, and most of the other criticisms were met by later legislation which increased the coverage and the size of the stipends.

Another part of the 1935 Act set up insurance against unemployment which was shared between the federal government and the states, as was also the aid to dependent mothers and children, the blind, and the indigent aged, as well as some public health services. The unemployment insurance was to be financed by a federal tax on employers of four (later of eight) or more persons. If a state set up a program which met federal standards, employers paid a state tax and received an offset of 90 percent of the federal tax. This encouraged the states to set up good systems and discouraged poor systems, and within two years all 48 states had unemployment compensation systems of some kind.*

In spite of the grave misgivings with which the social security legislation was viewed by many conservatives at the time of its passage, all major parties incorporated it into their promises to the electorate during each subsequent campaign. Like public education which a century earlier had been viewed as the beginning of socialism and the end of the family, social security has taken its place as one of the bulwarks of American democracy.

Congress also, with great reluctance, passed the Fair Labor Standards Act which became law on June 25, 1938. It set minimum wages for work on goods entering into interstate commerce at 40 cents an hour, and working hours at a maximum of 40 per week. It also, after years of unsuccessful attempts to stop this disgraceful practice, forbade the use of child labor in interstate commerce. Since two years were permitted to elapse before these laws went into operation, the immediate effect on the economy was negligible. Nevertheless, by the end of 1938 there was a definite improvement in national income.

After every war, veterans tend to form a pressure group to obtain from the government more adequate compensation for the sacrifices they made in defense of their country. As early as 1924, Congress had authorized a payment to them based upon length of service, but not actually to be paid until 1945. When the veterans had marched on Washington during the Hoover administration, in an effort to enforce their claims to immediate assistance, they had been fired on and routed by the police and, to add insult to injury, the bonus bill they demanded had been vetoed by the President.

The deepening depression and continuing political pressure made further action necessary. But, when Congress passed a bonus bill in April 1935, it provided the funds by the printing of greenbacks, a solution

---

* See p. 375.

which was equally unacceptable to the President and to Secretary Morgenthau. The bill was vetoed on the grounds that veterans in need were already provided for, and that the precedent of paying bills by irredeemable paper money would do great harm. The veto was not overruled by Congress, but a year later another bonus act was passed, specifying that the payment was to be made in bonds which would accumulate interest if held. When this also was vetoed, Congress speedily overrode the veto and the Treasury issued an additional 2.3 billion of bonds to meet the cost.

Aid to Agriculture

The farmers had been the first sufferers from the depression. All through the 1920s, farm prices had been falling from their inflated war peaks, and the farmers' share of the national income had steadily declined. After 1929, farm prices fell even more rapidly than those of other commodities. Corn went to 5 cents a bushel, eggs to 5 cents a dozen, and wheat could not be sold at any price so that farmers burned it for fuel rather than allowing it to rot in piles beside the freight tracks. It became almost impossible for farm mortgages to be paid off, and by 1932 it was reported that 20,000 farms were being foreclosed each month.

In 1929 the Agricultural Marketing Act created the Federal Farm Board with a fund of half a billion dollars to be loaned to farm cooperatives so that grain could be marketed gradually throughout the year. It was a plan well adapted to smoothing out the seasonal fluctuations in prices, but it could not cope with a steady decline in prices over the years. Moreover the high tariff of 1930 almost destroyed the ability of European manufacturers to sell their products in the United States and earn enough to pay for American farm produce. By the middle of 1931 the government found itself the owner of so much wheat (acquired as collateral for loans which farmers were unable to repay) that it began to sell, and the price fell to 40 cents and less per bushel. In 1932, in spite of government holdings of 3 million bales, the price of cotton fell to less than 5 cents a pound. Pressure from the desperate farmers explains much of the early legislation of the New Deal.

A new plan devised by government officials and representatives of farm organizations was embodied in the Agriculture Adjustment Act of May 1933. In order to raise prices and increase farmer purchasing power up to the 1910–14 level, farmers were to be paid for reducing their acreage of certain staple crops. The cost of this program was to be met by a tax on the processing of farm products, a tax which was declared unconstitutional by the Supreme Court in 1935. Easier and cheaper credit was also to be provided for farmers. Attached to this bill was the Thomas amendment which gave the President power to inflate the currency as an additional device for raising prices.

One of the best features of this legislation was that it concentrated in one organization, the Farm Credit Administration, the farm credit operations which had been scattered among five agencies. No longer would farmers have to shop around to find the lowest rates and the easiest terms for the type of credit they needed. Under the supervision of the FCA the Federal Land Banks, established in 1916, were to handle all the financing of farm mortgages; the Federal Intermediate Credit Banks, set up in 1923, were to rediscount loans on crops in the hands of farm cooperatives or warehouses. A new Production Credit Corporation was created to handle disaster relief and make loans for seed, and a new Central Bank for Cooperatives would finance farmers' cooperatives. Twelve regional district offices would bring these agencies within easy reach of every farmer, and would reduce the cost of farm credit.

The success of the new plan was evidenced by the increase in federal loans to farmers. Three hundred loans daily, by November 1933, were preventing foreclosures, and the total loans were amounting to 30 million dollars monthly. About one-fifth of the farm mortgage debt was refinanced by the Farm Credit Administration during its first eighteen months of operation, and the worst of the immediate farm crisis was over.

From this time on, the federal government became increasingly involved in programs for the relief of agricultural producers, programs which became a heavy burden to urban taxpayers.*

---

* See Chapter 16.

Federal Receipts and Expenditures

There was almost nothing of conscious fiscal policy during the depression. Expenditures for relief and social security were very large for the time, but their effect was offset not only by tax rate increases but also by several sudden shifts from expansion to contraction in monetary policy. In 1940 the Secretary of the Treasury classified the federal expenditures during these years as shown in Table 8. These figures do

TABLE 8. FEDERAL GOVERNMENT EXPENDITURES FOR YEARS ENDING JUNE 30, 1933 TO 1940 (*in million of dollars*)

	1933	1934	1935	1936	1937	1938	1939	1940	Total
Total	3,864	6,011	7,010	8,666	8,177	7,239	8,707	8,998	58,672
National defense	651	540	710	912	935	1,028	1,163	1,559	7,497
Interest on public debt	689	757	821	749	866	926	941	1,041	6,790
Social Security[a]	—	—	—	28	167	271	320	357	1,143
Aid to agriculture	209	780	1,076	938	976	860	1,235	1,567	7,643
Relief and work relief	350	1,845	2,267	2,292	2,376	1,869	2,602	1,906	15,507
Public works	442	698	883	730	1,024	783	992	948	6,500
All other	1,523	1,391	1,253	3,017	1,833	1,502	1,454	1,620	13,592

Source: Annual Reports of the Secretary of the Treasury.
[a] Grants made to states under Social Security.

not include the subscriptions to capital stock of the RFC and other government-sponsored corporations, nor the loans by the Commodity Credit Corporation and other agencies, all of which were repayable, and most of which were actually repaid.

The deficit in the federal budget, which had appeared in 1931 for the first time since 1919, continued to appear every year until after the war, in spite of increased revenues from many sources. Tax rates were raised almost every year in a futile effort to provide adequate funds. The Revenue Act of 1934 increased the tax on gifts and estates, and on earnings of corporations above 12.5 percent of the value of their stock. The personal income tax was made more sharply progressive. The Revenue Act of 1935 increased the surtax rate on individual incomes and on estates; the corporation income tax was graduated and made progressive. In 1936 a tax on undistributed profits of corporations was added to the income tax. The 1937 Act was devoted primarily to stopping leaks in the previous laws. In 1939 the undistributed profits tax was abolished, and a flat rate of 18 percent was levied on corporations with net income of more than 25,000 dollars.

Customs revenues and corporate and personal income tax revenues reached their lowest point in 1933 and increased slowly thereafter; only in 1939 was the upward trend halted for a year. Agricultural processing taxes produced significant amounts in 1934 and 1935, and the tax on alcoholic beverages was adding 600 million to the revenue by 1940, as much as the tax on tobacco. Social Security taxes added more than they cost the federal government after 1937. By 1940 the need for defense expenditures caused nearly all rates to be increased and personal exemptions to be decreased. The sources of federal income for 1933–1940 are given in Table 9.

Even before the New Deal, the national debt had begun to rise; from a low point of 15.9 billion dollars on June 30, 1930, it was already

TABLE 9. SOURCES OF FEDERAL INCOME FOR YEARS ENDING JUNE 30, 1933 TO 1940 (*in millions of dollars*)

	1933	1934	1935	1936	1937	1938	1939	1940
Total	2,080	3,116	3,801	4,116	5,294	6,242	5,668	5,925
Income taxes	747	820	1,106	1,427	2,180	2,629	2,185	2,130
Internal revenue	873	1,481	1,650	2,004	2,189	2,272	2,237	2,360
Agric. proc.	—	371	526	68	—	—	—	—
Social Security	—	—	—	—	253	755	741	833
Customs duties	251	313	343	387	486	359	319	349
Misc.	209	131	176	230	186	227	186	253
Net deficit	1,784	2,896	3,209	4,550	3,149	1,384	3,542	3,611
Interest-bearing debt	22,158	26,480	27,645	32,989	35,800	36,576	39,886	42,376

Source: Annual Reports of the Secretary of the Treasury.

more than 22 billion when President Hoover left office in 1933. Inevitably the relief projects of the New Deal had to be met by borrowing. Much of the borrowing took the form of short notes with maturities of 1 to 5 years, certificates of indebtedness, and Treasury bills which usually ran for 15 days. In 1930, the last year with a surplus, threefourths of the gross debt (12 billion of the 16 billion) had been in the form of bonds. As the debt increased, it became difficult to avoid issuing short-term obligations, but the Treasury made some headway after 1938 and long issues increased faster than short. This eased the problem of debt management until the war broke out.

Securities and Exchange Commission

The strengthening of the Reserve system by the legislation of 1935 had been in the nature of locking the door after the horse was stolen. In this category belonged also the new legislation regulating the securities exchanges. The first of these Acts, in May 1933, established the principle, adopted from the English Companies Act of 1900, that the issuer of a security was responsible for giving adequate publicity to all relevant facts, and that an investor who suffered loss from failure to get the facts might sue the issuer. The penalties of the American law were drastic, and were somewhat lessened when the law was revised in 1934. This new Securities Exchange Act took the administration from the Federal Trade Commission and entrusted it to a new Securities and Exchange Commission. Large exchanges were required to register with the Commission and furnish information to it about their membership and their operation.

The most important function of the new agency was to approve all new public offerings except federal and state bonds, railroad issues which were controlled by the Interstate Commerce Commission, bank issues which were under special federal or state authorities, and small issues below specified totals (100,000 dollars at first, later 300,000). The issuing group had to file a registration statement and wait twenty days for approval; then a public offering might be made. The Commission was made responsible also for the maintaining of a genuine market, without manipulation or rigging of the sort which had so often created scandal in the past.

A year later the duties of the Commission were enlarged by the Public Utility Holding Companies Act of 1935. This was the "death sentence" law, designed to eliminate the evils of the elaborate corporate structures like the Insull empire which had reached their climax in the boom period. The Act required geographical integration and corporate simplification of public utilities so that there would be only one layer of holding company above any operating company. For many companies this was a difficult task. The unscrambling of the Associated Gas and Electric Company, for example, which had twenty classes of securities outstanding when the Act was passed, was not completed until the late 1940s. The experience of the Commission in administering these provisions led it in 1941 to rule that public utility offerings should thenceforth be subject to competitive bidding. The Investment Company Act and the Investment Advisers Act of August 1940 provided for the registration and regulation by the SEC of investment companies and advisers, except banks.

The financial community protested against most of these changes at the start, but gradually came to realize that regulation was a protection for themselves and in their own best interests in the long run. The general public approved the measures, especially after the disclosures of fraud and finagling which were made by the various Congressional committee hearings after the stock market collapse.

The Securities and Exchange Act of 1934 had given the Federal Reserve Board the responsibility of regulating credit based on any security registered on a national securities exchange. In Regulation T of October 1, 1934, the Board spelled out the rules for margin accounts of brokers, and adopted a complicated formula under which about 75 percent of the market value of a security might be borrowed, or a margin of 25 percent be paid in cash at the time of purchase. The stock market was relatively inactive at that time, and a survey by the Board showed that most customers were borrowing 50 percent or less. As business began to revive in 1935 and 1936, stock prices also rose, and in January 1936 the Board increased the margin requirements to about 45 percent. Several months later the Board adopted Regulation U, which brought loans made by banks for purchasing or carrying securities under the same rules as loans by brokers and dealers. At the same time the previous formula was abandoned and a flat percentage of current market value was used to state the margin requirement. For the rest of the year 1936 the margin of cash payment was set at 55 percent; in November 1937 this was reduced to 40 percent, and there it remained through 1944.

The depression of 1937–38 created an atmosphere in which the old suspicion of monopoly as the cause of all the economic ills was strengthened. Congress therefore authorized an inquiry into the concentration of economic power under a Temporary National Economic Committee chaired by Senator Joseph O'Mahoney of Wyoming. The inquiry required nearly three years, with months of public hearings and hundreds of witnesses, and left a monument of thirty-one volumes of testimony and forty-three monographs. Students of business and financial practices found this material invaluable. Unlike the work of its predecessor, the National Monetary Commission, however, that of the TNEC resulted in little legislation.

The real attack on the evils of monopoly came from Thurman Arnold, Assistant Attorney General after 1938. He built up his staff to a total of 190 lawyers and brought suit against restrictive patents and monopolistic practices even when they involved such powerful giants as General Electric and the Aluminum Company of America. The courts found his interpretation of the Sherman Act unconvincing and refused to support him in many cases. When the war started, firms with government contracts could plead that their actions were necessary even if monopolistic, and the campaign against them had to be abandoned.

Devaluation of the Dollar

During the last months of the Hoover administration a conference had been held in Geneva to prepare for the Economic Conference scheduled for June 1933 in London. The agenda included the reduction of armaments, the lowering of trade barriers, the stabilization of currencies, and the reestablishment of friendly relations among nations; the question of war debts was explicitly excluded. During the first months of Roosevelt's term, eleven representatives of participating nations came to Washington one at a time to learn what attitude the United States would take at the conference. France and Italy were still on the gold standard, and Great Britain was hoping to return to it. The first of the foreign visitors was

Check signed by Franklin D. Roosevelt

Prime Minister Ramsay MacDonald but, by the time he arrived, the United States was also off the gold standard and any conversation was futile. This action had been taken in order to improve the domestic situation with little or no regard to its effect on other countries.

The conference, however, met as planned in London in June. President Roosevelt had just announced that there would be no tariff legislation in that session of Congress. This action destroyed any bargaining power that Secretary of State Cordell Hull might have had in obtaining trade concessions from other nations. Moreover, when on July 1 the principal European representatives declared themselves in favor of a gold standard, the reply came from the United States, dictated by the President, that it would be a "catastrophe" if the conference "allowed itself to be diverted . . . by a purely artificial and temporary experiment affecting the monetary exchange of a few nations only" and that the "old fetishes of international bankers" were being replaced by national currencies with constant purchasing power.[2] The conference, like its twenty-seven predecessors since World War I, recessed indefinitely with little to show for its pains. That little consisted of an agreement, pushed through by Senator Key Pittman of Colorado, that the nations would buy and sell limited quantities of silver, in order to stabilize the world silver market.

It seemed certain from the President's message to London that a policy of price inflation was to be followed in the United States. At the end of August an Executive order gave permission for newly mined domestic gold to be sold through the Federal Reserve banks, and two months later this activity was entrusted to the RFC. The price of gold was gradually raised until by the end of the year it was about 35 dollars an ounce as compared with the $20.67 mint par.

The gold price increase was brought to a halt by the passage of the Gold Reserve Act of 1934 which replaced the Gold Standard Act of 1900. All monetary gold was thereafter to belong to the government, and only the Treasury might buy or sell gold. The power of the President to reduce the weight of the gold dollar, under the law of May 12, 1933, was limited; the new dollar might not exceed 60 percent of the old weight. The next day a presidential proclamation fixed the weight at 59.06 percent of the former 25.8 grains, making the new dollar $15\frac{5}{21}$ grains nine-tenths fine, the equivalent of $35 per ounce.

The gold in the Federal Reserve banks was turned over to the Treasury in exchange for gold certificates; only the Reserve banks and the Treasury might hold these certificates, and only the Treasury might hold gold. The dollar value of all the monetary gold was increased from 1.4 billion to 4.2 billion dollars, a paper profit of 2.8 billion. Two billion of this was appropriated to the financing of the Stabilization Fund, and 640 million to retirement of the national bank notes. In 1945 the United States paid its share of the World Bank and the International Monetary Fund capital out of this profit.*

In thus devaluing gold, the United States put an end to the long and futile struggle, which had been waged ever since the end of World War I, to restore the prewar system of currencies based on stable exchange rates. It had been a heroic if ill-advised struggle accompanied by hardships to many. England had already been forced to abandon the gold standard in September 1931. The action of the United States triggered a series of similar actions abroad, and a cycle of devalution began. Inflation was not a reversible process; deflation put new elements of disequilibrium into the economic system rather than correcting the disequilibria produced by the preceding inflation.

The least defensible part of the American action was the joint resolution of Congress of June 5, 1933, declaring the gold clause in contracts "to be against policy" and therefore void. Although this action was upheld by the Supreme Court in one of its 5 to 4 decisions, it was unhappily reminiscent of the greenback wavering after the Civil War.

---

* See p. 363.

United States Stabilization Fund

The stabilization fund of 2 billion dollars which had been set up by the Gold Reserve Act of January 31, 1934, had been put under the exclusive control of the Secretary of the Treasury and had given him the responsibility of carrying on any sales or purchases of foreign exchange necessary to maintain the stability of the dollar. During May 1935 the fund aided the French by supplying dollars to prevent a run on the franc. In late 1936 the franc again lost ground and devaluation became inevitable. In order to prevent wild fluctuations in the exchange rates, England agreed to use her equalization fund (created in 1932 to prevent wide swings of the pound sterling after the devaluation of 1931) in co-operation with the United States and France to "maintain the greatest possible equilibrium in international exchange."[3] This Tripartite Agreement was announced on September 25, 1936, and was greeted with enthusiasm as a step toward the ultimate stabilization of world currencies and the end of the round of competitive devaluation.

For the next couple of years the funds were actively engaged in purchases and sales to keep exchange fluctuation within narrow bounds. Holland and Switzerland soon joined, and Belgium was also admitted although it was still on the gold standard. The worsening state of Europe, where Hitler and Mussolini were growing bolder and the government of the French was growing weaker, brought a new crisis to the franc in early 1938. Rather than resort to exchange controls, the French, with the reluctant approval of the United States and Great Britain, devalued again in May. The Pact was still unbroken, but it was becoming clear that it was far too weak an instrument to protect its participants. Its greatest achievement for the United States was that it reversed the policy of isolationism which had caused so much damage at the London conference a few years earlier.

Silver

The silver interests were not slow in taking advantage of the changed atmosphere of the New Deal. When the Agricultural Adjustment Act was pushed through Congress in May 1933 in order to bring immediate assistance to farmers, Senator Elmer Thomas of Oklahoma was able to tack on to it his amendment which gave the President power to inflate the currency by four different methods: reduce the weight of the gold dollar by 50 percent or less; issue greenbacks up to 3 billion; sell the same amount of government securities to the Federal Reserve banks; and order unlimited coinage of one or both metals at a fixed ratio.

Senator Carl Hayden of Arizona was able to obtain another provision on silver which permitted foreign governments to pay their maturing war debts in silver at a valuation of 50 cents per ounce. The market price was then far below that figure, and this generous arrangement gave Britain a saving of nearly 3 million dollars, with smaller savings to five other European countries which were still repaying their debts; most of the rest had long since defaulted.

As the pressure to do something for silver mounted, the administration decided to implement the silver agreement of the London Conference. In December 1933 the Secretary of the Treasury was directed to buy all newly mined domestic silver and coin it into dollars. Although the statutory price was the 1.29 dollars that had been set in 1837, the Treasury was to retain 50 percent of that amount as seigniorage, paying the seller 64.5 cents per ounce—still a handsome profit.

Very little silver was actually purchased under this proclamation. The next stage was the enactment of the Silver Purchase Act of June 19, 1934. Many other silver bills had been presented to Congress in this period, and there had been active speculation in the metal since it had become increasingly certain that some action would be taken to raise the price. Among the speculators was a Detroit priest, Father Charles E. Coughlin, who in his weekly radio broadcasts made emotional appeals for increased use of silver. The purchases he made were in the name of his radio station rather than of himself, but the exposure of his activities and others in the silver market indicated that much of the agitation was not disinterested. Nevertheless, the Act was passed by Congress, and it required an increase in the Treasury purchases of silver until one-fourth of the metallic monetary stock should consist of silver. The price was not to exceed 1.29 dollars for new silver, and old stocks were to be purchased at not more than 50 cents. Any profits from speculation in silver were to be taxed at the penalty rate of 50 percent. Silver might be nationalized like gold at the discretion of the Treasury; this was done at the end of August when the price had reached 49.5 cents.

Although the passage of this Act was a triumph for the silver interests and their inflation-minded supporters, it accomplished relatively little. The silver certificates based on the newly purchased silver were issued on the actual cost of the silver, not on the statutory value of 1.29 dollars. The result was to limit the volume of new currency put into circulation; moreover Federal Reserve notes were retired as silver certificates were issued. The gold stock increased so rapidly after this date that silver was never able to catch up, and the one-quarter ratio was never attained. After six years of buying, silver was further from the one-quarter ratio than it had been in 1934.

The purchases of silver by the Treasury raised the price of silver and encouraged speculation abroad. Production in the United States increased, and copper, lead and zinc mines, from which silver was a by-product, found it profitable to resume operations. By this time the general business situation was improving slightly, but the production of silver was so small in comparison with other metals that it could not claim credit for the improvement.

The rising price of silver, which had seemed to the silver interests a step in restoring silver to its former monetary position, actually had the opposite effect. The few countries in the world which were still on a silver standard were not silver producers, and now they found that the high price of the metal (which they had to buy in the world market) made it impossible to maintain that standard. China, which produced no silver, threw 200 million ounces on the market as a prelude to deserting the silver standard, which she did in November 1935. Mexico found that its silver coins were being melted down for bullion when the price of silver rose to 72 cents, and was forced to call them in for exchange with paper. Thus the principal demand for monetary silver was destroyed and was never regained. The Treasury let the price decline to 45 cents during most of 1936 and 1937, but it was too late to reverse the demonetization of silver by the foreign governments.

After 1935 no serious effort was made to carry out the Silver Purchase Act. Nevertheless, by 1938 Treasury purchases had amounted to 40,000 tons and storage presented a problem. Finally a depository was built on the grounds of the military academy on the Hudson river at West Point and 1.5 billion dollars worth of the metal was buried there, most of it to remain for a generation, until industry found a use for it in the 1960s.

Other countries whose currencies were threatened by the action of the United States in raising the price of silver were Siam, India, Indo-China, Australia, Japan, and Spain. India and China together in the 1920s had taken nearly half of the world production of silver. One of the objects of the Pittman Resolution at the London Conference of 1933 had been to stop the flood of silver which India threatened to pour into the world market. India lived up to her agreement and the danger was removed for the time.

Secretary Morgenthau became thoroughly disillusioned with the silver policy which he was obliged to follow. Attempts to repeal or amend the silver legislation were thwarted by the powerful silver bloc. Although the number of stockholders and employees of silver mines was relatively small, and the production of silver was less valuable than the peanut crop, the word seemed to have a magic power to evoke protective emotion. In fifteen years the silver industry with fewer than 5000 employees was able to obtain nearly 1.5 billion dollars from the government—more than was paid to millions of farmers to support agricultural prices during that period. It was not until 1963 that Congress finally repealed the Silver Purchase Act of 1934.

The Reciprocal Trade Agreements Program

The Economic Conference at London, from which he had hoped so much, had been a failure, but Secretary Hull did not abandon his effort to obtain freer trade for the world. It would have been impossible for him to obtain a general reduction of tariff duties by the United States in the middle of a depression, and the mere suggestion of such a move would have started one of the lengthy Congressional wrangles which had usually accompanied tariff changes. Instead, Secretary Hull revived the reciprocity idea of the McKinley tariff of 1890 and won support for a method of bypassing Congress and giving the President the right to negotiate tariff agreements with one country at a time, one commodity at a time. Any duty of the Smoot Hawley tariff of 1930 might be lowered by as much as 50 percent for a country which would give a similar concession to some American product. Since the most-favored-nation clause was operative in these agreements, any concession to one country automatically benefited all countries which produced that commodity.

By mid-1939, twenty-one treaties had been concluded under the Trade Agreement Act of June 1934. It ran originally for three years and was prolonged for terms of one to three years thereafter, with varying provisions for tariff reduction. The most important countries which entered into these arrangements with the United States were the United Kingdom, France, and Canada. Seven other European countries were included, and ten Spanish-American countries. The results during this early period were inconclusive. The preamble to the Act had declared that its purpose was that of "expanding foreign markets for the products of the United States," and Secretary Hull was pleased to observe that exports to trade agreement countries rose somewhat more rapidly than exports to other countries. American exports to all countries had also risen more than imports from all countries, thus improving the United States balance of payments. The trade agreements probably prevented further discriminatory measures against the United States, but the shadow of the impending European war soon made it difficult to distinguish clearly what the effect had been, if any.

More important than this slight financial result was the effect of the law in helping to remove the strangling network of trade and currency controls which were impoverishing all nations. After the war this became of great value. Another step in the same direction was the recognition in 1934 of the Soviet government, highly disapproved by the super-patriots of the American Legion and the Daughters of the American Revolution, but backed by sensible conservatives who saw in it an opportunity further to increase the market for American goods and improve international relations. A step in the wrong direction was the Johnson Act of 1934 which forbade American citizens to lend money to, or buy securities from, any foreign government which had defaulted in its payments to the United States. The outbreak of the war in Europe overshadowed all of these actions.

Steel penny, 1943

CHAPTER 15

WORLD WAR II

WHEN war broke out in Europe in mid-1939 the slow recovery from depression in the United States turned into a boom. The allied powers needed enormous quantities of American goods of all kinds. In order to circumvent the Neutrality Act of 1937 which forbade export of munitions to countries at war, Congress in November 1939 authorized such trade on a cash-and-carry basis. England and France, the heaviest purchasers, sold off the American investments of their nationals and sent gold to pay for the rest. Between August 1939 and November 1941 the United States stock of gold increased by 4 billion dollars. Britain had ordered 2 billion dollars worth of armaments by September 1940 and was planning another 2 billion in the next twelve months for planes, ships, chemicals, and machine tools.

In September 1940 also, President Roosevelt made his dramatic announcement of the trading of fifty overage destroyers to Britain in return for 99-year leases on eight Atlantic bases. Six months later, after heated debate, Congress passed the Lend-Lease Act which authorized 1.3 billion dollars worth of war materials to be sent to Great Britain and its allies, to be offset by goods and services supplied to the United States and its forces abroad. Almost before the bill was signed on March 12, the planes and destroyers were on their way and a request for another appropriation of 7 billion was before Congress. This lend-lease arrangement had many advantages over the aid which had been given during World War I in the form of loans. It went into operation far more quickly, it sounded far less ominous to the taxpayer, and it avoided most of the later wrangling over war debts which had dragged on for so many years after the first world war. The grand total of the aid given by the United States under this plan amounted to nearly 50 billion by the end of 1945; three-fifths of it to Great Britain, one-fifth to Russia, and the other fifth mostly to France and China. Under the terms of the law, any equipment which was still usable after the war was to be returned to the United States. Other offsetting items were the goods and services which amounted to more than 7 billion. Twenty years after the war only 2 billion was still outstanding, and agreements for settlement covered about half of that amount.

The United States had begun to increase its own defense expenditures very rapidly during 1939 and 1940, especially after the fall of France in mid-1940. Selective service was introduced, and Congress voted enormous sums for additional strategic and critical materials. The demand for war materials for allies and United States armies was soon outstripping productive capacity. To provide the funds needed for expansion in this emergency, the government turned again to the Reconstruction Finance Corporation as it had done during the depression. In June 1940 Congress gave the RFC such broad powers that it could do almost anything without waiting for special authorization. It was headed by Jesse Jones, who as Federal Loan Administrator had general supervision over the Federal Housing Administration, the Home Owners' Loan Corporation, and the Export-Import Bank in addition to the RFC. This centralization of financial power made rapid action easier. In August 1940 the RFC organized the Defense Plant Corporation as a subsidiary, and this was soon followed by the Metals Reserve Company, the Rubber Reserve Company, the Defense Supplies Corporation, the Rubber Development Corporation, the United States Commercial Company, and the War Damage Corporation. At the request of government agencies, loans were made to 2300 projects in forty-six states and several foreign countries, which totaled more than 9 billion dollars by the end of the war. They ranged from the collection of milkweed fibers for life preservers to the building of whole factories for manufacturing airplanes. Most of the synthetic rubber and much of the magnesium and aluminum were produced under these auspices. Businessmen and technical experts were brought together in such enterprises, which had to comply with the policies of the War Production Board set up under Donald M. Nelson in January 1942 and the Controlled Materials Plan which allocated scarce materials to the Army, the Navy, and the Maritime Commission.

In addition to the financing of defense production by the RFC and its subsidiaries, another approach was made by the guaranteeing of defense loans by government agencies. During 1941 the Reserve system began working with the Council of National Defense to help small firms and local banks obtain and finance war contracts. A further step was taken in 1942 when the War and Navy departments and the Maritime Commission agreed to guarantee credit extended by banks to producers who would not otherwise have been able to obtain loans. At the peak of this program in 1944 about 2 billion of such guaranteed loans were outstanding under Regulation V of the Federal Reserve Board. Later a new type, the VT loan, was introduced in order to give contractors assurance that, if the war ended, their working capital would be released promptly to permit immediate return to normal peacetime production. In August 1944 a T loan was provided to give contractors immediate funds when the war was terminated. Most of these V, VT, and T loans were small, from 400 dollars up, and they brought into the war production system a great number of small plants which greatly increased its total capacity.

The combined efforts of public agencies and private enterprises was so effective that, by the time the United States entered the war, 15 percent of the country's industrial production was already devoted to military purposes. The proportion continued to expand, and the peak of the munitions program was reached toward the end of 1943. Altogether the value of the war product reached a total of 186 billion through the war years.

Federal Tax Policy

War expenditures increased far more rapidly than taxes could be raised to meet them. Customs revenue was almost negligible because of the decline in imports, and internal excise taxes in spite of higher rates made up only a small part of federal revenues. The main reliance had therefore to be on individual and corporate income taxes.

The first of the war revenue acts was passed on June 25, 1940, a year after the war had begun in Europe but long before the United States became directly involved. Personal exemptions had been 1000 dollars for individuals and 2500 for heads of families, and rates on income above these figures had started at 4 percent normal tax, with surtaxes from 1 percent for income above 6000 dollars to 75 percent for income over 5 million. The 1940 law decreased exemptions by 20 percent and increased rates all along the line about 10 percent. The next year exemptions were still further reduced, and rates were raised slightly higher. The Act of 1942 increased some rates and added a Victory Tax of 5 percent of gross income above the exemption, to be withheld by employers from wages and salaries.

The Act of 1944 was even more severe. An exemption of only 500 dollars was granted to an individual whether married or single; a 3 percent normal tax was levied on income above that figure; surtaxes began with 20 percent on the first 2000 dollars and rose to 91 percent on the surtax net income over 200,000. For a married man with two dependents and an income of 5000 dollars, the tax amounted to 755 dollars; with an income of 10,000, the tax was 2245; with 100,000 the tax was 68,565, and at 1,000,000 the total federal tax was 900,000. By the end of the war, the revenue from the individual income tax was twenty times as great as it had been in 1940. This was of course in addition to the state and local taxes, mostly on property and retail sales, which also rose during the war, although less rapidly. The English and the Canadians were paying still higher taxes and enjoying far less food, clothing, tobacco, and gasoline.

The income tax paid by corporations was also increased in nearly every revenue measure during the war and by 1945 had increased its yield fifteenfold. Late in 1940 the basic rates which for several years had stood at 12.5 to 16 percent of adjusted net income, if 25,000 dollars or less, and at 19 percent if more than that, were increased and made more progressive, and an excess profits tax was added to "take the profit out of war." This was a very popular move, since the report of Senator Nye's Committee to Investigate the Munitions Industry in 1936 had disclosed a sordid tale of profits made by shipbuilders and manufacturers during World War I. This new tax took the place of the undistributed profits tax which had been eliminated in 1939. The capital stock tax of 1 dollar per share was increased by 10 percent, and most of the taxes were subject to elaborate legal qualifications which made them difficult to calculate.

In 1942 the basic rate for the smaller corporations was increased to a range of 15 to 19 percent. Larger corporations paid 24 percent on net profits, with a surtax of 6 or 7 percent and an excess profits tax beginning at 35 percent of the first 25,000 dollars of surtax net income and rising to 60 percent on such income over 500,000. These rates with some slight changes remained in effect until the end of the war. One of the most important innovations in the treatment of corporate profits during the war was the clause included in many war contracts for renegotiation of the contract if cost of production turned out to be lower than the original estimates. By the end of 1947 over 6 billion dollars had been returned to the government through renegotiation proceedings.

The most constructive and far-reaching change made in the federal tax system during the war was that enacted in the Current Tax Payment Act of June 1943. Henceforth tax payments were to be made as income was earned; employers were required to withhold 20 percent of wages and salaries beyond exemptions, and other income had to be reported by the taxpayer and the tax paid quarterly. Corporations had to report to the Treasury all dividends paid to their stockholders. In order to ease the transition period, three-fourths of the previous year's tax was forgiven, and the taxes for 1944 were put on a pay-as-you-go basis. The change was an enormous improvement from all points of view. For the taxpayer, there was no longer the strain of trying to pay in a lean year the high tax on income earned (and probably already spent) in a previous good year. The computation of his tax was also eased for the individual with less than 5000 dollars annual income by the use of simplified tables with standard deductions. For the Treasury the new system made possible rapid response to rate changes, so that true fiscal policy could be used; inflation could be countered by an increase in taxes, and depression could be met by lowering rates to increase consumer purchasing power.

Estate and gift taxes were also increased as the war went on. The former exemption of 40,000 dollar estate and 40,000 life insurance was changed to a combined exemption of 60,000 in 1942. Rates were increased from a range of 2 to 70 percent on net estates of 10,000 to 50 million dollars, up to a range of 3 to 77 percent on net estates of

5000 to 10 million in 1941. In the same year, gift taxes were increased to 2.25 percent on the first 10,000 after the exemption of 40,000 dollars, to 57.75 percent on gifts in excess of 10 million. In 1942 the exemption was reduced to 30,000 dollars, to be taken all in one year or over a period of years.

Excise taxes, especially on articles considered to be luxuries, rose during the war, both by increases in rates and by the inclusion of more articles to be taxed. Alcoholic beverages and tobacco contributed 55 percent of the total excise revenue by 1945; gasoline, admissions, and communications together made up another 20 percent. Excise taxes tripled their yield during the war but made up only one-seventh of the internal revenue by 1945.

The most important loophole in the federal system, the exemption of state and municipal securities, was not closed during the war. Exemption of income from future issues of federal securities had been abolished in 1941, but local government issues continued to serve as a tax haven for the very wealthy. Had their exemption from federal taxation been ended, they would have had to be issued at slightly higher rates of interest, but this might well have been an advantage in encouraging greater fiscal responsibility on the part of local governments. Moreover the federal tax structure would have become more truly progressive.

It was occasionally suggested that a federal retail sales tax should be included in the array of war taxes, but the idea never gained support. Local governments would have resented the intrusion of the federal government into this field. The expense of collecting such a tax over so wide a territory would have been heavy, and an army of administrators would have been required to enforce it. Since it is a regressive tax, bearing most heavily on the lowest-income groups, it was also opposed on grounds of social policy.

In spite of the good intentions of government and financial authorities, the proportion of war expenditures raised by taxation did not reach the level achieved during World War I and amounted to only 46 percent of the total, as compared with the former 55 percent.[1] Total federal tax receipts rose from 8 to 48 billion dollars in the five war years, but expenditures mounted from 13 to 100 billion, about the same proportionate increase but a very much larger absolute increase for expenses than for income.

The receipts and expenditures of the federal government for the years 1941 through 1946 are given in Table 10.

TABLE 10. FEDERAL GOVERNMENT RECEIPTS AND EXPENDITURES IN MILLIONS OF CURRENT DOLLARS, FOR YEARS ENDING JUNE 30, 1941 TO 1946

	1941	1942	1943	1944	1945	1946
			Receipts			
Individual income tax	1,416	3,216	6,505	19,779	19,146	18,331
Corporate income tax inc. excess profits	2,053	4,744	9,589	14,876	16,027	12,554
Internal revenue	2,967	3,847	4,553	5,291	6,949	7,725
Social Security	932	1,194	1,508	1,751	1,793	1,714
Customs duties	392	389	324	431	355	435
Other (inc. renegotiation)	508	277	906	3,280	3,470	3,480
Total	8,269	13,668	23,385	45,408	47,740	44,239
			Expenditures			
Defense	6,301	26,011	72,109	87,039	90,029	48,542
Veterans' pensions	563	556	602	730	2,060	4,253
Interest on debt	1,111	1,260	1,808	2,609	3,617	4,722
Social Security	588	659	735	803	815	852
Public works, relief, aid to agriculture	3,307	3,038	2,023	1,359	1,085	1,387
Other	840	873	901	1,203	2,799	5,263
Total	12,711	32,397	78,179	93,744	100,405	65,019
Total gross debt at end of fiscal year	48,961	72,422	136,696	201,003	258,682	269,422
Gross national product (in billions)	125.8	159.1	192.5	211.4	213.6	210.7

Source: Annual Report of the Secretary of the Treasury, 1946, pp. 398-99.

Government Borrowing during the War

The practical impossibility, for financial as well as for political reasons, of meeting all the war expenses by taxation forced the federal government to borrow heavily, and the Treasury became the chief factor in the money market for many years. Secretary of the Treasury Morgenthau, like war Secretaries Chase and Mellon before him, was determined that interest on government loans should be kept low, on the assumption that low interest charges would reduce the cost of the debt and thus lighten the burden on the nation. This was an assumption which overlooked the inflationary effect of a low-interest policy.

When war borrowing began, interest rates were low, because commercial banks had sizable excess reserves as a result of the heavy gold imports. The rates formed a curving pattern, with short-term Treasury bills up to 91 days maturity at three-eighths of 1 percent and certificates of indebtedness up to 1 year at seven-eighths of 1 percent. Treasury notes maturing in 1½ to 2¾ years were yielding 1¼ percent, and bonds with maturities of 5 to 27 years were yielding 1½ to 2½ percent. If short issues could be used for a large part of the debt, the Treasury would have to pay a lower average rate on its debt.

Since there was less commercial business for the banks to finance during the war, the Treasury believed that the short issues would be suitable for banks and other institutional investors. At first the banks resisted, and quotas had to be allotted by the Reserve banks in order to clear the market. However, when the banks found that Treasury bills could be sold back to the Reserve banks without loss, so that they were the practical equivalent of reserves, they were willing to buy bills in large amounts.

In spite of the Treasury's desire to place the longer issues in the hands of permanent investors, a large proportion of them were held by the banking system at the end of the war. Seven war loan drives and a final Victory loan between November 1942 and December 1945 were designed to reach individual and institutional purchasers and reduce inflation by draining off the increased purchasing power arising from government spending. Commercial banks were excluded from these loans except for limited amounts in proportion to the time deposits they held. They did, however, purchase bonds in the open market and were encouraged to do this by Federal Reserve policy, which kept them supplied with ample reserves.

By the end of 1945 the marketable part of the national debt was held as shown in Table 11.

TABLE 11. MARKETABLE PORTION OF NATIONAL DEBT AT END OF 1945 (*in billions of dollars*)

	Bills, Certificates, and Notes	Bonds	Total
Federal Reserve banks	23.3	1.0	$24.3
Commercial banks	36.3	46.5	82.8
Savings banks and insurance companies	1.3	32.4	33.8
Others	17.3	33.6	51.0
Total	78.2	113.5	191.8

Source: Federal Reserve Bulletin, March 1946, p. 318.

The Treasury policy of low interest rates was largely responsible for the high proportion of the debt which was of short maturity. In 1940 bonds had comprised 77 percent of the marketable issues, but at the close of 1945 they made up only 60 percent. The same policy accounted for the small part of the long debt which was in the hands of "Others," the individual and corporate investors who were the most apt to hold their securities. With so much of the debt in short form, the Treasury was under the almost constant obligation of arranging refunding, an expensive and also an uncertain operation which put the Treasury at the mercy of the financial market.

The large proportion of the debt in the portfolios of the commercial banks was unfortunate for the Treasury, since banks had to dispose of it after the war when business loans were again needed. It was also unfortunate for the banks, because so much of it was in long-term bonds which made their portfolios illiquid; this presented a genuine danger if market rates of interest rose (as they were bound to do) and pushed the price of the low-yield bonds downward.

In addition to the marketable debt of short and long maturities, several types of savings bonds were offered by the Treasury. Series E, F, and G were aimed to attract the small investor. The first two kinds were sold at 75 percent of par; the value built up to the full face value only if they were held 10 years to their maturity date, when the yield would amount to 2.9 percent for the E bonds and to 2.53 percent for the F series. Bonds of the G series were issued at par, and yielded 2.5 percent if held for 12 years. Only limited amounts might be purchased by any individual, but about 50 billion altogether were taken between 1941 and 1946. They were anti-inflationary because they were paid for out of income, many of them through payroll deduction plans.

The total federal debt increased about tenfold from the peak of World War I to the high point after World War II; the increase during the first world war had been about the same. In both cases a part of the nominal increase was caused by the increase in prices during the war; the true burden of the increase becomes difficult to measure, but is certainly somewhat less than the nominal one. The interest-bearing debt had been reduced from its 1919 high of 25 billion dollars to a low of 16 billion by 1930. The increase during the depression years brought it to 49 billion by mid-1941 before the war started, and by mid-1946 it stood at a new high of 269 billion.

Federal Reserve Policy

No central bank can with impunity refuse to follow the policy of its government in time of war; the accusation of disloyalty is too grave to be risked. The Reserve banks therefore felt obligated to support the Treasury policy of low interest rates on government issues, even after the market rates had risen. This involved the Reserve system in heavy purchases in order to keep the prices from falling with a corresponding increase in yield which would have made further issues at low interest rates, at par value, impossible.

In 1939 when the war started in Europe, the Reserve authorities agreed, in order "to maintain orderly conditions in the market for United States Government securities," that they would make advances to non-member as well as to member banks on government securities at par, at the discount rate.[2] At the same time the Reserve banks began to increase their own portfolios of governments, mostly long-term bonds. This action had no relation to member bank reserves, which were still far in excess of legal requirements, but was taken to prepare the market for the foreign borrowing which would be needed to finance war expenditures.

With the prospect of United States involvement imminent, in December 1940 a letter was sent to the Senate and the House of Representatives, signed not only by the Governors of the Federal Reserve Board, but also by the Presidents of the twelve Reserve banks and by the members of the Federal Advisory Council, who had become concerned about the danger of inflation. After describing the responsibilities which the banking system would have to face in the near future, the letter requested authority for the Reserve system, through its Open Market Committee, to set reserve requirements for all commercial banks, members or not, up to twice the statutory ratios of 7-10-13 percent. At the same time Congress was urged to avoid the dangers of inflation by financing the war as far as possible with taxation rather than borrowing. This letter, in spite of its impressive list of signers, made little impression on Congress.

Gold imports between 1936 and 1942, as the situation in Europe worsened, had doubled the monetary gold stock of the United States, bringing it to 23 billion. Member banks therefore had ample reserves and interest rates remained low, so that there was no occasion for Reserve bank intervention. Nevertheless in March 1942 the Reserve authorities requested and obtained from Congress restoration of the power to purchase up to 5 billion of Treasury obligations direct from the Treasury, if this were necessary to maintain stability in the market. This authority was used to a limited extent on several occasions to ease periods of tax payments or offerings of new Treasury obligations.

The policy of the Reserve Board in these months was ambivalent. On the one hand, it raised reserve requirements to the limit of the law at that time, to 14, 20, and 26 percent against demand deposits in the three classes of member banks. On the other hand, a month later in April 1942, the Reserve authorities agreed to repurchase Treasury bills bought by member banks, at three-eighths of 1 percent. A further easing of reserve requirements was made possible by an amendment to the Reserve Act in July 1942 which permitted changes for one class of member banks at a time. Under this provision the requirements for central reserve city banks, those in New York and Chicago, were reduced by steps during the summer and autumn of 1942 from 26 to 20 percent. This increased excess reserves about 1.2 billion dollars for the group of banks which was under the heaviest pressure, not only because of Treasury borrowing but also because of increased demand for currency. Early in 1943 the Board further eased reserve requirements for all member banks by ruling that War Loan deposit accounts were not subject to reserve requirements. This encouraged banks to lend to their customers the funds with which to purchase war bonds and bank loans increased heavily during the bond drives.

By this time the excess reserves of all member banks had fallen to 1 billion, and the Reserve system adopted a policy of maintaining them at that level through open-market operations. During World War I the Reserve banks had followed an alternative course to facilitate Treasury borrowing—that of rediscounting the member banks' own notes secured by government obligations as collateral.

The Treasury policy of low interest rates, and the further insistence on the particular pattern of low rates that had happened to be in existence at the beginning of the war, resulted in many problems for the Reserve system in its efforts to maintain the pattern. The sharply ascending interest rate curve, with its wide differential between short and long rates, induced a form of speculation in government securities known as "riding the curve." As the long securities approached maturity, their price rose because their yield fell to the point on the curve which was being maintained by the Reserve authorities through pegging operations. A profit could be made by borrowing on margin the funds with which to purchase these securities to be sold later at a premium. As long as investors believed that the curve would be maintained, they could also profit by reaching out for the longer maturities with higher yield, which in a pegged market were as liquid as the short obligations with lower yields. Investors could sell Treasury bills, certificates, and notes to the Reserve banks, which were under obligation to buy them in order to keep the yield pegged; the purchase of the longer issues with these funds tended to raise the price and lower the yield, which tended to flatten out the interest rate curve.

The constant need to purchase securities forced the Reserve system to a policy which it did not approve, that of pumping more reserves into the hands of banks regardless of their situation. Although the Board had pointed out the dangers of this policy in a number of its reports during the war, it was not until 1945 that it began a more vigorous protest. The debt had grown sixfold in five years, and by 1945 amounted to nearly two-thirds of the entire indebtedness of the country, private, local, state, and federal. The end of the war did not put an end to government borrowing, and the danger of monetizing this growing debt increased with its size.* It was another six years before the Reserve authorities regained a measure of independence in dealing with the money market.

Direct Credit Controls

It was impossible for the Federal Reserve system to exercise any general control over credit by the customary instruments of discount policy, reserve requirements, eligibility rules, and open-market operations as long as it had to support the low interest rate policy. It was, however, given a new tool with which to work, by the Executive Order of August 9, 1941, which empowered it to regulate consumer credit. It immediately issued Regulation W to set minimum and maximum limits to down payments on purchases and maximum maturities for each type of commodity. At first these limits applied only to installment sales, but a few months later they were applied to charge accounts and single-payment loans as well.

The total of consumer credit outstanding when the controls were initiated had reached nearly 10 billion dollars, a figure which in comparison with the 40 billion total of demand deposits represented an obvious danger to the stability of the economy. Within two years this form of credit had been reduced by half, a reduction which cannot be ascribed entirely to the controls since many consumer durable goods had disappeared from the market. Automobiles and refrigerators, for example, were no longer available. When the war was over and the veterans began to return with their pockets full of money to be spent for clothing and furniture, the total rose very rapidly and by the end of 1947, in spite of controls, was again above 10 billion, never to return to a lower level. Consumer credit must be held responsible for at least a part of the postwar inflation of consumer prices.

---

* That is, the bonds were paid for with deposits created by the banks, and these deposits increased the total of purchasing power used by the Treasury.

Another form of direct control over credit was exercised by the Federal Reserve Board under the legislation of 1935 which permitted it to set margin requirements for loans on securities. Under its Regulations T and U, purchasers of securities at the outbreak of the war had been permitted to borrow up to 60 percent of their market value with a cash payment of only 40 percent. The stock market was relatively inactive during the war and the volume of bank loans to brokers reported at the New York Stock Exchange declined to less than half a billion during 1942. It rose during the next two years to 1 billion, and the market became increasingly active with the end of the war. In order to prevent any such speculative upsurge as had occurred in the late 1920s, the Board raised margin requirements three times during 1945, to 50, 75, and finally 100 percent. This cut off credit to speculators and caused the total of brokers' loans to decline again to half a billion.

Both consumer and stock market credit controls were necessary complements to any anti-inflation program, but by themselves they were far too weak to offset the strong inflationary pressures of other factors. The relative stability of prices during the war depended primarily on the direct price controls and the rationing of commodities.

Price and Production Controls and Rationing

The need to economize in the use of scarce materials and increase the output of war supplies led to the establishment of the War Production Board by Executive Order early in 1942. All federal agencies were obliged to comply with its policies. Automobile and typewriter production for civilian use was soon stopped, along with that of many other non-essentials. A Controlled Materials Plan set up a few months later assigned to the Army, the Navy, and the Maritime Commission the scarce materials which they might allocate to their contractors. The Office of Defense Transportation took over the problem of moving the goods, and the financial organizations described earlier provided the funds needed at all stages.

The War Food Administration was responsible for providing the food for millions of American and allied soldiers in the field, and for the millions of citizens at home. This inevitably required rationing of many foodstuffs, especially the imported sugar and coffee, and the scarce butter,

Gasoline and food ration books, World War II

cheese, meat, and vegetable oils. Since food production in the United States increased during the war by more than one-third over the 1935–59 average, civilian food consumption increased on a per capita basis in spite of the large amount needed for the army. Rationing simply distributed the food more equitably among civilians and postponed for a time the full effect of the shortages. In January 1942 the Emergency Price Control Act authorized the issuance of a General Maximum Price Regulation which attempted to freeze the prices of many commodities at the levels prevailing in March. Gradually ceilings for individual products were substituted for the general freeze, but it became increasingly difficult to hold the line against the pressure of shortages on the one hand and high incomes on the other.

Wages also were put under control by an Executive Order of October 1942. The original intention of the order was to place a ceiling on wages, but the increasing cost of living forced many adjustments. The War Labor Board in the so-called Little Steel case adopted a formula of 15 percent increase and attempted to keep other wage adjustments within that limit. In spite of these efforts the average weekly pay in manufacturing industries, including overtime but before tax deductions, rose from 23.64 dollars in 1939 to 44.20 by 1945. The increase in income taxes did not offset the higher earnings and purchasing power in the hands of consumers steadily increased.

The Office of Price Administration fixed ceilings on rents during 1942, since the shortage of new housing aggravated the demand for living space. The OPA and the Department of Agriculture attempted to satisfy the demands of farmers by setting farm prices according to formulas based on previous periods when farm prices had been high in relation to other commodities.

The net result of the efforts to prevent prices from rising was to slow down the rate of increase during the war period. Defense materials, under strict allocation and price regulations, did not greatly increase in price. Twelve basic foodstuffs, on the other hand, had suffered an increase of 61 percent from August 1939 to the end of 1941, even before the United States was directly involved in the war. Wholesale prices as measured by the Department of Labor index (on the base of 1926) showed a ten-point rise from 77.1 in 1939 to 87.3 in 1941, and by 1945 averaged

105.8. In that year the new index of consumer prices averaged 128.4 on the base of 1935–39 as 100.

Both price indices were unsatisfactory for the war period. Changes in the kinds of goods produced occurred so rapidly that it was impossible for the price indices to keep up with them. Changes in weighting were made in an attempt to mirror actual conditions, as for example the increase in the weight given to automobile repairs in the retail price index, and the elimination of new car prices when there were no longer new cars in the market. Changes in the quality of consumer goods, painfully apparent in such commodities as children's shoes, were also impossible to represent adequately in the index numbers. Black markets introduced a factor with which the index did not even attempt to cope, since black markets were not only illegal but immeasurable; for a few commodities, like butter and gasoline, they were certainly important. The wholesale price index was probably less affected by all these factors than the retail price index. The latter, which had always been called the Cost of Living index, became so unsatisfactory that the Bureau of Labor Statistics finally gave up any pretense of measuring a concept so difficult to define and renamed it as the Consumers' Price Index for Moderate Income Families in Large Cities.

The joyful news that the war was finally over in late summer 1945 made it almost impossible to enforce price and rationing controls any longer. President Truman therefore abolished most of them during 1946 and the reaction of prices was immediate. Currency in circulation had increased rapidly during the war, as more workers earned more money in war industries. Much of this money was neither invested in government bonds nor deposited in checking accounts, but was held in cash either because the worker was unaccustomed to the use of banks or because the banking service was inadequate in many of the new production centers. The result was that the total currency in circulation nearly tripled between 1941 and 1945, rising from 9.3 to 26.2 billion dollars.

At the same time the volume of demand deposits was increasing from 38.6 to 76.2 billion, and time deposits were also doubling from 15.9 to 30.2 billion. A large part of the increase in bank deposits arose from the "monetization" of the public debt, as new Treasury issues were purchased by banks with credit entered on their books to the account of the

Treasury. The government used the deposits thus created to pay its creditors, and the circulation was proportionately increased. The total of the money supply, including demand and time deposits with currency, rose during the war years from 63.8 to 132.6 billion dollars, more than doubling. This rate of increase was greater than that of the Gross National Product in the same period, which rose from 126 billion in 1941 to 214 billion in 1945.

The ending of wartime controls released the great volume of purchasing power into a market in which consumer goods were not yet being produced in large volume. It was inevitable that prices would surge upward. The Consumers' Price Index rose from 129.9 to 167.0 during 1946 and 1947, and wholesale prices increased even more, from 107.1 to 163.2, all on the 1926 base of 100.

Cost of World War II to the United States

Modern wars are so destructive for so long a period, and their after-effects are so severe, that it is impossible to make precise estimates of their cost. At the end of World War II in mid-1945 Secretary of the Treasury Morgenthau estimated the war expenditures of the United States at 325 billion dollars or about one-half of the gross national product during the years of conflict. This figure he compared with World War I expenditures of about one-fourth of GNP.

His total included the interest on the war debt up to that time but did not of course include all the costs which the United States had to cover in the years after the war. War debts of allies had to be scaled down or completely forgiven in order to ward off economic collapse. Former enemies as well as allies had to be given billions of dollars in aid in order to save them from violent disorders at home and breakdown of economic patterns abroad. The cost of the war to all the countries involved is simply incalculable.

Reconversion

One of the costs of World War I was, however, avoided. The long and painful process of reconversion to peacetime production, with the unemployment, litigation, and general distress it involved, was warded off by the determination of government officials and business leaders. The peak of war production was passed in 1943, when it became apparent that supplies were being made and shipped as fast as needed by the armies. The end of the war was in sight, and the return of twelve million persons from the armed services presented serious problems of adjustment in the whole economy.

In October 1942 President Roosevelt had established the Office of Economic Stabilization (later the Office of War Mobilization and Reconversion) under the management of James F. Byrnes, who was soon succeeded by Frederick M. Vinson and then by John W. Snyder. Snyder, with the aid of economist Robert Nathan, drew up a plan for the postwar period which included public works, tax relief for corporations, and minimum wages and unemployment benefits for workers. In the meantime, Congress had been considering a number of proposals to ease the readjustment to a peace economy. One of the most constructive of these was the so-called GI Bill of Rights passed in June 1944. It gave the returning veterans up to 300 dollars in mustering-out pay, provided for 52 weeks of unemployment insurance at 20 dollars per week, made loans for housing, and guaranteed loans for acquiring farms or small businesses. Most important, it offered tuition and maintenance costs to veterans who wanted to obtain further education; this kept them out of the labor market at a time when it would be most crowded, and increased their earning ability when they returned to it by upgrading their skills. For many men and women this opportunity for advanced education was the fulfillment of a lifetime dream, and the presence of these serious and mature students was an inspiration to teachers and younger students in the institutions they attended.

On the industrial front, businessmen themselves, through their Committee for Economic Development, drew up plans for rapid reconversion of plants which had been diverted to war production. Floor plans were ready, tools were ordered, and materials acquired, so that when the war was over and the contracts for war goods were canceled, there was no long hiatus in the production like that which had occurred after World War I. The loans guaranteed by government agencies and the Federal Reserve system provided immediate funds, and legal questions about war contracts were settled quickly. Gross National Product in 1946 was only slightly less in volume than in 1945, and by 1950 it was greater than in 1944. It was an enormous achievement of government and business working together.

International Financial Cooperation

On the international as well as on the domestic front, preparations for peace were being made. The experience of the United States during the years following World War I, with the ineffectual efforts to restore stable currencies and revive world trade, had convinced financial leaders that preparations must be made before the war ended. Existing arrangements were obviously not enough. The Treasury was still using the Stabilization Fund set up in 1936, but this was competent only to aid friendly nations with their currency problems. During 1941, for example, the Treasury agreed to purchase from the Central Bank of China 50 million dollars worth of *yuan*, from the Central Bank of Argentina 50 million dollars worth of *pesos*, and smaller amounts from Mexico, Iceland, and Ecuador. The next year three gold purchase agreements totaling 63 million dollars were made with Soviet Russia to finance her purchases of war materials in the United States, and 500 million more were loaned to China. Cuba and Liberia were similarly aided during 1943, and the original loan to Brazil in 1937 was increased.

These scattered benefactions, important as they were to the countries receiving them, were quite inadequate to solve the larger problems which the war would bequeath. Not only would world production have to be shifted from military to consumer goods, but also the channels of trade and credit on which the distribution of the goods depended would have to be reopened. During 1943 several draft proposals were passed around among the treasuries of the allied powers, and a lively and sometimes acrimonious discussion began. There was general agreement that two kinds of institution were required, one to concern itself with currency stabilization, the other to provide long-term loans. The former provoked the greater controversy since it had overtones of economic and political prestige. Should all the currencies be valued in terms of gold, or should there be several "key currencies" such as the pound and the dollar, around which others could be grouped, with the ratio between the key currencies to be settled later?

In the summer of 1944 representatives of forty-three nations met at the invitation of the United States Treasury in Bretton Woods, New Hampshire, and for three weeks worked out the details of the two plans. The International Monetary Fund was devised to handle currency problems, providing advice to nations trying to stabilize their currencies and funds with which to meet temporary needs during the process. The dollar emerged as the currency in terms of which the others would eventually be defined; since the dollar was legally defined in terms of gold (although gold was not in circulation and could not yet be exported without license), this provision amounted to international recognition of the gold standard.

The International Bank for Reconstruction and Development, which soon came to be known as the World Bank, was provided with capital by sale of its stock to member nations in rough proportion to their share in world trade. It was to make loans to members on "banking principles," that is, not as grants but as loans approved by a Bank committee sent out to evaluate the situation and determine if the project could repay the borrowed funds within the life of the loan. No nation might borrow from the Bank unless it was also a member of the Fund.

Much to the dismay of the British delegation headed by Lord Keynes, who had hoped that London would be chosen, the offices of both the Fund and the Bank were located in Washington. This was a tactical necessity, since the United States was putting up the largest share of the capital of the Bank and the quota of the Fund, about 35 percent in each, with the same proportion of voting strength. Congress would never have approved United States membership in either had they been located abroad. As it was, Congress was persuaded to permit the United States to join only by setting up a National Advisory Council on International Monetary and Financial Problems consisting of the Secretaries of the Treasury (Chairman), State, and Commerce, the Chairman of the Board of Governors of the Federal Reserve System, and the Chairman of the Board of Trustees of the Export-Import Bank. This Council was to act as liaison between the international institutions and the Congress and to prevent any sacrifice of the sovereignty of the United States. The Act was passed on July 31, 1945, after lengthy discussion not only in Congress but also in the country at large. The United States paid 1.8 billion of its 2.75 billion subscription to the Fund out of the profits of devaluation of the dollar.

All the other nations which had sent delegates to Bretton Woods eventually became members of the Fund and the Bank except the USSR, which declined membership. Other nations joined the group when they saw that it would be to their advantage to do so. Both the Bank and the Fund performed invaluable services in the postwar period in making loans for reconstruction and later for redevelopment, and in advising on currency management.*

---

* See Chapter 16 for later activities of these institutions. Switzerland did not send a delegate and did not join.

CHAPTER 16

Kennedy half dollar

THE TWENTY YEARS AFTER WORLD WAR II

Reconversion

THE two decades following the end of the war were marked by almost steadily rising prosperity, erratically rising prices, a sharp change from net gold imports to net gold exports, and increasing governmental responsibility for the solution of problems, domestic and international, with which private enterprise was unable to cope. All of these developments had financial implications.

The feared unemployment crisis did not develop after the war. The careful planning for reconversion of industry, sparked by the Committee for Economic Development, and the arrangements by the federal government for prompt settlement of 35 billion dollars of cancelled war contracts made it possible for new jobs to be provided very quickly. Moreover, although 8 million members of the armed forces were released within 12 months, the labor force did not have to absorb them all at once. Many young men and women went to school for a time. Older workers retired, and many women withdrew from the labor force when their husbands returned. Unemployment rose from 1 to 2 million between 1945 and 1946, but actually declined slightly during 1947 and 1948.

The value of the Gross National Product showed similar resilience.

In 1946, because of the reduced war expenditures, it fell by 2 percent from the war peak of 214 billion dollars in 1945. Then it rose again steadily except for a fractional decline in 1949, and stood at 684 billion in 1965. With the price inflation of these years eliminated, so that the figures measured the relative changes in volume, the peak came in 1944, declined by about one-tenth through 1947, rose in 1948, and after a very small drop in 1949 rose almost steadily, with small declines only in 1954 and 1958.

Two years after the war, production of civilian goods had exceeded all previous records, in spite of the shortages which still existed in housing and automobiles, agricultural machinery, electrical equipment, and fuels. These categories soon caught up, and the total volume of consumer goods doubled by 1965; because of inflation, its value in current dollars had tripled. Personal consumption expenditures on goods and services showed even less variation from the upward movement in these two decades. After postwar adjustments, the nondurable goods settled into a pattern of annual increase which was interrupted only in 1952. Services purchased by consumers were even less variable. Durable consumer goods took up the slack, with larger absolute and relative variations.

Federal Government Finance

The great depression of the 1930s and the world war of the 1940s had made it impossible for the federal government ever again to assume that posture of bland indifference to the public welfare which had characterized even such a tenderhearted president as Taft. Social security legislation had become so deeply embedded in the economic structure that even conservatives seldom opposed it openly, and the subsidies to agricultural producers were almost equally invulnerable.

Another expression of this responsibility was the Employment Act of 1946, which reflected the view that depression was the result of reduced purchasing power of the masses. Since this was beyond the control of private enterprise, it was the obligation of the government to take action; not as an interference with free enterprise, but in support of it. The Act which emerged in 1946 with the backing of members of both parties did not guarantee a job for every citizen, much less the "right to work" which had come to mean restrictions on trade unions. What it did assert was the obligation of the federal government to "promote maximum employment, production and purchasing power" by using all practical means and enlisting the cooperation of industry, labor, agriculture, and local government units. The President was directed to appoint a Council of Economic Advisers to study and report annually on the state of the economy; a Joint Committee on the Economic Report of fourteen members of Congress was to study the report and make recommendations to Congress for needed action.

Although military expenditures were rapidly reduced after the war, total federal budgets never again returned to prewar levels. This has been true after every war, in part because of the upward trend of prices, but also because of the expanding function of government. In addition to these domestic factors, the United States as the richest nation in the world needs in its own self-interest to provide large amounts to help in the restoration and reconstruction of other nations. All of these demands on the federal purse meant that the need for large revenues continued.

Nevertheless, the Revenue Act of 1945 took an estimated 12 million persons off the tax rolls by increasing the normal tax exemption to 500 dollars, and it reduced by 3 points the surtax rates in each bracket; the total computed tax was further reduced by 5 percent. Service men and veterans below officer grade were not taxed on their pay during the war.

The taxpayers were understandably eager to have their burden lightened further, and the first Republican-controlled Congress since 1929 was equally eager to oblige them. A bill to reduce individual income taxes for 1947 was vetoed by President Truman as unsatisfactory, and even the delay of the reduction to 1948 was unable to win his approval but was passed by Congress over his veto in April 1948. The reduction took effect just as the recession of 1949 occurred and was probably a factor in cutting it short. The upturn which started in October 1949 was further aided by the Marshall Plan expenditures.*

These tax bills reduced the rates on individual income very little, but they introduced one important reform; they permitted husband and wife each to report one-half of their total income, regardless of which one had actually received it. The previous requirement in some states that the wife's earnings be added to the husband's to determine the income

* See p. 399.

tax bracket, in many cases brought the wife's earnings to such a high rate of taxation that it was hardly worth her while to work at all, especially if by her work additional household help was necessitated. Trained personnel in teaching, nursing, and other professions frequently chosen by women were desperately needed, and any device which made such activity more attractive to married women was far more important to society than the relatively slight additional revenue which might have been obtained otherwise. The question of equal rights also played a part in such decisions by the tax legislators.

The postwar period offered opportunity for general taxation revision as military expenses declined. A discussion of tax theory not only in Congress, but also in such business groups as the CED and in academic circles, opened the possibility of a more realistic approach to the problems of how different rates of different taxes would affect the economy. It was confidently expected that the budget could be balanced and the debt reduced, but it was also now accepted that fiscal policy as well as monetary policy could be used as an instrument to control cyclical movements which might threaten the economy with inflation or deflation.

The United States had developed a tax system which relied heavily upon direct taxation of individual and corporation earnings rather than on indirect sales and excise taxes. In many European countries about 1950 there had begun a shift from the elaborate combinations of indirect taxes to a tax on value added at each stage of the production process, the TVA as it is known. France was one of the first to adopt this and gradually extended it from manufacturing and wholesale trade to practically all commerce. The other countries of the Common Market agreed to work toward this type of taxation, and others in the European Free Trade Association followed suit. The advantage of the TVA is that it can be exactly calculated, can be passed on to the consumer without pyramiding, and is not inconsistent with the rules of GATT.

The CED advocated consideration of the TVA method for the United States in a statement in 1966 as a way of encouraging saving by consumers by shifting the tax in effect from earnings to spending. It would also reward efficiency of industry and eliminate the problem of expense account and other deductions.

The question of taxation had also to be considered in the context of social policy. One of the reasons for President Truman's veto of the 1947 bill[1] had been the fact that 40 percent of the income tax decrease would go to 5 percent of the taxpayers. The law was criticized also because it continued the exemption of income from state and municipal obligations, so that they continued to provide a tax refuge for the very rich. Another example of tax favoritism to the rich was the high depletion allowance granted to oil, gas, and some mining industries, ever since 1927, which enabled them to report high costs and thus reduce their taxable income.

A different line of attack was directed against the other end of the income tax schedule because of the steep graduation of the tax, which carried the rate from 20 percent in the first bracket up to 91 percent of net income over 200,000 dollars. Not many taxable individuals fell into this class but, since they were the persons who might otherwise have provided the risk capital needed for new and experimental enterprises, it was often urged that the volume of risk capital should be increased by lowering the top tax rates. There was little convincing evidence on this point, and there seemed to be no real shortage of risk capital after the war.

In spite of efforts at reform, the individual income tax continued to be the principal source of federal income, and the bulk of it came from the lowest income tax brackets. The Revenue Act of 1951, as a result of the Korean war, increased personal income tax rates in three steps; by 1954 they were above the 1945 level, with exemptions at 600 dollars for each taxpayer and each of his dependents. In 1954, as part of the program of tax reform, rates were reduced by about 10 percent. This encouraged consumer spending to rise as military spending declined, and aided in recovery from the depression which had begun in the second quarter of 1953.

The rapid growth in national product, especially after 1958, resulted in increased federal revenue without any change in tax rates. In 1964 there was even fear that this might produce a "fiscal drag" on the economy, a growth-inhibiting budget surplus. The future cost of the South Vietnam involvement was grossly underestimated in calculating total expenditures. This, combined with the high rate of unemployment, brought about the tax reductions in the Revenue Act of 1964. It was estimated that nearly 8 billion would be added to disposable personal income in 1964 by the reduction in taxes. Families with gross incomes of less than 3000 dollars benefited most, with a 39 percent reduction in their taxes. Families with incomes of more than 50,000 dollars obtained a reduction of only 13 percent. Unemployment did decline, but the youthful unskilled and the victims of racial discrimination still had difficulty in securing employment.

The corporate income tax, even more than the individual income tax, had shown itself sensitive to economic change and therefore raised more questions for public policy. How much of it, for example, could be shifted forward to consumers and thus turned into a concealed sales tax; or conversely, be shifted back to suppliers of the corporation? Where should the dividing line be drawn between large and small business so that the formation of new firms would not be hindered? What was the effect of business taxes in general on monopoly? on economic stability? on capital formation? on economic growth?

In addition to these large issues, there were many technical problems. The law changed frequently in its treatment of losses, permitting them to be spread over a period of years in order to reduce tax liabilities of good years. Depletion allowances for mineral and petroleum production, depreciation methods for capital assets, valuation of assets, special taxation for undistributed profits and its effect on methods chosen for corporate financing, were discussed at great length with each change of the law.

Several provisions of the corporation tax had already been changed in order to aid reconversion to peace production, especially of small firms. By the Revenue Act of 1945, refunds were speeded up, the excess profits tax was repealed, the capital stock tax was eliminated, and the corporate income tax was reduced. The result of these changes was to lower corporate taxes by more than 5 billion dollars.

The corporate income tax was second only to the personal income tax as a source of federal revenue during these years, and the general trend of the combined normal and surtax yields was upward. The excess profits tax which had been restored in 1950 was dropped again after 1953, chiefly because of difficulties of definition and interpretation. Depreciation allowances were given new and simplified guide lines in 1962 to permit more rapid write-offs for machinery and equipment. Further stimulus to modernization of equipment was given by the 7 percent tax credit granted for investment in depreciable machinery and equipment used in the United States; this was designed to help companies to meet the competition of foreign firms which had similar tax advantages. The Revenue

Act of 1964 reduced the combined normal and surtax rate on corporations by 4 percent, from 52 to 48 percent. In spite of these reductions in rates, revenue increased slightly as a result of increased national income.

Excise taxes produced about one-eighth of federal revenue in the postwar period, as much as 10 billion dollars in many years. Liquor and tobacco produced about two-fifths of the total excise revenue, and automotive vehicles and fuels about one-third. The rate at which excise taxes were set often depended upon estimates of what the traffic would bear without causing a resort to smuggling, illegal distilling, black-marketing, and the like. The 10 percent retailers' excise tax on luxury items such as jewelry, furs, and toilet articles was removed by the Excise Tax Reduction Act of 1965, and the manufacturers' excise tax was eliminated or reduced on many articles.

There was far less concern over federal gift and estate taxes, since they provided only 2 or 3 percent of the revenue in most years, and applied to a relatively small number of taxpayers. The estate tax rates were steeply graduated and rose in 1962 from 3 percent on the first 5000 above the exemption of 60,000 dollars to 77 percent on the share of the estate above 10 million. On gifts the rates after 1962 were 2.25 percent above 5000 dollars and 57.75 percent above 10 million.

State and Local Finance

Although federal tax receipts doubled in amount in the twenty years after the end of the war, the tax rate and the share of national income taken by federal taxes remained below the peak of the war years. In the case of state and local taxes, however, both rates and national income share rose steadily and brought the total figure close to that of the federal government by 1965.

For a few years after the war, state and local units had surplus funds at their disposal because they had been unable to carry on road building and other construction during the war. This money was soon used up, and the demands of a growing population for increasing services put a heavy strain on their resources. Between 1945 and 1965 expenditures for education increased nearly tenfold from 2.8 to 26.5 billion dollars. Not only were there more children to be educated, but also they often had to be given free books, free transportation, and, in some cases, free lunches.

Highways represented the next largest share and also increased tenfold to 8 billion.

Another fast-growing item was health and welfare. Rural residents, displaced by machinery and hoping for more opportunity for their children, moved into cities where there was little work for the unskilled. The wide differentials in welfare payments among the states tended to concentrate the rural poor in relatively few metropolitan centers, thus aggravating the effect of the population explosion. Police and fire protection, garbage disposal and sanitation, also cost more per capita as population density increased.

In meeting many of these needs, state and local units shared expenses. Total state and local expenditures rose in two decades from 9 to 74 billion (including interest on their debt but not the debt itself, which in the same period grew from 16 to 107 billion). In 1945 these state and local expenditures had represented 4 percent of the Gross National Product; in 1965 they were up to 11 percent of GNP.

There was wide variation among the states in the tax burden which these expenditures represented for their people. The wealthier states like New York and California were able to collect far more than the poorer states like Mississippi, Alabama, and South Carolina. In 1965 the ten highest states had an average per capita total for state and local taxes of 372 dollars, while the ten lowest averaged only 238 dollars.[2]

In obtaining revenue, the states were far more successful than the local units. In most years the states enjoyed a small surplus of receipts over expenditures. Their chief source of income was the general sales tax, which had been adopted in 42 states by 1965, and the specific sales taxes on gasoline, tobacco, and liquor; these taxes on consumers brought in more than half of the state tax revenues in the later years of this period. The second largest source was the income tax, levied in 36 states by 1965. Since states feared they might drive away their citizens, their rates were low in comparison with the federal income tax and the progression was moderate. Thirty-eight states levied corporate income taxes; 44 states still used property taxes, but these were declining in relative importance. Death and gift taxes were also used in some states, and the iniquitous poll tax lingered on in 9 states.

The overlapping with the central government of such taxes as those on inheritance, and excises on liquor and tobacco, caused some confusion, but methods of cooperation were developed in many cases. The federal government, for example, gave deductions for inheritance taxes collected by states. The states, on their part, aided federal agents in tracing illegal stills for making alcoholic liquors or in detecting smugglers carrying cigarettes across state borders. In some states the form for income tax reporting was made parallel to that of the central government to make life simpler for the harassed taxpayer.

Unlike the states, in most years after 1948 local governments faced a deficit which had to be made up by borrowing or by subsidies from state or federal government. These subsidies gave local units almost twice as much to spend as the states, although their tax revenue was no larger. Many of them were subject to rigid and often antiquated state legislation on taxing and borrowing, and they were unwilling to use heavy sales taxes which might hurt local business. The property tax continued to be the mainstay. In spite of problems of equity and administration which it presented, rising land values caused it to bring in twice as much in 1966 as in 1956, about seven-eighths of the total local revenue in both years. The remainder came from sales taxes, licenses, and in 20 large cities and 171 municipalities, income taxes.

The more serious problems both for the 50 states and for the 90,000 local governments arose from the shifts in population from farms into central cities, and from central cities into suburbs. Central cities lost the higher-income residents; many who remained were low-income families with little education and few skills. The lowered tax base of the cities made subsidy from the state essential but, even after the reapportionment forced by the Supreme Court decision, farmers and suburbanites in state legislatures were able to vote down aid to the cities, which faced the problem of educating millions of disadvantaged children with funds quite inadequate for training them to be useful and self-supporting citizens. The results of this neglect did not become immediately apparent; not until the late 1960s did violence break out in the cities.

Another problem for state and local governments was the increasing realization that many problems could not be solved by small local units. Water and air pollution, highways and transportation, cut across political boundaries. Inevitably the pressure for more funds shifted from local to state to federal government, which was finding the income tax so lucrative. The idea of federal grants was not new; the federal government had spent large sums on internal improvements in the days before Andrew Jackson; its Rivers and Harbors appropriations had long provided more or less useful sums to the states, and in 1890 it had made specific grants for education in agriculture.

The New Deal with its myriad forms of social legislation had greatly enlarged the field of federal grants and, even under the Republican administration of Eisenhower, eleven new programs had been added. The process continued under Kennedy and Johnson, raising the number of programs to 162 by the end of 1965. In that year the federal government was giving 10.9 billion dollars as grants-in-aid to state and local governmental units, in addition to 4.4 billion to private institutions and individuals for research and education. Federal funds were financing two-fifths of state expenditures for housing, more than half of state expenditures for public assistance, and nearly half of those for highways. A large part of these funds sifted down to local governments, which received four-fifths of their public assistance expenditures and two-fifths of education, transportation, and housing expenses from state or federal sources; these amounted to three-tenths of total local government expenditures.

One of the chief benefits of the conditional grant-in-aid was its ability to enforce minimum standards on the recipients, especially in the fields of welfare and education. Schools which did not meet desegregation standards, hospitals which were inadequate, found it difficult to obtain federal funds.

Some academic experts, emphasizing the superior efficiency and competence of the central government in this area, advocated that it should collect all the income taxes and give back to the states on a per capita basis, what they needed. This was a system used by Australia, but that fortunate country had a relatively homogeneous population of only 12 million, in only seven states.

Another possibility was suggested in 1965 by the Advisory Commission on Intergovernmental Relations: that the federal government give credit up to 40 percent of the federal personal income tax liability for state income taxes. A similar device had been adopted for death and unemployment taxes. It would give the states greater access to the more elastic and equitable income tax, without subjecting them to the kind of control exercised by most of the grants-in-aid.

Unemployment Insurance and Social Security

An area in which local, state, and federal governments cooperated very closely was that of unemployment insurance. The states set the tax rate to be paid by the employer, and in some states this was based on experience rating so that a firm which was able to keep its work force stable was granted a lower rate. By 1965 all of the states had approved programs and about 87 percent of all workers were included in the system. The average weekly payment was 37 dollars; the number of weeks covered varied from state to state. The federal unemployment tax on wages was 3.35 percent for 1963–65 but, after credit for state unemployment tax contributions, only a fraction of this had actually to be paid to the federal government. Unemployment trust funds totaled 7.8 billion by mid-1965, in addition to railroad unemployment insurance funds.

The different social security programs also required close cooperation of local, state, and federal governments. Taxes collected under the original modest legislation of the depression had developed into an important adjunct of fiscal policy. Old Age and Survivors Insurance started with a tax of 1 percent on employer and employee on the first 3000 dollars of annual earnings in firms employing at least eight (later four) workers. By 1965 the rate had risen to 3.625 percent on the first 4800 dollars for both worker and employer.* Farm and domestic workers, teachers and social workers, had been brought into the system, and even self-employed persons were included if they wished. Railroad and federal employees continued to have their own systems. Aid to dependent children and aid to the blind and the disabled were included, and the name of the system had been stretched to OASDHI—Old Age, Survivors, Disability and Health Insurance. Net proceeds of the tax were placed in a trust fund which had accumulated more than 20 billion by 1965, invested in securities which were direct obligations of the federal government or

---

* The rate was increased to 4.4 percent for 1967, and to 4.8 percent for 1969 on the first 7800 dollars.

guaranteed by it. In that year 16 million families or individuals were receiving benefits of 60 to 220 dollars monthly.

The payments made to retired persons and to dependent children, the blind, the disabled, and others, combined with unemployment insurance to maintain consumer purchasing power even in times of depression. This was of special importance in the case of the aged, since their numbers were rising in proportion to the rest of the population. Increased longevity for the retired put a heavy burden on the wage earner in the middle life span who had to produce enough goods and services to maintain the old as well as the young. By 1965 these two nonproducing groups made up 40 percent of the total population.

In contrast to the progressive income tax, the payroll tax gradually developed into a form of regressive taxation, since it was proportionally heavier on small than on large wage earners, and there were no exemptions. For families with two children, for example, the payroll tax exceeded the income tax if family income was below 5000 dollars. The regressive nature of the payroll tax tended to dampen consumption in a large number of families where the propensity to consume was highest, and for this reason exaggerated rather than counteracted the effect of cyclical changes in the economy. For employers, this tax and the unemployment insurance tax tended to stimulate the adoption of laborsaving machinery.

In spite of the rising prosperity of the country there were the usual complaints about the tax "burden"—the share of the national product spent by governmental units in providing a growing population with the increasing services which it demanded. A very large part of the increase, however, consisted of "defense" expenditures.

By 1965 total tax collections of all kinds were calculated as taking more than one-fourth of the Gross National Product. It was small comfort to most taxpayers to know that nine nations paid a still higher proportion, and only Canada and Japan among the major industrial nations had a lower fraction. Canada was only slightly below the United States, but Japan, because under the peace treaty she was not permitted to rearm, was significantly lower.[3] All of these countries, like the United States, enjoyed a rising standard of living during these years to which the expenditures of their governments, except those for armaments, largely contributed.

Management of the Federal Debt

The impact of the large government debt on the money market was a matter of continuing concern in the first decade after the war. Treasury policy was dictated by its determination to keep interest cost low and to prevent the price of its bonds from falling, as they had done after World War I.* These two aims were of course contradictory. In addition, the Treasury hoped to reduce the total of the debt and get it into the hands of permanent investors (rather than of financial institutions). This was made more difficult by the limit of 4.25 percent for bonds of longer maturity than 5 years set by Congress in 1918 and never repealed. Congress also legislated a ceiling on the total debt; this was 300 billion dollars by the Public Debt Act of 1945, but was reduced to 275 billion in 1946. The only effect of such legislation was to necessitate a change in the law every time the total approached its ceiling.

During the first few years after the war the Treasury was able to achieve some reduction of the debt. From the peak of 280 billion dollars in February 1946 there was a decrease of 20 billion to the end of the year, simply because the Treasury was able to reduce its cash balance by that amount. The decrease continued through 1948, carrying the total down to almost 250 billion. Commercial banks sold off their long bonds but, with the support of the Federal Reserve, bond prices did not go below par.

This modest reduction was soon wiped out when the United States Congress voted to join with the United Nations forces in Korea in June 1950. Inevitably the United States had to provide a major portion of the necessary funds. Since this was the period in which Federal Reserve authorities were insisting that support of low interest rates be abandoned, the Treasury had henceforth to tailor its offerings closely to market demand.

The gross debt rose almost steadily to about 320 billion by 1965. Small reductions occurred in a few years, but 1956–57 was the only period in which two successive years showed a decrease. The per capita debt stood at 1650 dollars in 1965. Debt management therefore involved providing for new issues and for refunding maturing issues. Since

---

* See p. 281.

a large portion of the debt was still short-term, the turnover was rapid, and efforts were made to lengthen maturities by increasing the proportion of bonds. These were designed to appeal to insurance companies and savings banks, while the short tax anticipation bills were aimed at corporations with funds temporarily being built up to meet tax payments.

In spite of Treasury efforts, the total of bonds outstanding did not increase either absolutely or relatively, but declined until 1951, and then remained almost constant for a decade while issues of less than 5 years maturity increased. This reduced the average maturity of the marketable debt from 9 to 5 years. The bills, certificates, and notes together continued to make up more than half of the marketable debt, and in 1961 and 1962 were more than 60 percent of the total. After 1963 some improvement in this ratio was accomplished by the policy of advance refunding, but it still remained above half. The Congressional limit of 4.25 percent on bonds was a serious hindrance to increasing their issue when market rates were above that figure, and forced recourse to the short issues which were subject to no such arbitrary ceiling on yield. The high proportion of short obligations also interfered with another aim of the Treasury, that of placing more of the debt in the hands of permanent investors.

Federal Reserve Policy

It had been feared that, when the war ended and government expenditures suddenly declined, there would be a depression. Instead, there was a rapid increase in prices when controls were removed; funds saved during the war poured into a market still unsupplied with consumer goods. This stimulated the demand for credit which banks were able to meet by replenishing reserves from the sale of their government securities. They had little need for Federal Reserve credit and an increase in the discount rate would have been ineffective.

The Reserve System was fully aware of the danger of uncontrolled credit expansion. It increased stock margins from 75 to 100 percent, but hesitated to take other action since the Treasury was still borrowing and refinancing and wanted low interest rates to continue. The main objective was to maintain stability in the government securities market; this necessitated the continued support of bond prices.

Gradually the central banking authorities shifted their position and began to emphasize, as in the Board report for 1947, the need "to absorb bank deposits and bank reserves and to restrain further over-all monetary expansion." The inflow of gold and the large amounts of government issues still in the hands of the commercial banks made control impossible without more drastic measures. The Board pointed out the inadequacy of its powers and the monetary instruments at its disposal, but Congress was unwilling to make changes in the law.

During 1948 the discount rate was raised and reserve requirements were increased for banks in the two central reserve cities (New York and Chicago) from 20 to 22 percent. But prices, especially for farm products, declined through 1948 and 1949 and credit was immediately eased. Reserve requirements were reduced in three stages, consumer credit terms were lightened, margin requirements went down, and open-market purchases of government securities were employed to lower interest rates.

The outbreak of hostilities in Korea in mid-1950 produced a great increase in federal expenditures and a corresponding increase in inflationary pressures. Prices rose to new highs during 1950 and early 1951. By this time the Reserve officials were determined to free themselves of the obligation to support the price of Treasury issues in order to keep interest rates below the market. The controversy between the Reserve and the Treasury continued through 1950 and finally was resolved by the Accord of March 1951.

The statement agreed on by the Secretary of the Treasury and the Board of Governors of the Federal Reserve System announced simply that they had "reached full accord with respect to debt management and monetary policies" in furthering "their common purpose to assure the successful financing of the Government's requirements and, at the same time, to minimize monetization of the public debt." It was a masterpiece of understatement, for it summarized years of controversy and recognized the importance of a monetary authority which could act as a brake on credit expansion even when that involved the government. The Reserve System no longer had to support the price of government bonds in order to maintain the fiction that the Treasury could borrow at low rates regardless of the state of the money market; it did, however, continue to ease the money market over temporary situations created by refunding of Treasury obligations or tax collection dates.

Fiscal Policy versus Monetary Policy

The Congressional investigations and the newspaper publicity which accompanied this controversy were valuable in educating the public to the importance of monetary policy and to the limitations of both monetary and fiscal policy in stabilizing, not only the government security market, but also the economy.

Fiscal policy, which included taxation, borrowing, and spending, had a direct effect on consumer income and a less direct effect on corporate income. However, changes in tax rates and in budgets were subject to several lags. Congress had first to be convinced that a change was necessary or desirable; reductions were more popular and more quickly voted than increases. After a change was enacted, there was a lag before it could be put into full operation. A reduction in personal income tax rates or an increase in exemptions for the great number of taxpayers in the lowest income bracket, taxed at 20 percent, was a relatively quick way to increase consumer purchasing power and stimulate business activity, thus reducing structural unemployment. An increase in social security payments also had rapid results; increases in other government expenditures usually operated more slowly on demand.

Monetary measures on the other hand acted quickly on selected features of the economy—bank reserves, interest rates, and the like—but their effect upon employment, production, and national income was much slower and less certain. Checking inflation is the particular province of monetary policy, since if the authorities are sufficiently courageous they can raise interest rates and check business expansion in the early stages. In depression, monetary measures are relatively ineffective, as was shown during the 1930s. Lowering interest rates and pumping funds into the economy by open-market operations were not able to persuade business enterprises to borrow in the face of wide unemployment and low consumer demand.[4]

Advocates of both monetary and fiscal policy tend to view the economy as an aggregate and fail to analyze the situation into the factors which have produced the problem. Unemployment, for example, if it is functional, arising from illiteracy, lack of technical skill, or discrimination, demands remedies quite different from those needed to correct structural unemployment caused by reduced consumer purchasing power or sudden reduction of government spending. Both policies have their place in a well-balanced financial armory, but even the use of both together cannot cure all the ills resulting from social and other non-economic factors.

During the Korean war both monetary and fiscal measures were used to prevent inflation. The Reserve Board, by the Defense Production Act of September 1950, had been given temporary controls over consumer and real estate credit. Margin requirements for stock trading were increased, and reserve requirements were raised. The combination of these monetary policies with the fiscal measures of tax increases and the general price freeze of January 1951 was effective in causing prices to fall slightly and then to remain almost stable for several years. War expenditures were thereby kept down and further borrowing by the government was unnecessary. This was one of the few military ventures of the United States which was paid for by taxes rather than loans.

When price controls were again lifted in January 1953, the Reserve authorities took advantage of their new freedom under the Accord and raised the discount rate from 1.75 to 2 percent in order to counteract any inflationary result. A month later, since stock prices had declined and bank loans had not increased, the margin requirements were reduced from 75 to 50 percent, but the money market was still under pressure from the tighter monetary policy. Open-market purchases were therefore used to provide additional funds, discount rates were again lowered, and reserve requirements were twice reduced. Tax reductions in 1954 and accelerated depreciation allowances, with increased government spending on highways and education, encouraged a new period of expansion which lasted until July 1957; a decline carried industrial activity down until April 1958; the following rise lasted until May 1960.

Throughout this period the Reserve authorities used frequent discount rate changes, many of them by one-quarter of 1 percent, staying usually above the Treasury bill rate but below the prime commercial paper rate, following them down in 1952–53, up in 1954–57, down again in 1958, up in 1959, down in 1960, then remaining nearly stable until 1963. In that year and the following year, the rate was raised only once each year, by steps of one-half of 1 percent. The small changes were evidence of Federal Reserve hesitation and lack of confidence. Lowered rates were backed up by open-market operations and by reductions in reserve requirements in the years when business activity was declining. Cash in vault could be counted as part of reserves after November 1960, and after July 1962 central reserve city banks kept only the same reserves as reserve city banks; the difference between them was abolished.

From 1953 to 1961 the Reserve system followed the "bills only" policy, confining its open-market purchases and sales to short issues, in order to emphasize its unwillingness to support bond prices. The short operations were used to stabilize the money market over short periods of stress such as tax payment dates. The "bills only" rule was dropped when the deficit in the balance of payments began to cause alarm.

If interest rates in the United States had been permitted to rise, funds might have been attracted from abroad, but fear of recession prevented any such action. Instead "Operation Twist" was attempted. The Reserve system began to purchase intermediate and longer maturities of government issues in order to raise the price and lower their yield, while at the same time the short rate was permitted to rise. This, it was hoped, would twist the interest rate curve, keeping the long rate low but raising the short rate enough to attract foreign deposits. However, all market rates tended to rise together, and this policy failed in its purpose. When the Bank of England rate was raised from 5 to 7 percent late in 1964, Operation Twist had to be abandoned, and the Reserve rediscount rate was raised to 4 and then to 4.5 percent, because inflationary pressures were mounting and gold exports were continuing. Market rates on bonds and mortgages inevitably rose.

In spite of the steady drain of gold and the steady increase in consumer prices of about 1 percent annually, the central authorities were reluctant to jeopardize "prosperity" and possibly increase unemployment by adopting adequate measures either monetary or fiscal. Through 1964 the Reserve system, instead of permitting gold exports to reduce member bank reserves, used open-market operations to offset the gold loss. The Reserve banks were beginning to feel concern over their own reserves, and early in 1965 the requirement of a 25 percent gold certificate reserve against member bank deposits was repealed by Congress. (In March 1968 the similar reserve requirement for Reserve notes was repealed.)

Rather than take any effective action at home, the Administration resorted to artificial controls on foreign investment by Americans.

Because of the slow inflation and changing monetary habits, the
Treasury was again faced after 1960 with the problem which had for
half a century been rarely troublesome—that of hand-to-hand circulation. After a spurt during the war years, the volume of currency outside
the Treasury and the banks leveled off until 1960; then it increased
within 5 years from 30 to 37 billion dollars. Much of this was due to
the use of small coins in automatic vending machines and to the hoarding of dollars and Kennedy half-dollars. The Treasury stock of silver,
which had been built up to a peak of more than 2 billion ounces in 1958
after the drain of the war years, was down to 800 million ounces by
1965 and it became necessary to reduce the use of silver in coins. By
the Act of June 4, 1963, as a first step, Federal Reserve notes of 1
dollar were authorized to take the place of the silver certificates which
had to be redeemed for the legal .77 ounce troy of silver no matter
what the price of the metal. This did not, however, meet the problem
of increasing demand for coins, and the Coinage Act of 1965 therefore
changed the proportion of silver from 90 to 40 percent in the half-dollars,
and from 90 percent to no silver at all in quarters and dimes. The dollar
was left unchanged, but its coinage was prohibited for 5 years.*

Commercial Banking

The commercial banks at the end of World War II had held both
demand and time deposits in unprecedented amounts, at 76 billion and
30 billion dollars, respectively. The combined total was more than twice
the peak of 43 billion in 1929. Demand deposits (exclusive of interbank
and federal deposits) showed a steady upward trend during the two
decades 1945–65 to 161 billion. Time deposits during the first decade
showed an upward trend at about the same rate as demand deposits,
but after 1955, and even more rapidly after 1960, the growth of time
deposits was so great that by 1965 their total of 147 billion almost
equaled that of demand deposits. One factor was the increase in interest

---

* In 1967 the Treasury permitted sales only to domestic industrial users,
and forbade the melting and export of silver coins.

paid on deposits of 90 days or more, from 3 percent to 4 percent in 1962, to 4.5 in 1964, and to 5.5 in December 1965, for banks subject to the control of the Federal Reserve Regulation Q. Nonmember state banks paid even higher rates.

Although commercial banks continued to be the leading financial intermediary, their rate of growth was less than that of some others. Their share of all deposits in financial institutions declined, reflecting the unwillingness of the public to hold large amounts of non-interest-earning demand deposits as interest rates rose.

In an effort to counteract this trend, a number of larger banks began to issue negotiable certificates of deposit in denominations of 100,000 dollars or more with maturities of 30 days to 1 year. Their yield was limited to the same figure as that of time deposits, but their marketability gave them some of the advantages of the demand deposit. From the issuing bank's point of view, this was a possible danger, since the CD's were often used as a placement for temporarily idle funds, making them volatile and unpredictable. Banks had also to maintain reserves against them as against regular time deposits. The total outstanding rose nevertheless from little more than 1 billion in 1960 to 16 billion by mid-1965, almost 10 percent of total time and savings deposits of commercial banks.

The development of the CD was encouraged by the monetary authorities because it reduced the incentive for corporations to invest their liquid funds abroad when interest rates there were higher than at home, and thus helped to relieve the pressure on the balance of payments. For many large corporate investors the CD was an attractive alternative to the Treasury bill, and the development of a dealer market in CD's still further facilitated their use. This was not entirely without danger, however. Several banks, already weak, offered bonuses to brokers for placing their issues, and failed during 1965.[5]

No radical changes occurred in the commercial banking structure in the two decades after 1945. The number of commercial banks declined by about 2 percent, leaving the total at 13,804. Most of the large state-chartered banks—16 percent of the number and 60 percent of the deposits of all state banks—were members of the Federal Reserve system by the end of 1965, a slight decline from the corresponding ratios in 1945. National banks, required to be members, constituted 35 percent of the total number of commercial banks and held 58 percent of total deposits. Only 263 commercial banks were not members of the Federal Deposit Insurance Corporation, a decline of two-thirds from 1945 to 1965. Most of them were insured under other systems (like the mutual savings banks of Massachusetts) or were ineligible for FDIC insurance.

The most striking change in banking structure was the increase in the number of branch offices of commercial banks from 3723 in 1945 to 15,486 in 1965. Texas and Illinois each had more than 1000; Iowa, Kansas, Minnesota, Missouri, Ohio, Pennsylvania, and Wisconsin each had more than 500. More than one-half of these were associated with national banks. This reflected a change in public attitudes in the century after the organization of the national banking system. The small independent bank had been found unable to meet the credit needs of the increasingly large corporations. Many small banks had failed during the 1930s, and their place had been taken by branch banks and holding companies. This development was encouraged by the 1952 legislation which reduced requirements for capital and surplus of a member bank branch to the same level as those for a branch of a state bank in that state. In 1962 the law went still further and permitted a state bank with branches to retain its branches if it converted to a national charter; it also permitted a national bank which purchased a state bank with branches to retain the branches. Only 11 states in 1965 prohibited branch banking; the rest were about equally divided between statewide and limited branch banking.

Another popular device for enlarging the scope of a commercial banking corporation was the bank holding company. The legislation of 1934 had given Reserve authorities the right to deny to such companies voting privileges for the bank stock they held unless they submitted to examination. It was not until 1956 that bank holding companies were required to divest themselves of nonbanking interests. By 1965 there were 53 bank holding companies in 32 states (5 of the holding companies were held by other holding companies) operating 468 banks with 1486 branches (6.7 percent of all commercial bank offices) with 27.6 billion dollars of deposits.

The one-bank holding company was also utilized in a new variation of financial merger. A large corporation or conglomerate might acquire a bank in order to have its assistance in corporate operations. In other cases a bank itself might organize the holding company and become its

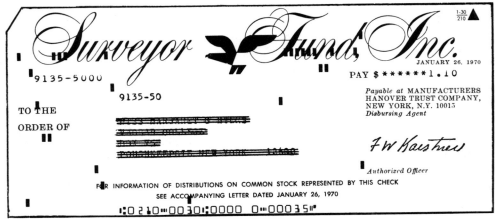

Modern automated bank check, 1970

principal component in order to combine several types of financial services. The third and simplest kind of one-bank holding company was that in which the owner was a corporation rather than a group of individuals. In all cases the bank itself was subject to the usual examination and supervision, but there was no legal control over the holding company which held only one bank. Bank mergers were controlled by the Bank Merger Act of 1960, amended in 1966, and companies holding more than one bank were required to register with the Board of Governors of the Federal Reserve system.

A number of the larger banks expanded their activities also into foreign countries. By 1965, 13 member banks had more than 200 branches in 50 countries scattered over four continents. Other corporations which engaged in foreign banking were those organized under Section 25 (a) of the Reserve Act to specialize in operations abroad although they might have their head office at home. In 1965 there were 37 of these. The rapid growth of the Eurodollar market during the 1960s gave an incentive to this development.

The growing demand for banking service caused many banks to look for increased capital. Banks in the United States, whether under national or state charter, had long been required to raise their capital funds through equity issues, except during the 1930s.* The cost of increasing

---

* See p. 323.

capital by the usual means of selling additional stock had discouraged capital growth, and the ratio of capital to deposits had gradually declined from the 80 percent of the early nineteenth century to about 10 percent in the 1950s.

The Comptroller of the Currency was impressed with the need of many banks for more capital and the difficulty of raising it by increasing their capital stock. He therefore in 1962 followed the example already set by New York, New Jersey, and Minnesota for their state banks and issued new regulations for national banks which permitted them again to issue senior securities; some other states followed suit. The advantage to the banks was the greater flexibility it gave them in meeting conditions in the money market. By 1965, 102 banks had issued capital notes or debentures, with most maturities between 20 and 25 years. The average borrowing was 25 percent of total capital, well within the statutory limit of 100 percent of capital plus 50 percent of surplus. As could be expected, the smaller banks paid the higher rate of interest. The total capital borrowed by banks was 1.6 billion dollars at the end of 1965, as compared with total capital and surplus of 30.3 billion.[6]

Commercial bank portfolios reflected the general prosperity of the postwar decades. At the end of World War II, United States government securities had made up nearly three-fourths of bank loans and investments, and the ratio of loans to deposits was only 20 percent. By the end of 1965 the government securities held by commercial banks made up only one-fifth of their total portfolio, and the ratio of loans to deposits had risen to 65 percent.

The absolute growth in loans from 30 to 200 billion dollars during these years was the result of increased credit to almost every sector of the market. Commercial and industrial loans went up fourfold, security loans fourfold but in much smaller totals, agricultural loans fivefold, real estate loans sixfold; consumer credit even more rapidly. The increase in loans to business resulted from the greater flexibility of bank credit. In some cases, this took the form of loans on commercial receivables; in other cases, banks provided intermediate- and longer-term credit by loans based on earning power of a firm rather than on a specified asset. Banks in the larger centers also entered the field of direct leasing of equipment. All of these developments, like the certificates of deposit, were efforts of the commercial banks to adapt to competitive conditions in a situation in which their time deposits had increased much faster than the demand deposits.

Although consumer credit was nothing new in the United States, its rapid growth after 1945 gave it a new importance in the total credit picture. In twenty years the total outstanding rose from 5.6 to 87.8 billion dollars, an almost constant rate of increase of 4 percent annually. Nearly four-fifths of this amount was installment credit, with automobile loans the largest single kind. The noninstallment types of charge accounts and single payment loans made up most of the rest. More and more this type of credit was used not only for commodities, but also for services such as travel and education, although it seldom went as far as the "Die Now, Pay Later" of the French novelist.

The borrowers were in great part young families, most of whom had few financial assets. The trend toward early marriage and parenthood encouraged borrowing, as did also the widespread use of credit cards. The volume of consumer credit outstanding can be judged also by its ratio to annual personal consumption expenditures which rose from less than 5 percent in 1945 to more than 20 percent in 1965. In the United States, prestige seemed to depend on how much one owed rather than on how much one owned.

Commercial banks and sales finance companies granted half of the consumer credit; the rest came from retail stores and distributors. The feature which caused most concern for the financial system was the steadily declining quality of consumer credit, i.e., the increasing risk inherent in credit transactions, as down payments were reduced and maturities lengthened. The Federal Reserve after 1952 no longer had control of these transactions and indeed was not eager to undertake control, according to its testimony before Congressional committees. Fortunately there were no serious business depressions during these years, and the flimsy structure of consumer credit was not shaken.

Another development in the field of commercial credit was the revival of commercial paper, sometimes called a "second banking system." This type of promissory note, in round sums up to 50,000 and even 100,000 dollars was issued for a few days or up to nine months by large corporations. For the issuing corporation the commercial paper provided funds at a better rate than that of the commercial bank loan; moreover the banks were hampered by the legal limit on loans to any one borrower. For the purchaser of the paper, the investor, the return was attractive as compared with Treasury notes of similar maturity. Sales finance companies handled much of this paper and acted as middlemen between automobile and appliance dealers, for example, and the investor. The volume of paper in the market increased very rapidly, doubling during the five years 1960–65 to a total of more than 10 billion, with no indication that the increase would not continue.

Increased activity in Federal funds also became a conspicuous feature of the money market in this period. Member banks which held excess reserves, even small member banks, were able to channel such funds through dealers in the large centers, where they were purchased as short-term investments or as adjustments for reserve positions. Small rate differentials caused such funds to be shifted back and forth between Treasury bills and Federal funds, with gross purchases and sales averaging up to 3 billion daily in an active period in the autumn of 1964.

The development of this market began about 1921 when several New York City banks adjusted reserves among themselves. Interdistrict trading began a few years later and was active during the boom period of the stock market in the late 1920s. Low interest rates prevailing during the 1930s and 1940s discouraged further use, and it was not until the early 1950s, when short-term rates were higher, that the market revived. The pressure on reserves created by the more rigorous policy of the Reserve authorities after the Accord of 1951 stimulated the use of the funds market. This more efficient use of reserves helped also to achieve greater uniformity of credit conditions throughout the country.[7]

Other Financial Intermediaries

In addition to central and commercial banking systems, investment bankers, and government lending institutions, many other financial intermediaries were operating in the money market during the two decades following the war. They included mutual savings banks, savings and loan associations, life insurance companies, credit unions, sales and personal finance companies.

The common characteristic of these intermediaries which distinguished them from the banking system was that they could not "create" deposits as did the commercial and central banks. Their operations therefore depended on what they could borrow from individuals or other institutions. While the war lasted, shortages of consumer goods resulted in a large amount of saving but this was soon exhausted after the war. In the postwar years the share of disposable personal income which was saved varied between the high of 7.6 percent during 1951 and 1952 and the low of 4.9 percent in 1960 and 1963. The absolute amount saved increased with GNP and was 25.7 billion dollars by 1965.

The largest share of private savings went to life insurance companies which had doubled their assets between 1945 and 1955 and almost doubled them again by 1965 to reach a total of 159 billion. Forty percent of this sum was invested in mortgages and real estate, 42 percent in corporate bonds and a few stocks, the rest in various governmental issues. The legal limit of common stock investment for life insurance companies was also raised in New York and by 1957 was 5 percent. Even savings banks were granted the right to buy a limited amount.

Savings and loan associations, about equally divided between federal and state charters, saw their assets quadruple between 1945 and 1955 and triple again by 1965 to 129 billion dollars. Mutual savings bank assets arrived at only 58 billion in 1965 from 17 billion in 1945. The investment of both these groups was largely in mortgages. Smaller amounts of other savings went into private pension funds and into mutual funds.[8]

The interrelationships among the intermediaries made a complex structure, and competition among them was keen. Changes in interest rates paid by commercial banks on time deposits affected their drawing power for funds. The corporate income tax imposed on savings and loan associations after 1951 affected them in the same manner as commercial banks, which had long been subject to this tax. Life insurance companies, although not directly subject to control by the monetary authorities, were nevertheless influenced in their investment policies by easy or tight credit, by selective credit controls on mortgages, by federal debt management, and by tax rate changes. The volume of funds entrusted to the insurance companies by their policyholders was influenced by alternatives presented in other parts of the money market. During the latter part of this period, many of the financial intermediaries were occasionally faced with the results of what was rather clumsily called "disintermediation"— the tendency for savings to be withdrawn from the intermediary institutions and invested directly in stocks, bonds, and the like in order to obtain higher yields.

Federal Credit Agencies

The federal government had established a precedent for filling some of the credit gaps left by private enterprise as early as 1917 when it set up the Federal land banks to make long-term land mortgage loans to farmers from funds originally supplied by the government. During the following fifteen years, ten more credit programs were initiated. More were added during the depression of the 1930s, and others grew out of war and postwar needs in the 1940s and 1950s. By the mid-1960s there were 74 different credit programs under seven departments and seven independent federal agencies, with more than 100 billion dollars in outstanding loans. Of the programs, 49 of the 74, and 30 percent of the total amount, was in direct loans; the rest were federally insured but the actual funds were from other sources.

When direct loans were involved, the funds were sometimes obtained by borrowing in the capital markets; Federal land banks, Federal intermediate credit banks, home loan banks and cooperatives were able to do this. Fourteen other direct loan programs borrowed their funds from the Treasury, most of them under revolving arrangements because of ceilings on the amount that might be outstanding at any one time. The programs which gave loan insurance or guarantees did not have to provide funds but were in most cases limited as to total commitments, and were subject to annual review by Congress.

In some cases the need for government credit facilities arose from a lack of banking offices in areas where branch banking was not permitted. In other cases there were banks but they were unwilling to lend because of assumed high risk, or would lend only at very high rates of interest. This was especially true of small business and of low-income housing. The Small Business Act of 1953 and the Small Business Investment Act of 1958 were designed to aid small companies unable to borrow elsewhere. For housing there was one program after another, some providing subsidies to private builders, in addition to grants to local governments for slum clearance and rehabilitation. Many states had housing credit plans also, but the need was so great that the problem remained.

Because of the multiplicity of programs for housing credit, there was bound to be duplication among agencies and shopping around by borrowers to find the lowest terms and the longest maturities. A committee under the Secretary of the Treasury in 1963 attempted to set up guide lines, and recommended that loans be shifted whenever possible to private institutions, but little progress was made in that direction. Private capital was not at all eager to enter a field in which the returns were so low.

Although many of the federal credit agencies had too recently been established to be able to compute their loss ratio by 1965, the record of the earlier agencies was surprisingly good. Disaster loans made between 1933 and 1953 had understandably shown the highest rate, nearly 7 percent, and the Federal Farm Mortgage Corporation down to 1951 had more than 3 percent loss. But none of the other agencies had more than 1.3 percent, five had 1 percent or less, and the Home Owners Loan Corporation had none to 1950. This record had been made in spite of the fact that many of the government agencies had less stringent regulations than those of private agencies, and had sometimes eased maturity and other requirements for the borrower.[9]

Subsidies to Agriculture

One of the least successful, and most expensive, of the federal aid programs was the agricultural one. For many Americans the concept of the "independent farmer," a "horny-handed son of toil" had a sentimental appeal which made it difficult for the government to take a common-sense approach to farm problems. The farming community itself has never been reconciled to the fact that as the nation became more prosperous a smaller proportion of its income was spent on food. Moreover improved technology had increased productivity in agriculture as in industry and had reduced the need for farm labor. In 1945 farmers still comprised 16 percent of the civilian labor force; by 1965 the number of farm workers had been cut in half and they were only 6 percent of the total.

The best solution to the farm problem would have been the withdrawal of marginal farms from production, and a shift of farm labor to the service industries which were the growing sector of the economy.

The increased productivity of agriculture should have been reflected in lower prices to consumers. Instead, the policies which were adopted tried to achieve two contradictory results, that of keeping farmers on the farm, and at the same time keeping their income at the same proportionate level as had prevailed a half-century earlier. When the high prices of the war period ended, the Commodity Credit Corporation was empowered to make loans against commodity collateral. If its price in the market fell below the price at which the collateral had been valued, the borrowing farmer simply forfeited the collateral in lieu of payment. The CCC was left with the task of disposing of the commodity as best it could, and very large surpluses accumulated in wheat, feed grains, and cotton.

The cost of continued storage was very high. The wheat surplus, for example, reached a maximum of 1.4 billion bushels in 1961. Much of it was stored in the holds of the "mothball fleet" anchored in the Hudson River and had to have chilled, poisoned air pumped through it to keep out vermin.

In 1954 another approach was tried by the Agricultural Trade Development and Assistance Act (Public Law 480). By donations to needy nations, by barter arrangements with others, and by sales for soft currencies to countries which had irredeemable money, it was hoped that the accumulated commodities could be disposed of without reducing domestic prices. Had any other country followed a similar policy, it would have been labeled "dumping." The surpluses did not disappear, and these subsidized sales caused damage to the markets of other countries. Between 1955 and 1965 the United States provided 14 billion dollars worth of farm products to 116 nations.

In the Agricultural Act of 1956, payment was given farmers for the land which they took out of cultivation, in the hope that such a "Soil Bank" would reduce the amount produced. Contracts for such agreements were signed up to 1960, some of them running until 1970, but the plan was then abandoned. The Food and Agriculture Act of 1962 continued the policies of production control and price support but, as the acreage was reduced, the amount of fertilizer and cultivation was increased and in some years not only did the yield per acre increase, but also the total crop. This intensive cultivation was especially appropriate for large farms, so that half of all the farms accounted for 90 percent of the product. This meant that the high-income commercial farmers received the major share of the subsidy payments, some individuals obtained as much as 50,000 dollars in a year, while a really poor farmer got a mere pittance.

None of the solutions to the farm problem was satisfactory to everyone. Farmers themselves began to be dissatisfied, and in 1963 the wheat farmers voted down a plan which would have controlled production and supported prices; they evidently preferred to take their chances with the market. Complicated arithmetic was involved in setting the parity price (the ratio of prices received by farmers to prices paid by farmers, compared with the same ratio in 1910–14) on which loan valuations were based. Consumers complained of the high price of food, but as taxpayers they complained even more of the high cost of subsidies. Foreigners resented the inconsistency of the United States in advocating lower tariffs on goods it sent abroad and at the same time restricting imports of many agricultural products into the United States. Even when they were the beneficiaries of Public Law 480, many foreign countries were of the opinion that the American food did more harm than good in the long run, since it enabled them to postpone serious consideration of the legal and technical difficulties of their own food production. Drought and crop failures created a demand for American supplies and by the mid-1960s the surplus food was nearly gone. The farm "problem" still remained nevertheless.

Securities and the Exchanges

Increasing prosperity and slow inflation were reflected in the rising volume and value of stock exchange activity after the war. At five-year intervals the growth was as shown in Table 12.

Some of the trading continued to be financed by customers' debit accounts with their brokers, but the margin requirements set by the Federal Reserve Board had taken the fever out of this market, and the call loan rates had long ceased to be of crucial importance. There were occasional flurries, but the general trend of prices was so steadily upward after 1950 that it soon wiped out the relative declines of 1953, 1957, and, sharpest of all, that of 1962. The 500 common stocks of

TABLE 12. STOCK EXCHANGE ACTIVITY, 1945 TO 1965

	Value of All Stocks Registered	Value of Share Sales	Number of Shares Sold (in millions)
	(in billions of dollars)		
1945	88.2[a]	16.3	769
1950	111.0[b]	21.8	893
1955	238.8[b]	38.0	1321
1960	335.3[b]	45.3	1441
1965	573.1[b]	89.5	2671

Source: Reports of the Securities and Exchange Commission.
[a] New York City only.
[b] All exchanges.

the Standard and Poor's Index went from an annual average price of 20 in 1950 (on the base of 1941–43 = 10) to 90 by 1965.

The increase in trading was not matched by the volume of new issues during this period (see Table 13). Common stock offerings totaled 397

TABLE 13. VALUE OF NEW ISSUES, 1945 TO 1965 (*in millions of dollars*)

	Common Stock	Preferred Stock	Corporate Bonds and Notes	State and Municipal Securities
1945	397	758	4,855	795
1950	811	631	4,920	3,532
1955	2185	635	7,420	5,977
1960	1664	409	8,081	7,230
1965	1547	725	13,720	11,148

Source: Reports of the Securities and Exchange Commission.

million dollars in 1945; reached a high point of 3294 million in 1961, but fell off again and amounted to only 1547 million in 1965. New issues of preferred stock in most years were only one-half to one-quarter as large. Since bond issues have a limited life, the volume of new bonds offered each year is much larger than that of new stocks; in four of the twenty years it was more than ten times as large. By the end of 1965 there were 3139 different issues of stocks admitted to trading, and 1291 issues of bonds.

The volume of new issues of both stocks and bonds was reduced by the fact that corporations no longer depended entirely on the capital

markets for increases in their funds, but financed much of their growth
from internal sources. Undistributed profits of all private corporations
during this period rose from 4.4 billion to 25.4 billion dollars by 1965,
exceeding their dividend payments in most years. Another internal source
of funds was the allowance for depreciation, depletion, and the like; this
amounted to 35.3 billion by 1965, a steady rise from the 6.5 billion of
1945.

The trend toward urban living, the longer life expectancy, and the
inexorable slow inflation created a demand for employee pension plans,
and the federal income tax legislation, especially that of the Revenue
Act of 1942, gave an incentive to corporations to meet it. Corporate
pension funds (as distinguished from industry-wide funds administered
by unions and employers jointly) gradually increased their holdings of
common stocks. The law of New York State, which set the pattern for
much of the country, in 1950 broadened the authorization for common
stock investment to 35 percent of the market value of their funds, and
funds which specifically exempted their trustees from this limitation
were permitted to go even higher.

Although these pension funds did not move in and out of the market
in speculative maneuvers—and were therefore no threat in a sudden
collapse of prices—their purchases were of sufficient volume to cause
concern. After the bull market of 1953–55 the Senate Committee on
Banking and Currency under Senator Fulbright investigated and found
that in some years they accounted for more than one-quarter of the net
purchases of common and preferred stocks. Even more concern was expressed over the fact that the pension funds tended to concentrate their
purchases in 200 to 250 issues which consisted largely of the "blue
chips," thus narrowing the potential market for issues of smaller corporations.[10]

Another important sector of the securities market consisted of the
mutual funds which had shown such rapid growth during the 1920s
when they were called investment trusts.* Their number doubled between 1945 and 1965, from 366 to 727, but their assets showed far
greater increase, rising from an estimated 3.3 billion dollars at the end
of 1945 to 44.6 billion by 1965. Their size gave them obvious power

---

* See p. 299.

to affect the market, although a study of the mutual funds made in 1962 by the Wharton School of Finance and Commerce found no evidence that the power had been misused; it concluded only that they should make more detailed reports and that the distribution of their capital gains should be limited or controlled.

The role of the investment banker continued to decline relative to the growth of the securities market as a whole as a result of all these developments. Moreover corporate borrowing by means of bonds, debentures, and notes was often accomplished by direct placement. During the early 1950s the volume of privately placed bonds and notes exceeded that of the public issues; then it tapered off to 40 percent in 1960 and rose again to nearly 60 percent in 1965. These private placements were less costly for the borrower, but had the disadvantage that they could not be disposed of in the market or retired at will.

There was no significant change in the legislation on security trading for many years after the Investment Companies Act of 1940. In 1963, however, the Commission published a "Special Study of the Securities Markets" in five volumes of 3000 pages, on the basis of which they made 175 recommendations for improvements. They were directed especially toward protecting investors in the over-the-counter market and raising the standards for dealers who wished to operate in that market. As a result, the Securities Acts Amendments Act of 1964 was passed by Congress. Among its provisions were disclosure requirements for 2500 companies which had not hitherto reported to the Commission; stricter and more detailed reports for conglomerate companies; more uniform accounting methods for companies whose securities were publicly traded. The new law aimed also to get more competition into the security business and to give insiders less opportunity to profit by their prior knowledge. The security markets voiced little objection to these changes, many of which had been brought about by recent scandals. Another development of concern to the Commission was that which was referred to as the "third market," the off-board trading in common stocks which were listed on an exchange but traded by broker-dealers outside the exchanges. The Commission had little power over such activity, but in 1965 it did rule that such dealers must make reports to them.

Court decisions in interpreting the antitrust legislation were still concerned with protecting business rather than consumers from unfair competition. The Clayton Act of 1914 had attempted to prevent mergers which lessened competition or tended toward monopoly by acquiring the stock of another corporation. Since this had not been effective in preserving small competitors, the Robinson-Patman Act of 1936 attempted to prevent price discrimination, the Wheeler-Lea Act of 1938 outlawed unfair or deceptive practices, and the Celler-Kefauver Antimerger Act of 1950 forbade acquiring the assets (as well as the stock) of a competing corporation.

The new legislation strengthened the antitrust agencies and enabled the courts to support the Federal Trade Commission's efforts more effectively. Nevertheless, the number of mergers in manufacturing and mining was increasing at such a rate that it was impossible for all of them to be investigated. During the 1940s they averaged about 240 a year; in the 1950s about 480 a year; and in the early 1960s were more than 900 each year. In 1965 alone there were 2100.

Moreover there was an increase in the proportion of large mergers involving assets of 10 million dollars or more. There was also an increase in the proportion of "conglomerates"—mergers which united companies in quite unrelated fields. It was difficult to prove that such mergers substantially decreased competition, although it was possible that one product of such a corporation might be sold at a loss, in order to drive out a competitor, because of the high profits derived by the merger from its other lines. There was also the constant threat of a takeover of an unwilling corporation by such an enormous financial giant.

Of special concern to the financial community and the governmental authorities was the use of complicated financial maneuvers in organizing a conglomerate. Paper pyramids of convertible preferred stocks, convertible and nonconvertible debentures, warrants, and the like were unhappily reminiscent of the late 1920s. The bidding-up of stock prices which accompanied many mergers was an unhealthy factor in the security markets. Existing legislation and tax laws seemed impotent in the face of this new threat to economic stability.[11]

Foreign Financial Developments

As the United States grew in wealth and financial power it was inevitably forced to take more responsibility for the rest of the world, if only to protect its own interests. The international financial organizations which had been created at Bretton Woods as the war was ending were effective within their limited spheres but were not able to cope with problems beyond those. The International Monetary Fund could assist in stabilizing currencies affected by temporary imbalances but was powerless to correct sustained capital outflows. Much of its activity was carried on quietly without fanfare as it offered advice for currencies in trouble. Teams of experts on economic and financial problems visited such areas and made recommendations which went far beyond purely monetary matters. In many cases the Bank for Reconstruction and Development made loans for specific purposes on the basis of these studies, from its own funds or from funds it borrowed. During the first years after the war these loans all went to western industrialized countries for reconstruction purposes.

In addition to this indirect aid through institutions to which it had contributed the major share of funds, the United States also made a direct loan to England of 3.75 billion dollars in mid-1946. Also, the capital of the Export-Import Bank was increased to 3 billion dollars so that it could increase its loans, and some of these loans went to France.

Two years after the end of the war, Europe outside of Germany had restored much of its industry and its transportation system and had revived its export markets; it seemed well on the way to economic recovery. The United Nations Relief and Rehabilitation Administration, which since 1943 had contributed about 4 billions in money and supplies to European countries, was being phased out as its work seemed to be done; 72 percent of this aid had come from the United States.

This optimistic outlook was changed by the damage of two very severe winters, especially hard in Great Britain, and by summer droughts which cut food production and necessitated increased imports. In the new emergency Secretary of State George Marshall, familiar with Europe after his wartime service there, suggested in a Commencement address at Harvard University in 1947 that, if the European countries would agree among themselves on their needs and priorities, stabilize their currencies and lower their trade barriers, the United States would assist them. During that summer, representatives of sixteen countries (Western Germany later became the seventeenth) met in Paris to form the Organization for European Economic Cooperation and hammer out a plan.

Check signed by Harry S. Truman

The United States meanwhile was studying its own needs and resources to determine what it could spare. By April 1948 the Congress approved the Foreign Assistance Act which authorized expenditures of 16 billion dollars over the next four years to be spent on the European Recovery Program.

Wheat, cotton, tobacco, and other agricultural products made up about half of the shipments; coal, steel, tractors, locomotives, and freight cars made up the rest and were rushed to the areas where need was greatest. With this assistance, West European industrial production for the year 1949 was 10 percent above its prewar level and it increased by about 10 percent in each of the next few years. Agriculture improved more slowly but each of the years to 1953 was better than its predecessor. So rapid was the recovery that the aid actually given by the United States never reached the amount which had been authorized. By mid-1952 the Economic Cooperation Administration, created to handle the project, had spent 13.6 billion dollars in western Europe; all but one-tenth of this sum was in the form of grants which did not saddle the recipients with debt. The United States had seen its own Gross National Product increase from 234 to 347 billion in the five years before 1952, profiting indirectly by the increasing prosperity of Europe, one of its best markets.

European recovery on the one hand, and the outbreak of war in Korea on the other, caused the ECA to be transformed into a new body, the Mutual Security Administration, and emphasis was put on military rather than economic aid. The line of demarcation between military and economic is difficult to draw precisely; a new road may be designed to take farmers to market or soldiers to the front. The shift toward military assistance was nevertheless obvious; it was based on the hope that it would increase friendliness toward the donor. It was accompanied by a parallel shift of areas, from Europe to the "underdeveloped" countries of Asia, Africa, and South America which were now referred to as "developing." In the decade 1956–65 the United States economic aid to such countries totaled 30 billion dollars, military aid about half as much. Other countries contributed about 22 billion to these areas during the same period, a higher proportion of GNP for some of them than for the United States.

The name of the American agency was frequently changed, reflecting changes in policy. MSA became the International Cooperation Administration, within which in 1957 the Development Loan Fund was created. By 1961 the ICA had become the Administration for International Development, with the appropriate abbrevation of AID.

As the United States balance of payments became increasingly unfavorable, the attitude of Congress stiffened. More of the aid was given in the form of loans rather than of grants, and both interest rates and terms of repayment were made more severe. For both loans and grants, it was required that all or part of the funds be spent in the United States, although prices of agricultural and industrial products were often higher in the United States than in other markets. The tying was justified in the view of Congress by the need to prevent further gold drain. There was also increasing demand for repayment of the loans in dollars rather than in the soft local currencies which were not redeemable in gold. More than one-tenth of the foreign aid was given as dollar loans made by the Export-Import Bank, and one-sixth of the total through Public Law 480, the "Food for Peace" plan which accepted local currencies in payment for American food, especially wheat.

The international financial institutions, as well as the United States, were obliged to shift their attention to the developing nations. Since the IBRD was unable under its charter to make loans except on principles of sound banking, it could not help countries with inconvertible currencies. It therefore, with the help of the United States and other economically strong member nations, organized several affiliates. The International Finance Corporation was established in 1956; it was empowered to invest in stocks and bonds of going industries, even without governmental guarantees; by 1965 it had put 137 million dollars into 103 corporations in 32 countries. In 1960 the International Development Association was inaugurated as another affiliate empowered to make loans repayable in soft currencies.

In 1959 the Inter-American Development Bank under the auspices of the Organization of American States was set up to channel both hard and soft loans into Latin America. It had 850 million dollars in capital, of which the United States provided 350 million. The capital was increased in 1965 to 2150 million, half in dollars and half in local currencies; the United States share rose to 762 million. The Bank was permitted to make only hard loans from its capital funds, or from funds borrowed on the international capital market, but might make soft currency loans from its Fund for Special Operations and its Social Progress Trust Fund. By 1965 the IDB had made 238 loans for 1.3 billion.

In spite of the massive aid from the United States (see Table 14) and the increase in their productivity, European countries found it difficult in the first years after the war to export enough to pay for their imports from the United States, and they complained of the "dollar gap." Insofar as United States imports were impeded by tariffs and other trade bar-

TABLE 14. UNITED STATES FOREIGN ASSISTANCE,[a] 1946 TO 1965 (*in millions of dollars*)

	Total	Europe	Near East and South Asia	Far East	Latin America	Africa	Other and Non-regional
Total	115,875	44,676	23,600	25,842	10,343	3,237	8,178
Economic							
Total	81,197	30,292	17,324	16,191	9,430	3,051	4,910
Loans	32,008	11,494	9,366	2,925	6,720	1,285	218
Grants	49,189	18,797	7,958	13,267	2,710	1,766	4,692
Military							
Total	34,678	14,384	6,276	9,651	913	186	3,268
Loans	586	126	150	35	132	11	134
Grants	34,092	14,259	6,126	9,616	781	175	3,134

Source: Economic Report of the President, February 1968.
[a] Including AID and predecessor agencies, Food for Peace, Export-Import Bank, and others.

riers, the querulous tone was excusable, but much of the gap was caused by the relative poverty which had resulted from the war. Many countries were forced to reconsider the level at which they had hoped to keep their currencies when they joined the International Monetary Fund in 1945–46. Great Britain was under special pressure because of her heavy war debts and, in spite of the loans from the United States and Canada, found her reserves dwindling. With great reluctance in September 1949 she again reduced the value of the pound, from 4.03 to 2.80 dollars. Her trading partners in the Commonwealth (except Canada and Pakistan) and eleven countries in western Europe followed her example, although Belgium, Italy, and France, which had already suffered a devaluation, adopted smaller ratios. West Germany had undergone a currency devaluation in 1948, but in 1961 had revalued its mark upward by 4.75 percent.

The need to economize their limited resources of dollars and foreign exchange, and the tapering off of Marshall Plan aid, led to the formation in 1950 of the European Payments Union by the countries in the OEEC. Started off by the United States ECA with 350 million dollars, the organization cleared payments among the member countries through an account with the Bank for International Settlements in Basel. Each member had to pay only its net balance to the Union, and only a part of it in gold, instead of settling individual balances with each of its trading partners. The Union also granted short-term credits to members with temporary deficits. The plan worked so successfully that it was extended year after year to 1960. By that time most of its members had achieved convertibility of their currencies, and for the Union they therefore substituted the European Monetary Agreement, a loose arrangement which required no outside help.

In the meantime six of the OEEC member countries, France, Italy, West Germany, Belgium, Luxembourg, and the Netherlands, had taken the first steps toward creating the European Economic Community. The Treaty of Rome signed in March 1957 provided for gradual abolition of tariffs among the members, equalization of member tariffs on exports from outsiders, and eventual unification of the economic life of the area. On the whole, the United States benefited by the increasing prosperity of this more efficient economic unit, but also faced heavier competition in some agricultural products, steel, and coal.

Another development in Europe with far-reaching results for the United States was that of the Eurodollar market. Although banks in financial centers had long held small amounts of deposits in foreign currencies, the amplitude of the market and the predominance in it of the dollar were new phenomena. The change started in the mid-50s when Russia and its satellites found themselves in possession of dollars which they preferred to hold in Europe rather than transfer to the United States. When the deficit in United States payments increased, the dollar gap disappeared and more dollar balances accumulated in European banks. They could obtain higher interest by lending the dollars in Europe than by transferring the deposits to the United States.

As the market developed, eight other European currencies began to play a role in Eurocurrency transactions, but the dollar continued to be of prime importance. Periodic difficulties of the pound and the franc and the smaller absolute size of Continental money markets limited the supply of their currencies, while the restrictions on credit in the United States increased the dollars available abroad. Eurodollars were loaned not only by European banks and European affiliates of American banks but also by American corporations and even individuals. They were borrowed by banks, foreign traders, oil companies, and governments. By 1965 the dollar liabilities in the market were estimated at more than 10 billions and still rising.

The wide swings in interest rates and in supplies of funds, coupled with the fact that short-term funds were often loaned on long term, became a source of concern to central banks and governments. The usual monetary controls were ineffective in this international market. If a liquidity crisis were to occur, there was no lender of last resort which could rescue those in difficulty.[12]

International Investments of the United States

Funds invested abroad by individuals and corporations increased very rapidly during the two decades following the war and made the balance of payments still more "unfavorable." Some of this took the form of portfolio investments, purchases of securities issued by foreign corporations or governments. An increasing portion, however, was in the form of direct investment in foreign affiliates of American corporations. Firms manufacturing inside the European Economic Community had a tariff advantage which gave an incentive to this method for European investment, and the interest equalization tax of 1964 provided further reason. The foreign affiliates of United States firms were able to provide about half of their new financing from internal sources of retained earnings and depreciation allowances. By 1965 only one-quarter of the needed funds had to be raised in the United States by bank loans and security sales. Moreover these direct investments resulted in a large return flow of funds in the form of dividends and royalties. In 1961 a policy of discouraging and restricting these operations was adopted, although in the long run this was more harmful than helpful to the balance of payments problem.

United States Trade Policy

The United States, in addition to its direct aid programs after the war, recognized the need for avoiding the strangling restrictions on international trade which had produced such harmful results during the 1930s. War controls over exports of strategic materials were gradually lifted; imports were encouraged in order to enable European buyers to pay for American goods, and "Trade Not Aid" became a slogan. A charter for an International Trade Organization was painstakingly drafted in a series of international conferences with the hope that it would parallel the IMF and the IBRD, but it was never able to gain the approval of the United States Congress and so had to be abandoned. However, the General Agreement on Tariffs and Trade, concluded among twenty-three nations in Geneva in 1947, was able to save the principle of trade cooperation, and in spite of its ambiguous legal position and its limited resources it became an effective and persistent instrument for elimination of trade discrimination.

An important step in the direction of freeing trade was taken in October 1962 by the passage of the Trade Expansion Act, which replaced the often-renewed Trade Agreements Act of 1934. Under the new legislation the President was given authority to reduce by 50 percent any existing rate of duty and to modify other types of restrictions. Duty on a commodity might be eliminated entirely, by negotiation with the European Economic Community, if the EEC and the United States together accounted for more than 80 percent of its total export from non-Communist countries. Other provisions of the Act gave protection for cases of undue hardship on individual firms or industries resulting from the change and provided for carrying out the negotiated tariff reduction in stages. The "Kennedy Round" of tariff negotiation instituted by this Act did not end until 1967, barely meeting the deadline set by the Act. In return for reduced tariffs on American exports, the United States agreed to lower rates on nearly 6000 items by an average of 35 percent over a period of five years, beginning in January 1968.

New devices were adopted in order to increase exports, reduce imports, tie foreign aid grants and loans so that they had to be used for purchase of American products, and encourage foreign tourists to visit the United States. There was also increasing clamor for protective tariffs and other measures to reduce foreign competition; this occurred at the same time that the United States was taking part in the Kennedy Round of conferences to reduce trade barriers among all the nations. Fortunately the Administration took a strong position against a return to protectionism. It did not, however, eliminate some of the administrative tariff practices to which foreign sellers objected, such as the American Selling Price method of customs evaluation for certain chemicals.

The United States was less dependent on foreign trade than most countries—exports amounted to only 5 percent of GNP in 1965—but the trade balance became an increasingly important part of the total balance of payments as military expenditures in foreign theatres of war increased. It was favorable in the old sense of the word, with exports greater than imports in almost every year, but not large enough to offset the unfavorable movement of funds.

Financial Position of the United States in 1965

The monetary gold stock of the United States, which had reached 23 billion dollars just before the war, remained high for a few years after the war. Then it began an almost steady decline which carried it down to 14 billion by 1965. This was still one-third of the world's stock of monetary gold (excluding the Soviet bloc and China), and in many ways it was a healthier distribution of the metal than formerly, since it permitted many other countries to hold adequate reserves. But it presented serious problems to the United States, which was still following an inflationary policy at home and was unwilling to permit interest rates to rise sufficiently to attract funds from abroad.

The financial position of the United States would have been considerably improved had it been able to collect the debts outstanding from the two world wars. Twenty countries in 1965 still owed more than 23 billion dollars on the indebtedness incurred during the first war, nearly half of it being accrued interest. Since many of these countries no longer had a separate existence but had been absorbed into the Russian complex or reorganized in some other way, there was little probability that the debt would ever be paid or even recognized. In addition, West Germany owed 52 million in 1965, which was being paid off at the rate of 4 million annually; most of the reparations debt had been written off.

The difficulty of collecting debts after World War I had produced a more realistic approach to the subject during World War II so that much of the aid to allies was given in the form of Lend-lease. Nevertheless in 1965 the accounts still unsettled under that arrangement amounted to 1.5 billion dollars and the total of all war debts, not including the World War I accounts, amounted to more than 18 billion. Even for the sums due from western Europe, about 40 percent of the total, there was small probability of eventual repayment. The United States had entered both world wars late, and many of its allies believed that they had contributed more than their share by the time the United States entered.

The continuing deficit in the balance of payments and the loss of gold should have been counteracted by an increase in interest rates in order to bring funds into the United States. Instead, in September 1964, it was met by an interest equalization tax designed to discourage American investment in foreign securities by increasing the cost about 1 percent over domestic issues. The tax was applicable to purchases by Americans of foreign securities maturing in 3 or more years. (In October 1968 the tax was extended to cover maturities of 1 year and over.) Canada and Japan protested strongly against the tax and their issues were exempted. Most of the foreign securities purchased by Americans during 1964 and 1965 were Canadian.

A further effort to slow the gold drain was taken early in 1965 when commercial banks were asked to use voluntary restraint and limit the increase in their foreign loans to 5 percent for the year. Although the amount of new European securities purchased by Americans was reduced by the tax and the voluntary control program, the net effect was small. Undistributed earnings of American corporations operating abroad were reinvested to an amount of 1.5 billion dollars in several years.

In the absence of effective monetary measures to stop the gold drain, the government resorted during 1962 to a number of petty and embarrassing devices to conserve gold. European countries were encouraged to prepay their long-term debts; the United States Treasury borrowed in Italy and Switzerland; the Reserve banks arranged with central banks abroad to obtain foreign currencies and thus reduce foreign purchases of gold. The deficit for 1963 was somewhat reduced by these devices, but such "swap" arrangements were continued through the next two years with eleven central banks and the Bank for International Settlements. It was not until late in 1964, after the Bank of England had raised its rate sharply from 5 to 7 percent, that monetary policy was adopted in the effort to prevent the outflow of volatile foreign balances without restricting domestic credit.

Another measure which could have been employed to stop the gold loss was that of devaluation, or raising the price of gold to make the same amount of the metal appear to be more valuable. This had been done once before in the United States, in 1934, not because there was any shortage of gold at that time but because there was a desire to raise the price level as a cure for the depression. Other countries have frequently resorted to this device; it gives a temporary boost to the economy by sending some prices higher and creating an illusion of prosperity. Those who lose are the individuals living on fixed incomes.

In the 1960s any increase in the price of gold would have benefited the gold-producing countries, which were chiefly South Africa and Russia. Most Americans found the racist policies of South Africa abhorrent and were unwilling to follow any policy which would increase her wealth; others were not willing to make Russia's economic position any stronger.

As it entered the last third of the century, the United States was still facing many problems. The conflict between stable price levels at home versus stable exchange rates abroad was still unresolved. The rate of inflation was rising. The inability of private enterprise to cope with the urban crisis of unemployment, and the shadow of the costly undeclared war in Asia, focused attention on the federal budget, and there was no prospect of relief for the taxpayer, even when (and if) the military establishment was reduced.

NOTES

1. The Colonial Period

1. *Documents relating to the Colonial History of New York,* I, 303.

2. *Ibid.,* II, 218, 371, 594, 697.

3. Henry Bronson, M.D., *Connecticut Currency* (New Haven, 1865; paper read before the New Haven Historical Society; 25 copies printed), p. 4.

4. Robert Proud, *The History of Pennsylvania in North America* (2 vols., Philadelphia, Z. Poulson, Junior, 1797), I, 133 ff.

5. Hening, I, 204; IV, 251 ff. William Z. Ripley, *The Financial History of Virginia,* pp. 18 ff.; 147 ff. (Columbia University Studies in History, Economics and Public Law, New York, 1893, III, 1), John Howard Hickcox, *Historical Account of American Coinage* (Albany, Joel Munsell, 1858).

6. Douglass, *Discourse,* II, 291 ff. Sylvester S. Crosley, *The Early Coins of America* (Boston, 1875).

7. The petition to the Board of Trade from the merchants is given in Robert Chalmers, *A History of Currency in the British Colonies* (London, Eyre and Spottiswoode, 1893), p. 12. His first chapter is one of the best concise summaries of early American coinage. He was an officer in the British Treasury.

8. Charles J. Bullock, *Essays on the Monetary History of the United States* (New York, The Macmillan Company, 1900), p. 25. Proud, *History,* p. 174. William Graham Sumner, *The Financier and the Finances of the American Revolution* (New York, Dodd, Mead and Company, 1891), Vol. II, Ch. XVIII.

9. The Potter pamphlet is on microfilm at the New York Public Library; the Woodbridge pamphlet is in *Colonial Currency Reprints,* I, 107. See also Joseph Dorfman, *The Economic Mind in American Civilization* (New York, Viking Press, 1946), Vol. I, Chs. VII and IX.

10. Andrew McFarland Davis, "Currency Discussions in Massachusetts in the Eighteenth Century," *Quarterly Journal of Economics,* Vol. 11, pp. 70-91, 136-60, and in Joseph Felt, *An Historical Account of Massachusetts Currency* (Boston, Perkins and Marvin, 1839), 88 ff. The phrase "immoderate quantities" was applied by Governor Shirley of Massachusetts to the paper money of the neighboring states in his speech to the Massachusetts

Assembly on February 9, 1743; in *Colonial Currency Reprints,* IV, 205. Burnaby, *Travels,* p. 92. Theodore Thayer, "The Land-Bank System in the American Colonies," *Journal of Economic History,* XIII (1953), 2.

11. New York and New Jersey were closely associated during the colonial period. Their experience with paper money may be followed in *Colonial Laws of New York,* I, 666; II, 1015, 1036, 1047; V, 638; and in *Documents Relating to the Colonial History of New York,* Vol. XI, which contains under the heading "Currency" in the index a full list of all the legislation.

12. Quoted by Richard Lester from a book by the governor of Pennsylvania, Sir William Keith, *Journal of Political Economy,* 46 (1938), 339.

13. Franklin's pamphlet can be found in *Papers,* I, 141-157. William R. Shepherd, *History of Proprietary Government in Pennsylvania* gives figures for the amounts of paper money (New York, Columbia University Studies in History, Economics and Public Law, 1896), VI, 414 ff. Other accounts of the early years in Pennsylvania may be found in Hickcox, p. 20; Proud, II, 151-77; and in Richard Lester, *Monetary Experiments* (Princeton, Princeton University Press, 1939).

14. William Z. Ripley, *The Financial History of Virginia,* pp. 154 ff: (Columbia University Studies in History, Economics and Public Law, IV, 1, 1893), pp. 154 ff. Kathryn L. Behrens, *Paper Money in Maryland, 1727–1789* (Johns Hopkins Studies in Historical and Political Science, 1923).

15. Douglass, *Summary,* I, 497; II, 14 ff. Thomas Hutchinson, *History of the Colony of Massachusetts Bay* (3 vols., London, 1764; reprinted Cambridge, Mass., Harvard University Press, 1936). *Historical Statistics of the United States,* p. 773. Charles J. Bullock, *Essays on the Monetary History of the United States* (New York, The Macmillan Company, 1900), p. 45. Good summaries of this controversy may be found in Bray Hammond, *Banks and Politics in America* (Princeton, N. J., Princeton University Press, 1957) and in Joseph Dorfman, *The Economic Mind in American Civilization* (New York, Viking Press, 1946), Vol. I, Ch. IX.

16. Details of credit given by merchants are to be found in Simon L. Adler, *Money and Money Units in the American Colonies* (Rochester, The Rochester Historical Society Publication Fund Series, VIII, 1929), p. 147; Susie M. Ames, "A Typical Virginia Business Man of the Revolutionary Era," *Journal of Business and Economic History,* III, No. 2, 407; W. T. Baxter, *The House of Hancock: Business in Boston 1724–1775* (Cambridge, Mass., Harvard University Press, 1945); Alva Conkle Burton, *Thomas Willing and the First American Financial System* (Philadelphia, University of Pennsylvania Press, 1937), p. 29; Edward Edelman, "Thomas Hancock," *Journal of Business and Economic History,* I, 1; Franklin, Papers, II, 178-235, 270-81; Virginia D. Harrington, *The New York Merchant on the Eve of the Revolution* (New York, Columbia University Press, 1935); William B. Weeden, *Economic and Social History of New England, 1620–1789,* p. 315 (2 vols., 1890, reprinted 1963 by Military House Publishers, New York).

17. Simeon E. Baldwin, *American Business Corporations before 1789:* American Historical Society Annual Report, 1902, Vol. I; Andrew McFarland Davis, *Currency and Banking in the Provinces of Massachusetts Bay* (American Economic Association Publications, 3, I, 1; II, 2; 1901). *New York Times,* January 6, 1968, gives date of founding of New York Chamber of Commerce.

18. C. H. J. Douglas, *Financial History of Massachusetts* (Columbia University Studies in History, Economics and Public Law, 1892), I, 4. Delos O. Kinsman, *The Income Tax in the Commonwealths of the United States* (Publications of the American Economic Association, New York, Macmillan, 1903), Ch. I.

19. *Colonial Laws of New York,* I, 60, 92, 666. Edwin P. Tanner, *The Province of New Jersey 1664–1738* (New York, Columbia University Press, 1908).

20. Shepherd, *History,* p. 437.

21. Hening, *Laws of Virginia,* I, 128, 143, 144, 305. Ripley, *Financial History of Virginia,* p. 44.

22. C. H. J. Douglas, *Financial History of Massachusetts,* 96 ff. John S. Ezell, *Fortune's Merry Wheel: The Lottery in America* (Cambridge, Mass., Harvard University Press, 1960).

23. Massachusetts Acts and Resolves, II, 10, 559. Records of the Colony of Massachusetts Bay, I, 186; II, 106, 269.

24. W. J. Ashley, *Surveys, Historic and Economic* (London, Longmans, Green and Company, 1900). Robert Beverley, *The History and Present State of Virginia* (ed. by Louis B. Wright, Chapel Hill, University of North Carolina Press, 1947), p. 1705. Albert Anthony Giesecke, *American Commercial Legislation before 1789* (Philadelphia, University of Pennsylvania Publications in Political Economy and Public Law, No. 23, 1910). John Dean Goss, *History of Tariff Administration from Colonial Times to McKinley* (Columbia University Studies in History, Economics and Public Law, 1891), I, 2. William Hill, *First Stages of Tariff Policy* (Publications of American Economic Association, VIII, 6, 1893).

25. Douglass, *Summary,* I, 540.

26. Macpherson, *Annals* of 1764.

27. Discussions of the effect of mercantilst policies on the American colonies may be found in Ashley, *Surveys,* pp. 313, 332; Douglass, *Summary,* I, 540; Eleanor L. Lord, *Industrial Experiments in the British Colonies of North America* (Baltimore, Johns Hopkins Press, 1898); Herbert Levi Osgood, *American Colonies in the 17th Century,* III, 33 (New York, The Macmillan Company, 1904–1907); and in Adam Smith, *Wealth of Nations* (1776), Book IV. Edmund S. Morgan, in *The Birth of the Republic* (Chicago, University of Chicago Press, 1956), Ch. IV, discusses the real and nominal function of British troops in the colonies.

2. Revolution and Confederation

1. The discussions on finance may be followed in the *Journals of the Continental Congress,* especially II, 207, 221–23; III, 390, 458; V, 546 ff., 674 ff.; VII, 354; XI, 415; XV, 1225; XXIII, 824. Benjamin Franklin described the depreciation in a letter to Samuel Cooper of April 22, 1779 (*Works,* VI, 354). Samuel Breck in 1843 wrote *Historical Sketch of the Continental Currency* (Philadelphia).

2. The depreciation of state and Continental notes is summarized in *State Papers on Finance,* V, 764–74, and is discussed in *Journals of the Continental Congress,* VI, 915; VIII, 124; IX, 955, XII, 930; Bolles, I, 147, 159, 165; William G. Summer, *The Financier and the Finances of the American Revolution* (New York, Dodd Mead and Company, 1891); Henry Bronson, *Connecticut Currency* (New Haven, 1865), Ch. VI.

3. *Journals of the Continental Congress,* VII, 36; XV, 1053.

4. *Secret Journals,* I, 145, 150. Also in *Journals,* XVI, 386.

5. E. James Ferguson, *The Power of the Purse* (Chapel Hill, University of North Carolina Press, 1961). Marquis de Chastellux, II, 293. *State Papers on Finance,* I, 54–62.

6. John Adams, *Familiar Letters* (New York, 1876), pp. 293, 365. Richard F. Upton, *Revolutionary New Hampshire* (Hanover, N. H., Dartmouth College Publications, 1936), p. 137.

7. *Journals of Congress,* XVI, 74, 136, 173, 280, 289, 319, 339, 402. Elliott, *Funding System,* p. 53.

8. Clarence L. Ver Steeg, *Robert Morris, Revolutionary Financier* (Philadelphia, University of Pennsylvania Press, 1954).

9. Bolles, I, 223. Pitkin, *Political and Civil History of the United States,* I, 411. *Secret Journals,* II, 7 ff.; 58–89. *Diplomatic Correspondence,* III, 91, 114, 192. John Adams, *Works* (1853 edition), VII, 588. Benjamin Franklin also complained of the state loan commissioners in Europe, *Works,* Bigelow edition, VI, 400.

10. Chastellux, I, 38; II, 255.

11. *Journals of the Continental Congress,* II, 200; III, 314, 362, 478. Robert East, *Business Enterprise in the Revolutionary Era* (New York, Columbia University Press, 1938), pp. 239 ff. McMaster, I, 206.

12. Thomas Anburey, *Travels through the Interior Parts of America, 1776–1781* (2 vols., Boston, Houghton Mifflin Company, 1923), II, 180.

13. *Diplomatic Correspondence of the American Revolution,* xii, 91. The Morris and Jefferson plans are also reprinted in the Report of the International Monetary Conference of 1878. Hepburn, p. 38. *Journals of the Continental Congress,* XXXI, 682 ff. The pennies were known as Franklin pennies because it was he who devised the motto they bore: *Mind Your Business.*

14. Merrill Jensen, *History of the United States during the Confederation* (New York, Knopf, 1950), Ch. 16. Nathan Miller, *Enterprise of a Free*

People (Ithaca, N. Y., Cornell University Press, 1962), p. 11. New York State Laws, Ch. XI, 9 Sess. Samuel Greene Arnold, *History of the State of Rhode Island* 4th ed., II, Ch. 24 (Providence, 1874). Frank Greene Bates, *Rhode Island and the Formation of the Union* (New York, Columbia University Studies in History, Economics and Public Law, 1898), pp. 119 ff. Rhode Island Colonial Records, Vol. X, May 1786.

15. Hamilton, II, 400–418, 604–635. Paine, II, 153. Burnett, V, 220. *Journals of the Continental Congress,* XVII, 542, 549; XX, 545 ff. Pelatiah Webster, *Political Essays,* 447 (Philadelphia, Joseph Crukshank, 1791).

When the national banking system was established in 1864, the Bank of North America was the only bank allowed to take out a national charter without altering its name to include the word "National"; this in recompense for its long and honorable service. Bray Hammond, "Banking before the Civil War," in *Banking and Monetary Studies,* ed. by Deane Carson (Homewood, Ill., Richard D. Irwin, 1963).

16. Broadus Mitchell, *Alexander Hamilton,* I, 346 ff. (2 vols., New York, The Macmillan Co., 1957–62). Allan Nevins, *History of the Bank of New York and Trust Company* (New York, privately printed, 1934). M. H. Foulds, "The Massachusetts Bank," *Journal of Business and Economic History,* II (1929), 256 ff.

17. Joseph S. Davis, *Essays in the Earlier History of American Corporations,* II, 257, 344 (Cambridge, Harvard University Press, 1917).

18. Burnett, *passim.* Charles J. Bullock, *Finances of the U.S. from 1775 to 1789* (Madison, University of Wisconsin, 1895). Payson P. Treat, *The National Land System* (New York, E. B. Treat and Company, 1910). *Journals of Congress,* IX, 807; XII, 931; XXVI, 279. Jefferson, II, 325 (Ford edition). Gallatin, III, 124. Washington (Bicentennial edition), XXVII, 485 ff. "Letter to Jacob Read."

19. *Journals of the Continental Congress,* I, 43, 51, 76; II, 200, 253; III, 464; IV, 258; XIX, 110; XXIV, 257. William Hill, "First Stages of Tariff Policy," *Publications of American Economic Association,* VIII (1893), 6. M. E. Kelly, "Tariff Acts under the Confederation," *Quarterly Journal of Economics,* 2 (1887–88). John D. Goss, *History of Tariff Administration from Colonial Times to McKinley* (Columbia University Studies in History, Economics and Public Law, 1891, Vol. 1, No. 2). Gordon C. Bjork, "The Weaning of the American Economy," *Journal of Economic History,* XXIV (December 1964, 541–60), p. 4.

20. *Journals of the Continental Congress,* III, 545 ff.; XXII, 12, 88, 328, 376, 384. Ferguson, Ch. 9 (note 3).

21. Rafael Bayley, *National Loans of the U.S.* (Washington, Government Printing Office, 1880). William Graham Sumner, 133 ff. John Durand, *New Materials for the History of the Revolution* (New York, Henry Holt and Company, 1889). *Diplomatic Correspondence of the Revolution,* vi, 470 (November 1782). Harold A. Larrabee, *Decision at the Chesapeake* (New

York, Clarkson Potter, 1964). Cleona Lewis, *America's Stake in Inter-national Investments* (Washington, D.C., The Brookings Institution, 1938).

22. The Franklin letter is in *Works* VII, 137. Breck, 22.

23. Hamilton, III, 420–426, IV, 40–65.

24. *Journals of the Continental Congress,* XXXI (September 20, 1786); 676; XXXII (February 21, 1787), 73.

3.   A New Constitution and a New Era in Finance, 1789–1811

1. Nathan Schachner, *Alexander Hamilton* (New York, D. Appleton-Century Co., 1946). 1 Congress, 1 Session, Ch. 12, Act of July 2, 1789, to establish the Treasury, in *Annals of Congress,* I, 436, 643. Tenth Census, VII, 322.

2. Jefferson, VI, 470, "Report on the Privileges and Restrictions on the Commerce of the United States in Foreign Countries, December 16, 1793."

3. Seybert, *Statistical Annals,* pp. 537–59; Timothy Pitkin, *A Statistical View of the Commerce of the United States of America,* 1835 (New Haven, Durrie and Peel, 1835). *Annals of Congress,* 1 Congress, 1 Session, I, 381; II, 2183, 2186; 5 Congress 2 Session III, 3777. A summary of trade statistics and a discussion of their adequacy is to be found in *Historical Statistics,* 529 ff. Leland D. Baldwin, *Whiskey Rebels, The Story of a Frontier Uprising* (University of Pittsburgh Press, 1939).

4. Hamilton's *Report on the Public Credit* is in *American State Papers on Finance,* I, 15, as well as in *Papers,* VI, 51. This volume also contains the case for assumption of the state debt (146 ff.). The *Annals of Congress* give summaries of the debates and the results of votes in the House; especially II, 1586, 2303, 2369. The Refunding Act is in 1 Congress, 2 Session, Ch. 34. Bolles, II, Chs. 3 and 4. Ferguson, *passim.* His interpretation contrasts with the earlier classic by Charles Beard in *Economic Interpretation of the Con-stitution* (New York, The Macmillan Co., 1913). Miller, 15 ff.

5. Annual Reports of the Secretary of the Treasury, 1800–1812. Pitkin, pp. 315–36. Seybert, 534, 727. *American State Papers on Finance,* I 30, 181, 183, 231. Raymond Walters, Jr., *Albert Gallatin* (New York, The Macmillan Co., 1957), Ch. IV. Alexander Balinky, *Albert Gallatin, Fiscal Theories and Policies* (New Brunswick, N. J., Rutgers University Press, 1958).

6. Wolcott's Report as Secretary of the Treasury, 1796, in *American State Papers on Finance,* I, 414 ff.

7. Hamilton, IX, 538. Jefferson (Ford edition), VIII, 172.

8. Jefferson's objections are found in *Writings,* V 284 ff., February 15, 1791. *Annals of Congress* contain the public debates on the charter, which are summarized and analyzed in: Wayne H. Morgan, *Business History Review,* XXX, No. 4 (1956), 472–92; Hammond, Chs. 5, 8; *American*

State Papers on Finance, I, 183–89; II, 217–18; Elliott, 172–215; James Hamilton, *Reminiscences,* p. 265; Lewis, *passim;* Domett, *passim;* Noah Webster, *Sketch;* James O. Wettereau, "The Branches of the First Bank of the United States," *Journal of Economic History,* II (1942), Supplement 66–; Kenneth L. Brown, "Stephen Girard's Bank," *Pennsylvania Magazine of History and Biography,* LXVI (1942), 29–55; Neil Carothers, *Fractional Money* (New York, John Wiley & Sons, 1930); John T. Holdsworth, *The First Bank of the United States.* (Washington, D.C., Government Printing Office, 1910) pp. 42, 51, 90, 92.

9. Annals of Congress, II, 2111; McMaster, I, 589; *American State Papers on Finance,* I, 102, 105; Seybert, pp. 543–44; Ernest Bogart, *Financial History of Ohio* (University of Illinois, Studies in the Social Sciences, 1912), I, 2.

10. Myers, 74; *An Appeal to the Public on the Conduct of the Banks in the City of New York,* 1815; Elliott, pp. 445–48; Bolles, II, 60.

4. War of 1812 and the Second Bank of the United States

1. Annual Reports of the Secretary of the Treasury for 1807 and 1813, in *American State Papers on Finance,* I, 493; II, 374, 527, 564–65, 569, 622, 662, 919. Philip Walters and Raymond Walters, Jr., "The American Career of David Parish," *Journal of Economic History,* IV, 1944; Stuart Bruchey, *Robert Oliver, Merchant of Baltimore, 1783–1819* (Baltimore, Johns Hopkins Press, 1956).

2. *American State Papers on Finance,* III, 229; *Annals of Congress,* 13 Congress, 3 Session, III, 656–57; Bogart, 189; Bolles, I, 254; David M. Cole, *The Development of Banking in the District of Columbia* (New York, The William-Frederick Press, 1959).

3. *The Adams–Jefferson Letters,* II, 424 (Chapel Hill, University of North Carolina Press, 1959).

4. Gallatin, *Considerations,* p. 43; Hammond, pp. 162, 227; Carey, p. 19; Rothbard, p. 58; Walter B. Smith, p. 232; Report of the Secretary of the Treasury, Dec. 3, 1816, *American State Papers on Finance,* III, 129 ff.

5. Hammond, Chs. 9 and 10; Dewey gives the charter in full; Secretary Crawford's "Report on the Bank of the United States and Other Banks, and the Currency," in *American State Papers on Finance,* III, 338, 494–508; Raymond Walters, Jr., "The Origins of the Second Bank of the United States," *Journal of Political Economy,* 53 (1945), 115.

6. McMaster, II, 314–15.

7. Report of the Committee Appointed To Examine the Books of the Bank, Jan. 16, 1819, 15 Congress 2 Session, H. R. 547, in *American State Papers on Finance,* III, 306–391; *ibid.,* IV, 495–1077, Correspondence Relative to the Public Deposits.

8. Catterall, 64 ff.; Hammond, 258–66.

9. Gouge, II, 110. Examination of the President, Cashier, and Directors of the United States Bank, with the Report of the Committee appointed on the 30th November, 1818, to inspect the books and examine into the proceedings of the Bank; 15 Congress, 2 Session, House Document 92, V.

10. Raguet, Appendix to *Currency and Banking*.

11. Chevalier, I, 96, 226.

12. Hammond, p. 310. For these and other points see Richard H. Timberlake, Jr., "The Specie Standard and Central Banking in the United States before 1860," *Journal of Economic History*, XXI No. 3 (1961).

13. Report of the committee . . . to inspect the books, and examine into the proceedings of the Bank of the United States, April 30, 1832, 22 Congress, 1 Session, House Report 460, 434–37. The quotation from the Biddle papers is in Hammond, p. 307 and Myers, p. 51.

14. Hammond, p. 411. Gallatin, III, 333–45.

15. 21 Congress, 1 Session, December 1829, Appendix 10, p. 18.

16. Niles' *Register*, May 12, 1833, p. 198. The majority and two minority reports from the committee and the veto message of the President are in the Appendix of Gales and Seaton's *Register of Debates in Congress*, Part III, Vol. VIII, 33 ff.

17. Catterall, pp. 303–304. Govan, p. 245.

18. Benton, I, 371; Harry N. Scheiber, "The Pet Banks in Jacksonian Politics and Finance, 1833–1841," *Journal of Economic History*, XXIII, No. 2 (1963). Govan, 282.

19. Bourne, 122–23, includes a tabular summary of the use made of the surplus in each state.

20. Total sales of public lands rose to nearly 15 million dollars in 1835, and to 25 million in 1836, more than the customs receipts of that year.

The *New York Journal of Commerce* reported on June 24, 1837, that the Lexington and Ohio Railroad Company had had to suspend its construction because Kentucky could not pay up the subscription it had made on the basis of the expected federal surplus distribution.

Arthur Cole, "Variations in the Sale of Public Lands, 1816–1860," *Review of Economic Statistics* 44 (1927); Hammond, 457 ff.; Myers, pp. 66–69.

21. This letter is in the Manuscript Division of the New York Public Library, in the Phelps Dodge Papers.

22. McCulloch, 57.

23. Jeffrey G. Williamson, *American Growth and the Balance of Payments, 1820–1913*. (Chapel Hill, University of North Carolina Press, 1964). Peter Temin, *The Jacksonian Economy* (New York, W. W. Norton and Company, 1969), stresses the increased volume of silver imports as a factor in the inflation.

5. Public and Private Enterprise Before the Civil War

1. Ripley, p. 21; Davis, II, 178, 197; Shaw Livermore, "Unlimited Liability in Early American Corporations," *Journal of Political Economy,* 43 (1935); W. C. Kessler, "A Statistical Study of the New York General Incorporation Act of 1811," *Journal of Political Economy* 48 (1940); Simeon E. Baldwin, "American Business Corporations before 1789," *American Historical Association,* 1902, Part I, p. 271. The anonymous pamphlet on corporations is in the Seligman Collection at the Columbia University Library. Evans p. 11, Table 5.

2. Commons, I, 88–91; *American State Papers on Finance,* II, 425, April 17, 1810.

3. Gilbert Livingston Papers, Taylor–Cooper Letters, New York Public Library Manuscript Division; Third Annual Report of the President and Directors of the Chesapeake and Delaware Canal, 1806 (Seligman Collection); *Niles' Weekly Register,* Jan. 8, 1814, 306; Jan. 18, 1817, 341 ff.; Meyer, 219.

4. Congressional Register, 19 Congress 1 Session, Appendix p. 6. Jefferson's recommendation was in his Sixth Annual Message, Dec. 2, 1806. Monroe reiterated this in his First Message.

5. Goodrich, pp. 35, 40; Annals of Congress, 11 Congress, 1 Session, 1390 ff., February 8, 1810; Maryland General Assembly Documents, 1843, R, February 17, 1844; Ohio, 46th General Assembly, Document No. 6; Annual Reports of the Secretary of the Treasury, 1826, 37–39; 1828, 10; 1829, 3; 1831, 7; *Niles' Weekly Register,* 22 (May 18, 1822), 179; 23 (Sept. 14, 1822), 27; *Maryland Senate Journal,* 7:4 (Jan. 8, 1810); 242 (Dec. 7, 1812); Public Documents relating to the New York Canals (New York, A. Mercein, 1821); New York State Assembly Documents, Session 1906, No. 129, V, 1030; Samuel Breck, *Sketch of Internal Improvements of Pennsylvania* (1818); Bishop, Ch. IV and Appendix VI; Ohio, 35th General Assembly, 1836/7, Document No. 72; 36th Assembly, No. 27. The Bayard Correspondence in the Manuscript Division of the New York Public Library contains many letters regarding the financing of Ohio canal stocks from 1825 on.

6. Davis, II, Ch. IV; Goodrich, p. 21; Miller, *passim.*

7. Lane, *Laws of New Jersey,* 39 Session, 2 sit., p. 68; Maryland, General Assembly Documents 1836, *Memorial of the Baltimore and Ohio Railroad Company, Praying a Further Subscription on the Part of the State,* February 10, 1836; *Report of the Majority of the Senate Committee on Internal Improvements,* 1839; Annual Message from the Governor to the Legislature, 1839; William P. Smith, pp. 19, 23; Phillips, pp. 173, 189, 226 ff.; *New York Journal of Commerce,* Jan. 3, Feb. 19, 1838; April 17, July 4, 12, 15, Aug. 5, Sept. 2, 3, 1839, April 29, May 14, Nov. 16, 1840; March 10, 1841.

The Seligman Collection at Columbia University contains the published proceedings of many of these railroad conventions and early annual reports of directors of railroads. Anon., *Brief Statement of Facts in Relation to the Western Rail-road,* Feb. 6, 1841 (Seligman Collection); Anon., *The Rail-road Jubilee, An account of the Celebration Commemorative of the Opening of Railroad Communication between Boston and Canada, Sept. 17–18, 1851* (Boston, J. H. Eastburn, 1851) (Seligman Collection); *American Railroad Journal,* July 7, 1832; *New York Times,* July 2, 1966.

8. Livermore, p. 43; Alfred D. Chandler, Jr., "Patterns of American Railroad Finance 1830–1850," *Business History Review, 28–29* (1954–55), 248–63; Hidy, Ch. III; G. S. Callender, "State Enterprise and Corporations," *Quarterly Journal of Economics,* 17 (1902–03), 111–62; Ohio, 38 General Assembly, Report of the Canal Fund Commissioners, Feb. 3, 1840, p. 144; Maryland, General Assembly Documents, 1839 Senate, Annual Message from the Governor to the Legislature, December 1839; New York Public Library Manuscript Division, Bayard Correspondence, *passim;* Henrietta M. Larson, "The Beginning of an American Private Bank," *Journal of Economic and Business History,* IV (May 1932); *Hunt's Merchants Magazine,* I (July 1839); VIII (Jan. 1843); New York *Daily Tribune,* May 7, 1850; McGrane, *passim.* Annual estimates of foreign investment in the United States are given by Douglass North in *Trends in the American Economy in the Nineteenth Century* (New York, National Bureau of Economic Research, 1960).

9. The securities markets of this period are discussed by Armstrong, Clews, Hemming and Martin.

10. Hammond, pp. 68, 193, 625. "Finance and Capital in the United States, 1850–1900," *Journal of Economic History* (Dec. 1967), 621.

11. Annual Reports of the Secretary of the Treasury; Annual Reports of the New York State Superintendent of Banking; *Bankers Magazine, passim;* Brown; Gibbons.

12. Brown, p. 218.

13. Van Vleck; *Report on Currency,* New York Board of Currency, May 16, 1859 (New York, privately printed).

6.   Federal, State, and Local Finance Before the Civil War

1. Congressional Globe, 25 Congress, 1 Session, III, 11–29; Benton, II, 27, 33, 318, 347, 406; Hammond, pp. 497 ff.

2. Myers, Ch. IX; Knox, p. 62; Report of the Secretary of the Treasury, 1846, 6, 7; 1854, Appendix 30, p. 255.

3. Gallatin, *Writings,* III, 304; Hepburn, pp. 54 ff.; Director of the Mint, Report for 1886, 279–82; Myers, Ch. IV; Laughlin, Ch. V; 32 Congress 2 Session, Congressional Globe Appendix, pp. 190 ff., gives the speech of

Congressman Dunham of Indiana on the coinage bill; Report of the Secretary of the Treasury, 1847, 133; 1852, 11; 1898, 300, gives details of coinage from 1793.

4. Taussig, *Tariff History,* 109 ff.; *Niles' Register,* XXXVI, 113; XXXVII, 81.

5. Sumner, p. 166; Justin H. Smith, pp. 255 ff.; Bolles, II, 577–99; New York *Daily Tribune,* Oct. 18, 1845; April 8, 13, 17, 26, 29, August 7, 1847; November 25, 1848; October 17, 1849; Benton, II, 406, 413, 726; Larson, p. 69.

6. Bolles, II, 596; Myers, p. 188; Comptroller of the Currency, Annual Report for 1896, I, 544.

7. Adams, pp. 326 ff.; Tenth Census, 1880, VII, 526.

8. Letter of Frank Thomas, President of Chesapeake and Ohio Railroad, to Wm. A. Spencer, Chairman House Ways and Means Committee, Feb. 12, 1840 (in Seligman Library); New York *Herald,* April 2, 1843; *Hunts Merchants Magazine,* 14, 177; 21, 157.

9. McGrane, pp. 28, 62, 82; *New York Journal of Commerce,* August 21, 1839. "Debts of the States," *North American Review,* 1844.

10. Scott, pp. 230 ff.

11. 27 Congress, 1 Session, Congressional Globe, X, 7, 1841; 27 Congress, 3 Session, H. R. 296, March 2, 1843; Benton, II, 240–43.

12. George Rogers Taylor "American Urban Growth Preceding the Railway Age," *Journal of Economic History,* XXVII (Sept. 1967), 3.

7. *Financial Aspects of the Civil War*

1. Report of the Secretary of the Treasury, July 4, 1861, p. 14.

2. The text of this law may be found in Huntington and Mawhinney, pp. 64–65.

3. Letter from Secretary Chase to House Committee on Ways and Means, quoted by Spaulding.

4. Spaulding, p. 181.

5. Spaulding, p. 27.

6. Spaulding, p. 188; Sherman, *Speeches,* p. 245.

7. Third Report of Special Commissioner of the Revenue, 1868, p. 21.

8. Annual Report of the Secretary of the Treasury, 1863, p. 10.

9. Spaulding, pp. 189–90.

10. Sherman, *Recollections,* p. 220.

11. London *Economist,* 20 (February 22, 1862), 197.

12. Laugel, p. 114.

13. For the effect of the war on economic growth, see Andreano, Engerman and Gallman.

8.   From the Civil War to Resumption

1. The failure of the banking house of Overend-Gurney and Co. was the most dramatic incident of the panic of May 1866 in London and the one which gave it its name. Rumors of war in Europe, excessive speculation in cotton, and a drop in its price from 20 d. to 12.5 d. in the course of a few weeks were background for suspension of the Bank Act by the Bank of England, a sharp rise in its discount rate, and the failure of a number of financial houses.

2. Report of the Secretary of the Treasury, 1866, p. 9.

3. Report of the Secretary of the Treasury, 1869, p. 3.

4. Huntington and Mawhinney, p. 201.

5. 41 Congress, 2 Session, House Report 31. Adams, pp. 100–135.

6. Strong, *Diary,* IV, 287.

7. Annual Report of the Comptroller of the Currency, 1868, xxiv.

8. Adams, p. 5.

9. 42 Congress, 3 Session, House Committee Report 77, February 18, 1873, 106 ff. Robert W. Fogel, *The Union Pacific Railroad* (Baltimore, Johns Hopkins University Press, 1960), points out that the promoters took heavy risks, and that the social return was large.

10. Manuscript letter to his wife, September 23, 1873, on stationery of London office of Jay Cooke, McCulloch and Company, now in manuscript division of library of University of Indiana.

11. Report of New York Clearing House Loan Committee, November 11, 1873, in Sprague, *Crises under the National Banking System,* pp. 91–103.

12. Sherman, *Recollections,* pp. 565, 702.

9.   The Struggle over the Standard

1. Good summaries of this troubled period are in Commons, Nevins, Josephson, Lauck, and Unger. North, Ch. 11, summarizes the farm situation.

2. Report of the Comptroller of the Currency, 1890, p. 381; 1894, p. 379.

3. New York *Nation,* 25 (Nov. 22, 1877), 314; Lawrence E. Godkin was then editor.

4. Congressional Record, 1876, 44 Congress, 1 Session, 4553, 4567.

5. 44 Congress, 2 Session, Senate Report 703, March 2, 1877.

6. The report of Comptroller Knox on reorganization of the Mint and change in the currency is in 41 Congress, 2 Session, Senate Misc. Document 132, April 25, 1870.

7. The debates in the House are recorded in the Congressional Globe, 42 Congress, 2 Session, especially pp. 322 (Chairman Kelley) and 2305 ff. (Mr. Hooper).

8. The best discussion of the trade dollar is in John M. Willem Jr., *The United States Trade Dollar,* (New York 1959), privately printed. The report

of Mr. Linderman, first Director of the Mint under the 1873 law, is in *Bankers' Magazine,* March 1873, 710–16. "History of the Trade Dollar," *American Economic Review,* Porter Garnett, VII (1917), 91 ff.

9. Sherman, *Recollections,* 391 ff., 823 ff.

10. Report of the Director of the Mint (included as part of the Report of the Secretary of the Treasury), December 1, 1873.

11. The reports of the international monetary conferences are in: 1867 and 1878, 45 Congress, 3 Session, Senate Executive Document 58; 1881, 49 Congress, 1 Session, House Miscellaneous Document 396; 1892, 52 Congress, 2 Session, Senate Executive Documents 34, 82; 1893, Annual Report of the Director of the Mint, gives a summary of all these conferences.

12. *New York Times,* November 28, December 3, 1889; July 14, 1890.

13. The discussion on Representative Dockery's effort to get an investigation in the House is in 51 Congress, 2 Session, 1196 ff. (January 12, 1891) and the testimony before the House Committee on Rules, December 13, 1890, on pp. 1202 ff. The St. Louis *Globe-Democrat* had charged on September 20, 1890 that a million-dollar profit had been made by 12 Senators and 15 Representatives. The *New York Times* discussed the charges at intervals: December 2, 1890; January 2, 13, 18, 23, 24, 25, and February 4, 1891. The statement of Representative Conger is in 51 Congress, 1 Session, 6450 (June 24, 1890).

14. 46 Congress, 2 Session, House Executive Document 9, 467, 480, November 15, 1878.

15. Report of the Secretary of the Treasury, 1889, LXI. By an Act of August 4, 1886, Congress authorized the issue of silver certificates in denominations of 1, 2, and 5 dollars in place of the larger denominations, in order to increase the demand; the small denominations of greenbacks were at the same time replaced by larger sizes.

10. Trusts and Tariffs before 1900

1. Navin and Sears; Nelson, p. 3.

2. Thorelli, pp. 59, 154.

3. See, for example, the remarks of Senator Beck in 49 Congress, 2 Session, pp. 480 ff. The two committee reports are to be found in: Report of the Select Committee on Transportation Routes to the Seaboard, Senator William A. Windom, Chairman, 2 vols., 43 Congress, 1 Session, S. R. 307, April 24, 1874; and Report of the Select Committee on Transportation, Senator Shelby M. Cullom, Chairman, 49 Congress, 1 Session, S. R. 46, 1886.

4. Report of the Committee on Finance, Senator Aldrich, Chairman; October 4, 1888, 50 Congress, 1 Session, S. R. 2332. Senate Bribery Investigation, 53 Congress, 2 Session, S. R. 606, August 16, 1894.

5. *The Nation,* Aug. 16, 23; Sept. 6, 1888.

6. Carl Schurz, *Speeches, Correspondence and Political Papers* (New

York, G. P. Putnam's Sons, 1913), V, 62.

7. Report of the Tariff Commission, 47 Congress, 2 Session, House Misc. Doc. 46.

8. Taussig, p. 249.

9. *Harper's Weekly,* July 5, 1890. *New York Times,* January 17, 1896, p. 4.

10. *New York Times,* January 22, 1897, p. 1.

11. Financial Reform before World War I

1. Report of the Secretary of the Treasury, 1906, p. 40.

2. Sprague, p. 319. Jeffrey G. Williamson. *American Growth and the Balance of Payments* (Chapel Hill, University of North Carolina Press, 1964).

3. James G. Smith, *passim.*

4. Testimony taken before the Joint Committee of the Senate and Assembly of the State of New York to Investigate and Examine into the Business and Affairs of Life Insurance Companies doing business in the State of New York (7 vols., Albany, J. B. Lyon Company, 1906).

5. State of New York. Public Papers of Governor Hughes, 1909 (Albany, J. B. Lyon Company, 1910), pp. 288–330.

6. The report of the Pujo Committee is in 62 Congress, 3 Session, House Report 1593, February 28, 1913.

7. The text of the Aldrich plan may be found in 61 Congress, 3 Session, Senate Document 4, January 16, 1911.

8. First-hand accounts of the drafting and passage of the Federal Reserve Act (not always in agreement with each other) are to be found in Glass, Warburg, and Willis.

9. New York *Times,* October 5, 16, 1913

12. World War I and Its Aftermath

1. First Annual Report of the Federal Reserve Board, January, 1915, p. 3.

2. Second Annual Report of the Federal Reserve Board for the year 1915, p. 5.

3. 65 Congress, 1 Session, 103, April 2, 1917, and 65 Congress, 2 Session, 7137, May 27, 1918.

4. Hines, chs. I-IV.

5. Frank Taussig, "Price Fixing as Seen by a Price-fixer," *Quarterly Journal of Economics,* 19 (Feb. 1919), pp. 239 ff.

6. Two useful summaries of price changes during the war, in addition to those in *Historical Statistics of the United States* and the publications of the Bureau of Labor Statistics, are to be found in Hardy, *Wartime Control*

of *Prices,* and Litman, *Prices and Price Controls in Great Britain and the United States during the World War.*

7. 66 Congress, 1 Session, Senate Resolution 142, July 1919, Congressional Record, 3394, 3484–92, 3553. Report of the Secretary of the Treasury 1919, p. 17.

8. Harvey E. Fisk, *The Inter-Ally Debts,* computed the cost of the war for each of the countries as of 1924. Changes in the cost due to modification of reparations and debt settlements after that date of course not included.

The other estimate was made in 1919 by the Secretary of the Treasury in his annual report, pp. 25 ff. An earlier estimate by Ernest L. Bogart for the Carnegie Endowment for International Peace, *Direct and Indirect Costs of the Great War* (New York, Oxford University Press, 1919), set the total gross cost to all belligerents at 208 billion without taking into account the factor of inflation.

13. The New Era: Boom and Crash

1. Myers, *League Loans.*
2. Brown, pp. 404 ff.
3. *Stock Exchange Practices,* p. 125; *Sale of Foreign Bonds,* Pt. 3, 1579.
4. Lewis, p. 605; Berle and Means, pp. 76, 160, 194.
5. *Stock Exchange Practices,* p. 7.
6. *Stock Exchange Practices,* p. 339.
7. *Fortune,* March 1933.
8. *Stock Exchange Practices,* p. 13.
9. Annual Report of the Federal Reserve Board, 1923, p. 16.
10. "Big Ten" was the name applied to a prominent group of speculators. See Robert T. Patterson, *The Great Boom and Panic 1921–1929* (Chicago, Henry Regnery and Company, 1965), p. 33.
11. For a contrary opinion see Friedman and Schwartz, Ch. 7.
12. Edna Ferber, *Giant* (New York, Doubleday, 1952); *New Republic* (March 10, 1926).
13. Bird, especially Ch. 2.
14. *Fortune* (May, June, 1933; Nov., Dec., 1934).

14. Financing the New Deal

1. *Literary Digest,* CXV (March 11, 1933), 5.
2. Hull, *Memoirs,* pp. 246 ff.; *New York Times,* July 1, 4, 1933.
3. Blum, p. 165.

15. World War II

1. Paul, p. 395.
2. Annual Report of the Federal Reserve Board, 1939, p. 6.

16. The Twenty Years After World War II

1. Secretary of the Treasury, Annual Report for 1947, p. 55.

2. United States Department of Commerce, Bureau of the Census, *Governmental Finances 1965–1966.* C. 3. 191/2 G.F. No. 3.

3. Organization for Economic Cooperation and Development, 1965 Review.

4. The principal advocacy for stabilizing the rate of increase of money, as a preventive of deflation, is to be found in Milton Friedman and Anna J. Schwarz, *A Monetary History of the United States 1867–1960* (Princeton University Press, 1963).

5. *New York Times* January 24–March 18, 1965, *passim.* Report of the Federal Deposit Insurance Corporation for 1965, p. 10.

6. Federal Reserve Bank of New York *Monthly Review,* February 1966, p. 31.

7. *Federal Reserve Bulletin,* August 1964, pp. 944 ff. Parker B. Willis, *The Federal Funds Market* (Federal Reserve Bank of Boston, 1957).

8. Institute of Life Insurance, *Life Insurance Fact Book 1967.* United States Savings and Loan League, *Savings and Loan Fact Book 1967.*

9. 88 Congress, 2 Session, Subcommittee on Domestic Finance of the Committee on Banking and Currency of the House of Representatives, *A Study of Federal Credit Programs,* 2 vols. (Government Printing Office, 1964).

10. Daniel Holland, *Private Pension Funds* (New York, National Bureau of Economic Research, 1966). 84 Congress 1 Session, Senate Committee on Banking and Currency, *Hearings . . . on Factors Affecting the Buying and Selling of Equity Securities,* March 3–23, 1955.

11. One of the best studies of concentration in industry can be found in the Hearings before the Subcommittee on antitrust and monopoly of the Committee on the Judiciary of the United States Senate, 88 Congress, 2 Session, in 7 volumes beginning with July 1964 on *Overall and Conglomerate Aspects. Report on Mergers* by Federal Trade Commission, May 15, 1968. William N. Leonard, *Towards a New Policy on Mergers* (1968 Proceedings of the New York State Economic Association), *New York Times* July 10, September 1, 1968; February 16, 1969.

12. Roy L. Reierson, *The Euro-Dollar Market* (New York, Bankers Trust Company, 1964). The Annual Reports of the Bank for International Settlements contain the most complete summaries of the Eurocurrency markets.

BIBLIOGRAPHY

1. The Colonial Period

The most interesting materials for this period are the contemporary accounts, beginning of course with William Bradford's *History of Plymouth Plantation 1620–1647* (Boston, published for the Massachusetts Historical Society, Houghton Mifflin, 1912). The Rev. Andrew Burnaby, in *Travels through the Middle Settlements in North-America in the Years 1759 and 1760* (London, T. Payne, 1775; reprinted for Great Seal Books, Ithaca, N.Y., 1960), and Madame Knight, *The Private Journal Kept by Madame Knight on a Journey from Boston to New York in the Year 1704* (New York, Wilder and Campbell, 1825), give many useful glimpses into the economic life of the country. John Hull's *Diaries* (from the original manuscript in the collection of the American Antiquarian Society, Boston, J. Wilson and sons, 1857) and Benjamn Franklin's *Papers* (New Haven, Yale University Press, 1959), Vol. I, discuss the coinage and paper money problems.

Colonial Currency Reprints, ed. by Andrew McFarland Davis (4 vols., Boston, Prince Society, 1911, reprinted 1964 by A. M. Kelley, New York), includes a wide range of articles covering all points of view. One of the more important of these is "A Discourse Concerning the Currencies of the British Plantations in America," by William Douglass, M.D.; he was also the author of *A Summary, Historical and Political, of the First Planting, Progressive Improvements, and Present State of the British Settlements in North-America,* (2 vols., London, R. and J. Dodsley, 1760).

Official documents include the *Documents Relating to the Colonial History of New York* and the *Colonial Laws of New York; Statutes at Large, Being a Collection of All the Laws of Virginia,* ed. by William W. Hening (Richmond, Samuel Pleasants, Jr., 1809); *Massachusetts Acts and Resolves* and *Records of the Colony of Massachusetts Bay.*

Useful statistics for the period are given by David Macpherson, *Annals of Commerce, Manufactures, Fisheries and Navigation* (London, Nichols and Son, 1805), and by Pelatiah Webster, *Political Essays* (Philadelphia, Joseph Crukshank, 1791).

Historical Statistics of the United States (Washington, D.C., Government Printing Office, 1960) contains tables of the bills of credit and Treasury notes issued by the American colonies, 1703–1775.

2. *Revolution and Confederation*

The official sources for this period are the *Journals of the Continental Congress* (34 vols., Washington, D.C., Government Printing Office, 1904–1937); the *Secret Journals of the Acts and Proceedings of the Congress of the Confederation* (4 vols., Boston, Thomas B. Wait, 1821); the *American State Papers on Finance* (5 vols., Washington, D.C., Gales and Seaton, 1832), *Diplomatic Correspondence of the American Revolution* (7 vols., Washington, D.C., F. P. Blair, 1833–34).

Edmund C. Burnett edited the *Letters of Members of the Continental Congress* (8 vols., Washington, D.C., The Carnegie Institution, 1921–36).

Jonathan Elliott, *The Funding System of the United States and Great Britain,* was published in 1845 as House Document 15, 28 Congress, 1 Session, with details of federal finance to that time.

Official papers of the states include *New York State Laws* and *Rhode Island Colonial Records.*

The published works of leaders during the Revolution which contain financial details include *The Works of John Adams,* ed. by C. F. Adams (10 vols., Boston, 1850–1856); *The Complete Works of Benjamin Franklin,* John Bigelow ed. (New York and London, The Knickerbocker Press, 1887–88); Albert Gallatin, *Writings,* 3 vols., ed. by Henry Adams (Philadelphia, J. B. Lippincott and Company, 1879); *The Papers of Alexander Hamilton,* ed. by H. C. Syrett and J. E. Cooke (New York, Columbia University Press, Vols. I–XV, 1961–68, more in preparation); *Writings of Thomas Jefferson,* 9 vols., ed. by Paul Leicester Ford (New York, G. P. Putnam's Sons, 1892–99); Thomas Paine, *Writings* (New York, G. P. Putnam's Sons, 1893); George Washington, *Writings,* 39 vols., ed. by John C. Fitzpatrick (Bicentennial Edition, Washington, D.C., Government Printing Office, 1931–44).

For general historical background, one of the best sources is John Bach McMaster, *History of the United States from the Revolution to the Civil War* (8 vols., New York, D. Appleton and Co., 1894–1913). More specialized histories are A. Barton Hepburn, *A History of Currency in the United States* (New York, The Macmillan Co., 1915), and Albert Bolles, *Financial History of the United States* (3 vols., New York, D. Appleton and Company, 1892), are useful, although Bolles must be used with caution, as his statistics are not always correct.

Contemporary records include Marquis Francois Jeane de Chastellux' *Travels in North America in the Years 1780, 1781 and 1782* (London, G. G. J. and J. Robinson, 1787) and Timothy Pitkin's *Political and Civil History of the United States* (2 vols., New Haven, 1828) as well as his *A Statistical View of the United States of America* (New York, James Eastburn and Co., 1817).

A facsimile of George Washington's *Account Book with the United States*

1775–1783 was published by The American Publishing Company, Hartford, Connecticut in 1857.

The final text of the Articles of Confederation is to be found in the *Journals of the Continental Congress,* IX (Nov. 15, 1777), pp. 907 ff.

A useful statistical study is that of Arthur H. Cole and Walter B. Smith, *Fluctuations in American Business, 1790–1860* (Cambridge, Mass., Harvard University Press, 1935).

3. A New Constitution and a New Era in Finance, 1789–1811

The *Annals of Congress* and the *American State Papers on Finance* continue to be basic sources for this period. The annual reports of the Secretary of the Treasury for the years before 1825 are in the latter.

Contemporary accounts with financial details are those of Tench Coxe, *A View of the United States of America* (Philadelphia, W. Hall, 1794); Adam Seybert, *Statistical Annals* (Philadelphia, Thomas Dobson and Son, 1818); and Noah Webster, *Sketch of the History and Present State of Banks and Insurance Companies in the United States,* in his *Miscellaneous Papers* (New York, E. Belden and Company, 1802), Vol. IV.

James Hamilton, son of Alexander, published his *Reminiscences* (New York, Charles Scribner and Company) in 1869.

Useful historical accounts of this period include Bray Hammond, *Banks and Politics in America* (Princeton, N.J., Princeton University Press, 1960); E. James Ferguson, *Power of the Purse* (Chapel Hill, University of North Carolina Press, 1961); John C. Miller, *The Federalist Era* (New York, Harper and Row, 1960);Henry W. Domett, *History of the Bank of New York, 1784–1884* (New York, G. P. Putnam's Sons, 1884); Lawrence Lewis, *Bank of North America* (Philadelphia, J. B. Lippincott and Company, 1882); and Margaret G. Myers, *History of the New York Money Market to 1913* (New York, Columbia University Press, 1931).

4. The War of 1812 and the Second Bank of the United States

In addition to the official sources mentioned in previous chapters, the annual Reports of the Secretary of the Treasury are available in separate bindings after 1825. Probably no period of nineteenth century American history has been so well covered by books and pamphlets.

Contemporary writings of this period include: Thomas Hart Benton, *Thirty Years View* (2 vols., New York, 1861–62), one of the most consistent supporters of "hard money"; Mathew Carey, *Essays on Banking* (Philadelphia, 1816, published by the author), advocate of the "American" high tariff policy; John Cleaveland, *The Banking System of New York* (New York, John S. Voorhies, 1857); William Gouge, *Short History of Paper Money and Banking in the United States* (New York, B. and S. Collins, 2nd ed., 1835) a rabid attack on banks, in support of Jackson's policies; and Hugh McCulloch, *Men and Measures of Half a Century* (New York, C. Scribner's Sons, 1888), a thoughtful review of the period.

Albert Gallatin, *Considerations on the Currency and Banking System of the United States* is included in his *Writings* Vol. III.

Michel Chevalier, *Lettres sur l'Amérique du Nord* (2 vols., Paris, 1838) and Condy Raguet, *A Treatise on Currency and Banking* (Philadelphia, Grigg and Elliott, 2nd ed., 1840), were also useful.

Historical studies which have been useful are: Robert G. Albion, *Square Riggers on Schedule* (Princeton, N.J., Princeton University Press, 1938); Ernest L. Bogart, *Financial History of Ohio* (Urbana-Champaign, Ill., The University, 1912); Albert Bolles, *Financial History of the United States* (New York, D. Appleton and Company, 1892), Vol. I; Edward Bourne, *The History of the Surplus Revenue of 1837* (New York, G. P. Putnam's Sons, 1885); Ralph C. H. Catterall, *The Second Bank of the United States* (Chicago, University of Chicago Press, 1903); Davis R. Dewey, *The Second United States Bank* (National Monetary Commission, Washington, D.C., Government Printing Office, 1910); Thomas Govan, in *Nicholas Biddle* (Chicago, University of Chicago Press, 1959), blames Jackson himself rather than the cautious Van Buren; Bray Hammond, *Banks and Politics in America* (Princeton, N.J., Princeton University Press, 1957); Reginald C. McGrane, *The Panic of 1837* (Chicago, Chicago University Press, 1924); John Bach McMaster, *The Life and Times of Stephen Girard* (2 vols., Philadelphia, J. B. Lippincott Company, 1918); Fritz Redlich, *The Molding of American Banking* (New York, Hafner Publishing Company, 2 vols., 1951); Roy M. Robbins, *Our Landed Heritage* (Princeton, N.J., Princeton University Press, 1942); Murray N. Rothbard, *The Panic of 1819* (New York, Columbia University Press, 1962); Walter B. Smith, *Economic Aspects of the Second Bank of the United States* (Cambridge, Mass., Harvard University Press, 1953); Arthur M. Schlesinger, Jr., *The Age of Jackson* (Boston, Little, Brown and Company, 1945). Jean Alexander Wilburn, in *Biddle's Bank, the Crucial Years* (New York, Columbia University Press, 1967), describes the feud between Van Buren and the Clay-Calhoun-Webster coalition which was so disastrous for the Bank.

5.   *Public and Private Enterprise Before the Civil War*

Contemporary sources for this period, besides the Annals of Congress and the Reports of the Secretary of the Treasury, include the New York daily *Journal of Commerce* and *Tribune;* the weekly *Niles' Register* and the monthly *Hunt's Merchants Magazine;* the Bayard Correspondence and the

Taylor-Cooper Letters in the Gilbert Livingston Papers, in the Manuscript Division of the New York Public Library, and the following books:

William Armstrong, *Stocks and Stock-jobbing in Wall Street* (New York, New York Publishing Company, 1848).

Samuel Breck, *Sketch of Internal Improvements of Pennsylvania* (Philadelphia, J. Maxwell, 1818).

Mathew Carey, *Brief View of the Internal Improvements of Pennsylvania* (Philadelphia, 1831).

Henry Clews, *Fifty Years in Wall Street* (New York, Irving Publishing Company, 1908).

James S. Gibbons, *The Banks of New York* (New York, D. Appleton and Company, 1859).

John A. Poor, *The Railway* (Boston, Little, Brown and Company, 1867).

Joseph G. Martin and Clarence W. Barron, *The Boston Stock Exchange* (Boston, 1893).

Joseph G. Martin, *A Century of Finance.* (Boston, published by the author, 1898).

William P. Smith, *The Book of the Great Railway Celebrations of 1857* (New York, D. Appleton and Company, 1858).

Historical studies consulted include:

Avard L. Bishop, *State Works of Pennsylvania* (New Haven, Connecticut Academy of Arts and Sciences Transactions, 1907), Vol. XIII.

John Crosby Brown, *A Hundred Years of Merchant Banking* (New York, privately printed, 1909).

John R. Commons, *History of Labor in the United States* (New York, The Macmillan Company, 1918).

Joseph Stancliffe Davis, *Essays in the Earlier History of American Corporations* (Cambridge, Mass., Harvard University Press, 1917).

George Heberton Evans, *Business Incorporations in the United States* (New York, National Bureau of Economic Research, 1948).

Carter Goodrich, *Government Promotion of American Canals and Railroads 1800–1890* (New York, Columbia University Press, 1960).

Carter Goodrich, ed., *Canals and American Economic Development* (New York, Columbia University Press, 1961).

H. G. Hemming, *History of the New York Stock Exchange* (New York, H. Glover and Company, 1905).

Ralph Hidy, *The House of Baring in American Trade and Finance* (Cambridge, Mass., Harvard University Press, 1949).

Reginald C. McGrane, *Foreign Bondholders and American State Debts* (New York, The Macmillan Company, 1935).

B. H. Meyer, *History of Transportation in the United States before 1860* (Washington, D.C., Carnegie Institution, 1917).

Nathan Miller, *Enterprise of a Free People* (Ithaca, N.Y., Cornell University

Press, 1962), gives a detailed survey of the building of the New York canals and their stimulus to the economy of the area.

Ulrich B. Phillips, *History of Transportation in the Eastern Cotton Belt to 1860* (New York, 1908).

William Z. Ripley, *Main Street and Wall Street* (Boston, Little, Brown and Company, 1927).

George W. Van Vleck, *The Panic of 1857* (New York, Columbia University Press, 1943).

Nathaniel Wright Stevenson and Waldo Hilary Dunn, *George Washington* (New York, Oxford University Press, 1940).

6.   *Federal, State, and Local Finance Before the Civil War*

In addition to the official documents and the periodicals which have been cited in earlier chapters, there is invaluable material for this period in the Reports of the Special Commissioner of the Revenue, Mr. David A. Wells, for the years 1866 to 1869 inclusive.

The Report of the Comptroller of the Currency for 1896 gives figures for specie and bank note circulation from 1800 to 1859.

Specialized studies of this period include:

Henry C. Adams, *Public Debts* (New York, 1887).

Charles J. Bullock, *Essays in the Monetary History of the United States* (New York, The Macmillan Company, 1900).

Delos O. Kinsman, *The Income Tax in the Commonwealths of the United States* (New York, The Macmillan Company, 1903).

John Jay Knox, *United States Notes* (New York, 3rd ed., 1888).

Henrietta Larson, *Jay Cooke, Private Banker* (Cambridge, Harvard University Press, 1936).

J. Lawrence Laughlin, *History of Bimetallism in the United States* (New York, D. Appleton and Company, 4th ed., 1897).

Marce C. Rhodes, *History of Taxation in Mississippi* (Nashville, Tenn., George Peabody College, 1930).

John C. Schwab, *History of the New York General Property Tax* (Publications of the American Economic Association, V, 5, 1890).

William A. Scott, *Repudiation of State Debts* (New York, Crowell and Company, 1893).

Edwin E. Seligman, *Essays in Taxation* (New York, The Macmillan Company, 1925).

Justin H. Smith, *The War with Mexico* (New York, The Macmillan Company, 1919).

Don C. Sowers, *Financial History of New York State from 1789 to 1912* (New York, Columbia University Press, 1914).

William Graham Sumner, *History of American Currency* (New York, Henry Holt and Company, 1874).

Nollie O. Taff, *History of State Revenue and Expenditure in Kentucky* (Nashville, Tenn., George Peabody College, 1931).

Frank W. Taussig, *Tariff History of the United States* (New York, G. P. Putnam's Sons, 1888).

7. Financial Aspects of the Civil War

The most important primary sources for Civil War financing are the annual reports of the Secretary of the Treasury and, after 1863, those of the Comptroller of the Currency. The reports of David A. Wells, Special Commissioner of Revenue, were published as government documents annually from 1866 to 1869 inclusive. The Annual Report on the Banks in the United States for January 6, 1863 (37 Congress, 3 Session, H. Ex. Doc. 25) gives the report of the New York Clearing House Loan Committee. The report on the cost of the war is in 46 Congress, 2 Session, S. Ex. Doc. 206.

Contemporary discussions can be found in the *New York Times,* the London *Economist,* and the *Bankers' Magazine* (Baltimore and New York, monthly, 1846–). Elbridge Gerry Spaulding, in *History of the Legal Tender Paper Money* (Buffalo, Express Printing Company, 1860) defends his part in writing the legal tender bills, while Simon Newcomb, in *A Critical Examination of our Financial Policy during the Southern Rebellion* (New York, D. Appleton and Company, 1865), takes a critical attitude toward the greenbacks. Auguste Laugel, a young French engineer, describes the social and political condition of the country as he saw it during the war in *The United States during the Civil War* (Bloomington, Indiana University Press, 1961).

The standard work on this period is Wesley Clair Mitchell's *History of the Greenbacks* (Chicago, University of Chicago Press, 1903). Irwin Unger, *The Greenback Era* (Princeton, Princeton University Press, 1964), and Robert P. Sharkey, *Money, Class and Party: An Economic Study of Civil War and Reconstruction* (Johns Hopkins Studies in Historical and Political Science, Ser. LXXVII, No. 2, Baltimore, Johns Hopkins Press, 1959), discuss special aspects of the greenbacks. Frank W. Taussig, in *Tariff History of the United States* (London, G. P. Putnam's Sons, 1888), and Frederic C. Howe, *Taxation and Taxes in the United States under the Internal Revenue System* (Boston, Thomas Crowell and Company, 1896), were also useful.

Background material was found in John Bach McMaster's *History of the People of the United States during Lincoln's Administration* (New York, D. Appleton and Company, 1927), Emerson Fite, *Social and Industrial Conditions in the North during the Civil War* (New York, The Macmillan Company, 1910), and James Ford Rhodes, *History of the Civil War* (New York, The Macmillan Company, 1917).

Useful articles in the professional journals include Charles F. Dunbar, "The Direct Tax of 1861," *Quarterly Journal of Economics,* 3 (1888–89); Joseph A. Hill, "The Civil War Income Tax," *Quarterly Journal of Economics,*

8 (1893–94); Robert T. Patterson, "Government Finance on the Eve of the Civil War," *Journal of Economic History,* XII (1952); Eugene M. Lerner, "Money, Prices and Wages in the Confederacy," *Journal of Political Economy* 63 (1955); and "The Monetary and Fiscal Programs of the Confederate Government," *ibid.,* 62 (1954).

Biographies which throw light on this period are John Sherman, *Recollections of Forty Years* (New York, Werner Company, 1895), and *Selected Speeches and Reports on Finance and Taxation* (New York, D. Appleton and Company, 1879). Hugh McCulloch, in *Men and Measures of Half a Century* (New York, Charles Scribners' Sons, 1900), gives details of his own activities. Of the several biographies of Chase, *Salmon Portland Chase* by A. B. Hart (Boston, J. T. Morse, 1899) is well-rounded. *Inside Lincoln's Cabinet: The Civil War Diaries of Salmon P. Chase,* ed. by David Donald (New York, Longmans, Green and Company, 1954), shows clearly that Chase's real interests were political and military rather than financial. Henrietta M. Larson's *Jay Cooke, Private Banker* (Cambridge, Mass., Harvard University Press, 1936) sheds light on the character of Chase as well as of Cooke and is extremely useful for details of war financing. Jefferson Davis describes with admirable candor the difficulties of the Confederacy in his two volumes, *Rise and Fall of the Confederate Government* (New York, D. Appleton and Company, 1881).

The effect of the Civil War on economic growth has been discussed in Stanley L. Engerman, "The Economic Impact of the Civil War," *Explorations in Entrepreneurial History,* 2nd Ser., III (Spring 1966); Ralph Andreano, ed., *The Economic Impact of the Civil War* (Cambridge, Mass., Schenkman Publishing Company, 1962); David T. Gilchrist and W. David Lewis, eds., *Economic Change in the Civil War* (Greenville, Delaware, Eleutherian Mills, 1965); and Robert E. Gallman, "Commodity Output, 1839–1899," *Trends in the American Economy in the Nineteenth Century* (National Bureau of Economic Research, Princeton University Press, 1960).

8.   From the Civil War to Resumption

Primary sources and government documents: The annual Reports of the Secretary of the Treasury and the Comptroller of the Currency are basic materials for this period. Special reports are those of 41 Congress, 2 Session, H. R. 31, of March 1, 1870, on the gold panic of Black Friday, and 42 Congress, 3 Session, House Committee Report 77 of February 18, 1873, on the *Credit Mobilier* scandal.

Biographies and autobiographies: Bouck White, *The Book of Daniel Drew* is not the autobiography it purports to be, but is solidly based on the facts of Drew's career. Hugh McCulloch, in *Men and Measures of Half a Century* (New York, Charles Scribner's Sons, 1900), and John Sherman, *Recollections of Forty Years* (New York, The Werner Company, 1895), deal discreetly with financial events of their respective periods. George Templeton Strong, *Diary* (4 vols., New York, The Macmillan Company, 1902), describes events of these years as he saw them from his New York law office; he was a member of the Sanitary Commission during the Civil War. Papers of Hugh McCulloch are in the library of the University of Indiana.

Studies of special financial features of the resumption period: Don C. Barrett, *The Greenbacks and Resumption of Specie Payments* (Cambridge, Harvard University Press, 1931); John Jay Knox, *United States Notes* (New York, Charles Scribner's Sons, 1888); and Robert T. Patterson, *Federal Debt-management Policies, 1865–1879* (Durham, North Carolina, 1954). Edward Stanwood, *American Tariff Controversies* (Boston and New York, Houghton, Mifflin and Company, 1903), is useful but less objective than Frank Taussig, *Tariff History of the United States* (New York, G. P. Putnam's Sons, 1923). O. M. W. Sprague, *History of Crises under the National Banking System* (National Monetary Commission, Washington, D.C., Government Printing Office, 1910), includes the Report of the Clearing House Loan Committee of November 11, 1873. Charles F. and Henry Adams, *Chapters of Erie* (Boston, James R. Osgood and Company, 1871), describes both the Black Friday and the Erie railroad scandals. Robert P. Sharkey, *Money, Class and Party; An Economic Study of Civil War and Reconstruction* (Baltimore, The Johns Hopkins Press, 1959, *Johns Hopkins Studies in Historical and Political Science,* Vol. LXXVII, No. 2), gives a new interpretation to some of the events of the period.

9. *The Struggle over the Standard*

Official Documents

"Documentary History of the Coinage Act of 1873" was prepared by the Director of the Mint in 1896 and published as part of the Report of the Secretary of the Treasury for that year, pp. 461–573.

The report of the Silver Commission appointed August 15, 1876, is to be found in 44 Congress, 2 Session, S. R. 703, dated March 2, 1877.

Biographies and Autobiographies

Oliver Carlson and Ernest S. Bates, *Hearst, Lord of Saint Simeon* (New York, Viking Press, 1936), trace the relationship of the Hearst newspapers to the silver campaign.

Paxton Hibben, *The Peerles Leader, William Jennings Bryan* (New York, Farrar and Rinehart, 1929).

Allan Nevins, *Grover Cleveland, A Study in Courage* (New York, Dodd Mead and Company, 1932).

Alexander Dana Noyes, *Forty Years of American Finance* (New York and London, G. P. Putnam's Sons, 1909).

Carl Schurz, *Reminiscences* (New York, McClure Company, 1907).

Don Seitz, *Joseph Pulitzer, His Life and Letters* (New York, Simon and Schuster, 1924), describes Pultizer's opposition to the "Silver Kings" in 1896.

John Sherman, *Recollections of Forty Years* (New York and Chicago, Werner Company, 1895).

John Sherman, *Selected Speeches and Reports on Finance and Taxation* (New York, D. Appleton and Company, 1879).

Henry Villard, *Memoirs* (Boston and New York, Houghton, Mifflin and Company, 1904).

Newspapers and Magazines

The New York *Nation* (weekly), purchased by Henry Villard in 1881, took a leading part in the campaign for "sound" money.

The *New York Times* continues in this period, as earlier, to be a prime source, in part because of its excellent index.

The Commercial and Financial Chronicle, weekly, New York, 1863–, gives the most complete coverage of financial news.

Public Opinion, Washington, D.C., 1886–1906.

Harpers' Weekly (New York, Harper and Brothers, 1857–).

Books and Periodical Articles

John R. Commons and associates, *History of Labor in the United States* (New York, The Macmillan Company, 1921), Vol. II.

Lance Davis, "The Investment Market 1870–1914," *Journal of Economic History,* XXV (1965), 3.

Willard Fisher, "Coin and His Critics," *Quarterly Journal of Economics,* X (1896), 187, summarizes the replies.

William H. Harvey, *Coin's Financial School* (Chicago, Coin Publishing Company, 1894. Reprinted with Introduction by Richard Hofstadter (Cambridge, Mass., Belknap Press of Harvard University Press, 1963).

Indianapolis Monetary Commission, *Report* (Chicago, University of Chicago Press, 1898).

Matthew Josephson, *The Politicos* (Harcourt Brace and Company, New York, 1938), includes an account of the Bryan campaigns which is colorful but not always precisely accurate.

W. Jett Lauck, *The Causes of the Panic of 1893* (Boston, Houghton, Mifflin and Company, 1907).

James Laurence Laughlin, *The History of Bimetallism in the United States* (4th edition. New York, D. Appleton and Company, 1897) is still a classic.

Jeanette Nichols, in "Silver Diplomacy," *Political Science Quarterly,* 48 (1933), 565, and in "Silver Repeal in the Senate," *American Historical Review,* 41 (October 1935), 26, fills in many details of the silver history.

Douglass C. North, *Growth and Welfare in the American Past* (Englewood Cliffs, N. J., Prentice-Hall, 1966).

Robert T. Patterson, *Federal Debt-management Policies 1865–1879* (Durharm, N. C., Duke University Press, 1954).

George E. Roberts, *Coin at School in Finance* (Chicago, W. B. Conkey Company, 1895).

Irwin Unger, *The Greenback Era* (Princeton, N. J., Princeton University Press, 1964), shows how complicated were the factors which brought about the demand for cheaper money.

10. Trusts and Tariffs Before 1900

Official Documents

First Annual Report of the Commissioner of Labor, Carroll D. Wright (Washington, D.C., Government Printing Office, March 1886).

Interstate Commerce Commission Activities, 1886–1937, Bureau of Statistics, Interstate Commerce Commission (Washington, D.C., Government Printing Office, 1937).

Report of the Tariff Commission, December 4, 1882, 47 Congress, 2 Session, House Misc. Doc. 46, 2 vols.

Customs tariffs, Senate and House Reports, 1888, 1890, 1894, 1897, 60 Congress, 2 Session, Senate Doc. 547.

Tariff Acts passed by the Congress of the United States, 1789 to 1909, 61 Congress, 2 Session, House Doc. 671, 1909.

Books

William Jennings Bryan, *The First Battle* (Chicago, W. B. Conkey Company, 1897).

Alfred D. Chandler, *Strategy and Structure* (Cambridge, Mass., M.I.T. Press, 1962).

Gabriel Kolko, *Railroads and Regulation, 1877–1916* (Princeton, N. J., Princeton University Press, 1965), which points out that the railroads preferred federal regulation to that by the states.

John Moody, *The Truth about the Trusts* (New York, Moody Publishing Company, 1904).

Ralph L. Nelson, *Merger Movements in American Industry, 1895–1956* (Princeton, N. J., National Bureau of Economic Research, Princeton University Press, 1959).

William Z. Ripley, *Railroads: Rates and Regulations* (New York, Longmans Green and Company, 1912).

Edwin R. A. Seligman, *The Income Tax* (New York, The Macmillan Company, 1911).

Edward Stanwood, *American Tariff Controversies in the Nineteenth Century* (Boston, Houghton, Mifflin and Company, 1903).

Ida M. Tarbell, *The Tariff in Our Times* (New York, The Macmillan Company, 1911).

Frank W. Taussig, *Tariff History of the United States* (New York, G. P. Putnam's Sons, 8th ed., 1931).

Hans B. Thorelli, *The Federal Antitrust Policy* (Baltimore, The Johns Hopkins Press, 1955).

Charles R. Van Hise, *Concentration and Control* (New York, The Macmillan Company, 1912).

Trends in the American Economy in the Nineteenth Century (National Bureau of Economic Research, Studies in Income and Wealth, Vol. XXIV, Princeton, N.J., Princeton University Press, 1960).

Periodical Articles

Alfred D. Chandler, "The Beginning of Big Business in American Industry," *Business History Review,* XXXIII (Spring 1959).

Lance Davis, "The Capital Markets and Industrial Concentration," *Economic History Review,* Ser. 2, XIX (1966).

John Heberton Evans, Jr., "The Early History of Preferred Stock in the United States," *American Economic Review* (March 1929 and March 1931).

Thomas R. Navin and Marian V. Sears, "The Rise of a Market for Industrial Securities," *Business History Review,* XXIX (June 1955).

Jeremiah Jenks, "The Michigan Salt Association," *Political Science Quarterly* (1888).

11.   *Financial Reform Before World War I*

George E. Barnett, *State Banks and Trust Companies since the Passage of the National-Bank Act.* 61 Congress, 3 Session, Senate Doc. 659 (National Monetary Commission, Washington, D.C., Government Printing Office, 1911).

Roy G. Blakey and Gladys C. Blakey, *The Federal Income Tax* (New York, Longmans Green and Company, 1940).

Louis D. Brandeis, *Other People's Money and How the Bankers Use it* (New York, Frederick A. Stokes Company, 1914).

Solomon Fabricant, *The Trend of Government Activity in the United States since 1900* (New York, National Bureau of Economic Research, 1952).

Carter Glass, *An Adventure in Constructive Finance* (New York, Doubleday, Page and Company, 1927).

Mabel Newcomer, *Separation of State and Local Revenues* (New York, Columbia University Press, 1917).

Henry R. Seager and Charles A. Gulick, Jr., *Trust and Corporation Problems* (New York, Harper and Brothers, 1929).

James G. Smith, *The Development of Trust Companies in the United States* (New York, Henry Holt and Company, 1928).

O. M. W. Sprague, *History of Crises under the National Banking System*

(National Monetary Commission, Washington, D.C., Government Printing Office, 1910).

Paul M. Warburg, *The Federal Reserve System* (New York, The Macmillan Company, 1930).

H. Parker Willis, *The Federal Reserve System* (New York, The Ronald Press Co., 1923).

12. World War I and Its Aftermath

The principal sources for the events of this period are the annual reports of the Secretary of the Treasury, of the Comptroller of the Currency, and of the Federal Reserve Board. The monthly Federal Reserve Bulletin gives some additional details, as does *Banking and Monetary Statistics* published by the Federal Reserve Board in 1943. Political events are best followed in the *New York Times*.

Books which have been useful for specialized topics are:

Benjamin Haggott Beckhart, *The Discount Policy of the Federal Reserve System* (New York, Henry Holt and Company, 1924).

Roy G. and Gladys C. Blakey, *The Federal Income Tax* (New York, Longmans Green and Company, 1940).

William Adams Brown, Jr., *The New York Money Market: External and Internal Relations* (New York, Columbia University Press, 1932).

Harvey Fisk, *The Inter-Ally Debts* (New York, Bankers Trust Company, 1924).

Charles O. Hardy, *Wartime Control of Prices* (Washington, D.C., The Brookings Institution, 1940).

Walker D. Hines, *War History of American Railroads* (New Haven, Yale University Press, 1928).

Cleona Lewis, *America's Stake in International Investments* (Washington, D.C., The Brookings Institution, 1938).

Simon Litman, *Prices and Price Controls in Great Britain and the United States during the World War* (New York, Oxford University Press, 1920).

Randolph E. Paul, *Taxation in the United States* (Boston, Little, Brown and Company, 1954).

Earl Sylvester Sparks, *History and Theory of Agricultural Credit in the United States* (New York, Thomas Y. Crowell Company, 1932).

H. Parker Willis and John Chapman, *The Banking Situation* (New York, Columbia University Press, 1934).

13. The New Era: Boom and Crash

The annual reports of the Federal Reserve Board, the Secretary of the Treasury, and the Federal Farm Loan Board are the basic sources for this period. Hearings before Congressional Committees contain a great amount of detail. The pertinent ones are:

Sales of Foreign Bonds or Securities in the United States: Hearings before the Committee on Finance, United States Senate, 72 Congress, 1 Session (4 parts, 1931–33).

Stock Exchange Practices: Hearings before the Senate Committee on Banking and Currency, 73 Congress, 2 Session, June 6, 1934.

Investigation of Concentration of Economic Power: Hearings before the Temporary National Economic Committee, Congress of the United States, 76 Congress, 2 Session, Part 23 on Investment Banking (December 1939).

United States Congress, Joint Commission of Agricultural Inquiry (Washington, D.C., Government Printing Office 1921–22).

World Economic Survey (Geneva, League of Nations 1932–44).

Periodical Articles

Margaret G. Myers, "The League Loans," *Political Science Quarterly,* LX (Dec. 1945), 4.

"Ivar Kreuger," *Fortune* (May, June, July, 1933).

Books

Benjamin Haggott Beckhart, *The New York Money Market* (New York, Columbia University Press, 1932), Vol. IV.

A. A. Berle and Gardner Means, *The Modern Corporation and Private Property* (New York, Commerce Clearing House, 1932), describe some of the changes in corporate structure and their results.

Caroline Bird, *The Invisible Scar* (New York, David McKay Company, 1966).

Roy G. and Gladys C. Blakey, *The Federal Income Tax* (New York, Longmans Green and Company, 1940).

Williams Adams Brown, Jr., *The International Gold Standard Reinterpreted, 1914–1934* (New York, National Bureau of Economic Research, 1940), gives in great detail the changes during and after the war in the currency systems of the principal countries.

Lester V. Chandler, *Benjamin Strong, Central Banker* (Washington, D.C., The Brookings Institution, 1958), has a sympathetic account of the dilemma of a cosmopolitan conscience in the mid-20s.

Milton Friedman and Anna Jacobson Schwartz, *A Monetary History of the United States 1867–1960* (Princeton, N.J., National Bureau of Economic Research, Princeton University Press, 1963).

John Kenneth Galbraith, *The Great Crash* (Boston, Houghton, Mifflin Company, 1955), a brief and lively, sometimes superficial, account of what happened around 1929.

Cleona Lewis, *America's Stake in International Investments* (Washington, D.C., The Brookings Institution, 1938).

Margaret G. Myers, *Monetary Proposals for Social Reform* (New York, Columbia University Press, 1940).

Ferdinand Pecora, *Wall Street under Oath* (New York, Simon and Schuster, 1939), summarizes the hearings he conducted on Stock Exchange practices in 1934.

14. Financing the New Deal

The Annual Reports of the Treasury, the Federal Deposit Insurance Corporation, and the Federal Reserve Board are basic sources for the New Deal period, as is also the *New York Times*.

Useful historical studies and memoirs include:

John Morton Blum, *From the Morgenthau Diaries: Years of Crisis 1928–1938* (Boston, Houghton Mifflin Company, 1959).

Allan Seymour Everest, *Morgenthau, the New Deal and Silver* (New York, King's Crown Press, 1950).

Cordell Hull, *Memoirs* (2 vols., New York, The Macmillan Company, 1948).

William E. Leuchtenburg, *Franklin D. Roosevelt and the New Deal 1932–1940* (New York, Harper and Row, 1963).

Arthur M. Schlesinger, Jr., *The Coming of the New Deal* (Boston, Houghton Mifflin Company, 1958).

Charles J. Tull, *Father Coughlin and the New Deal* (Syracuse, N.Y., Syracuse University Press, 1965).

Among the official summaries of the period are:

Final Report on the Works Progress Administration (Washington, D.C., Government Printing Office, 1946).

Final Statistical Report of Federal Emergency Relief Administration (Washington, D.C., Government Printing Office, 1942).

Final Report on the Reconstruction Finance Corporation (Washington, D.C., Government Printing Office, 1959).

15. World War II

The Annual Reports of the Secretary of the Treasury, the Annual Reports of the Board of Governors of the Federal Reserve System, the monthly *Federal Reserve Bulletin*, and the *New York Times* are the principal sources for the material of this chapter.

Useful books written by those who participated in some of the events of the period include:

Jesse H. Jones with Edward Angly, *Fifty Billion Dollars: My Thirteen Years with the RFC* (New York, The Macmillan Company, 1951).

George S. Lincoln, William S. Stone, and Thomas H. Harvey, *The Economics of National Security* (Englewood Cliffs, N.J., Prentice Hall, 1950).

16.   *The Twenty Years After World War II*

In addition to the agencies whose reports have been used in previous chapters, the following cover the years after 1945:

Annual Reports of the Securities and Exchange Commission, 1934–, and *Monthly Statistical Bulletin of the Securities and Exchange Commission,* 1962– (Washington, D.C., United States Securities and Exchange Commission).

Economic Report of the President, 1947–, annual or semiannual (Washington, D.C., Government Printing Office).

Survey of Current Business, monthly, 1921– (Washington, D.C., United States Department of Commerce, Office of Business Economics).

Bulletin of the Social Security Administration, monthly 1938–, (Washington, D.C., Government Printing Office).

Annual Reports of the *Organization for European Economic Cooperation* 1948–1961, and its successors, *OECD Observer,* bimonthly, 1962–.

Annual Reports of the *Economic Cooperation Administration* and its successors, the *Mutual Security Administration, Administration for International Development* (Washington, D.C., Government Printing Office, 1948–).

Annual Reports of the *International Monetary Fund* and the *International Bank for Reconstruction and Development* and their affiliates, the *International Finance Corporation* and the *International Development Association,* 1946–.

Special Study of the Securities Markets, Securities and Exchange Commission, 1963, 88 Congress 1 Session, House Doc. 95.

Annual Reports of the *Federal Trade Commission* (Washington, D.C., Government Printing Office, 1915/16–.)

Recent books on special aspects of finance include:

Arthur F. Burns, *The Business Cycle in a Changing World* (New York, National Bureau of Economic Research, 1969).

Geoffrey H. Moore and Philip A. Klein, *The Quality of Consumer Instalment Credit* (New York, National Bureau of Economic Research, 1967).

Carl Kaysen and Donald F. Turner, *Antitrust Policy* (Cambridge, Mass., Harvard University Press, 1959).

George W. Stocking and Myron W. Watkins, *Monopoly and Free Enterprise* (New York, The Twentieth Century Fund, 1951).

Robert Tilove, *Pension Funds and Economic Freedom. A Report to the Fund for the Republic,* 1959.

INDEX

DATE DUE

New Books	4-5-73		

DEMCO 38-297